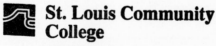

St. Louis Community College

Forest Park
Florissant Valley
Meramec

Instructional Resources
St. Louis, Missouri

THE RISE AND FALL OF CLASS IN BRITAIN

UNIVERSITY SEMINARS
Leonard Hastings Schoff Memorial Lectures

The University Seminars at Columbia University sponsor an annual series of lectures, with the support of the Leonard Hastings Schoff and Suzanne Levick Schoff Memorial Fund. A member of the Columbia faculty is invited to deliver before a general audience three lectures on a topic of his or her choosing. Columbia University Press publishes the lectures.

1993
David Cannadine: The Rise and Fall of Class in Britain

1994
Charles Larmore: The Romantic Legacy

1995
Saskia Sassen: Sovereignty Transformed—States and the New Transnational Actors

THE
RISE
AND
FALL
OF
CLASS
IN
BRITAIN

DAVID CANNADINE

COLUMBIA UNIVERSITY PRESS

NEW YORK

COLUMBIA UNIVERSITY PRESS
Publishers Since 1893
New York   Chichester, West Sussex

Copyright © 1999 David Cannadine

All rights reserved

Library of Congress Cataloging-in-Publication Data
Cannadine, David, 1950–
The rise and fall of class in Britain / David Cannadine.
p.   cm. -- (University seminars/Leonard Hastings Schoff memorial lectures)
Includes bibliographical references (p.   ) and index.
ISBN 0-231-09666-6
1. Social classes--Great Britain. 2. Social mobility--Great Britain.
I. Title.   II. Series.   HN400.S6C356   1999
305.5´0941--DC21   98-28611
                                           CIP

Casebound editions of Columbia University Press books are printed
on permanent and durable acid-free paper.
Printed in the United States of America
c 10 9 8 7 6 5 4 3 2 1

*For my colleagues and friends in the
Department of History, Columbia University, 1988–98,
in admiration, gratitude, and affection.*

*The main message of this book is that in studying class . . .
one cannot escape from history.*

—A. Marwick, *Class: Image and Reality in Britain, France and the USA
Since 1930* (London, 1980), p. 363

*The emergence of class is one of the great themes, perhaps the great
theme, of modern English social history.*

—K. Wrightson, "Estates, Degrees and Sorts: Changing Perceptions of Society
in Tudor and Stuart England," in P. Corfield (ed.),
Language, History and Class (Oxford, 1991), p. 31

*I had originally called this book The Fall of Class. . . . There is a powerful
sense in which class may be said to have "fallen."*

—P. Joyce, *Democratic Subjects: The Self and the Social in
Nineteenth-Century England* (Cambridge, 1995), p. 2

The appropriate discipline for studying "class" is not sociology but rhetoric.

—P. N. Furbank, "Sartre's Absent Whippet," *London Review of Books*, 24
February 1994, pp. 26–27

Nobody knows for sure what the word class *means.*

—P. Fussell, *Caste Marks: Style and Status in the U.S.A.*
(London, 1984), p. 24

CONTENTS

It is widely believed, both in Britain and abroad, that the British are obsessed with class in the way that other nations are obsessed with food or race or sex or drugs or alcohol. According to John Betjeman, it is "that topic all-absorbing, as it was, is now and ever shall be, to us—CLASS."[1] It is impossible to tell whether the British are more preoccupied with class than other European nations, and it is difficult to imagine how to devise, or to carry through, a research project that would subject this well-known cliché to the sort of rigorous comparative examination that it certainly deserves. This book makes no claims to attempt such an undertaking but concerns itself with the second matter to which Betjeman's remark directs us: what, exactly, is this thing "class" with which the British are undeniably so obsessed? Stein Ringen has recently sketched this preliminary, provocative answer: "What is peculiar to Britain," he suggests, "is not the reality of the class system and its continuing existence, but class psychology: the preoccupation with class, the belief in class, and the symbols of class in manners, dress and language." "This thing they have with class," he continues, "is a sign of closed minds, and it is among what is difficult for a stranger to grasp in the British mentality." "Britain," he concludes, "is a thoroughly modern society, with thoroughly archaic institutions, conventions and beliefs."[2]

Class, Ringen seems to be implying, is rather like sex: it is to some extent in the eyes of the beholder and in the British case takes place at least as much inside the head as outside.[3] As someone who has lived for ten years in the United States, with the lengthening vista on Britain that this perspective lends, I find it difficult not to be impressed by these remarks. This undoubted British preoccupation may be varyingly regarded as admirable, appropriate, essential, inevitable, regrettable, unhealthy, ignorant, snobbish, petty, small-minded, or mean-spirited.

But whichever of these it is, or whichever combination of these it is, most British thinking about class is vague, confused, contradictory, ignorant, and lacking adequate historical perspective. The purpose of this book is to suggest some ways in which those in Britain—and else-where—might begin to think about class more seriously, more deliber-ately, more historically, more reflectively, and more creatively; to try, in short, to get a better sense of what class is and was and of what it means and what it meant. "History," Keith Thomas once observed, "enhances our self-consciousness, enables us to see ourselves in perspective, and helps us towards that greater freedom and understanding which comes from self-knowledge."[4] This book is written in full agreement with those views and seeks to open up those minds "closed" to class of which Stein Ringen complains.

As such, the book can be read in a variety of ways and by a variety of audiences. At one level, it is an interim report from the historiographical battle front, an account of what historians have been thinking (or increasingly *not* thinking) about class during a twenty-year period that has seen the collapse of Communism as a system of would-be world dominion and Marxism as a system of would-be world explanation and, in Britain, the rise and fall of Thatcherism, the lingering aftermath of John Major, and the more bracing advent of New Labour. Writing against, and responding to, this changing national and international background, many scholars have concluded that class doesn't matter anymore, which seems, to put it mildly, rather odd. It is not a conclusion that I (or most Britons) share.[5] At another level, this book attempts to provide an account of the different senses of social identity as they have evolved, competed, and changed in the greater British world across the last three centuries, identities for which the word "class" is both the best but also the most misleading shorthand. As such, the book represents an attempt to write history that is genuinely British (though I am well aware how far it falls short of that objective) and to produce a new master narrative of class, built not around one (Marxist) identity but around multiple identities. Finally, it is written to provide a historical perspective on the contemporary debate about the meaning and impor-tance of class in Britain and to offer some suggestions as to what would have to be done to achieve a "classless society," assuming—and this is a very large and debatable assumption—that such a society is possible or desirable.

This book breaks new ground in that it tries to sketch out a history of class as the history of changing (and unchanging) ways of looking at society rather than as the more familiar history of changes (or lack of change) in society itself. It is concerned with economic history in that it recognizes that there have been many developments in what Marx would have called the mode of production, but it is mainly interested in assessing their impact on the ways society has been seen rather than their impact on society itself. It is concerned with social history, not as the old grand narratives of class formation, class consciousness, and class conflict, narratives around which the law of diminishing returns long ago seems to have set in, but rather as the history of the varied and varying ways that Britons envisaged and described their social world. And it is concerned with political history, not as an account of ministerial maneuvering and government administration but as a study of the visions of society entertained by British politicians and of the ways in which they conceived their task to be that of imposing their vision of the people on the people. In short, this book hopes to offer a history of class primarily as a cultural history of the ways in which Britons observe and understand, think about and discuss, the unequal society to which they belong. It is not yet another book about toffs and nobs, social climbers, or working-class heroes.

When Jilly Cooper published her *Class* in 1979 (of which more later), she admitted herself to be "very aware of the inadequacies" of what she had written. "The subject," she went on, "is so vast and so complex that I have only touched on a few aspects which seemed important to me."[6] All those writing about class are bound to echo this disclaimer about their own work, especially when, as in this case, they are trying to breathe new life into an old subject. Moreover, the argument unfolded and developed here could have been made more briefly, or alternatively it could have been extended to several volumes. In seeking a compromise between these two scales of exposition, I have tried to combine the virtues of both approaches (brevity and detail) rather than their shortcomings (superficiality and overkill). But there is one shortcoming of which I am especially aware: these pages do not specifically address the question of what *women* have thought about class. If Jilly Cooper's book is any guide, they think about it very much as men do, which is hardly surprising, because for most of recorded history, the social position and social identities of women have been determined first by their fathers and then by their husbands. But I do not feel entirely happy with this formulation, and having recently reread, side by side, *The Classic Slum* (1990), by Robert Roberts, and *Hidden Lives* (1995), by Margaret Forster, I think it likely that women visualize the social world, and their place within it, in some ways that are different from men. This "serious gap in our knowledge" still awaits its historian, and perhaps the shortcomings of this book will provoke someone else to fill it.[7]

In the course of preparing *The Rise and Fall of Class in Britain*, I have incurred many obligations, which it is a pleasure to be able to acknowledge here. The book began life as the inaugural series of the Leonard Hastings Schoff Memorial Lectures, which I delivered at Columbia University in the autumn of 1993, and I am deeply grateful to Professor Kenneth Jackson and his co-electors for their generous invitation, which gave me the opportunity to think about the subject in a more deliberate and systematic way than I might otherwise have done. Since then, parts of the book have been delivered as the Raleigh Lecture to the British Academy and the George Orwell Memorial Lecture at the University of Sheffield and also as seminar papers at Cambridge, Southampton, and the Johns Hopkins Universities. Most of the writing was undertaken while I was a visiting fellow at the Whitney Humanities Center of Yale University, and I owe a particular debt to Professors David Marshall and Peter Brooks for providing me with such congenial colleagues and stimulating surroundings. I also wish to thank the master and fellows of Pembroke College, Cambridge, who kindly elected me a visiting scholar for the Lent term of 1996, which enabled me to get the whole project into better perspective. And I am especially grateful to the Andrew W. Mellon Foundation of New York, without whose financial support this book would not have been completed this side of the millennium.

The personal debts I have accumulated are no less great. The study of class in Britain has been transformed during the last twenty years, and my obligations to the many historians now working in the field are extensively and appreciatively acknowledged in the notes. Like them, I have relied on, and responded to, the writings of an earlier generation of scholars, who first made the history of class a serious subject, among them, Asa Briggs, John Foster, Eric Hobsbawm, the late Henry Pelling, Harold Perkin, Dorothy Thompson, the late Edward Thompson, and Michael Thompson. I owe particular thanks to Andrew Adonis, Andrew August, David Armitage, Susan Bayly, Christopher Bayly, David Bell, Joanna Bourke, Bill Bowen, Richard Bushman, Robert Darnton, Eric Foner, Roy Foster, Kevin Kenny, Jonathan Parry, Sally Shuttleworth, Quentin Skinner, Sir Keith Thomas, James Thompson, Roberta

Guerriero Wilson, Jay Winter, Isser Woloch, Sir Tony Wrigley, and Harriet Zuckerman. My editors at Columbia University Press, initially John D. Moore and more recently William Strachan, have shown great forbearance and resourcefulness as this book slowly but inexorably evolved into something much larger than they (or I) originally intended. My agent, Mike Shaw, has provided support and encouragement in endless and bountiful abundance, and Linda Colley has, as always, made life worth living and books worth writing.

While working on this subject and this book, I have often been reminded of some wise but rather discouraging words of R. H. Tawney's: "the word 'class,'" he rightly noted, "is fraught with unpleasing associations, so that to linger upon it is apt to be interpreted as the symptom of a perverted mind and a jaundiced spirit."[8] There is much to be said for this remark, from both a social viewpoint and a scholarly perspective. Class can be nasty, and class can be boring. In Britain, it is often both. But I must record, by way of unapologetic confession, that I have found this book an enormous pleasure to write and the subject a source of endless fascination, constant stimulus, and unfailing surprise. I hope I have been able to convey some of this pleasure, fascination, stimulus, and surprise in the pages that follow. And since the British persist in lingering on this subject, and often do so in a rather unpleasing manner, it is surely neither a perverted aim nor a jaundiced ambition to try to shed some fresh historical light on it. Accordingly, I offer this book in the belief that it will enable the British to understand class better, to understand their society better, and to understand themselves better; and also in the hope that it will enable those who are *not* British to understand *them* better. If it makes only a modest contribution to the achievement of these objectives, it will have more than served its turn.

David Cannadine

THE RISE AND FALL OF CLASS IN BRITAIN

CHAPTER ONE

INTRODUCTION

Beyond Class—Forward to Class?[1]

"The rise and fall of class in Britain" is both an allusive and ironic phrase, totally correct yet also at least half mistaken. It is allusive (and correct) because, during the last twenty years or so, the once-fashionable and widely accepted view that class structure and class analysis provide the key to understanding modern British history and modern British life has been disregarded by many historians and abandoned by almost all politicians. Yet it is also ironic (or mistaken), because it remains a generally held belief, not just in Britain but around the world, that class, like the weather and the monarchy, is a peculiarly and particularly British preoccupation.[2] It certainly has been in recent years at 10 Downing Street. For was it not John Major who declared, shortly before becoming prime minister in November 1990 and in a phrase that has continued to resonate ever since, that his aim was to bring about what he called the "classless society"?[3] One does not have to be a master logician to conclude that Major thought—and surely, in this regard, thought rightly—late-twentieth-century Britain to be a class-bound and class-obsessed nation. In which case, of course, the irony is that there has been no "fall of class" at all. It is still very much *there* in Britain.[4]

This means there is a tension—indeed, a contradiction—between the allusive and the ironic messages conveyed in the phrase "the rise and fall of class in Britain." Has class "fallen" or hasn't it? If it has, why do some people maintain that it hasn't? And if it hasn't, why do others insist that it has? Two quotations may serve to sharpen this tension and heighten this contradiction, one from a nineteenth-century male political theorist and the other from a twentieth-century female political practitioner. Here is Karl Marx: "The history of all hitherto existing society is the history of class struggles"—a confident, grandiloquent, all-encompassing, much-quoted (and often misquoted) phrase, which has resounded down the decades since it was originally coined and has inspired much political activity, some good and some bad, and much historical scholarship, of which essentially the same may be said. And here, more recently, but no less self-assuredly, is Margaret Thatcher: "Class," she insisted, "is a Communist concept. It groups people as bundles, and sets them against one another."[5] These could hardly be more divergent views, and they could scarcely be more trenchantly expressed. For Marx, class was the essence of history and of human behavior; for Thatcher, class has been the perversion of both.

As these contrasted quotations imply, the last two decades have witnessed a fundamental rethinking of the economic, social, and political history of modern Britain, with the result that class analysis and class conflict, which had until recently seemed so central to it, have ceased to carry the conviction they once did. Instead, an alternative interpretation has come to prevail that, although not always explicitly Thatcherite, certainly shares her assumption that class should be downplayed, disregarded, and denied and that grouping people in confrontational collectivities is a subversive rhetorical and political device rather than an expression or description of a more complex, integrated, and individualist social reality. Whether these developments are for the better or the worse, these pages must hope to show. But before getting to the historical substance of the matter, it might be helpful to sketch out the class-based orthodoxy that held sway in Britain and elsewhere from the Second World War until the mid-1970s and to describe the ways in which it has since then been undermined and discredited.[6] This is also the appropriate place to reaffirm the unfashionable view that class is still essential to a proper understanding of British history and Britain today, provided it is appropriately defined, properly understood, imaginatively treated, and openly approached.

Class as History

The class-based account of Britain's recent past relied heavily on the categories and concepts associated most famously (or most notoriously) with Karl Marx, which have been elaborated and developed by his self-confessed disciples and have also been used, much more critically and selectively, by many social historians who did not regard Marxism as dogmatic, self-evident, incontrovertible truth.[7] In trying to understand and explain the evolution of past societies, Marx believed it was essential to deal not just with the politics of their ruling elites but also with the histories of their whole populations. But how were these whole populations to be encompassed and described in a comprehensive and convincing way? What were the abstract concepts and collective nouns he thought it appropriate to employ for this purpose?[8] Marx's solution—which proved exceptionally influential—was to classify individuals in collective groupings according to their different relations to the means of production. This enabled him (and his followers) to place everybody in one of three categories: landowners, who drew their unearned income from their estates as rents; bourgeois capitalists, who obtained their earned income from their businesses in the form of profits; and proletarian workers, who made their money by selling their labor to their employers in exchange for weekly wages. For Marx, these were the three fundamental, constitutive classes of human society, and it was in the conflicts among them, which had raged unabated across the centuries, that the essential motor of the historical process was to be found.

These primordial classes, as discerned and understood by Marx, were possessed of a double identity, and so they had to be viewed in two different yet complementary ways: both as class "in itself" and as class "for itself."[9] Class "in itself" was no more (and no less) than an objective social category that grouped individuals together on the basis of their shared economic characteristics: the source of their incomes, the extent of their wealth, and the nature of their occupations. Thus described, these classes had no corporate identity or shared sense of themselves. They were inert, inanimate social aggregations; they did not do, feel, or achieve anything collectively; they were not locked in perpetual struggle with other classes; and so they neither made history nor changed its course.[10] As such, these classes anticipated and resembled the groups into which all individuals are placed in a national census, which are used to provide a comprehensive picture of society based on income, wealth, and occupation. They also lie behind the work of successive generations of sociologists, who continue to refine and debate the number and nature of such classes to be found in modern Britain.[11] *Pace* John Major, these classes will always be with us, as long as there remain inequalities in income, differences in occupation, and variations in wealth that can be objectively observed and precisely measured.

But Marx, and most social historians who have followed him with varying degrees of faithfulness and fidelity, was less interested in class as objective social description ("in itself"), than in class as subjective social formation ("for itself"). By what processes, on what occasions, and with what results, did these inert statistical aggregates become transformed into historical actors, alive and aware of themselves as a class, with a shared identity, collective history, group trajectory, and common objectives? For Marx, the answer lay in the perpetual struggle among landowners, capitalists, and laborers for rent, profit, and wages. Sooner or later, he believed, this inevitable economic conflict over the spoils of production was bound to give rise to social conflict, which would in turn lead to political conflict. Thus regarded, these struggles were both caused by, and helped to consolidate, that active, adversarial sense of collective identity known as class "for itself" or, better still, as class consciousness. Class formation, or the making of a class, was the shorthand term regularly employed for describing this shared process of self-discovery and self-realization.[12] Transformed and energized in this way, classes were not lifeless sociological categories; over time, they came into being, battled with each other for the historical initiative, scored victories and suffered defeats, and so became either the makers or the victims of the historical process.

It was, Marx believed, these deeply rooted and momentous struggles among class-conscious classes, arising directly and inevitably out of the conflicts inherent in the productive activities of the economy, that gave history its basic dynamic, hence his famous dictum, already quoted. And the climax of these class conflicts was political revolution, when the balance of power shifted decisively and irrevocably between one defeated class on the way down and another triumphant class on the way up. According to this interpretation, the modern world had come into being when a succession of bourgeois revolutions[13] led to the overthrow of the traditional, feudal aristocracy: in Britain in the 1640s, in the United States after 1776, and in France after 1789. The result was the creation of that nineteenth-century, middle-class civilization of which Marx himself was both product and pundit, citizen and critic. Yet he was equally certain that this was no more than another temporary stopping place on Clio's class-based progress toward the millennium. There would, he felt sure, be more revolutions. But in future they would be proletarian, with the industrial workers overthrowing the bourgeoisie just as the middle class had earlier overthrown the aristocracy. This, he was no less certain, would lead to the socialist utopia, in which both the state and class would wither away. It is an intriguing irony that, long before John Major made the phrase fashionable during the 1990s, Marx had predicted that a "classless society" would one day come into being.[14]

Drawing with varying degrees of conviction and plausibility on Marx's ideas and insights, the class-based account of modern British history begins with the social origins of the bourgeois revolution of the mid-seventeenth century—otherwise known as the Civil War or the Great Rebellion—that witnessed the transition from feudalism to capitalism and thus from late medieval to early modern times.[15] The victims and beneficiaries of these changes were, respectively, the declining aristocracy and the rising bourgeoisie (or, in other versions, the rising gentry), and it was during the Civil War that these two classes, set on very different historical trajectories, first clashed directly. But although in the short term the bourgeoisie vanquished the monarchy, the peerage, and the established church, its revolutionary movement was curiously incomplete. By the late seventeenth century, after the Restoration and the "Glorious Revolution," the traditional forces of authority were back in control, and for much of the eighteenth century the aristocracy, by now transformed into a quasi-bourgeois elite of agrarian capitalists, reasserted themselves.[16] The stable, oligarchic world of early Georgian politics gave little opportunity for the middle class to improve its position in what remained a preeminently patrician society.

It was only as the industrial revolution gathered momentum in the 1770s and 1780s that Britain's social and political structure was more drastically and more permanently transformed.[17] As new nonlanded wealth was created in unprecedented abundance, the aristocracy began to enter a second and much longer era of decline, which this time was indeed terminal. The middle class, by contrast, became more vigorous, more numerous, and more ambitious, largely thanks to the advent of a new breed of heroic entrepreneur, part creator and part beneficiary of the economic developments that were rapidly changing Britain into the first industrial nation and the workshop of the world. And in turn, the growth of manufacturing meant that the first industrial proletariat also came into being: an exploited working class, crowded in cities and slums, subjected to stern factory discipline, and often degraded, disoriented, and discontented as a result. Inevitably, the workers and their employers were locked in conflict that was bitter and violent, and the factory owners almost invariably won. Moreover, the passing of the Great Reform Act of 1832 confirmed that the middle classes had superseded the aristocracy as the chief power in the state, dominating the economy, politics, and ideology of the nineteenth century as surely and securely as the landowners had previously dominated the eighteenth.[18]

Here at last was a triumphant bourgeoisie, vanquishing the aristocracy, subduing the workers, and entering into the inheritance it had
been denied in the mid-seventeenth century: the age of capital, of
machinery, of railways, and of Marx was at hand.[19] But as with the
Civil War, the passing of the Great Reform Act turned out to be
another incomplete revolution. For the working class, whose vigorous
collaborative agitation had been essential in forcing the measure
through a reluctant but intimidated Parliament, was denied its just
deserts: the proletarian revolution, which Marx had foretold would
follow inevitably in the wake of the bourgeois revolution, did not
materialize. The world-historical role that he had wished on the workers and predicted for them was one that they proved unwilling and
unable to play, as their class "in itself" disappointingly refused to
become a class "for itself." To be sure, the Chartist agitations of 1839,
1842, and 1848 brought with them what seemed to be serious social
upheaval and quasi-revolutionary political activity.[20] But they eventually fell almost farcically flat, and it was decades before the working
classes recovered any collective sense of identity and political will.
By contrast, the entrepreneurial middle classes enjoyed a second great
triumph, as they compelled the patrician Parliament to repeal the Corn
Laws in 1846, thereby both demonstrating and consolidating their grip
on Victorian Britain.

For some social historians, the failure of the working class to carry
through a successful proletarian revolution during the early part of
the nineteenth century was not only a source of deep regret: it also
obliged them to explain why something that Marx had said should
happen and would happen had not happened. They offered several
ingenious reasons for the lamented nonevent. They argued that on
many occasions from the 1800s to the 1840s, Britain *did* come close
to revolution and that it was only bad luck, or bad weather, or the
coercive power of the state, that prevented it from occurring. They
suggested that the unprecedented prosperity of the 1850s, 1860s, and
1870s, the so-called mid-Victorian boom, blunted the revolutionary
ardor of the working class. And they claimed that the most prosperous
proletarians, the "labor aristocracy," who should have provided the
revolutionary leadership during the mid-Victorian era, lost sight
of their own true class interests, succumbed to "false consciousness,"
submitted to the "social control" of their betters, and so traitorously
acquiesced in the liberal bourgeois compromise of the "age of
equipoise."[21] As with the seventeenth-century bourgeoisie, so with the

nineteenth-century proletariat: theirs was a revolution manqué, a turning point in history that had failed to turn.

It was, so this interpretation continued, only during the late nineteenth century that the pace of social change began to pick up again, bringing with it a renewal of class consciousness and class conflict. The rising bourgeoisie and the declining aristocracy fused together into a composite capitalist ruling class, hence the era of Tory dominance, high imperialism, Joseph Chamberlain, and the Boer War. The unprecedented growth of big business and the scale of production meant that the working class developed into a new and self-conscious force: it was remade, not, this time, as the would-be revolutionary movement of the earlier nineteenth century but as a more reformist body, which found two interconnected institutional expressions.[22] The first was the trade unions, whose membership exploded during the 1880s and 1890s, again on the eve of the First World War, and yet again both during and immediately after it and which gave a powerful collective voice to the organized workingman. The second was the creation of the Labour Party, which in 1918 pledged itself, in clause four of its constitution, to bring about "the common ownership of the means of production" in the name of ordinary men and women. With the demise of the Liberals after 1914, the way was open for renewed class conflict, as the party of industrial capital (the Conservatives) confronted the party of organized workers (Labour). This was the basis of the economic, social, and political conflicts of the twentieth century, culminating in such bitter, class-ridden confrontations as the General Strike of 1926 and the miners' strikes of 1974 and 1985.[23]

For the best part of a generation—the welfare state generation of 1945–79—this interpretation of Britain's past carried almost everything before it.[24] Whether Marxist, Marxisant, Whig, or liberal, there was among social historians and sociologists a shared presumption that economic change was the key to social change, that social change was concerned with the rise and fall of classes and the conflicts between them, and that it was the outcome of such battles that determined both the changing structure and the developing issues of politics. The conflict between the classes was the direct, inevitable consequence of the conflict between those who were differently related to the means of production, and it was this struggle that in the end determined the nature and working of the political structure. Even if the dictatorship of the proletariat had not yet arrived, as Marx had predicted it should have done, his insights still seemed to offer the best way of understanding the broad contours of the economic, social, and political development of modern Britain, insights to which, it bears repeating, class formation, class identity, class consciousness, and class conflict were central.[25]

This approach to the British past not only seemed intrinsically appealing: it was rendered additionally attractive because it was neither parochial nor insular. During the 1950s and 1960s, the era of decolonization, the Vietnam War, and student protest, such concepts as class formation, class conflict, and political revolution became essential features of many national histories and historiographies. In France, the events of 1789 were presented as the paradigmatic bourgeois revolution, the momentous outcome of a long-term battle between the rising middle classes and the declining aristocracy that changed the world forever and for the better.[26] In Mexico, the revolution of 1910–11 was depicted in essentially Marxist terms, as a popular, progressive, anticlerical, class-based movement successfully directed against a repressive and reactionary old regime.[27] And, in Russia, a similar social-historical interpretation was eventually advanced about the upheavals of 1917, which, it was argued, witnessed the first-ever triumph of a self-consciously revolutionary proletariat, thanks to Lenin's inspired leadership as he gave history a helping hand in a Marxist direction.[28] In this broader perspective of national history writing, the class-based interpretation of the British past was merely part of a general, widespread postwar pattern.[29]

Class Dismissed

Even in the late 1970s, this remained very much the prevailing orthodoxy. Yet today there is almost no one among a younger generation of British historians who would unquestioningly endorse this once-paramount interpretation. Why has it ceased to carry conviction?[30] Part of the explanation lies in the massive amount of detailed empirical research that has progressively undermined these earlier, confident, but often highly speculative generalizations. For it is now clear that the pattern of economic development that provided the materialist motor for the Marxist model was neither as neat nor as simple as was once claimed. The development of capitalism in the seventeenth century, the industrial revolution of the late eighteenth and early nineteenth centuries, the rise of new technologies during the late nineteenth and early twentieth centuries, the growth of consumer-oriented industries during the interwar years, and the decline of the great Victorian staples since 1945: all these phases of economic change turn out, on closer inspection, to have been extremely complex, varied, and gradual developments.[31] In turn, this meant that changes in the economy were never so momentous, so straightforward, or so pervasive as to make possible or bring about the creation of those homogeneous, self-conscious classes of landowners, capitalists, and laborers locked in perpetual conflict with each other that Marx and his later followers among British historians hoped (and claimed) to discern.[32]

On closer inspection, the best that could be said of Marx's three class-conscious classes was that they were ideal types, historical abstractions that grossly oversimplified the way in which the social structure of modern Britain had actually evolved and developed. One difficulty was that the shared class characteristics and clear-cut class boundaries that Marx and his followers had posited had rarely if ever existed in fact. Landowners did not only enjoy agricultural rents: they also drew profits from their mines, docks, urban estates, and industrial investments. In the same way, successful middle-class businessmen often set themselves up as broad-acred gentlemen, thereby straddling the supposedly deep and unbridgeable divide between the country house and the countinghouse.[33] Another problem was that within Marx's three supposedly inclusive class categories, there were many internal divisions: between aristocrats and landed gentry, between bankers and businessmen, between industrialists competing for the same markets, and between the many different gradations of skilled and unskilled labor. Yet a third qualification was that during and since Marx's time, old occupational groups have expanded, and new occupational groups have come into being that do not easily fit into his three-level model: rentiers, managers, professionals, domestic servants, and the whole of the lower middle classes. Thus described, the social structure of modern Britain was more elaborate, and also more integrated, than Marx had allowed.[34]

But this was not the only way in which it turned out that he had been a heroic and misleading oversimplifier. For as particular episodes were more fully examined, it soon emerged that the grand, linear narrative— of class formation, class conflict, and political revolution—failed to sustain its credibility across the centuries, instead collapsing amid a welter of short-term, internal contradictions. How could the aristocracy have been in apparently terminal crisis by the 1640s yet still be the dominant class in the country on the eve of the passing of the Great Reform Act one hundred and eighty years later?[35] If the working class had been so successfully "made" by the 1830s, then why (and how) was it necessary for them to be "remade" during the last quarter of the nineteenth century?[36] As for the ever-rising middle class, how was it possible for them to have gained so much in power and self-consciousness in every century, to have pioneered a bourgeois revolution in the seventeenth century, to have been "made" during the early eighteenth century and then "made" again a hundred years later, and yet to have achieved so little?[37] In the short-run, self-enclosed historiographies of the seventeenth, eighteenth, and nineteenth centuries, these problems could largely be ignored. But the longer-run national narrative, built around rising and falling classes that persistently failed to rise and fall and centering on political revolutions that were invariably incomplete, was shot through with both logical and chronological inconsistencies.

The class interpretation was also in error in placing so much stress on the unifying experience of laboring activity in the creation of class consciousness. As soon as historians began to study work, it turned out, like so much else, to be a more complex subject than the Marxists had appreciated. The growing range and number of occupations made people's circumstances more differentiated rather than more alike; many men frequently changed jobs and were often unemployed; and many women did not work at all. *Pace* E. P. Thompson, it was thus not clear that class "eventuates," as he had claimed it did, as "men and women live their productive relations."[38] Even for the working class, there was always more to life and living than work and working. Historians of leisure, of domesticity, and of consumption have discovered social groupings and social relationships that were often significantly different from those found by historians of work and those of "social control." And historians of housing have found patterns of residential segregation and social zoning in towns and cities that were often far less clear than the conventional tripartite division into upper-class enclaves, middle-class suburbs, and working-class slums. The physical shapes on the ground, like the social shapes in society, were more varied than Marx recognized.[39]

It was never possible, moreover, as the interpretation built around the making of class consciousness crucially required, to collapse social categories into political groupings, to elide class into party, in any convincing, coherent, and credible way. As detailed research soon began to show, the Civil War was neither caused by nor fought out between rising bourgeois roundheads on the one side and declining aristocratic cavaliers on the other. In eighteenth-century Britain, it was impossible to read off

Whig or Tory political affiliations from their different positions in the economic and social structure. In nineteenth-century Britain, which had supposedly witnessed the final triumph of the bourgeoisie, politics remained a largely patrician pursuit, and there was never a hegemonic middle-class political party.[40] And in twentieth-century Britain, many workers have voted Conservative (how else, indeed, could the Tories have won elections so frequently on a full adult franchise?), while the leadership of the Labour Party has for most of the time been middle class rather than proletarian.[41] Now, as in earlier times, political parties are not dominated, as Marx had too readily assumed, by the exclusive interests of a single class, and politics is never merely the direct, unmediated expression of class identities and class conflicts.[42]

But the class-based interpretation of modern British history has not been undermined only by the detailed empirical research that it has stimulated and provoked. During the last two decades, a second and no less serious challenge has been mounted by women's historians and devotees of the new literary theory. Feminist scholars rightly observe that very few women appeared in the canonical texts of social history written in a Marxist mode. How odd it seems to them that books ostensibly about a whole class were only concerned with one half of it. Yet in many ways, they insist, women's experiences of work and life were very different from those of men, and there were also tensions and conflicts between the sexes that eroded any sense of class solidarity they might feel. As a result, a great deal of effort has been spent by some feminist historians in trying to reconcile[43]—and by others in seeking to deny[44]—the competing claims of class and gender. So far, on balance, gender has destabilized class as a category of historical analysis rather than revived or reinforced it. During the 1950s and 1960s, pioneering social historians were Marxists interested in class. During the 1980s and 1990s, they have more usually been feminists interested in gender. For them, the history of all hitherto existing society is no longer the history of class struggles; instead it is the history of gendered identities and interpersonal relationships.

Equally subversive of the traditional view of class has been the rise to prominence of postmodernist literary theory. As the result of their discovery of what is called the "linguistic turn," many historians no longer regard class as the study of the vexed relations among land, capital, and labor and of the political conflicts arising out of them. Instead, they see class as the study of the language that people used, because it was the words they employed that provided the essential source of their social and political identities.[45] Thus conceived, class was neither an objective guide to social reality nor a shared subjective experience. Classes never actually existed as recognizable historical phenomena, still less as the prime motor of historical change. They were nothing more than rhetorical constructions, the inner imaginative worlds of everyman and everywoman, seeking as best they could to explain their social universe to themselves.[46] And not only was social perception ultimately the product of language; it did not even have to be the language of class. For there were—and are—many other words in which people envision the social order. Thus regarded, the history of all hitherto existing society is no longer the history of class struggles; rather, it is the history of a limitless number of individual self-categorizations and subjective social descriptions of which class is only one among a multitude of competing and frequently changing vocabularies.[47]

All this is merely to say that we now live in a postmodern era of decentered and deconstructed discourse in which grand, traditional master narratives are no longer fashionable because they no longer seem credible. On the contrary, they are now widely dismissed as being deeply and fatally flawed: too teleological, too anachronistic, too Whiggish, too reductionist, too masculinist, too all-encompassing, too overdetermined, too simplistic. Among the prime casualties of this new mode of thinking have been those bold, confident, overarching, Marxist-liberal histories built around class formation, class conflict, and political revolution. The simple, direct connections so easily assumed but so rarely demonstrated between economic change, the making of a class, and revolutionary politics have very largely been given up.[48] Accounts of class making and class formation are by their very nature hopelessly and helplessly blighted by the distorting vision of hindsight.[49] And the once heroically regarded political revolutions are now seen as the result of accident and contingency, with no long-term social causes or far-reaching political consequences. In its postwar heyday, class was the grandest and most masterly narrative available. But today the only master narrative left is that there is no master narrative whatsoever, only the "chaotic authenticity" of random happenings and unforeseeable events.[50]

As is so often the case in the writing and interpretation of modern British history, these recent scholarly developments have coincided with, and have undoubtedly been influenced by, broader changes in public affairs, in Britain and elsewhere. Since 1980, one of the most conspicuous domestic developments has been the defeat of organized labor, in both its professional and its political guises. The final, precipitous collapse of the great Victorian staple industries, and of the traditional working class, means that the number of trade-union members has fallen dramatically, and that their political influence is much diminished. Support for the Labour Party declined significantly in the twenty years from 1974, and until it reinvented itself during the 1990s, it showed a conspicuous inability to win general elections.[51] The old, ostensibly class-based politics that gave it coherence and purpose—improving the lot of industrial workers and nationalizing the means of production—were an inadequate basis on which to build a successful party of the Left in the closing decades of the twentieth century. As a result, today's Labour politicians are less interested than their predecessors were in the history of class consciousness and class conflict, a history that was once such an important prop to the party's collective identity and purpose. Instead, they have returned to an earlier notion of socialism by stressing cooperation and community rather than class and conflict.

This is well exemplified in the case of Tony Blair, who is at least as much a party leader and prime minister for our postsocialist times as was John Major. He is not saturated with Labour's traditional language and categories of class and has expressed no ambition to promote class consciousness or incite class conflict. On the contrary, these venerable party nostrums are the "great absence" from his political vision and his political vocabulary. Like John Major, only more so, he is primarily interested in talking about community, consensus, and conciliation, and class gets in the way of such talk. Hence his determination to rid Labour of its "Marxist intellectual analysis," with its "false view of class," which was "always out of kilter with the real world," and also its long-standing commitment to the "common ownership of the means of production."[52] He has accomplished all these objectives, persuading the party to accept that Thatcher's privatization of the 1980s is here to stay and successfully carrying through the abolition of clause four. As he proclaims it, the key to Blair's politics is the nurturing of the reciprocal relationship between the individual and society, and this culture of community and inclusivity leaves no room for the outdated and outmoded notions of class identity, class interest, and class war.[53]

Underlying this "fall of class" on the Left in Britain is a broader change in the conventional vocabulary of political discussion and social perception, namely, the shift from the traditional preoccupation with people as collective producers to the alternative notion of people as individual consumers. This was partly Margaret Thatcher's achievement, and she very much knew what she was doing. She attacked the trade unions, because they represented organized, collective, productive labor. She stressed the market, the public, the customer, and the individual, which undermined the language of social solidarity based on productive classes. She offered hope—in a way that Labour never had—to the working and lower middle classes of escaping the constraints of impoverished expectations and irremediable subordination. And by wrapping herself in the flag, she very effectively marginalized the politics of sectional interests and class conflict. As a result of her policies and her rhetoric, Thatcher thus went a long way toward achieving her ambition of banishing the language of class from public discussion and political debate about the structure and nature of British society.[54] And the fact that Tony Blair has no wish to resurrect this language is a measure of her achievement in changing the way people think about social structures, social relations, and social identities in today's Britain.

As in the earlier era of the welfare state, these developments in British politics, which have significantly influenced developments in British history writing, also need to be set in a broader, continental perspective. For the collapse of Communism in Eastern Europe has only dealt a further blow to any political or academic enterprise that is essentially class based in inspiration. The demise of the Soviet Union and its Warsaw Pact satellites during the late 1980s has discredited Marxism throughout Europe as an ideology, and today it only survives, increasingly beleaguered, introverted, and irrelevant in enclaves in North and South America and in certain departments of European universities devoted to art history, literature and linguistics, and cultural studies.[55] But as an all-embracing intellectual system that once confidently claimed to provide the key to all human society and all human behavior, past, present and future, Marx's doctrines now seem generally discredited beyond rehabilitation. Communism is dead, therefore Marxism is dead, therefore class is dead: thus runs the argument. Accordingly, the whole outmoded apparatus of class analysis has been consigned to the wastepaper basket of history, along with the cold war, the Berlin Wall, the Soviet Union, and the guards outside Lenin's mausoleum. In the light of these developments, class is no longer a way (let alone *the* way) of looking at history; it has become part of history.[56]

Not surprisingly, the recent decline in Marxist, Marxisant, and class-based history has been a European-wide phenomenon. As class formation, class conflict, and political revolution have been taken out of the British approach to the past, so they have also disappeared from the histories and historiographies of other countries. In France, the Revolution is no longer seen as the inevitable outcome of class war: the bourgeoisie was too weak, too diffuse, and too unself-conscious to have accomplished anything so single-mindedly significant or heroic in 1789.[57] In Mexico, the old regime has been rehabilitated, the revolution has been reappraised as a political not a social phenomenon, and its effects are now seen as having been distinctly limited.[58] And in Russia, recent accounts of 1917 have deliberately ignored the once-central class dimension. In each case, long-term social causes have been disregarded, class identities have been denied and set aside, and the upheavals themselves are lamented as the regrettable, unnecessary, and illegitimate work of rootless, unprincipled, and amoral conspirators.[59] Here, as in British history, class consciousness and class conflict have been decisively rejected as the essential motor governing and driving the historical process. Culture now matters more than class; chance and contingency are deemed to be more important than structure and pattern.

These are some of the reasons why class analysis has been dethroned from its previously central place in the social history of modern Britain in recent years. It never did explain what it purported to explain, namely, the broad contours of Britain's historical evolution from the sixteenth century to the twentieth. The idea that classes rise, struggle, and fall like Paul Kennedy's great powers no longer seems as convincing as it did.[60] It has been further undermined by feminist scholars, by those excited by the "linguistic turn," and by the loss of the credibility of traditional master narratives. And it has been additionally eroded by the marginalization of the old Labour Party in Britain, by the shift in emphasis from people as collective producers to people as individual consumers, and by the collapse of Communism in Eastern Europe. As a result, the view that the history of modern Britain—or the history of modern Anywhere Else—may best be understood in terms of conflicts between opposing armies of fully self-conscious class warriors has been overthrown. Rather than employ class to explain history, it now seems that we should employ history to explain class. Instead of using Marx to help us make sense of the nineteenth century, it is more appropriate to use the nineteenth century to help us make sense of Marx, assuming that anyone today still thinks that a worthwhile undertaking.[61]

Class as Social Description

Such is now the conventional historiographical wisdom. As deployed in its welfare state heyday, class was too crude a concept: it did not do justice to the refractory complexity of the historical process, and it never captured more than a part of the way in which ordinary men (to say nothing of ordinary women) lived out their lives. Small wonder that some historians are now talking of a terminal crisis in the concept of class and of the need to replace it with something else—or with nothing at all.[62] Today, they are much more inclined to stress the relatively high degree of consensus that seems to have prevailed in Britain, the general absence of clear-cut classes and clear-cut class conflict, and the way in which different social groupings and identities merged easily and imperceptibly into one another in the seamless web of the social fabric. At the same time, they have become increasingly aware of the associational richness and diversity of past people's lives: as men and women, husbands and wives, parents and children; as members of churches or trade unions or soccer clubs or political parties; as individuals with loyalties to their firms, their villages, their towns, their cities, their counties, their regions, their country. With so many fluctuating and sometimes contradictory senses of identity that constantly cut across each other, there no longer seems any justification for privileging class identity—or class analysis.[63]

Not surprisingly, then, Marx has been one of the most conspicuous casualties of our postindustrial, postsocialist, post–cold war, postmodern world, for it is a post-Marxist world as well.[64] Indeed, the reaction against Marxism and class analysis is now flowing so strongly that the most recent and authoritative social history of modern Britain, which runs to three large and otherwise comprehensive volumes, managed to leave out the subject completely, thereby giving an entirely new meaning to the injunction "class dismissed."[65] Even some of the old-guard Marxist historians seem to have retracted and recanted. Christopher Hill no longer insists that the English Civil War was the first bourgeois revolution.[66] Eric Hobsbawm has shifted his interests from class and class conflict in nineteenth-century Europe to nationalism, national identity, and the twentieth century. And in one of his last essays, E. P. Thompson declared that " 'class' was perhaps overworked in the 1960s and 1970s, and it had become merely boring. It is a concept long past its sell-by date." It is unclear from the context whether Thompson was expressing his own changed views or merely summarizing the altered state of contemporary opinion. For present purposes, it does not matter; either way, class today is not what it once was. It has had a great fall.[67]

But the difficulty with banishing class from modern British history in the way it has increasingly become fashionable to do is that it leaves us incapable of understanding what it was that John Major was talking about or why what he said resonated—and is still resonating—so widely. For if he was right in asserting that Britain is still a class-bound society, then it is little short of bizarre that in recent years historians have been spending so much time and effort denying that this was so and, by implication, that this is still so.[68] If we accept, as we are surely correct in doing, that class is one of the most important aspects of modern British history no less than of modern British life, then it is at best regrettable and at worst plain wrong for the current generation of historians to show minimal interest in the subject. Even if, in its crudest forms, the Marxist approach to class no longer carries conviction, that is no reason for dismissing class altogether. The baby, still kicking vigorously, should be retained, even though the bathwater, long since grown tepid, has rightly been jettisoned. For the most important and immediate task is neither that of denying nor rehabilitating old-style class analysis but of defining the subject afresh and envisioning it anew.

In order to do so, we need to be clear as to the central problem with the traditional approach to class. This was not that it sought to study or understand class, both of which are entirely worthwhile scholarly objectives. The difficulties were those arising from mistaken identity and excessive expectations. Most Marxists believed that a person's class identity was collective rather than individual and was primarily determined by his (or, just occasionally, her) relationship to the means of production. But this was clearly too narrow, too materialistic, too reductionist an approach, and it assumed that all social identities were shared rather than single. Moreover, these collective classes, as defined and understood by Marx, showed a high degree of internal coherence and homogeneity. Again, this seems to have been an oversimplification. And he also assumed a direct causal link not only between economic development and social change but also between social change and political events. This, too, seems excessively crude. In short, the sort of classes for which Marxists searched never existed as they hoped to find them. And so it is hardly surprising that class as it *has* actually existed did not fulfill its task as the animator and agitator of the historical process that Marx had wished on it.

But how has class actually existed? In seeking to answer that question, we should also recognize that where Marx was on to something was in his insistence that the material circumstances of people's existences— physical, financial, environmental—do matter in influencing their life chances, their senses of identity, and the historical part that they and their contemporaries may (or may not) play. Whatever the devotees of the "linguistic turn" may claim, class is not just about language. There is reality as well as representation. Go to Toxteth, go to Wandsworth, go to Tyneside, go to Balsall Heath, and tell the people who live in the slums and the council estates and the high-rise ghettos that their sense of social structure and social identity is no more than a subjective rhetorical construction, that it is nothing beyond a collection of individual self-categorizations. It seems unlikely that they will agree. Nor, for that matter, would the inhabitants of Edgbaston or Eastbourne, Belgravia or Buckingham Palace. Class, like sex, may indeed take place in the head, but it has never existed solely in the head or in the eyes or in the words of the beholder. Social reality always keeps breaking in. Classes, like nations, are sometimes more and sometimes less than imagined communities. All of which is simply to say that language is a necessary but insufficient guide, to both social circumstances and social consciousness. We need to get beyond the "linguistic turn."[69]

It is somewhere between the overdetermined reductionism of Marxist analysis and the free-floating subjectivities of the historians of language that we should seek to discover, describe, and discuss class as it has actually existed and developed in Britain during the last three hundred years. But where, in making such a fresh start, might we most helpfully begin? One appropriate place is with a long view of Britain's evolving—or, rather, nonevolving—social structure from the early eighteenth century to the late twentieth. If we borrow W. G. Runciman's recent typology, it is clear that across this long span, British society has been continually characterized by what he terms four "systactic" categories: a small elite; a larger group of managers, businessmen, and professionals; the general body of wage workers; and a deprived, impoverished, and sometimes criminalized underclass.[70] These general social-cum-occupational groups have been a constant across the centuries of modern British history, and an abundance of recent, more detailed research into patterns of wealth distribution and occupational structure amply bears this out.[71] Indeed, it has been the gradual piecing together of this long-term picture of *un*changingness that has done much to subvert the old Marxist or Marxisant notion that the historical process was built around the economically driven processes of rapid social development, sudden class creation, and abrupt class conflict. This is not, it now seems, the way in which things in the British past actually happened.

Class also has a geography as well as a history. Local studies of villages, towns, cities, and regions by definition tell us a great deal about particular places. But they are also, by definition, prone to parochialism and introversion, and they dislike and avoid making generalizations or seeking broader patterns. Yet we need to remember that across the last three centuries these localities were embedded in many wider worlds: not just the four nations of England, Ireland, Scotland, and Wales but also the larger identities of Great Britain and the British Isles. Moreover, for much of the period with which this book is concerned Britain was an imperial power and an expanding society. And for the entire period there were British-spawned nations across the seas that, with their shared backgrounds but different economies, both mirrored and distorted the social structure of the homeland.[72] Most British colonies remained agricultural and rural long after Britain was industrializing and urbanizing. In Canada and South Africa, British settlers and lawmakers encountered alien races with alien social structures. In Australia and New Zealand, they self-consciously transplanted British communities overseas, rejecting some aspects of the mother country while maintaining and extending others. And in India, the Raj evolved into the most elaborate imperial hierarchy of all, with its British proconsuls and officials, its native princely states, and its caste system. On the boundaries of empire, at the frontiers of dominion and settlement, much was revealed about the social structure of Britain itself.[73]

But these are merely the essential preliminaries to the central question about class as this book poses and address it. How, across a long time span and from a broad geographical perspective, can we recover the ways in which Britons saw and understood the manifestly unequal society in which they lived? For a suggestive answer, we might usefully turn to Montpellier in 1768, when a bourgeois citizen set out to "put his world in order" by describing the social structure of his town.[74] He concluded that there was no single comprehensive or authoritative way in which this could be done. Instead, he offered three very different yet equally plausible accounts of the same contemporary social world. The first was Montpellier as a procession: as a hierarchy on parade, a carefully graded ordering of rank and dignity, in which each layer melded and merged almost imperceptibly into the next. The second was Montpellier divided into three collective categories of modified estates: the nobility, the bourgeoisie, and the common people. And the third was a more basic division: between those who were patricians and those who were plebeians. Clearly, these were very different ways of characterizing and categorizing the same population. The first stressed the prestige ranking of individuals and the integrated nature of Montpellier society. The second placed people in discrete collective groups that owed more to wealth and occupation and gave particular attention to the bourgeoisie. And the third emphasized the adversarial nature of the social order by drawing one great divide on the basis of culture, style of life, and politics.

Thus Montpellier in 1768, *and thus Britain during the last three hundred years*. That, in essence, is the argument that I advance and unfold in the following pages. When Britons have tried to make sense of the unequal social worlds they have inhabited, settled, and conquered, across the centuries and around the globe, they have most usually come up with versions or variants of these same three basic and enduring models: the hierarchical view of society as a seamless web; the triadic version with upper, middle, and lower collective groups; and the dichotomous, adversarial picture, where society is sundered between "us" and "them." These were, and still are, the conventional, vernacular models of British social description used by ordinary people, by pundits and commentators, and by politicians, and it is with the history of these three models that this book is primarily concerned. Strictly speaking, they were mutually exclusive, using different criteria to describe the same unequal society in very different ways and often (though diminishingly) using their own specific languages. Thus regarded, these three depictions of society do not amount to what the sociologist Gordon Marshall would call "a rigorously consistent interpretation of the world."[75] Far from it; indeed, quite the opposite.

But in practice and like the Montpellier bourgeois, most people move easily and effortlessly from one model to another, recasting their vision of British society to suit their particular purpose or perspective. And one of the reasons they were able to do so was that they gradually came to use the same language, regardless of the particular model they were employing. Often it was the vocabulary of ranks and orders. But it was also, and increasingly, the language of class that was most commonly used for describing all three models of contemporary British society: class as hierarchy; class as "upper," "middle," and "lower"; and class as just "upper" and "lower." Thus regarded, the history of class is not the master key that unlocks the entire historical process: the history of class struggle as classes come into being and do battle with each other. Nor is it the history of innumerable subjective social identities exclusively constituted by language. Rather, it is the history of the three different ways in which, across the centuries, most Britons have visualized their society: the history of three models of social description that are often but not always expressed in the language of class. Redefined and understood in this way, the history of "class" should properly be regarded as the answer to the following question: how did (and do) Britons understand and describe their social worlds? It is that answer, and that history, that this book aims to provide.

"All societies," George Watson has rightly noted, "are unequal; . . . but they describe their own inequalities variously." In the British case, it is these three idealized models, not always but often articulated in the language of class, that have lain behind most popular perceptions and descriptions of social structure since the early eighteenth century.[76] Like all such popular perceptions, they were the jumbled product of custom and habit, history and experience, politics and inquiry, information and misinformation, ignorance and prejudice; then, as now, there were limits to what Britons knew about the social worlds in which they lived. None of these three idealized models constitute what Ernest Gellner recently called "real social knowledge."[77] All of them are ignorant oversimplifications of the complexity of society. Yet they have remained remarkably enduring, and they are still in existence in Britain today. Indeed, it is precisely because of their continued existence that Britain cannot possibly be described as a "classless society" and that historians are mistaken in dismissing class from their current agenda. For if we are to understand class historically, we need to understand how it is over time that these three models of society have coexisted and why it is that for different people, and at different times, one or another of these models has been the preferred account of how things are.

Part of the answer does lie in long-term changes to the British population, which did occur, notwithstanding the significant continuities in social structure of which we are now well aware. Over the long run, health, life expectancy, and standards of living all improved; the numbers of people increased more than tenfold; there was a shift in the distribution of the population from the country to the town; modes of employment, ownership, and production changed; inequality grew then lessened; a tiny electorate expanded to universal adult suffrage; a

Christian society became a secular society; at least two empires were made and lost. All these long-term changes are known, some of them can be measured, and each must surely have influenced and changed social perceptions in the long run, though we have yet scarcely begun to identify how or when or why. But a moment's reflection suggests that people living in a predominantly rural society with a scattered population, most of whom did not have the vote and many of whom believed in God, would see themselves and their world differently from people living in a predominantly urban society that was densely populated, where everyone had the vote and few of them believed in God.[78]

But another part of the answer lies in trying to understand, across the centuries, the ebb and flow of the appeal of the different descriptions of British society that were generally available. Why is it that ordinary people have seen their society in these three ways? What has persuaded them, at any given time, that one of these models seems more convincing than the other two? And what is the process by which they change their minds, moving from one view of society that has served them well in the past to another that now seems to make more sense of things? Part of the answer is clearly to do with discontent, which means that the version of society as it is becomes less appealing than a vision of society as it might be. But it is also, and increasingly, to do with politics and politicians. Indeed, it is one of the prime contentions of this book that politicians play a large part in the creation and articulation of social identities and in the process whereby one version becomes, for a time, more resonant than the alternatives.[79] From John Wilkes to Margaret Thatcher, one of the most important tasks that many politicians have tried to accomplish has been to get ordinary people to see their society differently, "to change the way we look at things," which in practice has meant moving them from preferring one of the three models of social description to another.[80]

Class Here, Now, and Then

One final point, by way of preliminary. Of these three models of British society that have been on offer since the early eighteenth century, it is class as hierarchy that has had the widest, most powerful, and most abiding appeal. In part this is because Britain retains intact an elaborate, formal system of rank and precedence, culminating in the monarchy itself, which means that prestige and honor can be transmitted and inherited across the generations. Even today, books are written about that system, setting out the five gradations of the hereditary peerage, explaining the relative standing of the younger son of a baronet vis-à-vis the elder son of the younger son of a duke, and pointing out whether a Master of Arts from Oxford ranks higher than a provincial mayor with no university degree.[81] But in addition, and more broadly, a Briton's place in this class hierarchy is also determined by such considerations as ancestry, accent, education, deportment, mode of dress, patterns of recreation, type of housing, and style of life. All these signs and signals help determine how any one individual regards him- (or her-) self, and how he (or she) is regarded and categorized by others. Taken together, it is these formal and informal hierarchies of prestige and status that people often have in mind when they speak of the "British class system": a model of society more elaborate than the two- or three-stage versions.[82]

One does not have to go to India to discover *Homo Hierarchicus*; he has been around in Britain for a very long time.[83] Nor should this come as any great surprise. Ever since the discovery of the pecking order among hens in the 1920s, ranked-status hierarchy has been seen as the main form of social organization among animals. More recent work suggests that this is especially marked in the case of primates, particularly chimpanzees, for whom aping their betters has always been more than just a metaphor. If this is right, then the implication is that humans are also intrinsically and essentially hierarchical animals, both by nature and throughout most of history. Thus regarded, men and women are predisposed toward rank and order—toward class as hierarchy—because, as Desmond Morris once put it, they are risen apes rather than fallen angels.[84] If this is right, then hierarchy is the primordial human mode of social structure and social perception. By comparison, the three- and two-stage models of society are much less deeply rooted, more fluid, flimsy, and fragile in their identities and more the product of deliberate, self-conscious articulation, as people seek for alternative ways of seeing and understanding their social worlds.

Throughout the last three centuries of Britain's history, there has been much less evidence of class consciousness and class conflict than Marx boldly—and mistakenly—asserted. But there has also been a great deal of *consciousness of class* as social description and social identity, most usually of class as hierarchy, sometimes of class as "upper," "middle," and "lower," and on other occasions of class as "upper" and "lower." For Britons are always thinking about who they are, what kind of society they belong to, and where they themselves belong in it. They have not always agreed about these things, but their disagreements have been within very limited parameters and perspectives, and they have often and increasingly been articulated in class terms and class terminology. All of which is merely to say that to write class out of British history and British life is to disregard or misunderstand one of its central themes. Class may not be the essence of history in the way that the Marxists and welfare state liberals once believed. But neither is it the perversion of history that Margaret Thatcher claims. Taking a long and broad view, changes in popular perceptions of British society have been at least as important as changes in British society itself, and it is in the evolving relationship between these social perceptions and social structures that the history of class is properly to be found and to be studied.[85] Hence this book. Enough of these preliminary reflections. It is time to turn to the thing itself and to move forward, not backward, to class.

CHAPTER TWO

THE EIGHTEENTH CENTURY

Class Without Class Struggle

Even in the heyday of the class-based history of modern Britain, Marxist scholars were never altogether at ease with the eighteenth century—a period that for these purposes may roughly be taken as beginning with the Glorious Revolution in 1688 and ending with the American Declaration of Independence in 1776. Before it came the supposed "bourgeois revolution" of the 1640s; after it was another ostensible middle-class triumph in the 1830s. This much, at least, seemed clear. But what happened during the intervening period? According to E. P. Thompson, Hanoverian society was deeply split between a dominant "patrician banditti" of Whig, agrarian capitalists and the plebeian working people, otherwise described as "the poor," "the crowd" or "the mob." And the relations between these two groups might best be understood, he insisted, as "crowd-gentry reciprocity," when things were quiet and settled, or as "class struggle without class," when this reciprocity broke down amid riots and popular protest. There was "class struggle" because these were two deeply antagonistic groups, whose relations were never less than tense and were often more overtly hostile. But there was no "class" because such fully self-conscious collectivities did not yet exist, as the industrial revolution was still to come and Marx was not alive and around to tell them this was who they were and what they were doing.[1]

This account of eighteenth-century social identities and political antagonisms has been justly influential. It was clever, eloquently articulated, and seemed to restore coherence and interest to a century that, in the aftermath of Sir Lewis Namier, had been atomized into myopic trivia and dissected into episodic tedium. But it never carried complete conviction, and since 1980 it has been undermined by criticisms from two different directions. One group of historians insists that eighteenth-century England was not polarized but instead a three-layer society and that it was the group in the middle that was the most important in holding the social fabric together and the most vigorous in pushing the nation toward modernity, improvement, and industrialization. Indeed, this interpretation has led some scholars to stand Marx on his head and to insist that it was in the eighteenth rather than in the nineteenth or seventeenth centuries that the rising bourgeoisie "played a most revolutionary part."[2] Alternatively, it has been argued that it is misleading to describe the eighteenth century in terms of collective class categories, whether two or three of them, because it was still overwhelmingly a hierarchical, individualist society. How, indeed, could it have been otherwise, given that neither 1642 nor 1688 had witnessed a bourgeois revolution, which necessarily meant that the traditional titled and territorial elite remained at the apex of a traditional, layered society of ranks and orders, station and degree?[3]

But this is not the only way in which scholarly thinking about the eighteenth century has changed and grown more complex. For in recent years, historians have become more aware that Hanoverian England was part of a much greater, bigger British world, encompassing not only Wales, Scotland, and Ireland but also the eastern seaboard of North America and large parts of the Caribbean.[4] Here again, however, there is similar confusion: were these eighteenth-century societies polarized into two struggling collectivities or divided into three with a dominant bourgeoisie, or were they still traditional, integrated hierarchies? And should these different—indeed mutually exclusive—ways of seeing these societies be understood in class terms or not? Historians have not been able to agree how they should describe these eighteenth-century social worlds, whether narrowly English or more broadly British, and it seems highly unlikely that they ever will.[5] But this should occasion no surprise, for contemporaries saw their social worlds in essentially the same three ways: hierarchical, three-layered, and polarized. Appropriately enough, all three visions were often expressed in different and particular vocabularies. But they were also increasingly expressed in two vocabularies that were becoming common to all three accounts: one was the language of ranks and orders; the other the language of class.

English Social Worlds

The most commonplace view of Hanoverian England's social structure was that it was providentially ordained, hierarchically ordered, and organically interconnected. This perception of society was generally associated with monarchs, aristocrats, courtiers, heralds, lawyers, clergy, and scholars: those who enjoyed prestige and wielded power. But it was also accepted by the majority of the population as the time-honored and authoritative way of seeing their world and understanding their place within it. It had originated in the Middle Ages, when all sorts and conditions of men were allotted their preassigned position in the unitary social order.[6] It was further elaborated by Tudor and early Stuart commentators into a world picture of a single, all-encompassing hierarchy of social ranks; this soon became widely accepted. One indication of this was Ulysses' speech, "Take but degree away, . . . and hark what discord follows," in Shakespeare's *Troilus and Cressida*. Another was the Prayer Book, with its divine injunction "to honour and obey the king, and all that are put in authority under him. . . . To order myself lowly and reverently to all my betters. . . . To do my duty in that state of life which it shall please God to call me."[7] To be sure, the Civil War had taken these orders and degrees and stations away, and terrible discord had duly followed. But the regicidal chaos of the 1640s and 1650s rendered this traditional social taxonomy more appealing rather than less, and it was restored along with King Charles II in 1660.

It was this venerable, layered, individualistic view of society that was most widely recognized and accepted in Hanoverian England. From the reigning monarch to the humblest subject ran unbroken this Great Chain of Being: via the five different ranks of titled nobility, to baronets, knights, esquires, gentlemen, leading citizens, and professionals, to yeomen, husbandmen, and artisans, and so finally to cottagers, laborers, servants, and paupers.[8] To those who lived at the apex, these gradations of rank and station provided what they regarded as an objective account of the world and their place within it, for it seemed to them that this was the natural order of things, that it mimicked on earth the celestial hierarchies of heaven, and that it was thus divinely sanctioned. People were ranked "according to the stations which it hath pleased God to allot them," and the resulting inequality was "not by chance, but by the sovereign disposer of the Lord of all." "In the course of His providence," wrote Thomas Broughton in 1746, "[God] has thought good to appoint various orders and degrees of men here upon earth." Samuel Johnson was of the same opinion, noting the "fixed, invariable external rules of distinction of rank, which create no jealousy as they are allowed to be accidental," by which he meant they were beyond human intervention or alteration because they were God's will and God's work.[9]

It was not only those at the top of eighteenth-century English society who were persuaded by this hierarchical model; these perceptions of the social structure were more widespread, appealing far beyond the confines of the privileged few. When Richard Gough wrote his *History of Myddle* in 1701, he began it with a description of the church seating plan, which extended in an unbroken sequence from the gentry at the front to the cottagers at the rear. This was how he saw society, and this was how society behaved and ranked itself. In 1733, when Sir Abraham Elton, Whig MP for Bristol, returned to the city having opposed Walpole's Excise scheme, he was welcomed by what were described as "all ranks and degrees of people."[10] Much more breezily and with a secular and meritocratic concern that was unusual for the time, Soame Jenyne wrote of "the wonderful chain of beings" that he envisaged extending "from the senseless clod to the brightest genius of human kind." Such examples could be multiplied many times over, for this picture of a graded society linked together in "one continued chain" was the conventional social wisdom. Here, indeed, was the customary hierarchy of a traditional, agrarian society, ordered, immutable, and "dogmatically validated."[11]

These vernacular descriptions of eighteenth-century English society were often articulated in the language of order, rank, station, degree, or estate. But as Harold Perkin long ago explained, in a suggestive insight that has never been given appropriate attention, another word was regularly, interchangeably, and increasingly used to describe this traditional, layered vision of the Hanoverian social world, and that word was class, class as hierarchy. As such, it carried no connotations of collective social categories or shared group identities, still less of deeply rooted social antagonisms; using this model of society and putting men into classes literally meant classifying them individually according to the prestige of their social rank.[12] In this connection, it is worth recalling George Watson's observation about the models and languages of nineteenth-century social description. "Much," he notes, "of the profusion of class terms and class discussion in the mid and late Victorian era becomes more intelligible and informative if it is seen as based on a general assumption of rank and hierarchy." If "Hanoverian" is substituted for "Victorian," this remark remains equally valid.[13]

But for all its popular resonance, this hierarchical picture of eighteenth-century England was, like any vernacular model of society, both idealized and partial. It sought to fix everybody—literally, everybody—with an assigned place in a single, linear, interconnected chain or ladder.

This was an appealing image, but it was indeed an image. Inevitably, it became less accurate and detailed the lower down the social scale it was applied, where minute gradations of status were often less apparent and it was more difficult to distinguish one person from another. It supposed all social relations to be individual rather than collective, presumed that prestige was largely inherited, took no account of social mobility, and paid inadequate attention to nonrural life and the nonrural professions. In its strictest form, this meant the hierarchical model of eighteenth-century English society was often too idealized and too inflexible to take account of the complex realities and shifting alignments of social structures and social developments.[14] Here is one example of its recognized limitations. During the 1770s, customs officers at English docksides recorded in detail the particulars of emigrants departing for the American colonies. In addition to describing their occupations, they were also expected to rank them hierarchically according to their "quality." But in practice it proved impossible to do so, in part because the emigrants came from a relatively narrow span of the social spectrum, and entries in this column were soon abandoned.[15]

The shortcomings of the hierarchical model meant that by the sixteenth and seventeenth centuries, commentators such as Sir Thomas Smith and William Harrison had begun to move toward modified versions of it, based on a more limited number of collective categories rather than the innumerable gradations of individual placings.[16] During the eighteenth century, as the population of England expanded and its wealth and occupational structure became more diverse, there were repeated attempts to update and adapt the traditional model in this way. In 1688 Gregory King divided English society into twenty-six ranks and degrees. Richard Gough modified his strict hierarchy by dividing the parishioners of Myddle into "the chief inhabitants," the "best of the parish," the "good and substantial persons," and the "poor people." In 1709 Daniel Defoe produced a seven-tier classification, from "the great," who "live profusely," to "the miserable," who "really pinch and suffer want." At midcentury, James Nelson proposed five categories ("nobility" to "peasantry"), while Joseph Massie preferred seven ("noblemen or gentleman" to "labourers and husbandmen"). And in 1770 the author of *The Cheats of London Exposed* postulated a fourfold division that ran from "The Nobs" via "The Citizens and their Ladies" to "The Mechanics and Middling Degrees" and eventually reached "The Refuse," an early, vernacular anticipation of W.G. Runciman's four systactic categories.[17]

Such modifications of the hierarchical model bring us, by scarcely perceptible development and increasing simplification, to the second way in which the eighteenth-century English saw their society: as broken up into three collective groups. Once again, there were ample precedents. There was Aristotle's "virtuous social middle," moderately placed between the two extremes and thereby holding society together; and there were the three functionally distinct yet interdependent medieval estates, consisting of those who prayed, those who fought, and those who worked, an arrangement that was "part of the original design of the universe, the immutable structure of society."[18] By the early modern period, this vision of society had become increasingly secularized, and by the second half of the seventeenth century, the three medieval orders had been superseded as collective categories by "sorts" or by "ranks," a word shared with the hierarchical model.[19] It was to this model that Gregory King resorted when he offered Robert Harley a much simpler taxonomy than his twenty-six ranks and degrees: the "poorest sort," the "middle sort," and the "better sort." Daniel Defoe, modifying his seven categories, settled for the "labouring sort," the "middling sort," and the "landowning sort." In 1753 *The Protester* wrote of "the middling ranks of the people," and William Thornton distinguished between "the middling ranks of this kingdom" and the "higher class."[20]

Self-evidently, this division of English society into three distinct and discrete categories into which everybody—again literally—could be fitted was as much an oversimplified image as the hierarchical model, to which it was on occasions preferred, albeit in rather a different way. As William Thornton's words suggest, by the third quarter of the eighteenth century, this triadic picture of the Hanoverian social order was not only being articulated in the vocabulary of "ranks" or "sorts" (or, occasionally, "sets"); it was also described in the language of "class," a word that, like "rank," was common to both the hierarchical and the three-layer models. An early and idiosyncratic anticipation of this was to be found in *The Spectator* in 1712, when "Hotspur" allocated women into three "distinct and proper classes": "the ape, the coquette, and the devotee." More conventionally, as early as 1748 Samuel Richardson employed the phrase "the middling class" in *Clarissa.* Almost ten years later, Joseph Massie, who reflected contemporary usage in mixing up the language of rank, degree, and class, modified his seven socio-occupational groups into "gentlemen" and middling and inferior classes." And in 1777 Josiah Wedgwood wrote of the importance of selling his goods to "the middling class of people, which class we know are vastly, I had almost said, infinitely, superior in number to the great."[21]

Since medieval times and especially since the Civil War, there had also been available a third model of English society, the most simplified of all, that assumed there was one single, deep division, in which people were polarized between high and low, the few and the many, gentlemen and nongentlemen, superior and inferior, polite and common, learned and ignorant, rich and poor, nobility and commoner, "laced waistcoats" and "leather aprons," and so on.[22] As this varied vocabulary suggests, there were many different ways in which society could be divided into these two unequal sections. In the most simplified version of his tables, Gregory King distinguished between those who were increasing the wealth of the nation and those who were lessening it. Here the criterion was economic. In Norwich, there was a service of thanksgiving to celebrate the failure of the Jacobite rebellion of 1745, and it was attended by two segments of society: "the nobility and gentry" and "multitudes of people of low life." Here the criterion was prestige. And Thomas Bewick did not enjoy London because the metropolis was so sharply divided: from one perspective (financial) between "extreme riches" and "extreme poverty"; from another (status) between "extreme grandeur" and "extreme wretchedness."[23]

Like sheep and goats, or the saved and the damned, or "one half of the world" against (or ignorant of) "the other half," this was a powerful and potentially adversarial model of a deeply riven society that was held together neither by the individualized relationships of an elaborately ranked and classified hierarchy nor by the middle class that bridged the social gap between those above and those beneath. As Henry Fielding made Jonathan Wild observe, this appeared in some ways the "great division," between those who used their own hands and those who used the hands of others, and it was often represented as a polarity between "the common sort of people" on one side and "the better sort of inhabitants" on the other.[24] At the time of Walpole's ill-fated Excise scheme, the *London Evening Post* opined that "the sense of the people" was against "the promotors" of the measure. And in 1741, at Wymondham in Norfolk, the rejoicing at Admiral Vernon's victories over the Spanish was an expression of "the general sense and free act of the People, being in no way promoted by any leading gentleman." But this dichotomous vision could also be inverted, as by Jonas Hanway who in 1772 published his dismissive and hostile *Obser-*

vations on the Causes of the Dissolution Which Reigns among the Lower Classes of the People.[25]

Hanway's choice of words and blending of vocabularies is as instructive as William Thornton's. For as with the hierarchical and the tripartite models, this polarized picture of Hanoverian society was also being articulated by the second half of the eighteenth century in the language of classes. César de Sassure divided the English into "the lower classes," who he claimed got drunk in the daytime on liquor and beer, and "the higher classes," who he thought preferred to get drunk at night on port and punch. More seriously, and more subversively, John Wilkes distinguished in the 1760s between "all peers and gentlemen" on one side and "the middling and inferior class of the people" on the other, in a manner that anticipated E. P. Thompson's subsequent formulation of "patricians" and "plebs," and he made it plain whose side he was on.[26] And in his novel *Sandford and Merton*, Thomas Day drew yet another single line across the complexities of English society when he put these words into the mouth of one of his characters: "Gentleman in your situation in life are accustomed to divide the world into two general classes—those who are persons of fashion, and those who are not." These were arresting and appealing antitheses: but if three categories were an idealization, then how much more was this true of two?

These, then, were the three basic, vernacular models of eighteenth-century English society, as they were of Montpellier in the 1760s: the hierarchical, the triadic, and the dichotomous. Of these, the hierarchical was undoubtedly the most appealing and the one against which the other two were propounded as alternatives. Inevitably, all of them were oversimplifications, albeit in different ways, of a complex social structure, which was gradually becoming ever more complex, and they were expressed in a range of vocabularies so varied as to lend ample support to Dr. Johnson's lament about "the boundless chaos of living speech." But while each model had its own richly specific language, there were also some words which were increasingly common to all three. The language of ranks, orders and degree, although nowadays most readily associated with the hierarchical vision of society, was by this time also used to describe the two- and three-layer models. And so, as Dr. Johnson himself recognized, was the vocabulary of class. In his *Dictionary of the English Language*, published in 1755, he recognized two very different meanings of the word: one individualist and hierarchical, the other collective. His initial definition of "class" was "rank or order of persons." But he also recognized its alternative use: "a set of beings or things, a number arranged in distribution, under some common denomination."[27]

Already, then, by the third quarter of the eighteenth century, the language of class was being so widely and indiscriminately used in England that it was impossible to infer from the word itself which model of society was being alluded to. When James Nelson noted in 1753 that "every nation has its custom of dividing people into classes," he was clearly using the word to refer to a variety of different models, as his own subsequent analysis, which was very eclectic and confused, served to show.[28] Nor is this the only problem. For the model chosen and the picture of society it conveyed often tell us as much about the perspective and position of the beholder as they do about the society beheld. Anglican clergymen and Tories like Samuel Johnson were enamored of the hierarchical view of society and the divinely ordained subordination of some individuals to others. Likewise, Gregory King was a herald, a Stuart sympathizer, an admirer of the traditional, landed world, and it is scarcely coincidence that he substantially underestimated the numbers and incomes of the "middle ranks" in his social survey. Daniel Defoe, by contrast, preferred the triadic model, regarding the mercantile classes as the leaders of the nation and giving them approving prominence in his writings. So did Oliver Goldsmith, who claimed that "in this middle order of mankind are generally to be found all the arts, wisdom and virtues of society" and that its representatives were "the true preservers of freedom."[29]

As the examples of Defoe and Goldsmith suggest, those who embraced the three-stage model of English society almost invariably belonged to what they saw as the "middle" part of it, and they were often trying to make the case that these people were "free from the vices of the highest and lowest part of mankind" and were thus entitled to a greater say in the affairs of the country than they at present enjoyed. In short, they were deploying the triadic model not as an objective description of the social order but as a way of constructing and proclaiming favorable ideological and sociological stereotypes of those in the middle.[30] When William Beckford offered a very capacious definition of the "middling people" as encompassing gentry, financiers, merchants, manufacturers, shopkeepers, and yeomen, he was wanting to make the political point that they were very numerous and very admirable.[31] And when William Thornton drew the contrast between "the public spirit of persons in the middling ranks of this kingdom" and "the depravity of those in a higher class" (note, incidentally, the familiar mixture of languages), he was doing very much the same thing: asserting, in a wholly unverifiable manner, the virtues of one "rank" or "class" at the expense of another.[32] In essence, these were collective social groups as "imagined communities," partly in the sense that no one actually knew just how many of them there were but also because claims were being made about their moral qualities and modes of behavior that were selective, exaggerated, and unverifiable.

We shall encounter many more instances of this middle-class ideological stereotyping in the years after the 1780s, but this activity was never confined to those who saw society in triadic terms and from the vantage point of the middle. In the same way, and as some of the examples already given suggest, those who embraced the binary model of society and were on the side of "the people" invariably stressed that they were virtuous, respectable, independent, and predominantly consisted of the "middling sorts," as in Thomas Day's novel, *Sandford and Merton*, where he inveighed, on behalf of the patriotic majority, against those he saw as the selfish, Frenchified, effete upper classes.[33] Once again, this was largely a rhetorical ploy, of which much more was to be heard during the late eighteenth and early nineteenth centuries. And it often provoked the predictable counterassertion from those at the top that, on the contrary, it was *they* who were virtuous, decent, public-spirited, and high-minded, whereas "the people" were merely "the rabble" or "the mob," drawn from the "lower sorts" rather than from the "middling sorts," whose views were of no significance whatsoever. Either way, these were unquantifiable numbers of people with unverifiable modes of behavior, collective groups that existed more in the eye of the beholder than in social reality.[34]

The two- and three-stage models were thus alternative accounts of eighteenth-century society, not just in the sense that they described it collectively rather than individually but also in that they were either latently or explicitly antihierarchical. Similar ambiguities emerge in the contemporary debate over who was or was not a gentleman. To the believers in the hierarchical model, he was a landowner, with a coat of arms, the direct descendant of the classical and Renaissance ideal type, renowned for his courage, chivalry, generosity, hospitality, and sense of duty.[35] To the believers in the tripartite model, the definition was more complex. Professional men liked to think of themselves as gentlemen, and this was increasingly the case. But those in trade or business or manufacturing were not so sure. Some wanted to claim that they were genteel, "town gentry" if not necessarily "country gentry." But, as Defoe discovered, this was not always accepted: the "born gentleman" and the "bred gentleman" were "two sorts or classes of men," obviously different.[36] In the case of the dichotomous model, there was a clear choice: those on the top were by definition gentlemen, provided those beneath were morally or culturally or financially inferior. But if the upper class was depicted as selfish, effete, and Frenchified, then the gentlemen were more likely to be on the other side. As was so often the case, it very much depended on context, circumstance, point of view, and polemical (or political) purpose.[37]

In their purest forms, these three models clearly conveyed very different pictures of society, and their political and confrontational implications were to become increasingly apparent during the years after 1776 and 1789. But for most of the eighteenth century, contemporaries were willing and able to meld and merge them one into another and to move backward and forward between them. Since the hierarchical model tailed off after the elite, it could be easily elided into the dichotomous picture of society: the gentry versus the people.[38] If the middle classes, whom the triadic model featured so prominently, were broken down into separate professions, they could be incorporated into the ladder of ranks and orders. Alternatively, they could be divided into two, with the richer and more important attached to the landed establishment, while the rest went with the majority of the population, thereby returning to the binary model again.[39] And these sociological meldings and taxonomical glissades were made increasingly easy as the languages of ranks and class were used interchangeably for all three of the prevailing models of society. The result was that, whichever model they used and for whatever purposes, most people did know what their place was in Hanoverian society. And it can hardly be coincidence that it is these same three models of eighteenth-century England to which historians have most been drawn, the bulk of them seemingly unaware that they are reproducing contemporary social descriptions that never amounted to "real social knowledge."

British Social Worlds

Geographically, politically, socially, and imaginatively, eighteenth-century Britain was a larger place than eighteenth-century England, spreading across the seas and half way around the globe. Contemporaries were well aware that they belonged to a dynamic and expanding society of diverse regions and multiple identities. But it is only recently that historians have begun to appreciate the archipelagic and transatlantic elements of this larger realm and started to explore the ways in which different parts of it were converging and coming together, as well as the ways in which they remained (and were becoming) unalike. In terms of connections and convergences, Wales and England have been linked since Tudor times, while Scotland and England have shared the same crown since 1603 and the same legislature since 1707. Ireland recognized a common sovereign, was tied to Britain by the Protestant ascendancy, and was incorporated into the United Kingdom in 1801. And the British colonies across the Atlantic were not only subordinate to the king in Parliament; they also absorbed hundreds of thousands of emigrants from the mother country during the seventeenth and eighteenth centuries. All were subjects of the same sovereign; most thought of themselves as being Britons.

Yet there were also many significant variations within and between the constituent societies of this pan-British community. Geographically, they were very different: large parts of Ireland, Scotland, and Wales were rugged and remote, with high mountains and thin soils, and the transatlantic colonies encompassed a wide range of landscape and climate. Economically, their performance varied: the American colonies were generally more prosperous than England, while the countries of the "Celtic fringe" were noticeably less so. Historically, they were of differing antiquity: Wales and Scotland boasted pasts as lengthy as England's; so did Ireland, but it had acquired a new landowning elite in the seventeenth century; and the American colonies had only been settled relatively recently by Britons. Numerically, they had separate histories: people were much more thinly spread on the land in Wales, Scotland, and Ireland than in England, and while this was also true of the transatlantic colonies, population grew more rapidly on the American mainland than it did in England between the 1700s and the 1770s. Culturally, linguistically, and ethnically, there were greater variations: the majority of the Irish population was Catholic; in Wales and Scotland, there were many who could not read or write or talk in English; and in the colonies, there were black slaves, native Americans, and immigrants descended from other European nationalities, as well as those of authentically British stock.

These similarities and differences carry important implications for the social structures and social identities of this greater British world and for the ways in which contemporaries (and historians) have envisaged and understood them and their place within them. Scotland, Ireland, and Wales were in some ways separate and distinct, yet they were also England's immediate and increasingly assimilated neighbors. The transatlantic colonies were peripheral, parvenu, polyglot communities half a world away from the metropolis, but in the decades before 1776 they were becoming more like England in their social structures and cultural aspirations, rather than less.[40] The models that contemporaries used to describe these similar but different societies were virtually identical to those employed by eighteenth-century Englishmen: models of hierarchy, of tripartite divisions, and of a great divide. So, with certain local modifications, were the languages in which these models were described. And, as with England, historians' interpretations have closely shadowed the accounts that were most popular and resonant at the time.

In colonial America, as in Georgian England, the traditional way of conceiving and describing society was hierarchical. As in England, this model was specially favored by clergymen, lawyers, and those at the top of the ladder, all of whom accepted that this was the ideal, God-given state of affairs. In 1700 the Boston merchant John Saffin opined that God "hath ordained different degrees and orders of men, some to be high and honourable, some to be low and despicable, some to be monarchs, kings, princes and governors, masters and commanders, others to be subjects and to be commanded; servants of sundry sorts and degrees, bound to obey; yea, some born to be slaves, and so to remain during their lives." "There is," agreed Jonathan Edwards later in the century, "a beauty of order in society, as when the different members . . . have all their appointed offices, place, and station." Thus regarded, the hierarchy of monarchical society, successfully transported and transplanted across the Atlantic ocean, was part of the great chain of existence that ordered the entire universe, part of what John Adams called that "regular and uniform subordination of one tribe to another down to the apparently insignificant animalcules in pepper water."[41]

Like the English imperial metropolis, colonial America was a monarchical culture, a title-conscious place with "a prestige order which corresponded roughly with economic rank order." "Esquire," "Gent.," "Master," and "Honourable" were regularly but sparingly used, reserved for those of great wealth, high political or civic office, broad-acred estates, or superior education, and titles in the militia were also important designations of status in an ordered system of dignity, honor, and obligation. Cadwallader Colden noted that New Yorkers were divided into different "ranks," beginning with the great proprietors owning over 100,000 acres; Philip Fithian thought New Jersey was dominated by "gentlemen in the first rank of dignity and quality"; and visitors were much struck by the "great disproportion and distinction of ranks and fortunes" from Maryland down to South Carolina."[42] Throughout the colonies, church pews were assigned on the basis of the social position of the family head, and entering students at Harvard and Yale were ranked according to the standing of their parents. So great was this concern with status that several colonial families obtained grants of coats of arms from the English College of Arms during the third quarter of the century, and there were requests for a colonial peerage in order to establish a "complete" social hierarchy on the British model.[43]

But as this abortive proposal suggests, the lack of a resident monarch, of a titular aristocracy, and of the legal recognition of the attributes of nobility, combined with the presence of indentured servants and black slaves, meant that the hierarchy in colonial America was significantly different from the English model. As Colden pointed out, rich merchants and broad-acred planters were often of obscure and undistinguished ancestry—"the most opulent families, in our own memory, have risen from the lowest ranks of people"—and at the other end of the scale, there was a "great interval" between poor whites and indentured servants and Negro slaves.[44] This led many observers, both colonial and English, to conclude that by the standards of contemporary Europe it was the *lack* of a fully articulated hierarchy in America that was most remarkable. "All mortifying distinctions of rank," observed a British official in 1760, "are lost in common equality," while Henry Hulton believed "the spirit of equality" prevailed throughout Massachusetts, where they "have no notion of rank or distinction."[45] These were clearly exaggerations. But it is easy to see why some chose to describe colonial America in these terms, in view of the contrast with the extensive English language of hierarchy.

The fact that "rank of birth" was generally "not recognized" and that there were "no such things as orders, ranks and nobility" meant that alternative models of social description were popular and well developed. In America, as across the Atlantic, there was the three-stage model, often expressed in the language of sorts: usually "the better sort," "the middling sort," and "the meaner sort." This was widely and imaginatively used, as when the Virginian Edward Stevens wrote of "the Rich," "the middling kind," and "the lower sort." By midcentury, in America as in England, "class" was being employed in addition to "sorts": a New York auctioneer felt able to describe the goods he sold as coming from "first, middling, and lower classes of householders."[46] In England, the tripartite model of "sorts" and "classes" was especially popular among those who belonged to the middle class or wished to assert their growing importance, and in colonial America, where the upper class was neither titled nor aristocratic and where the lower class was indentured or enslaved, the significance of the middle class was correspondingly greater. Indeed, some were already claiming that the thirteen colonies were almost wholly middle class; the *Pennsylvania Journal*, for example, in 1756, opined that "the people of this province are generally of the middling sort, and at present pretty much upon a level. They are chiefly industrious farmers, artificers or men in trade; . . . and the meanest among them thinks he has a right to civility from the greatest."[47]

The third model of colonial American society was the binary distinction, which rejected the picture built around a preeminent middle class and became more widespread and more inflected with adversarial implications as the century advanced. In 1693 Samuel White contrasted "persons of mean and low degree" with "persons of good parentage, education, ability, and integrity." "In a little time," one observer remarked apocalyptically in 1736, there would be "no middling sort": "We shall have a few, and but a very few Lords, and all the rest beggars." "Rapidly are you dividing," wrote "Brutus" half a century later, "into two classes— extreme rich and extreme poor."[48] As in England, the biggest difference was between those who were regarded as genteel and those who were common, between those who wore the periwig and those who did not, between those who rode horses and those who did not. "We were accustomed," Devereaux Jarrett recalled, "to look upon what were called gentle folks as beings of a superior order." But there were also specific local variations: between king and people; between those who were independent and those who were dependent; and between those who were free and those who were slaves. In colonial America, these "absolute antitheses" were very popular.[49]

As in Hanoverian England, there were three distinct accounts of the social order in colonial America that in practice were elided one into the other: the hierarchical into patricians and plebs, patricians and plebs into one great middle-class whole.[50] As in England, they were articulated in languages that were sometimes specific to each model but sometimes expressed in the shared vocabularies of ranks or classes. As in England, the hierarchical model was generally preferred by those at the top; the tripartite by those in the middle; and the binary by those concerned with (or sometimes fearful of) ordinary people's rights. As in England, these three models have been taken up by different schools of historians of colonial America, whose interpretations closely (though not always consciously) mimic those of contemporaries.[51] How much attention does the hierarchical account pay to social change? Who exactly was a gentleman?[52] How are the middle classes defined, and who belonged to them? Where are the bourgeoisie in the dichotomous model? Was colonial America on the eve of the Revolution becoming more hierarchical, more middle class, or more divided between patricians and plebs? The answers depend on which contemporary (or which historian) you read.[53]

Not surprisingly, contemporary descriptions of the social structures of the Celtic fringe sometimes drew comparisons with the thirteen American colonies or with England. But because they were to a considerable degree in the eye of the beholder, they did not always yield the same insights or results. In 1772, for instance, Benjamin Franklin made a tour of Ireland and Scotland, where he was impressed by the state of "landlords, great noblemen and gentlemen, extremely opulent, living in the highest affluence and magnificence." But he was also appalled by the straitened condition of "the bulk of the people," who were "tenants, extremely poor, living in the most sordid wretchedness, in dirty hovels of mud and straw, and clothed only in rags." How different this starkly polarized society seemed to him from "the happiness of New England, where every man is a freeholder, has a vote in public affairs, lives in a tidy warm house, has plenty of good food and fuel, with whole clothes from head to foot." For Franklin, the problem with Scotland and Ireland was that they were deeply riven societies, lacking the ample, prosperous, and unifying middle class that was the very essence of colonial America.

Yet at almost the same time, after making their visits to Scotland, James Boswell and Samuel Johnson drew exactly the opposite conclusions from those that Franklin had reached. As a Tory who believed in the importance of tradition and hierarchy, Boswell regretted that the spirit of "shocking familiarity" was now pervasive between what had previously been the different ranks of men. And for similar reasons Johnson feared that "money confounds subordination by overpowering the distinction of rank and birth." There had been, he later lamented, "a general relaxation of reverence."[54] For Boswell and Johnson, then, the problem with Scottish society was not that there was a large gap between those at the top and those at the bottom but that that gap had narrowed almost to the point of disappearance. From their perspective, everyone seemed to be increasingly alike, living on the same level with the extremes of rank and fortune much diminished. Theirs was a description of Scottish society as unlike Franklin's as it was possible to imagine. About the only thing the three of them seem to have agreed on was that hierarchy was conspicuous by its absence. But in rejecting that model of Scottish society, they were almost certainly in serious error.

For there were many on the Celtic fringe who believed their societies were traditional, rurally based, divinely ordained hierarchies of degrees, orders, and classes that were founded on esteem, prestige, and inherited position, views that, as in England, dated back to medieval times.[55] The vocabulary of nobility and subordination pervaded the reference books on the Scottish and Irish peerages, while Welsh landowners were renowned for their obsessive interest in "pedigree and pride." As in England, clergymen preached the need for pious acceptance of one's God-given station in life and spoke the language of "ranks and conditions." In the counties, subscription lists to books reflected the precise gradations of the local social ladder: the titled, esquires, gentlemen, higher clergy, parish clergy, and so on down the scale.[56] Nor was this vision of society confined to those at the top of it. In Anglesey, the Morris brothers set great store by such social niceties, and Lewis Morris was notorious for his snobbish obsession with rank and title. And in Scotland, in 1727, James Johnston, a cooper of Liberton, gave instructions in his will that his body was to be decently interred in the parish churchyard "according to my rank and degree." This was a standard burial custom, based on a standard social perception.[57]

Indeed, many of the foremost writers of the Scottish Enlightenment, although preoccupied with the virtues and dangers of the new, commercial society that was evolving in Edinburgh, were of an essentially traditional and hierarchical caste of mind, saw their society from this perspective, and gave expression to it in their use of the language of order and degree. Like his near-contemporary Samuel Johnson, David Hume believed in the importance of "birth, rank and station" as the proper way of organizing society and feared "the mischiefs consequent to an abolition of all rank and distinction."[58] In his *Essay on the History of Civil Society*, Adam Ferguson used the words "orders," "ranks," and "classes" interchangeably and made plain his belief in the importance of hierarchy: "the object of every rank is precedency." In a similar manner, and for similar purposes, James Millar devoted an entire book to *Observations Concerning the Distinction of Ranks*. And Adam Smith's *The Wealth of Nations* is shot through with the same hierarchical view of society. "Birth and fortune," he observed, were "the two circumstances which principally set one man above another." They were, he believed, "the two great sources of personal distinction," and they naturally established "authority and subordination among men."[59]

Yet while Celtic society was often viewed in this conventionally hierarchical way, this mode of perception was qualified by the fact that none of these hierarchies was as complex or as deeply rooted as in the original English model. In Ireland, the landed class was descended from alien, Scotts-English military adventurers who had only established themselves in the second half of the seventeenth century. As such, it lacked venerable legitimation and autochthonous credibility, and because many of the landlords were absentee, it was widely believed that the resident hierarchy was much depleted at the top.[60] In Wales, the territorial elite was authentically venerable, but the great magnates were few and far between, and they tended, like the duke of Beaufort, to be absentee. And because of the severe demographic crisis, many estates passed by marriage to distant, non-Welsh owners, which further depleted the resident hierarchy. In Scotland, the traditional clan system was visibly disintegrating (hence Boswell and Johnson's remarks); in the aftermath of the Act of Union of 1707 grandees such as the dukes of Argyll and Hamilton left for London; and as a result of the events of 1745, many highland titles and estates were for a time forfeit. Here, as in Wales and Ireland, the extended hierarchy that was supposed to exist according to the vocabulary of ranks and orders was in practice incomplete.

Many conservative commentators and local patriots lamented what they regarded as this hierarchical shortfall. In Wales, writers such as Ellis Wynne and John Byng described empty, crumbling mansions, their owners having departed for England, and yearned for the halcyon days of "the men that once were." In Ireland, Thomas Prior produced his famous (and exaggerated) *List of Absentees*, which went through seven editions between 1729 and 1783, and observers such as William King regretted that "no very topping noblemen or gentlemen" were to be found in his neighborhood. And in Scotland, David Hume lamented that "we have lost our princes, our parliaments, our independent government, even the presence of our chief nobility."[61] Undoubtedly, there was truth in all these claims. But to an even greater extent than the inflated accounts of the virtue and importance of the English middle class, these descriptions of incomplete Celtic hierarchies were examples of special sociological (and political) pleading. Those who regretted Irish land-lords' absenteeism, or the demise of the "ancient gentry" in Wales, or the departure of Scottish grandees south of the border undoubtedly exag-gerated the incompleteness of their indigenous hierarchies as a way of protesting the increasing dominance (and allure) of England, especially London.[62]

The traditional social picture of hierarchy was thus important and widespread in Scotland, Wales, and Ireland, even though there was disagreement as to the nature and extent of that hierarchy. By contrast, the tripartite model of "sorts" or "ranks" or "classes" was less in evidence than in England or colonial America, appropriately enough because those in the middle who were most inclined to use it were themselves less in evidence. In the Scottish highlands, there were those who divided society between the clan chiefs and their families, the "tacksmen" (or middlemen), and the "lower rank of tenants and cottars."[63] In Edinburgh, David Hume modified his hierarchical view of society by suggesting a tripartite alternative, the most important element of which was "the middling rank of men," who came between "gentlemen who have some fortune and education" and the "meanest, slaving poor." Notwithstanding his belief in hierarchy, Hume was enthusiastic about the growth of the commercial, self-supporting "middling rank," but like many men of similar views in England and America, he was not always clear or consistent in his description. Later luminaries of the Scottish Enlightenment were more equivocal about the growth of the middle class than Hume. The most famous of these was Adam Smith, for while he was prepared to acclaim the probity and propriety of the "middling sorts," he was increasingly concerned by the development of their exces-sive, self-interested, monopolistic affluence and influence.[64]

In Ireland, the tripartite model of society was even less in use, although there were abundant medieval precedents. Except in the case of the Dublin merchant community, which was the only large group of middling men in the country, it was rarely employed in a confident or favorable way. On the contrary, it was more likely to be invoked by those at the top of the social hierarchy to disparage the standing of those immediately beneath, especially the "middlemen" who came between the landlord and his tenants. These were the people the earl of Kenmare had in mind when he denounced "the pride, drunkenness and sloth of the middling sort among the Irish," a nice reversal of the English (or colonial American) mode, which was much more inclined to exaggerate the same "sort's" virtues. Arthur Young, who got most of his opinions on the subject from the Irish gentry and who probably invented the term "middleman," was no less critical.[65] Here was the use of the triadic picture of society for negative rather than positive stereotyping of those in the middle. In Wales, by contrast, this model seems to have been scarcely used at all (though again it had been in existence since medieval times), whether for negative or positive purposes.It is easy to see why. Of the five constituent parts of the greater British world, this was the one where the "middling sorts" were least in evidence.[66]

This brings us back to Benjamin Franklin's view, which many contemporaries shared, that the social structures of Wales, Scotland, and Ireland were best understood in polarized terms. According to one English visitor to Ireland, there was "no middle rank between the great man and the beggar," and it was widely believed that Irish society was divided between "the landlords" and "the ordinary sort," or "the poor." It was the same in Wales. In Cardiganshire, in 1684, a distinction was drawn between "the rich," who were "happy and high," and "the vulgar," who were "most miserable and low," and "both to an extreme." Sixty years later, in Glamorgan, there was still the same division between "gentlemen" and "the meaner sort."[67] In Scotland, *Forbes's Almanack* separated "noblemen, gentlemen, merchants and others" from "the vulgar," while Adam Ferguson drew the line between "the superior" and "the lower classes of men." Adam Smith distinguished between "the rich and the great" and the "poor and mean," or, in another formulation, between "a man of rank and fortune" and "a man of low condition." And he described Ireland in similar terms, as inhabited by superior and inferior "ranks of people," by "the oppressors and the oppressed," and by "the protestants and the papists," whom he saw (as if in partial anticipation of Benjamin Disraeli) as "two hostile nations."[68]

As this last quotation implies, these binary divisions and dichotomous identities were not just a replication of the Anglo-American pattern. They were also reinforced and reconfigured by local circumstances that were the product of history, culture, religion, and geography and were played out differently in each of the three nations. In Wales, the distinction between "patricians" and "plebeians" was accentuated by that between the native inhabitants who spoke Welsh and the elite, which was becoming increasingly Anglicized. During the eighteenth century, English became "the genteel and fashionable tongue," while Welsh was dismissed as "a poor, anonymous tongue," as "an incoherent jargon," as the language of "brutes." In Ireland, the same social division was initially reinforced by the division between those indigenous inhabitants who saw themselves as "Irish" and the new-comers whom they dismissed as "English." But as Adam Smith noted, this was gradually replaced by the more significant distinction between those who were "Papists" and those who were members of the "Protestant Ascendancy," a phrase first coined in the 1780s but a concept current long before.[69] In Scotland, by contrast, the horizontal gulf was undermined, rather than reinforced, by the division between the Highlands and the Lowlands, a distinction that was a function not just of geography but also of culture, with the clans, Catholicism, and Gaelic on the one side and a modernizing, Anglicized, urbanized world on the other.

Inevitably, these various ways of dividing up Celtic society involved a considerable degree of oversimplification, just as did the more familiar Anglo-American descriptions and identities that they usually reinforced but sometimes undermined. In Wales some squires continued to speak the native language, especially in those parts more remote from the English border. In Ireland "patricians" could not always be elided into Protestants and "plebs" into Catholics: some Catholic landowners managed to survive; there were middle-class Protestants in Dublin, Cork, and Waterford; and in Ulster the majority of the population was neither Catholic nor Anglican but Presbyterian. And in Scotland the social identities evolved in the Lowlands had more in common with England, whereas those of the Highlands in some ways more closely resembled Ireland. It was all very complex, more complex than in the case of Hanoverian England or colonial America. No wonder that Franklin and Boswell and Johnson did not see or did not understand everything and did not agree about what they had seen.

But notwithstanding these local variations (and there were doubt-less more than have been mentioned here), the general picture seems clear, and it is that which we need to keep in mind. In Wales, Scotland, and Ireland, the same models of society were available as in Hanoverian England and colonial America: the hierarchical, the three-layered, and the polarized. As in Hanoverian England and colonial America, historians have been drawn to these identical three models, most of them unaware that they have been replicating and reproducing them.[70] And as in Hanoverian England and colonial America, contemporaries were able to move from the hierarchical to the dichotomous model of their society with relative ease. Of course, there were differences: there were specialized vocabularies for Ireland, Scotland, and Wales, just as there were for America; the triadic model of society seems to have been less well developed on the Celtic fringe than in England or the thirteen colonies; and the language of class also seems to have been less in evidence with regard to all three models. Nevertheless, contemporaries in this greater British world were remarkably consistent in the models they used to describe the social structure of its constituent parts. And the result was that, whatever description they used, most people knew their place. As one Irishman explained, this was something that "no one was clear in, but which everyone understood."[71]

Social Life and Social Perceptions

Indeed, this phrase may be taken as applying more broadly to the whole of the greater eighteenth-century British world. For notwithstanding the local variations in social structures and the accompanying models of society, both within the British Isles and across the Atlantic contemporaries moved back and forth between the hierarchical, the triadic, and the polarized models with relative ease and widespread comprehensibility. But this merely begs another question. For how were they able to acquire, maintain, articulate, and communicate these multiple yet generally reconcilable perceptions of themselves and the world on the basis of their actions and experiences as *homines economici*, as social beings, or as political participants? Then, as now, social models and social vocabularies existed and evolved to facilitate not only social understanding but also the living of interactive lives. How, then, was it possible for Hanoverian Britons to conclude, on the basis of their getting and spending, their social relationships, or their involvement in politics that the society to which they belonged and in which they lived was best understood as a ladder of ranks or classes, or as three layers of "sorts" or "classes," or as divided between "the great" and "the people" or the "upper" and "lower" classes, or as a constantly changing mixture and meld of different bits of all three?

No one in the eighteenth century denied that the distribution of wealth in the greater British world was manifestly unequal, ranging from dukes with incomes well in excess of £10,000 a year to poor laborers getting by on £10 or less.[72] But there were different ways in which this economic inequality was socially envisaged. One way was to see it as an infinity of gradations extending from the very rich to the very poor, as a hierarchy of property and income that closely corresponded to, and helped reinforce, the hierarchy of social prestige: dukes were generally richer than barons, merchants than manufacturers, shopkeepers than artisans, skilled workers than laborers, servants than paupers. A second approach was to recognize three social groups on the basis of wealth and work: landowners; those in services, finance, the professions, and industry; and those with more humble occupations. Hence the tripartite model, which was especially appropriate for an economy that boasted the largest nonagricultural sector in Europe.[73] Or it was possible to envisage the structure of wealth as being divided along a single, elemental fault line that underscored many of the binary social divisions: between what Adam Smith described as "those who have some property against those who have nothing at all."[74] Not surprisingly, perceptions of the distribution of wealth and perceptions of the social forms to which it gave rise were closely interconnected.

These prevailing models of social description also resonated differently in the country and the town, for rural and urban society were not necessarily envisaged in the same way. Self-evidently, it was easiest to observe the ordered, traditional hierarchy of rank and degree in the countryside, where it had originated and still retained much of its credibility. Yet it was also in many parts of the countryside that the great gulf between those who owned landed property and those who did not was most striking, hence the easy interpermeability, in the rural world, of the hierarchical and dichotomous models. But this was only part of the picture. For eighteenth-century England was also the most urbanized nation in Europe, and there were large and growing metropolitan agglomerations elsewhere in the greater British world.[75] In London and Edinburgh, Dublin and Glasgow, Boston and Philadelphia, Norwich and Bristol, men and women were thrown together in their tens of thousands and sometimes in their hundreds of thousands. This was a totally different society: crowded, tumultuous, rootless, mobile, restless, sometimes segregated, sometimes not, where the customary models of hierarchy offered at best an inadequate and outdated guide to the social landscape.[76] It was necessary to find other ways of envisioning and explaining this fluid society, which is why it was in the towns and cities that the tripartite model most vigorously evolved and the binary model of social division acquired a new, specific, and keener articulation.

Notwithstanding party divisions and loyalties, politics also derived from and helped reinforce conventional ideas of social structure and social identity. It was commonly recognized that political activity and political influence were hierarchically determined: the further up the social scale one went, the greater the degree of involvement in elections, government, and administration and the more substantial the amount of power wielded over others.[77] But politics could also be convincingly explained in terms of the increasingly popular tripartite model: the upper classes influenced or controlled many constituencies; provided most of the parliamentary candidates; monopolized the Commons, the Lords, and the cabinet; and governed the country. The "middling sorts" dominated the local oligarchies that governed most towns; they were actively involved as voters, canvassers, and election agents in constituency politics; and they could even exert a certain influence on Parliament's legislative agenda. By contrast, the "lower orders" had walk-on parts as rioters, players in crowd scenes, and extras. Alternatively, there was the one great divide: between those who were officially involved in the formal political process and were "within the pale of the constitution," with the necessary property qualifications to vote or hold high public office, and those who were outside, "beyond the pale," who played no formal part whatsoever. Beyond doubt, these were approximate, idealized categories—there were some middle-class MPs, and many people who had the vote were, by various criteria, working class[78]—but they generally seem to have worked, in that they helped to render political activity socially credible and comprehensible.

Those who made, implemented, and encountered eighteenth-century law were also able to make some sense of it in social terms. In one guise, the legal system reflected and undergirded a stratified society: there were elaborate gradations of courts, assizes, and sessions, as well as complex ranks of judges and justices; and it was often claimed that those who were richer or of higher prestige got better justice and greater courtesy of treatment than those who were poorer or lowlier. From another sociological perspective, the working of the law could more appropriately be understood in triadic terms: the power of the "better sorts" was significantly limited by the laws they themselves made and applied; the prime users and beneficiaries of the legal system were the "middling sorts," as plaintiffs, defendants, and jurors; and the majority of criminals were drawn, as they always are, from the "meaner sorts."[79] But criminal law (and in Ireland the penal laws) could also be seen as an instrument of upper-class rule over the rest of society, because those who made the law and those who implemented it came from the same superior social stratum, because there were special pieces of class-specific legislation such as the game laws, and because the defense of property was a higher priority than the defense of life.[80] As with political activity, these were exaggerated accounts seeing the law as being the product of, and a reinforcement to, the hierarchical or tripartite or dichotomous views of society. But once again, they seemed to make some sense of things.

The same may be said of education, and not only in terms of the characteristics of its institutions but also in terms of the concepts and categories that it made available to those who were receiving it, which helped them establish their own social identities. Like politics and the law, teaching, learning, and literacy were intrinsically hierarchical.[81] There was an elaborate ladder of places of learning, from Oxford and Cambridge universities, via Eton and Harrow and the grammar schools of Manchester and Leeds, to the humblest parish schools. The higher up the social scale, the better, the longer, and the more expensive the education that was available. And this, too, could be understood in a more simplified (indeed, oversimplified) way, as a three-tier system, in which people from three basic social backgrounds went to three basic types of institutions: public schools and Oxbridge for the aristocracy and gentry, grammar schools and professional training for the middle classes, and parish schools (or nothing) for the rest.[82] There was also the more fundamental division: between those who had a university degree and those who did not, or between those who were "educated" and those who were not, or between those who were literate and those who were not. And however education was envisaged in social-structural terms, it was more concerned with teaching people their place than with giving them opportunities to advance. For education was a religious activity, and religion taught "rank, station, duty, and decorum" rather than social ambition or social mobility.

These were some of the ways in which eighteenth-century Britons could make social sense of themselves and their society on the basis of their experiences as workers and wealth holders, as town or country dwellers, as political activists or spectators, as lawmakers and litigants, or as pupils at school or undergraduates at university. Much of this continued to remain true during the nineteenth century, a great deal of it still holds good in Britain today, and throughout the pages that follow, this should be kept constantly in mind. Similar arguments could (and can) also be made with reference to (among other things) health, nutrition, life chances, accent, dress, transport, recreations, the armed services, and the church. With equal plausibility, all these varied realms of human activity and social experience could be comprehended and communicated hierarchically, or triadically, or dichotomously, or in ways that moved from one conventional mode of social description and social understanding to another. Thus did social structures, social activities, and social vocabularies mutually prop each other up.[83] Of course, as I have pointed out time and again, these social descriptions and social understandings were crude, selective idealizations. They always are and always will be. But in this greater British society, they worked, they made sense, and most people understood.

These perceptions, experiences, descriptions, and understandings were further underscored by the different ways in which Hanoverian society went public by putting itself ritualistically on display. Throughout the greater British world, hierarchy was constantly being dramatized, and the established order made visible. Royal entries, progresses, birthdays, weddings, coronations, and funerals provided the most magnificent displays of the formal hierarchy at its most complete and compelling, with elaborate processions in which the careful gradations of status ranking were observed and proclaimed.[84] From Birmingham to Boston, Manchester to Montreal, local celebrations and mimetic observances replicated order and reaffirmed degree. And it was not only the marking of royal rites of passage that occasioned such vivid hierarchical pageants and processions; in the country, and in some towns, the rites of passage of local notables were observed with similar splendor. The formal entry of the Lord Lieutenant of Ireland into Dublin, the state opening of Parliament, the installation of a university chancellor, the beginning of a new legal term, the processions marking the entry of electoral candidates into their constituencies: all these were opportunities for the pomp and circumstance of order and degree to be made public. And as Britons were confronted by, or participated in, these transcendent social dramas, it must have been easy to believe that this ritualized depiction of social gradations was indeed the real version of the natural order of things.[85]

But for all their claims to transcendence, these processional rituals of state and church, royalty and nobility, superiority and subordination were not the only versions of the social order that were acted out and theatrically displayed in the greater British world of the eighteenth century. There were alternative ceremonies of social structure, just as there were alternative models.[86] Many gatherings, whether political or social, formal or informal, deliberately staged or spontaneously acted out, affirmed a very different view of society, in which the old, traditional hierarchy was set aside in favor of public displays of middle-class oligarchy and assertiveness. In the large towns and cities, where the social hierarchy was incomplete, urban rituals and civic ceremonials were as likely to exclude as to include those at the very top: mayor making, saints' days, assize sermons, and the like. And many of the rituals surrounding bourgeois sociability were equally restrictive: theaters and balls, parks and pleasure gardens, libraries and reading rooms, all welcomed the urban patriciate, while the aristocracy stayed away and the "inferior sorts" were deliberately kept out, by fees, by membership requirements, or by direct proscription.[87] The result was a version of society, different from the inclusive procession, that proclaimed instead the dominance of the middle-class civic elite.

There was yet a third way in which the British social structure was represented and its social identities were dramatized, which derived from and reinforced the dichotomous vision of things. For riots, protests, and demonstrations offered a ritualized version of how society was and ought to be: that is, adversarial and oppositional rather than hierarchical or consensual. Instead of the deferential acceptance of subordination or the confident assertion of middle-class identity, "the mob," "the crowd," or "the people" might organize and take to the streets to protest against what were regarded as unacceptable abuses of power by those in authority.[88] Thus was the binary interpretation of the social order made real and actual: in demonstrations against food hoarding or turnpikes or the press gang; in opposition to Walpole's excise scheme or Henry Pelham's "Jew Bill"; or in support of Pitt the Elder or John Wilkes. Here was a form of public, collective behavior characterized by anger, dissent, protest, disaffection, and nonacquiescence; by the reassuring (or ominous) claims of solidarity between (to quote John Wilkes again) "the middling and inferior class of people"; and by hostility to social superiors, who were depicted and derided as the corrupt, self-interested, self-serving elite.[89]

Be that as it may, in the greater eighteenth-century British world, the models of social stability provided a more realistic guide and a more powerful imperative than the competing visions of social conflict or subversion. However much it was challenged, the hierarchical picture generally remained both pervasive and persuasive, and with it the attitudes of subordination and deference that it depended on and proclaimed. By contrast, the triadic description, with its stress on the socially specific nature of middle-class virtue, was rarely the vehicle of serious social grievance or realistic political demands. There may have been sporadic outbursts, as with those "middling sorts" who supported John Wilkes during the 1760s, but they did not amount to anything definite or permanent or socially specific.[90] And under these circumstances, there was little prospect of the polarized model of society being realized (as distinct from dramatized), with "the people" as a whole rising up in a mass movement to subvert the established order and overthrow their social superiors. One reason why the greater British world was generally so stable was that with alternative descriptions available, each of them credible but none of them entirely comprehensive, and with hierarchy as the most widely accepted, it was difficult to imagine how, or in whose interests, the existing social order might be fundamentally reconstructed.

To be sure, some contemporaries asserted the claims of the middle classes against their betters, of the triadic model of society against the hierarchical. But as other Britons observed, there was in reality no fundamental conflict between land and commerce, upper and middle classes, or between these two ways of looking at society. As Josiah Tucker opined in 1750: "These supposed distinctions of landed interest and trading interest are the most idle and silly, as well as false and injurious, that ever divided mankind." In the same way, the ephemeral protests that publicized and dramatized the dichotomous vision of society were more usually focused on single issues or particular individuals than on a thoroughgoing critique of the social structure that presumed a fundamental division into conflicting collective identities. For British society was not only seen as aristocratic and hierarchical; it was also regarded as bourgeois and triadic, and sometimes as dichotomous and plebeian. It was none of these things separately because it was all of them together.[91] From one perspective, many Britons saw themselves as subjects of a traditional monarchy; from another, they believed they were the citizens of the Venetian republic; from yet a third, there were those who sometimes—but only sometimes—felt alienated and excluded.

For the fact was that "the rich" and "the poor" were not going to come to blows, however much E. P. Thompson later argued (and wished) that they might have done and should have done. As Dr. Johnson observed, "There is no doubt that, if the poor should reason, 'We'll be the poor no longer, we'll make the rich take their turn,' they could easily do it, were it not that they can't agree."[92] In the end, and as this remark suggests, eighteenth-century Britain was *not* divided between two homogeneous, easily defined, and perennially warring collectivities. Nor (and this was Johnson's second insight) was the nation held down by force; with the exception of the Scottish Highlands in the aftermath of the 'Fifteen and the 'Forty Five, most people *did* acquiesce in what they most often understood as a hierarchical society of "ranks" and "classes," sometimes envisaged as a tripartite society of "sorts" or "classes," and now and then saw as a more polarized society of "the great" and "the people" or the "upper" and the "lower" classes.[93] Indeed, the Jacobite risings are very much the exceptions to this that prove the rule, for those protests were not built round collective social identities so much as geographical identities: the Gaelic, Catholic, highland clans in revolt against the modernizing world of the south.

With very few exceptions, therefore, eighteenth-century British politics was *not* concerned with the articulation, assertion, or conflict of collective social identities, beyond the usually unstated but accepted recognition that a hierarchical society was the best of all possible social worlds and that the people at the top of that hierarchy should be left to get on with governing it. Politicians did not talk about or try to create such identities in the way that their successors were to do in the nineteenth and even more in the twentieth centuries. And most people involved in popular protest had no intention of turning what they saw as a time-honored, providential, and credible hierarchy upside down. All of which is merely to say that Richard Pares's by-now-venerable remark about Hanoverian England retains much of its validity—"The distribution of political power between the classes was barely an issue"—not least because while people were sometimes thinking socially in terms of class, either hierarchically or collectively, they were rarely thinking *politically* in such terms. This in turn suggests that E. P. Thompson's formulation needs modifying to the point of total reversal. Instead of witnessing "class struggle without class," it is probably more correct to observe that eighteenth-century Britain saw class without class struggle.[94]

Creating a Classless Society

This society, seen in these three different but usually reconcilable ways, did not endure indefinitely unchanged and unchallenged, and its transformation in some areas and its termination in others were both prefigured in the amazing year of 1776, after which social structures, social perceptions, and the greater British world itself were never quite the same again. One reason was the signing of the Declaration of Independence by representatives of the rebellious American colonies, a declaration that contained the ringing affirmation that "all men are created equal."[95] Of course, it has long been known that the American Revolution was not about equality for everyone, least of all for women or slaves or native Americans: they had a long time to wait and a long way to go. But in the broader British context, it *was* an exceptionally audacious and subversive notion, serving notice on traditional conceptions of hierarchy and aristocracy, orders and ranks, deference and subordination and proposing a social structure not just (as colonial America already was) partially unlike that of the mother country but totally and deliberately unlike.[96] It also bears stressing that this revolutionary way of envisaging a nation and organizing its society were first portended thirteen years before the Bastille was stormed in Paris.

To be sure, the precise meaning of the Declaration of Independence and the significance of the subsequent Revolution depend on which of the characterizations of pre-1776 social structure one accepts as the starting point. For those who believe that colonial America was becoming more feudal, more hierarchical, more settled, more English, the Revolution wrought massive change, halting and then reversing these developments and directing the republic along a new path of social evolution in which ideas of equality and freedom vanquished those of deference and subordination and political leadership ceased to be the exclusive preserve of those of great wealth or high social status.[97] For those who believe that colonial America was already a preponderantly independent and middle-class society, the Revolution mattered less, for it merely "completed, formalized, systematized, and symbolized" what were largely the already accomplished facts of social structure and social perception.[98] And for those who believe that colonial America was becoming polarized between the haves and the have-nots, the Revolution did not change very much, as the new republic continued to be divided, as it had already been in colonial times, between a middle class and a working class that were becoming more numerous and (within limits) more self-conscious.[99]

These matters remain much debated by American historians, and it is neither appropriate nor possible to try to resolve them here. But some remarks are worth venturing. However limited may have been the hierarchy that existed in colonial America, the founding fathers deliberately rejected and overthrew it, by abolishing primogeniture and declaring titles illegal. And this antihierarchical impulse was strengthened by the subsequent failure of the Federalists to create a "natural" aristocracy or entrench it in the Senate.[100] To be sure, the American Revolution did not abolish distinctions between rich and poor, and during the nineteenth century, these economic inequalities would become greater than those in Britain itself. But it *did* assault political dependency, *did* undermine social inequality, *did* outlaw formal distinctions of status, and, by so doing, *did* create a new sort of society—and a new way of looking at it—increasingly unlike that in England (or anywhere else in Europe) that had originally settled and spawned it. As anyone knows who has crossed the Atlantic, Americans *are* more independent and less deferential than the English. Theirs is a republican, not a monarchical, culture, which means they do see their society differently and which is why, when they put their social structures on public display, they have parades (which are intrinsically egalitarian), whereas the British have processions (which are innately hierarchical).[101]

Of all the communities the British have created across the seas and around the world, America is unique in having so explicitly rejected the hierarchical social structure and the deferential social attitudes of the colonial metropolis and in having rejected along with them the languages both of ranks and of class as the prevailing forms of social description.[102] Indeed, it must have been just this prospect that George Washington had in mind when he observed in 1788 that "the distinction of classes begins to disappear"; that Timothy Dwight was thinking of when he noted in 1794 that "one extended class embraces all, all mingling, as the rainbow's beauty ends"; and that Charles Ingersoll was alluding to when he claimed in 1810 that "patrician and plebeian orders are unknown."[103] As is invariably the case, these social descriptions were much oversimplified and were themselves to become the bases for much subsequent American self-mythologizing. But for all their limitations, special pleading, and exaggerations, these remarks were—and still are—much more applicable to the United States, whose inhabitants are citizens, than to the United Kingdom, whose inhabitants are still subjects. That is a measure of the differences between these two countries, wrought by and in the aftermath of 1776.[104]

Anyone interested today in seriously attempting to transform Britain into something approaching a "classless society," or even in the more modest undertaking of creating a completely nonhereditary second legislative chamber, needs to study the making and aftermath of the American Revolution.[105] For it is the first and most significant occasion in the whole history of the greater British world when those in charge of one part of it envisaged, proposed, undertook, and accomplished both the greater and lesser of these two tasks. (In Ireland, after the Treaty of 1922, something similar did happen, as it did again in India after independence in 1947, but of these, more later.) And as a result, the Revolution not only brought about a new and self-consciously anti-British social structure in the United States that was deeply hostile to the idea of, and to government by, a leisured aristocracy and where most people thought of themselves and their society as "middle class"; it also detached the United States from the greater pan-British community, which means that the later history of American social structure and social description forms no part of this account.[106]

This was not the only way in which 1776 was a turning point in the history of British social structures and social perceptions. For that remarkably creative year also witnessed the publication of Adam Smith's *The Wealth of Nations*, a work that has already been quoted because of its conventional use of the hierarchical and dichotomous models of social description. But his book was at least as innovative as it was derivative, and it was its innovative aspects that were the more influential (and more exaggerated) in the long run. In the first place, Smith took an idea that had gradually but unsystematically been gaining ground during the eighteenth century and elevated it to the level of a fundamental principle when he advanced the proposition that social status and social identity were primarily determined not by honor or prestige ranking and still less by religion or politics or gender or family or leisure or locality but by occupation and relation to the means of production: "The understandings," he opined, "of the greater part of men are necessarily formed by their ordinary employments."[107] So far as is known, this was the first systematic attempt to argue that it is work that provides the key to social identities.

This account also enabled Smith to reformulate the traditional tripartite model into something less descriptive and more powerful and portentous. Society, he suggested, was fundamentally divided into landowners, businessmen, and laborers, because they were drawing their different incomes—respectively, rent, profits, and wages—from their different relations to the means of production, and as a result they were necessarily and inevitably competing with each other as to how much they obtained. It was, he concluded, these collective economic and occupational relationships that gave rise to collective social identities: "the three great, original and constituent orders of our modern society."[108] Here was the most sophisticated attempt yet to justify the three-stage model of human populations by offering a rigorous and consistent explanation of what the three collective groups in it were, how they came into being, and why they would always be there. But for all the novelty of the argument, Smith did not articulate it in a correspondingly novel vocabulary. On the contrary, he followed customary usage, writing, and thinking in the collective language of ranks and orders rather than that of classes.

In two ways, however, his analysis was an extreme (but very influential) oversimplification. It asserted that social identity was primarily determined by occupation and employment; but there were different views about that in the eighteenth century, just as there are different views about it in our own time. And like all tripartite divisions, however sophisticated, it did not do full justice to the complexities and diversity of the contemporary economic and social structure.[109] The best that could be said of Smith's three collective categories is that they were vague, ideal types that did not comprehensively describe society as a whole. Nevertheless, his analysis was taken up by James Millar in his later writings and by David Ricardo, who converted Smith's "orders" into the more usual word "classes," and it thereby reinforced the triadic vision of society that was to become extremely popular, resonant, and politicized in the half century ahead. It also lay behind the economic, social, and political analysis that was subsequently advanced so influentially by Karl Marx, who wrote the "history of all hitherto existing society" around the class wars among a feudal aristocracy, a capitalist bourgeoisie, and a laboring proletariat. As he later admitted, with Smith very much in mind, "no credit is due to me for discovering the existence of classes in modern society, nor yet the struggle between them."[110]

There are many ironies here for historians of social structure and social description, and especially for those Thatcherites who have sought to appropriate Adam Smith as the evangelist and celebrant of laissez-faire, middle-class capitalism. One is that, as a product of the Scottish Enlightenment, Smith had his doubts about the probity and wisdom of unbridled business culture. Another is that his very restricted references to the middle class were in no sense a celebration of their rising wealth or virtue.[111] Yet a third is that Karl Marx, the man

Lady Thatcher claims most to hate, derived his basic models of social structure and social identity, models that she so deplores and abominates, from the works of Adam Smith, a man whom she so admires. For the idea that society should be understood in terms of collective and conflicting social groups—sometimes three and sometimes two, sometimes expressed in the language of class but sometimes not—was well established as a capitalist concept long before it was appropriated as a communist concept. Far from being invented by a nineteenth-century revolutionary who looked forward to a proletarian utopia and a classless society, it had first appeared in a book by a Scottish political economist who was steeped in the hierarchical view of society. As the next hundred years were to show, that traditional way of visualizing British society still had a great deal of life left in it.

CHAPTER THREE

THE NINETEENTH CENTURY

A Viable Hierarchical Society

In the long perspective of British history, the period from the 1780s to the 1840s was once a teleologist's dream, but it has lately been turning into a postmodernist's nightmare.[1] According to the traditional class-based account, it had all been very simple and straightforward: the industrial and French revolutions together transformed social structures and social relations by destroying the old, individualistic, hierarchical world of ranks, orders, and degrees and bringing about an entirely new social system based on collective and conflicting identities, a system that resulted from the making of the working and middle classes, sometimes locally, sometimes in England, sometimes in Britain as whole. Never before—and never since—had classes so purposefully come into being, had class consciousness been so widespread, had class struggle been so prevalent, and had the results been so momentous.[2] From this perspective, the economic antagonisms generated on the factory floor between employers and employees led directly to an unprecedented upsurge of popular and near-revolutionary discontent, and this resulted in massive political disruption and constitutional change: the passing of the Great Reform Act, the repeal of the Corn Laws, and the Chartist movement. All these were the expression and end product of the intense struggle between the newly emerging classes as they battled for the mastery of early Victorian Britain, the greater British world, and the rest of the nineteenth century.

Here was an emphatically post–eighteenth-century society, where economic developments, social processes, and political events moved forward, interconnectedly and self-reinforcingly, to their necessary outcome: the collective and antagonistic identities found within the modern nation state, which were appropriately described in the new "language of class."[3] But by 1851 these bitter battles were over, giving way to the stable and secure world of "compromise" and "equipoise" dominated by a triumphant bourgeoisie, in which the classes resolved to live with each other rather than fight. This was, in short, the "viable class society" of the mid-Victorian era. Such academic disagreement as there was largely centered on explaining how these things had happened and the nature and number of the classes that formed this unusually stable society. Contemporaries may have been confused about this period, but the historical account was masterly in its confident simplicity.[4] Hierarchy was replaced by three classes (upper, middle, and lower) that battled and struggled from the 1820s to the 1840s but subsequently settled down to peaceful coexistence. Alternatively, it was argued that the upper classes were vanquished, or incorporated into the bourgeoisie, and that the two remaining classes (middle and lower) then made peace. Either way, there was a clear and apparently inexorable social-cum-political development: from hierarchy to three classes, or perhaps to just two.

But in recent years, this once-appealing interpretation has been seriously damaged. Historians still recognize that the decades from the 1780s to the 1840s were disturbed and momentous, but they no longer believe that the making of class-conscious classes provides a convincing master narrative that explains how and why things unfolded as they did.[5] Inevitably, this scholarly uncertainty about the first half of the nineteenth century has disrupted the established account of the period that follows. For if the working and middle classes had not been "made" by 1851, then what of the "viable class society" that supposedly came after, a society whose nature and stability had previously been explained in terms of the peaceful coexistence of collective groups? In short, the whole idea that this period witnessed a progression from hierarchy to three classes, or possibly to two classes, is much too overdetermined. Instead, it now seems clear that throughout the years from the 1780s to the 1870s, British society was envisaged by contemporaries in essentially the same ways that it had been during the century before. All three models remained, with hierarchy still the preferred version. Each retained its own specific vocabulary, but the languages of ranks and (especially) of class became increasingly common to all three. The significant difference was that these visions of society were now more consciously and contentiously politicized than before, at least until the 1840s. Why and how was this so? And why and how did this subsequently cease to be so?

Social Visions and Social Divisions

It bears repeating that the contemporary understandings of eighteenth-century British society had all been *latently* political: hierarchy because in a time of social disorder and political subversion it might need defending and reasserting; the triadic model because the middle classes might become more vigorous and aggressive in pursuit of their own sectional interests; and the binary account because conflict might actually break out between "us" and "them." Before the 1780s, these images had described and helped shape social structures rather than challenged or undermined them, as their political implications remained generally unrecognized and unrealized and the discrepancies between them were smoothed away by contemporaries more than they were sharpened up. But in the aftermath of the French Revolution, there was a clear and definite change, not so much because the working and middle classes were "making" themselves where no such classes had existed before, but rather because the proponents of different visions of the social order increasingly sought to assert their own, mutually exclusive notions of how society was—and how it should be.[6] In short, the novel feature of this period was not that new social structures were coming into existence and that new social vocabularies were being used to describe them; it was that the three traditional models of the British social order were being vigorously politicized.

Why did this happen? Notwithstanding the necessary and oft-cited qualifications, these *were* years in which the British social order was wrenched and transformed by a succession of seismic shocks. The French Revolution unloosed ideas of liberty and equality far more disruptive and subversive than those put about by the Americans in 1776. The agricultural and industrial revolutions brought significant changes in the rural and the urban economy, in productive processes, in occupational structure, and in the basic relationship between numbers of people and national resources. Population grew massively: in England it doubled between 1780 and 1836; in Scotland it rose by 5 percent between 1801 and 1831; and in Ireland it exploded from less than 2.5 million in 1753 to more than 6.5 million in 1821. During the 1810s and 1820s, such cities as Liverpool, Manchester, and Birmingham expanded more rapidly than in any period before or since, and most of their inhabitants were under twenty-four years of age. And in many parts of the British Isles, there was misery, hunger, protest, and discontent on a scale that had not been witnessed in the century since the

Glorious Revolution.[7] Small wonder that contemporaries found it difficult to understand or agree on what was happening to their society. Some feared chaos and collapse; some hoped for a new and better social order; many were merely bewildered and confused; most believed the changes to be more rapid and discontinuous than in any previous period.

It is, then, no coincidence that, as the social order was described, debated, and discussed with unprecedented urgency, intensity, and anxiety, the language of class, like the language of ranks, became more widely used, in both the private realm of everyday conversation and the public world of political discussion.[8] But this does not mean that new collective classes were being "made" and the old individualistic hierarchies were being overthrown. For the language of class was employed, as before, in connection with all three of the models of British society that had been available throughout the eighteenth century. Those attracted to the hierarchical vision continued to use class as an alternative to "rank," "station," "order," and "degree." Those who preferred the triadic model used class as a synonym for "sorts," "rank," or "degree" or, increasingly, instead of them.[9] And those who envisioned society as divided into two different groups often described them as the "upper" and "lower" classes. But whichever model was being used, most people who resorted to the language of class did so in the plural: "middle ranks," "middling sorts," "middle orders," and "middle classes" were regularly interchanged, as were "working classes," "lower orders," "productive classes," and "industrious classes." Even as they divided their society into these large collective groups, few Britons believed that there was one single middle class or one single working class, and they were right to be thus incredulous.[10]

This highly charged debate about how British society was and should be was joined with the publication of Edmund Burke's *Reflections on the Revolution in France* in November 1790, which was followed five months later by Thomas Paine's reply, *The Rights of Man*. Together, they provided the most powerful, competing versions of society and politics (and of society *as* politics) that would be available during the next fifty years. For Burke, the chaotic aftermath of 1789 lead him to champion traditional hierarchy, social subordination, and organic evolution in Britain and to deplore its overthrow and destruction in Robespierre's France.[11] Where, he wanted to know in his celebrated description of the execution of Marie Antoinette, was that chivalric inclination, that "generous loyalty to *rank*," that "proud submission," that had hitherto been so marked, so widespread, and so admirable? Nobility was, after all, the "graceful ornament to the civil order," the "Corinthian capital of polished society," and to do away with it was to subvert society as a whole. For Burke, hierarchy, station, and degree were the "unalterable relations which Providence has ordained"; the "social ties and ligaments" between different levels of society must be kept in place, and the "principles of natural subordination" properly observed.[12]

But Paine would have none of this. In the aftermath of 1789, he rejected Burke's arguments about the interconnectedness of past and present and his celebration of the organic nature of the existing social structure. Instead, Paine's writing recognized and released the conflict that had always been latent in the dichotomous model of society, a society that Paine saw, in heightened terms, as polarized between a corrupt, extravagant ruling establishment and a cowed and oppressed majority. "There are," he noted, in familiar phraseology, "two *classes* of men in the nation, those who pay taxes and those who receive and live upon taxes," and it was clear which side of this great social chasm Paine himself was on.[13] He dismissed hereditary hierarchy and plumaged nobility as mere "dishonourable rank" and thought titles marked "a sort of foppery in the human character which degrades it." The monarchy, the aristocracy, and the rest of the social-cum-political establishment should be overthrown, and the ordinary people should be given a say in government. By describing British society in these unprecedentedly stark and adversarial terms, Paine urged those who did not belong to the elite to rise up against it. Here was social description preaching political revolution.[14]

To Burke's established, traditional, organic version of the social order, Paine thus counterposed a novel, radical, confrontational alternative, and Burke sometimes replied in the same terms, understanding (or fearing) that Painite propaganda was breaking the graded, interconnected hierarchy apart into two antagonistic constituencies. But instead of Paine's virtuous "people" endowed with noble qualities and high aspirations, Burke depicted a "mob," "a swinish multitude," mindlessly threatening to rend asunder the integrated fabric of society. Others took the same view, including Christopher Wyvill, who, like Burke, was a once-moderate reformer turned establishment defender. "If Mr Paine should be able to rouse up the lower classes," he wrote in 1792, "their interference will probably be marked by wild work, and all we now possess, whether in private property or public liberty, will be at the mercy of a lawless and furious rabble." And the Rev. Thomas Malthus took in an even broader swathe of society, complaining that *The Rights of Man* had done "great mischief among the lower and middling classes of people in this country."[15] Here were disagreements about the nature and the future of the British social order that were more politically charged than anything seen earlier in the eighteenth century and that were to persist until the end of the 1840s. How were these arguments made, and who were they made by?

There were many conservatives who, like Burke, continued to envisage the British social fabric in terms of hierarchy and subordination. In 1793 Thomas Estcourt, JP, noted "the imperceptible gradation of the different orders of society which puts every person at his ease with the person who is a little above or a little below him," which meant that "no man can put his finger on any particular point of separation betwixt the one and the other." Likewise, in 1820 the Rev. William Otter felt that "the peculiar excellence of the admirable structure of society established in this country consists . . . in that singular coherence and adaptation of its several parts, by which many classes and ranks of men, rising in orderly gradation, and melting as it were into each other, . . . compose together one solid, well compacted and harmonious whole."[16] David Robinson agreed. "In most other countries," he felt, "society presents scarcely anything but a void between an ignorant labouring population, and a needy and profligate nobility." But in Britain, "the space between the ploughman and the peer is crammed with circle after circle, fitted in the most admirable manner for sitting upon each other, for connecting the former with the latter, and for rendering the whole perfect in cohesion, strength and beauty."[17]

These conservative contemporaries were not merely continuing to see society in traditional, idealized, hierarchical terms; what was new was that hierarchy was being aggressively defended and justified.[18] In January 1789 Bishop George Pretyman-Tomline insisted that the "subordination of ranks, and the relation of magistrates and subjects, are indispensably necessary in that state of society for which our creator has evidently intended the human species." Nine years later, William Wilberforce saluted Christianity's "grand law of subordination," which "renders the inequalities of the social scale less galling to the lower orders, whom she also instructs in their turn to be diligent, humble, patient, reminding them that their more lowly path has been allotted to them by the hand of God."[19] The novels of Sir Walter Scott and the writings of Sir Kenelm Digby urged "respect for rank, combined with a warm relationship between different ranks," and in 1830 Robert Southey, the ex-radical Tory romantic, celebrated

> That appointed chain,
> Which when in cohesion it unites
> Order to order, rank to rank,
> In mutual benefit,
> So binding heart to heart.[20]

These exhortations were matched by deeds. Among "all ranks of people" the venerable British hierarchy was successfully reasserted (and sometimes newly invented) against the challenge mounted by parvenu republican France. During the 1790s, the Loyal Association movement became the embodiment of hierarchical activism, as the "gentlemen of property in each county," each "according to his rank and station in life," rallied the people in defense of the king, the constitution, and the established social order.[21] Many of the philanthropic and evangelical societies of the decade urged the importance of deference and subordination. The Society for Bettering the Condition and Increasing the Comforts of the Poor, for example, aimed to "teach them the true virtue of those gradations of rank and condition which our creator has thought fit to establish." And this renewed belief in hierarchy came from the top down as well as the bottom up: the honors system was augmented and extended; the British peerage was consolidated, and its prestige enhanced; reference books on the aristocracy and the gentry proliferated; justifications were advanced "to prove the merit and utility of an hereditary race of nobles"; and Gothic castles were constructed, asserting the continuity between past and present, that the age of chivalry was not dead, and that tradition and subordination would prevail against the upstart egalitarianism of French republican classicism.[22]

The most convincing sign of this hierarchical revival was the efflorescence throughout the British Isles of grand ceremonials that made visible and reinforced the established view of the social order. In Dublin, the Lord Lieutenant's court witnessed the introduction of elaborate processions, entries, levees, and investitures following the creation of the Order of St. Patrick.[23] In London, there was a series of spectacular ceremonials: the thanksgiving services for the naval victories of 1797 and 1798; the state funerals of Nelson and Pitt the Younger; the Golden Jubilee of George III in 1809; the peace celebrations of 1814–15; and George IV's coronation in 1821. Here was the layered social fabric most vigorously and splendidly displayed, from the king himself down to the ordinary sailors and marines who appeared at the thanksgiving service of 1797. These metropolitan pageants were replicated throughout the land; they involved and embraced the whole community in a mixture of consensus and order; and they were presented as the very embodiment of traditional continuity. Completing and complementing these developments was the exaltation of King George III, living, appropriately enough, in his new-old Gothic castles at Windsor and Kew and personally legitimating the elaborate social hierarchy of "all classes of mankind."[24]

Nor were these new assertions and articulations of the traditional social order confined to Britain. In Canada, the younger Pitt's ministry sought to promote a ranked and religiously sanctioned social structure that would make impossible any revolution on the American model. Under the Canada Act of 1791, the Anglican Church was endowed and bishops were introduced, and a landed aristocracy was promoted and given a part in government via what was intended to be a hereditary upper house.[25] Elsewhere, as British dominions expanded during and after the successful wars against France, they had imposed on them the full panoply of proconsular pageantry, patterned after the viceregal court in Dublin and the British monarchy itself. In India, Lord Wellesley built a magnificent palladian Government House, modeled on Kedleston Hall in Derbyshire, and presided over a regime that rivaled the sovereign's in its rank and grandeur. In the recently conquered Cape of Good Hope, Lord Charles Somerset, the younger son of the duke of Beaufort, exploited his Plantaganet ancestry and created his own small court in what had previously been the severely Calvinistic surroundings of Dutch Cape Town. And in Britain's new Mediterranean empire, conquered after 1802, Sir Thomas Maitland reveled in the pomp of the Knights of Malta and later founded the Order of St. Michael and St. George.[26]

Thus was the imperial British hierarchy augmented and reinforced in conscious emulation and reinforcement of the metropolitan British hierarchy. But on the periphery of dominion, it also had its local articulations and indigenous extensions. For in India, South Africa, the Caribbean, and the Mediterranean, the British encountered and conquered for the first time many alien races, some European (French, Dutch, Spanish, Portuguese) but many not. As the imperial reach extended, these people were categorized, classified, and dealt with in a predictably hierarchical way: indigenous peoples were excluded from all but the lowliest offices of state; those of mixed parentage were treated with particular hostility; and native aristocracies were co-opted and encouraged. In practice, most colonial "reform" between 1780 and 1830 was concerned to create or confirm social and racial gradations. At the same time, the growth of trading communities in Calcutta, Bombay, and Madras, the codification of the rigid caste system in south Asia, and the consolidation of planters in the Caribbean and gentry in Canada meant that the "distinction of ranks" was everywhere becoming more marked.[27] In the words of Peter Marshall: "Empire reinforced a hierarchical view of the world, in which the British occupied a pre-eminent place among the colonial powers, while those subjected to colonial rule were ranged below them, in varying degrees of supposed inferiority."[28]

But while the hierarchical view of British society was being reasserted and reinforced, it was also being repudiated and rejected by a succession of radical writers who inveighed on behalf of the virtuous "people" whom they believed to be held down by corrupt hierarchy and tyrannical aristocracy. Paine's contemporary James Oswald bitterly attacked all hereditary distinctions, opining that "in a state really free, a privileged caste of men cannot possibly exist; for it could never enter into the minds of free people to establish so absurd a barrier between man and man. In a free state, there can be but one class of men, which is that of citizen; as there is but one will, which is that of the people."[29] In 1792 Thomas Cooper responded directly to Burke, insisting that the "swinish multitude" were the "most important part of the community, the most oppressed, the most industrious," who were being subjected by "an aristocracy of property, more or less extended." The young William Wordsworth agreed. "Hereditary distinctions and privileged order of every species," he declared, "must necessarily counteract the progress of human improvement." The same view was held by William Godwin. "I disapprove," he wrote, "of monarchical and aristocratical governments however modified. Hereditary distinctions and privileged orders of every species I think must necessarily counteract the progress of human improvement."[30]

This polarized analysis of contemporary society was most famously put about by William Cobbett, who converted from romantic Toryism to radical populism during the 1800s and denounced the "chain of dependence running through the whole nation which, though not everywhere seen, is everywhere felt." His alternative social vision was starkly simple. On the one side was "Old Corruption," "The Thing," or just "It," a parasitic amalgam of aristocracy and government, placemen and jobbery, finance and debt, the church and the law, the East India Company and the Bank of England. On the other was not "the mob, the rabble, the scum, the swinish multitude" but rather the "labouring classes," or "working classes," or "working people," or "the people," from whom "the real strength and all the resources" of the country had "ever sprung, and ever must spring."[31] For Cobbett, these two social constituencies were locked in perpetual conflict: "an insurrection of talents and courage and industry against birth and rank" or "one class of society united to oppose another class."[32] This Manichaean vision was exceptionally influential, for the whole "sociology of postwar radicalism," as found in the writing of such figures as John Wade and William Benbow, derived from the belief that there was one division in society, not just between "gentlemen" and "the people" but between the "useful" or "productive" or "industrious" classes on the one side and the idle courtiers, spendthrift aristocrats, irresponsible speculators, and parasitic middlemen on the other.[33]

The widespread popular discontent of these years drew its inspiration from this alternative social analysis, which at the same time reinforced and validated these perceived divisions still further. The crowds, the protests, the meetings, the demonstrations, the expressions of collective solidarity and confrontational hostility: all both dramatized and demanded a very different social order from that embodied in the graded processions of establishment ceremonial. The unprecedented riots over food in England in 1795–96, 1799–1801, 1810–13, and 1816–18 were a powerful (or ominous) portent that social polarization was intensifying.[34] The new, radical corresponding societies of the 1790s appealed for "active and useful citizens" to campaign against "idle drones in society." In the name of ordinary people, the Luddites attacked machines and their owners in 1811–12, 1816, 1822, 1826, and 1830: here was another manifestation of "us" versus "them."[35] The post-Waterloo "monster meetings" and the Peterloo "massacre" of 1819 intensified the confrontation between a repressive establishment and an oppressed "people" who sought reassuring symbolism in the Cap of Liberty.[36] And during the Queen Caroline affair, "the people" rioted in support of the queen and against the king in a subversive display of national "tumult and insurrection."[37]

This hope (or fear) that a deep division was opening in the social fabric was more widely entertained (or lamented) in Ireland, Wales, and Scotland, where the polarized model of social (and political) structure had always been especially popular and resonant, reinforced by language, religion, and nationality. As the Lord Lieutenant of Ireland anxiously noted in 1793, "The lower orders or Old Irish consider themselves as plundered and kept out of their property by the English settlers, and on every occasion are ready for riot and revenge."[38] Two years later, a loyalist newspaper surveyed the same social-cum-political structure more apocalyptically: "The lower order of papists," it thundered, "want equality, they will allow no lords or gentlemen." In 1799 George Canning made the same point a different way, regretting the absence in Ireland of "those classes of men who connect the upper and lower orders of society, and who thereby blend together and harmonise the whole . . . that middle class of men, of whom skill and enterprise, and sober orderly habits, are the particular characteristics." And in the mid-1820s Henry Goulburn advised the Irish secretary, Robert Peel, that the nation was once again dividing into "the people" on the one side and "their landlords" on the other, in such a confrontational mode that the old world of "deference and supremacy" was seriously threatened.[39]

It was the same in Scotland. In the Highlands, there was thought to be a growing social gulf between those described as "chiefs," "lairds," "lords," "gentlemen," or "heads of clans" and those referred to as "poor inhabitants," the "mob," the "lower orders," or the "lower class of people." More usually this was described as a direct clash between "the proprietors" on the one side and "the people" on the other. In the towns and cities, government informers such as Alexander Richmond depicted a social order no less riven. "Rank, and everything previously held sacred and venerable," he said, "was laughed at to scorn." "A line of demarcation was drawn between the different ranks of society," and "rooted antipathy and a ferocious spirit of retaliation was engendered in the minds of the working classes."[40] In Wales, too, the social gulf was widening, though neither the divisions nor the language seem to have been as extreme as in Ireland or Scotland. "The poor," John Ellis declared at Machynlleth in 1796, "are oppressed by the rich." In south Wales, Walter Davies regretfully observed the "want of confidence between higher and lower ranks in rural society," and in the mining villages of the valleys, the common refrain, echoing Canning's remarks about Ireland, was "we have no middle class of tradespeople here."[41]

As in England, these descriptions of Celtic society divided against itself were both the expression and the product of serious social and political protest. Ireland was the most polarized, and the last quarter of the century witnessed unprecedented disaffection, initially in outbreaks of rural violence associated with the Whiteboys and the Defenders and subsequently in the militia riots of 1793 and the United Irishmen's rebellion of 1798.[42] This tradition persisted into the new century, beginning with the Ribbonmen, and later became more politicized with Daniel O'Connell's Catholic Association in the 1820s. In Scotland, the protests by dispossessed crofters against their landlords' Highland Clearances were another tableau of social polarization, beginning in the 1790s and peaking in the 1810s. So were the riots that took place in Scottish towns over food, wages, military recruitment, or politics. Likewise in Wales, there were food and militia riots in the 1790s, enclosure riots from the 1800s to the 1820s, and serious industrial discontent in the south in 1816.[43] But did this widespread unrest mean that the hierarchical structure was collapsing and that the image of the social fabric being rent asunder was describing the reality?

Ever since the days of Burke, believers in hierarchy had feared that "the chains of connection," the "bonds of attachment," were being broken and that the social order was polarizing into two irreconcilable groups. This was why, as Frances, Lady Shelley, recalled, "the awakening of the labouring classes after the first shocks of the French Revolution, made the upper classes tremble." This was why, at the Dorset election of 1806, Henry Bankes urged that "the whole landed interest is essentially connected together, and those who endeavour to draw lines of division are not less the enemies of the lower order than of the higher." This was why, by the late 1810s, Whigs like Holland, Grey, Russell, Althorp, and Milton feared "a complete separation and enmity between the upper and lower ranks, the governors and governed, the rich and the poor in society."[44] This was why in 1820 William Otter worried that the laborers in the manufacturing towns were "an isolated class, without that due admixture of ranks and orders, which in all other cases tends, by the infusion of benevolence, respect and intelligence, to temper and soften the whole mass." And this was why Thomas Chalmers lamented that "there is a mighty unfilled space between the high and low of every large manufacturing city." Here was the language of the "two nations"—of "the rich against the poor"— long before that phrase became popular.[45]

Yet as the variety and imprecision of the language used implies, the idea that Britain was divided into two homogeneous, self-conscious, and permanently warring classes was precisely that: an idea. It was never easy for those who opposed "The Thing" to define it; at best it was a vague amalgam of the rich, the well born, and the powerful that sometimes included the middle classes and sometimes did not. And those who opposed "The Thing" were themselves very different and very diverse. The members of the corresponding societies were an amalgam of artisans and more prosperous leaders. The Luddites were artisans with a strong sense of local identity who were upset at losing their jobs to the new machinery. The people demonstrating against Peterloo or for Queen Caroline were different again, and different from each other. The social structure of the Scottish Highlands was more varied and more differentiated than the protesting crofters implied.[46] In Ireland, the stark dichotomies in which both participants and observers envisaged Hibernian society disregarded "numerous gradations in wealth and social status," as well as regional variations.[47] In all cases, it was no easier to define "us" than to define "them": there were many visions and versions of these two competing, antagonistic constituencies.

To be sure, there was a marked growth in the belief that British society was deeply, perhaps irrevocably, divided at this time. But this does not mean that contemporaries were witnessing or accomplishing "the making of the English [or Scottish or Welsh or Irish] working class." E. P. Thompson's claim that "the outstanding fact of the period between 1790 and 1830 is the formation of '*the* working class' " misreads what was happening and disregards the words in which contemporaries described what was happening. Significantly, the phrase "working class," as distinct from "working classes," appears very rarely at this time, even in Thompson's own book.[48] As this suggests, it was not so much the forging of a new, unprecedented, homogeneous working class, along with its correspondingly new, unprecedented, homogeneous consciousness and identity of interests, that was taking place during these undeniably troubled and tumultuous times. Rather, it was an intensification of the traditional, populist way of looking at the world as being irrevocably divided between "us" and "them." Neither rhetorically, nor organizationally, nor politically did this polarized picture of British society embody or portend a new-style Marxist "class war."[49]

Nevertheless, it bears repeating that for many people, hierarchy *did* seem at risk, and it is in this context that we might best understand the attractions of the triadic vision of society that was also being more aggressively promoted in these years, which stressed and asserted the growing importance of the middling ranks, sorts, and classes vis-à-vis those above and below, as well as their unique capacity to bridge the gap that many feared had opened up between "us" and "them." During the eighteenth century, members of the middling sorts had largely confined themselves to making occasional (and unverifiable) claims about their peculiar and particular virtues. But from the 1790s such claims became more frequent and more politicized, and the idea that the middle classes were a recent, important, and homogeneous social formation was widely put about. So in 1798 the *Monthly Magazine* sang the praises of the "middle ranks," in whom it was claimed "the great mass of information, and of public and private virtues reside."[50] In the same year, Vincentimus Knox opined that "the greatest instances of virtue and excellence of every kind have originated in the middle order," which prevented a community from polarizing into "rich and poor." And in 1799 George Canning praised the "sober, orderly habits" of "those classes of men who connect the upper and lower classes of society, and who thereby blend together and harmonise the whole"—in England, though not, of course, in Ireland.[51]

The next upsurge in this celebration of the rising middle class came late in the 1800s: in 1807 John Atkin insisted that the "middle ranks of people" were "the most valuable members of society," and in the following year, *The Examiner* argued that the "middling class" was where "the best strength and truest felicity of a nation resides," filling the space between the majority of the people beneath and the wealthy above. Ten years later, such opinions were more pronounced. In 1818 the Rev. Lionel Berguer claimed that the "middle classes" were placed between "ministers" and a "disorderly and disordered rabble" and that they constituted "the whole respectable and independent population of the country," committed to "peace, tranquillity and order." William Davis took the same view, averring that the middle classes were "the strongest links in the chain of society, which connect the rich and the poor together."[52] But their most ardent champion was James Mill. In 1820, in his *Essay on Government*, he described the "middle rank" as "the class which is universally described as both the most wise and the most virtuous part of the community." And six years later, he celebrated them as "the glory of England," whose "growing number and importance are acknowledged by all," because they contained "the greatest portion of the intelligence, industry and wealth of the state."[53]

These attempts at middle-class self-promotion were so successful that they were soon taken up by Whig politicians, who came to believe that the enfranchisement of the "middle ranks" was the best way of safeguarding the hierarchical social fabric that they feared was being rent in twain. In 1821 Lord Milton embraced the cause of parliamentary reform because "the great mass of the middle classes of society" were in favor of it. In the same year, John Lambton, the future Lord Durham, declared that "the middling classes of the nation, the very sinews of the nation, are eager and desirous of reform." A year later, the marquis of Tavistock presented a petition for reform that he claimed was supported by "the industrious and intelligent and moral middle class of society."[54] Lord John Russell urged reform because of the "tendency to increase the importance of the middle classes of society," whose wealth and intelligence offered the best hope for the future prosperity of the nation. And in 1826 Sir James Graham described "the seat of public opinion" as being "in the middle ranks of life," by which he meant "that numerous class, removed from the wants of labour and the cravings of ambition, enjoying the advantages of leisure, and possessing intelligence sufficient for the formation of a sound judgement."[55]

But this was not the only response to the supposed "rise of the middle classes." For at the same time they were being unprecedentedly praised, they were also being unprecedentedly disparaged. There was negative as well as positive social stereotyping. From the late 1770s, there was growing condemnation and ridicule of awkward, ill-mannered, underbred, middle-class upstarts who had made their money in business or trade, were obsessed with fashion and luxury, and bought their way into land in the vain hope of acquiring high social standing.[56] Thus regarded, the members of this new middle rank were not the sinew and fiber and best hope of the nation; they were selfish and vulgar parvenus who were undermining the social order rather than strengthening it. Such figures soon became the stock-in-trade of popular novelists, from Mr. Smith in Fanny Burney's *Evelina* (1778), to Mr. Crotchet in Thomas Love Peacock's *Crotchet Castle* (1831).[57] Even more disliked were returning adventurers from India, those bloated "nabobs" with their gold, diamonds, and ill-gotten gains who were deemed to be especially greedy, rapacious, and corrupt. And no one fitted this sordid specification more perfectly than Warren Hastings, whose protracted impeachment from 1788 to 1795 sparked off a spate of critical fictional renditions.[58]

This hostility to middle-class money making and social advancement was not just social; there were many Tories who, unlike the Whigs, saw this new group as a threat to the hierarchical fabric rather than a support. For Burke, the reason the French Revolution had broken out was that the middle-class "monied interest" had grown too big, had been corrupted by wealth, had been possessed by "the spirit of ambition," had elbowed its way into historical prominence, and had launched France down a bloody path of anarchy and tyranny.[59] During the 1810s, the Tory *Quarterly Review* regularly praised the virtues of the aristocracy and the lower orders while denying that those who came in between were as decent or able. Sir Kenelm Digby thought the middle portion of society brought only "disorder and confusion and tempest" and was the origin of virtually everything that was wrong with the country. And by 1827 Robert Southey had decided that the new industrial middle classes represented the most dangerous threat to the established social order, on account of their numbers and ambitions. At the same time, and especially in the aftermath of Peterloo, another attack was launched on the middle classes from a radical perspective: writers such as John Wade and publications such as *The Black Dwarf* denounced them as the selfish, supine slaves of the aristocratic governing cabal and as the enemies of the people.[60]

Whatever their differences of political perspective or polemical purpose and however varied and discrepant the stereotypes they constructed, all these commentators agreed that the new middle classes were rising. How true was this? Beyond doubt, there was an expansion in suburban living, voluntary societies, and newspapers: those very emblems and embodiments of middle-classness. But in the light of the discoveries and the arguments that eighteenth-century historians have recently been making about their forebears, it seems clear that much that was said and claimed by contemporaries (and later scholars) about the originality and importance of the middle class between the 1780s and the 1820s was exaggerated.[61] For there is little evidence that they suddenly arose as a new, coherent, and identifiable social formation that was obtaining greater self-consciousness through a sequence of experiences in which they discovered and increased their capacity for collective, independent action. On the contrary, if the middle class arose as anything during these years, it was largely as a new *rhetorical* formation. For the widely articulated claims (or denials) that this new middle class enjoyed a monopoly of decency, piety, charity, responsibility, judgment, intelligence, and sobriety were no more than idealized, imaginative assertions, incapable (as usual) of empirical validation.[62]

It should by now be clear that from the 1780s to the 1820s, the language of class did not vanquish every other form of existing social description.[63] To be sure, it was used more frequently than it had been for most of the eighteenth century. But so, in this contentious and confusing time, were all the other social vocabularies. And, like the language of ranks and orders, the language of class was very widely employed: by those who conceived of British society hierarchically, by those who conceived of it triadically, and by those who conceived of it dichotomously. These three ways of imagining and understanding the structure of British society remained very much part of the private and public language of conventional social description. What *had* changed was that they were being more vigorously and more adversarially articulated than ever before. But it was not just that the rise of the language of class did not vanquish other forms of social description. It was also that the rise of the language of class did not mean that the rise of new collective classes vanquished all other modes of social structure and social identity. "The making of class," be it the middle class or the working class, is not how the events and developments of these years may best be described, explained, or understood.[64] What *was* going on was an unprecedentedly agitated discussion of social structure that ebbed and flowed, as contemporaries could not agree—and did not want to agree—whether early-nineteenth-century Britain could (or should) be more appropriately described as hierarchical, three-level, or two-stage. During the passing of the Great Reform Act, this discussion was to become even more agitated.

The "Politics of Class" Propounded

Those who conceived of British society hierarchically—and this included virtually everyone in the court, the cabinet, the Lords, and the Commons, as well as many people lower down the social ladder—were united in their wish to see hierarchy preserved during and after the years 1830–32. But in the face of nationwide protest and discontent, the ruling elite was deeply divided as to how this might best be accomplished. Traditionalist Tories such as Wellington believed that hierarchy could only be safeguarded if hierarchy stood firm. Popular agitation must be faced down and suppressed, and the time-honored habits of "obedience, order and submission," without which the social order could not survive or function, must be reestablished.[65] Nor, in terms of the contents of the measure, should the vote be conceded to the new, upstart middle class. As Horace Twiss explained in the Commons during the debates on the Reform Bill, it would be a terrible wrong if "shopkeepers and attorneys, persons of narrow minds and bigoted views" were "now to be called in to the council of the nation." From a different perspective, Sir Robert Peel, while not sharing this hostile characterization of the middle classes, also feared the measure would damage hierarchy by threatening to disenfranchise those toward the lower end of the social spectrum.[66]

·The Whigs agreed that hierarchy must be preserved and that, as Lord Grey explained to the king, the "natural influence of property and station" must be safeguarded. The administration they formed in 1830 was one of the most aristocratic of the nineteenth century, and Grey himself, as befitted someone who had been born in 1764, was a firm believer in an ordered, traditional, stable society. The problem, as the Whigs saw it, was that growing discontent and dissatisfaction meant that hierarchy could no longer be left to take care of itself. They feared that popular revulsion against those aristocrats who controlled the return of MPs via their rotten boroughs meant that "all support for station and authority" had been "entirely lost."[67] The parliamentary system was discredited, which discredited the social structure on which it depended and that it, in turn, embodied. By diminishing the unacceptable face of aristocratic power, the Whigs hoped to strengthen "the legitimate influence of rank and station on which society, as they conceived it, rested." Without such reforms, they feared that the established hierarchy would buckle, collapse, and disintegrate amid what the young Macaulay described as "the confusion of ranks, the spoliation of property, and the dissolution of social order."[68]

But these were not the only steps the Whigs believed must be taken to preserve station and degree and restore "tranquillity and subordination." They also thought it necessary, as Lord John Russell put it, to "bind firmly and kindly the different classes of society together." The alternative was the continued wrenching and rending of the social fabric, and, as the Whigs had been arguing since 1820, the way to prevent this was to "associate the middle with the higher orders of society in the love and support of the institutions and government of the country" by giving them the vote.[69] It was this belief—that society could only be knit together again by giving prominent recognition to its "middling ranks"—that underlay the extravagant encomiums the Whigs heaped on them as "the pride and flower of England" during the debates on the Reform Bill. According to Lord Brougham, they constituted "the wealth and intelligence of the country, the glory of the British name." Lord Grey agreed that they formed "the real and efficient mass of public opinion, . . . without whom the power of the gentry is nothing." Likewise, Lord Durham saw them as the "most steadfast allies" of the constitution, which justified giving them the vote: "to property and good order we attach numbers."[70]

In celebrating the rising middle class, the Whigs were rehearsing remarks about the tripartite British social structure that had become commonplace since the 1790s. This celebration remained an idealization. For the claims of Grey, Brougham, Russell, and Durham—that the middle classes were uniquely decent, independent, responsible, and industrious—were still no more than unverifiable behavioral imaginings. Statistically and sociologically, that information was simply unavailable.[71] But the Whigs did believe that the enfranchisement of this imagined middle class was the best—indeed the only—way to bridge the gap between the upper and lower orders that they feared was opening up. To that extent, they invoked the triadic model of society in the service and support of the hierarchical. And, in a way, the dichotomous could be used similarly. For when the Whigs spoke of "the people," as they regularly did during the Reform Bill debates, they did not mean the workers or "the rabble" or "the mob" but "the great majority of the respectable middle classes of the country," whose respectability entitled them to the privilege of the vote and whose enfranchisement was the best hope that hierarchy might be preserved.[72]

But this was not how those outside the charmed circle envisaged "the people" during the years from 1830 to 1832. The people's conception of "the people" was very different from that of the politicians'. For the popular agitation in support of "the Bill, the whole Bill, and nothing but the Bill" embodied the traditional Manichaean vision of society: "the people" in general raging against "Old Corruption" in particular. Thus understood, "the people" was a very ample constituency indeed, including (as with the Whigs) those from the "middling ranks" but also (unlike the Whigs) the laboring classes. And this broader, more inclusive concept of "the people" was most powerfully and menacingly proclaimed in the aptly named "Political *Unions* of the Middle and Working Classes" (my italics), the first of which had been founded by Thomas Attwood in Birmingham late in 1829 and subsequently proliferated throughout Great Britain. The message these Unions sent out made plain the yawning and unacceptable divide between a united "us" and an excoriated "them." The House of Commons "in its present state" was "too far removed in habits, wealth and station from the wants and interests of the lower and middle classes of the people to have any just views respecting them, or any close identity of feeling with them." Accordingly, the object of reform was "to obtain a full, free and effectual representation of the middle and working classes in the Commons' House of Parliament."[73]

Throughout the unprecedented unrest of the period 1830–32, there were meetings, protests, and demonstrations, from Bristol to Birmingham, Glasgow to Merthyr, and there were the "Captain Swing" riots in the countryside.[74] For a time, it did seem that they represented a consolidated popular revulsion against exclusive oligarchy and outmoded hierarchy. "The important feature in the affair," wrote Cobbett in December 1830, "is that the middle class, who always, heretofore, were arrayed, generally speaking, against the working class, are now with them in heart and mind, though," he added, ominously and presciently, "not always in act." Here was the widespread popular hostility to aristocracy and government that had been sketched out and advocated by Paine forty years before and had now become disturbing reality. We shall never know whether it really portended social and political revolution in the most stressful months of the Reform Bill crisis. But there were some who hoped, and others who feared, that the social fabric was seriously at risk. "The lower orders," averred the duke of Wellington, "are audacious and excited by a thirst for plunder; the upper orders timid, and excited alone by a thirst for popularity." Macaulay used the same model to draw a different conclusion: if the bill was not passed, he feared nothing would remain "but an insolent oligarchy on the one side, and infuriated people on the other."[75]

For contemporaries then (as for historians since), the Great Reform Act thus meant many different things, as people judged the need for it, and its substance, in the light of their own preferred vision of British society as it was and as the measure might change it. The same was true of its consequences. To anxious, alarmist Tories, its passing portended the eclipse of the traditional order. Alexander Baring feared the end of "the whole aristocracy of the country," while J. W. Crocker thought it would mean "No King, no Lords, no inequalities in the social system": hierarchy, rank, and station would all be dead.[76] Not to be outdone, Wellington had long since predicted that the passing of the measure would mean "a total change in the whole system of that society called the British Empire." But, predictably, the Whigs took a more optimistic view. Earl Grey had always been determined to defend his fellow patricians and the social order of which they were the apex. He had succeeded: hierarchy had been safeguarded and rehabilitated. Not for nothing did Grey claim that the Great Reform Act was "the most aristocratic measure that ever was proposed in parliament." As the *Westminster Review* admitted in 1833, "the landed interest" still exercised "great sway in public affairs."[77]

But from another perspective, there were those who regarded the measure as having been a triumph of and for the middle classes. "The Great Reform Act," stated one pamphlet, "has transferred the government of these kingdoms from the grasp of a greedy oligarchy, in effect to the middling classes." "The middle classes," agreed Richard Cobden, were those "in whom the government of this country is now vested." So sudden and significant was the assumed arrival of the middle class on the post-1832 political scene that it is easy to appreciate this observation of Dror Wahrman: "It was not so much the rising 'middle class' that was the crucial factor in bringing about the Reform Bill of 1832; rather, it was more the Reform Bill of 1832 that was the crucial factor in cementing the invention of the ever-rising 'middle class.' " For invention it certainly was. As the Whigs had determined, the Reform Act did not hand over power to the middle classes, however much they admired them. But it was widely believed that it had done so, as the middle classes were thought to occupy a separate and superior position of political power that was both the expression and recognition of their assumed moral worth.[78]

The obverse of this rather fanciful perception of middle-class triumph was the sense of working-class disappointment and betrayal. As the *Poor Man's Guardian* concluded, "the promotors of the Reform Bill projected it, not with a view to subvert, or even re-model, our aristocratic institutions, but to consolidate them by a reinforcement of sub-aristocracy from the middle classes." Bronterre O'Brien took the same line: "We forsaw that its effect would be to detach from the working classes a large portion of the middle ranks, who were *then* more inclined to act with the people than with the aristocracy that excluded them." The result was to unite "all property against all poverty."[79] Robert Lowery agreed. "The enfranchised middle classes," he felt, "looked more to their own class interests than to those of the unenfranchised who had helped them to attain the bill," and this "produced feelings of disappointment and vexation among the working classes towards the middle classes." In turn, this meant that the concept of "the people" was reformulated and downgraded. Instead of meaning the respectable middle class that the Whigs had celebrated during the parliamentary debates of 1830–32 or the whole of the nation opposed to an aristocratic cabal, "the people" now referred only to the "working" or "laboring" classes: those who did not vote.[80]

Because it was a political not a social measure, the passing and the provisions of the Great Reform Act did not change the structure of British society itself, nor the basic, competing models of this society that were available to contemporaries. But they *did* change perceptions of society, which powerfully influenced the politics of the years that followed. Those who believed in hierarchy did not forget that it had seemed to tremble between 1830 and 1832 (or worse), and thereafter they redoubled their efforts to safeguard it. But they also feared that the deep social and political chasm of those years might open up again, and they were right to do so. Those who preferred the triadic model of society convinced themselves that the middle classes had indeed "arrived" and that there was nothing in politics that they could not achieve. And those who favored the polarized picture of the social order felt obliged to rethink their identities and objectives now that the line between "the people" and the voting and governing elite had been redrawn to their disadvantage. From 1832 to 1848, these competing visions of how British society was, and of how it should be, were constantly debated and articulated.

For those who believed the Great Reform Act had witnessed the triumph of the middle classes, the three-stage model of British society remained very appealing. According to the *Edinburgh Review*, the middle classes were now at the very center of things: "the hope, the stay, the comfort, and the true ornament of their country." According to Matthew Bridges, they were "in importance paramount, in fact all but everything." As Edward Baines Jr. announced in 1840, "We do not believe that there is in the world a community so virtuous, so religious and so sober minded as the middle classes of England."[81] Pundits such as Edward Bulwer-Lytton, Edward Gibbon Wakefield, and Thomas Arnold stressed in the 1830s "the growing power of the middling classes of society." Writers as varied in their viewpoints as John Wade, Macaulay, and Montague Gore produced historical accounts of the "rising middle classes" that appeared to confirm this view, arguing that they had been responsible for every great leap forward in British history and liberty, from the Reformation to the Glorious Revolution to the Great Reform Act itself.[82]

In what seemed an appropriately self-validating way, two more middle-class campaigns were fought to a triumphant conclusion in the aftermath of 1832. The first was the battle for local autonomy and civic democracy in urban England. Incorporating one's borough was seen as a way of emancipating both old and new towns from the thralldom of aristocracy, corruption, and inefficiency and of accomplishing locally what 1832 had already accomplished nationally. Once again, the fight was against "the Lords of Clumber, Belvoir and Woburn," against "monopoly and privilege," and against the "booby squirarchy" who were their civic lackeys. From this perspective, the Municipal Corporations Act of 1835 completed the work of the Great Reform Act by bringing about democratic, urban self-government and making possible the subsequent incorporation of such great industrial cities as Manchester and Birmingham. In terms of the composition of the electorate and the background of the councillors, the middle classes were now in charge. Indeed, Cobden believed that "the corporation act" was "the most democratic act upon our statute book."[83]

Even more self-consciously middle-class was the campaign against the Corn Laws. First passed in 1810, they were seen as a "symbol of aristocratic misrule" and patrician self-interest that, like the rotten boroughs, had to be abolished. Hence the campaign of the Anti–Corn Law League, based in Manchester and led by Richard Cobden and John Bright, which was as favorable to the middle class as it was hostile to the aristocracy.[84] As Cobden claimed, "we were a middle-class set of agitators," and the league was administered according to "those means by which the middle class usually carries on its movements." There were many attacks on "aristocratic tyranny," on "hereditary opulence," and on "the lords and great proprietors of the soil."[85] When repeal came in 1846, it was seen as witnessing "a great social transition": the final triumph of the middle classes. "Do you shrink from governing through the bona fide representatives of the middle class?" Cobden wrote euphorically to Peel. "The Reform Bill decreed it; the passing of the Corn Bill has realized it." John Bright made the same point when he told the Commons: "No government can long have a majority in this house which does not sympathise with the great middle class of this country."[86]

All this had been said in 1832. The fact that it was being repeated fourteen years later suggests that it remained a powerful belief in certain quarters. But did this mean that the middle classes had triumphed politically as well as rhetorically? Were they now the dominant element in a society understood in terms of three distinct and antagonistic classes? It seems not. For no more than 1832 did 1835 or 1846 create a world that corresponded to the extravagant statements regularly being made about the controlling power and unmatched importance of the middle classes. In terms of its content and consequences, the Municipal Corporations Act was very small beer. In some towns, aristocratic control continued as before. In others, the citizenry merely exchanged one set of middle-class oligarchs for another. Either way, the new authorities were originally given very limited power, which was only gradually augmented during Victoria's reign. And far from being the cynosure of middle-class dominance and self-consciousness, these municipal corporations were often the cockpit for bitter squabbles between middle-class factions that were deeply divided by politics, religion, and occupation.[87]

In the same way, historians have long since discredited the idea that the Anti–Corn Law League embodied and enhanced a unified middle-class consciousness, under the heroic leadership of Cobden and Bright, as has the view that it was the League's irresistible pressure that brought about repeal. In fact, these were contemporary middle-class self-mythologizations: many members of the middle class did not actively support the League; the leadership of Cobden and Bright was far from unchallenged; and Peel had many reasons for repeal, of which the League provided only one. Once again, middle-class power, consciousness, and identity were greatly exaggerated.[88] And how could it have been otherwise? For the tripartite model of British society that gave special prominence to one united and homogeneous middle class was rhetoric rather than reality, based on a crude and vague vision of how things actually were. As far back as 1834, J. S. Mill had made this point. Commentators, he noted, "revolve in their eternal circle of landlords, capitalists and labourers, until they seem to think of the distinction of society into these three classes, as if it were one of God's ordinances, not man's, and as little under human control as the division of day and night."[89] It was a shrewd remark.

While apologists for the middle classes after 1832 still favored the triadic version of society that gave them particular prominence, the working classes and their leaders perforce embraced a much more divisive social vision, in which "the real people" were equated with "the labouring classes," those who were excluded and denied the vote and of whose thwarted aspirations Chartism was the eventual outcome and expression. The People's Charter was drafted by representatives of the London Working Men's Association, and the aim of universal male suffrage and annual parliaments was to enfranchise and empower "the people" over and against the corrupt ruling oligarchy. In Leicester, they toasted "the people, the legitimate source of all power."[90] In Nottingham, they drank to "the sovereignty of the people" and "the memory of that immortal patriot, Thomas Paine." In 1848 the *Bradford Observer* opined that the Charter was "a symbol which expresses not the political faith only, but the social wants and hopes of the working classes." The meetings, the riots, the demonstrations, and the parliamentary petitions of 1839, 1842, and 1848: all these proclaimed Chartism to be a working-class movement, and it was accepted as such by most contemporaries.[91]

Inevitably, this meant the social vision of the Chartists projected and intensified the deep divide between workers and men of property, producers and consumers, the industrious classes and idle parasites, the poor oppressed and the rich oppressors. There were many more detailed variants, as when "the honest, sober and reflecting portion of every town and village in the kingdom linked together as a band of brothers" were distinguished from the "exclusive and demoralising influence" of "a corrupt government," "a vicious aristocracy," and "the gambling influence of money." In 1838 the *Northern Star* contrasted "the working classes" who were the "beasts of burden" with "the aristocracy, Jewocracy, Millocracy, Shopocracy, and every other Ocracy which feeds on human vitals."[92] In Manchester, in the same year, the divide was between "the handloom weavers, the poor of Great Britain and Ireland, and the factory children" on the one side and "their masters" on the other. Ten years later, in London, the confrontation was between "the people" and "the queen, her progeny, the present government, with that of the late premier's, the constitution of the country, the representatives of Parliament, and the lords spiritual and temporal." More ominously, Ernest Jones and George Julian Harney described this animosity as "The War of Classes."[93]

The difficulty with this picture of a fundamentally riven society was that it was no more credible in the troubled 'thirties and Hungry Forties than it had been during the 1820s. On the one side, the rhetoric of working-class unity and solidarity was not matched by reality. Indeed, the rhetoric failed to realize the reality. The working classes were too sectional, too localized, and too fragmented. There were craftsmen, factory operatives, domestic outworkers, agricultural laborers, and it was impossible to create a sense of unified collective identity by grouping these people together. As W. T. Thornton, the economist, noted in 1846, "The labouring population has been spoken of as if it formed only one class, but in reality it is divided into several." In industrial areas such as Tyneside mass participation was never better than patchy and ephemeral, while rural Chartism was virtually unknown. The movement attracted different people in different areas for different purposes, but never a majority of the working class.[94] It was never the embodiment of collective proletarian consciousness that some contemporaries hoped or feared or that some historians have vainly sought to depict. It was another version of traditional populism, which saw society as irrevocably divided between "us" and "them," rather than the belated making of *the* English working class.[95]

Nor, as in the 1820s, was it clear what groups on the other side the Chartists were opposing. The quotations already given vividly illustrate the variety and confusion with which "them" was now characterized. Some Chartists, attuned to recent economic and social developments, thought the battle was between labor and capital, but they never worked out a coherent theory of exploitation and production, and they were not generally hostile to capitalists and employers. Most were not concerned with the new economic divide but with the traditional political divide. For them, the battle remained, as it always had been, with "Old Corruption": the amalgam of peers, politicians, landowners, and fundholders. In short, and as usual, it was no easier to define (or unify) "them" than to define (or unify) "us." Inevitably, as one contemporary observed, this meant "there are great differences of opinion as to where the line should be drawn which separates the working classes from the other portions of society." As in the 1820s, there was no single fault line with homogeneous class crusaders on each side.[96] The stark social analysis that lay at the heart of Chartism grossly misrepresented and misunderstood the complexities of Britain's social structure.

Yet notwithstanding the fact that the Chartist notion of a deeply divided society was too crude, this vision was also embraced, as it had been in the 1820s, by some on the other side of the great—if vague—divide. Thomas Carlyle revived and made respectable the distinction between the productive and the unproductive classes. In *Sartor Resartus* (1833–34), he called them "the dandies" and "the drudges" and predicted they would one day divide England between them, "each recruiting itself from the intermediate ranks, till there be none left to enlist on either side." Friedrich Engels, having investigated conditions of life in Manchester, reached the same conclusion. The workers and the bourgeoisie were "two radically dissimilar nations, as unlike as differences of race could make them." Here were two irreconcilable classes, with class war and revolution the only really possible outcome.

"The cities," Engels opined, "first saw the rise of the workers and the middle classes into opposing social groups."[97] For him, as for Marx, Chartism was thus the first powerful manifestation of this new phase of the universal class struggle. The contradictions of capitalism meant society was "more and more splitting into two great hostile camps, into two great classes directly facing each other: bourgeoisie and proletariat."[98]

Thus regarded, Marx and Engels were articulating and universalizing a commonplace view of social divisions that increasingly prevailed among the educated people of Britain. Disraeli had not read Engels— he may not even have read Carlyle—and neither did he invent the idea of the "two nations," which had been around at least since the 1820s. But he certainly popularized it, along with the view, dating back to the 1790s, that the social fabric was being rent in twain.[99] In *Sybil* (1845), the hero, Egremont, is told the facts of sociological life by Stephen Morley, who divides the nation into the rich and the poor, "between whom there is no intercourse and no sympathy; who are as ignorant of each other's habits, thoughts and feelings as if they were dwellers in different zones, or inhabitants of different planets; who are formed by different breeding, are fed by different food, and are not governed by the same laws." But Disraeli was not alone in popularizing such an image of British society in fiction. In Mrs. Gaskell's *Mary Barton* (1848), the Chartist John Barton complains of the "great gulf" between "the rich" and "the poor": they were, he opined, "as separate as if we were in two worlds; aye, as separate as Dives and Lazarus." "Class distrusted class," we are told, "and their want of mutual confidence wrought sorrow to both."[100]

This idea of one new, deep, fundamental, unbridgeable social gulf was exceptionally resonant during the 1840s, as many commentators deplored what they saw as the great and growing gap between the rich and the poor in the increasingly crowded cities. In 1843 G. C. Holland declared that in Sheffield, "the rich lose sight of the poor, or only recognise them when attention is forced to their existence by their appearance as vagrants, mendicants or delinquents." In Manchester, in 1844, William Cooke-Taylor divided society into the "Haves" and the "Have-nots" and claimed that the "higher ranks" knew no more of the working classes than they did of "the inhabitants of New Zealand or Kamchatka." In Leeds, in 1845, James Smith noted that there was no "useful intercourse" between "the working class" and "the higher class" because they lived in separate parts of the city.[101] In Bradford, in the same year, the town seemed divided between those who lived "in comfortable healthy houses" and those who dwelt in "dens of pestilence." And London itself was no different. Between 1845 and 1848 G. W. M. Reynolds published *The Mysteries of London,* a series of sub-Gothic melodramas in which the metropolis was inhabited by only two classes: a decadent aristocracy and a "lowest class" of outcast criminals.[102]

Many contemporaries clearly believed that this was how their society was: as in the 1820s, the loss of the "old social bonds" and the "links in the social chain" that were supposed to bind every one together was widely reported and generally lamented.[103] This analysis also received powerful reinforcement from those who, using similar concepts and vocabularies, described the structures of Ireland, where the famine and the abortive "Young Ireland" rising of 1848 reinforced the traditional picture of a society deeply riven between what Disraeli called "a starving population" and an "absentee aristocracy." Of course, this had for long been a commonplace formulation. According to de Tocqueville, there was "an upper class and a lower class. The middle class evidently does not exist." *The Times's* Dublin correspondent agreed: "On the one hand I find a turbulent, demoralised population about to be famine-stricken. . . . On the other, I find a landed aristocracy entirely separated from the sympathies of the people. . . . Between these warring extremes of society, there interposes in the south of Ireland no middle class."[104] Here, as much as in the new industrial towns, were two nations: rich and poor.

But this analysis was profoundly flawed, being much stronger on emotional appeal and rhetorical attractiveness than it was on describing the complex substance of the British social structure. As with the Chartists, this way of seeing things presumed and proposed two monolithic social blocs locked in latent or perpetual conflict. Yet there were no such monolithic blocs, and there was no such war. The "two nations" of Carlyle, Disraeli, and Mrs. Gaskell—and of many other social commentators—were the stark overreactions of febrile social imaginings. Marx and Engels were no less in error in universalizing a primordial class war between proletariat and bourgeoisie on the basis of the British (and French) experience of the 1830s and 1840s.[105] But they were merely the most influential offenders, their social analysis and political predictions casting their long shadows down subsequent decades, until the 1970s. Instead of transcending their times, they merely misunderstood their times: "For every single individual who adhered to the Marxian view that society was becoming polarised into two great classes, thousands would have insisted upon the gradations and status distinctions to be found within each of those groups."[106]

In fact, the physical conditions of life and the spatial patterns of the great early Victorian cities were never as segregated as the extravagant "two nations" imagery suggested; the social and residential configurations were much more nuanced. For notwithstanding the claims made about "exclusive" suburbs and slums, most urban dwellers lived in mixed communities and neighborhoods. The "two nations" image was a shape more in people's minds than on the ground, where different levels of income and status were mixed up, flowing imperceptibly one into the other. Thus regarded, cities like London or Leeds or Liverpool were better envisaged as seamless webs rather than as fabric being rent asunder because of segregated housing patterns. As some experienced locals admitted, these "bonds by which society is united" were to be found in towns like Bradford as well as the countryside.[107] It was simply untrue to say there was no contact between these different worlds; much middle-class time was spent supporting local voluntary organizations to strengthen the bonds that held society together.

The image of Ireland as a riven society was no less misleading. This belief had been gathering force since the 1790s, it remained a cliché of the British official mind for the rest of the century, and it was often to be invoked (and thus corroborated) by Irish nationalist leaders. But this description ignored the fact that Ireland was characterized by "a myriad of subtle distinctions," both economic and social, between landlords of varying acreage and wealth, middlemen who sublet from landlords to farmers, farmers whose holdings ranged from less than twenty to more than eighty acres, cottiers, and laborers. This was how it had been in the eighteenth century, and this was how it remained during the nineteenth. In the early 1840s the Devon Commission more perceptively described Ireland as a hierarchical society where "every class in this country oppresses the class below it."[108] Yet this never became conventional political wisdom, in London or in Dublin. On the contrary, the powerful but mistaken belief that Ireland was more a riven than a hierarchical society was generally accepted on both sides of the Irish Sea and lay behind (or got in the way of) all British efforts to solve the "Irish question" from the early 1840s on. Here more than anywhere in government, social perceptions formed and informed political prescriptions and government legislation.

For all the continued appeal of the three-stage and polarized models during the years 1832 to 1848, hierarchy remained for many people the natural, omnipresent, time-honored, and divinely sanctioned way of seeing British society and of understanding their own place within it.[109] The coronations of King William IV and Queen Victoria, although not among the grandest of royal spectacles in nineteenth-century Britain, put the layered social order on ceremonial display and legitimated and reinforced the finely graded world that extended down and out from royal London across the whole of Britain and its empire. William IV's coronation took place in the midst of the Reform Bill agitations, and Victoria's almost coincided with the Chartist disturbances; both spectacles provided a very different vision of society from that of the rioting multitudes. And in his *Art of Colonization* (1833), Edward Gibbon Wakefield called for the creation of hereditary titles in the colonies. In short, it is an exaggeration to claim that by this time "the complex interacting hierarchy of older perceptions of the social system" had disappeared and that "the vocabulary of social description was far more concerned with aggregating individuals than with identifying the sections of a cohesive idea of the social order."[110]

This impression is reinforced by any glance at contemporary directories, national and local newspapers, or those many early Victorian novels where, instead of the "two nations," the finely layered hierarchy of status is still to be found thriving and comprehensible. The world according to Dickens was riven neither by one single great divide nor by a tripartite social structure of upper, middle, and lower. His concern was more with individual character and family relationships than with collective social categories. He was preoccupied with the nuances of accent, deportment, status, and hierarchy and with the way in which people of different social standing were jostled and jumbled together in great cities.[111] Likewise, Thackeray was mainly concerned with manners, social ambition, high fashion, and pretensions to gentility. The 1840s were the decade in which he published both *The Book of Snobs* and *Vanity Fair*. And in *Middlemarch*, published in 1872 but set forty years earlier, George Eliot envisaged society in a similar manner. There were, she noted, certain families in the town who were "conscious of an inherent social superiority which was defined with great nicety in practice, though hardly expressible theoretically," and much of the novel is a nuanced exploration of those niceties of hierarchy, rank, status, and degree.[112]

As this suggests, there were many in church and state who still believed that the best way of envisioning British society was as a traditional, finely graded hierarchy, in part because they thought this description the most plausible but also because they felt the arrangement was religiously sanctioned. "We have every reason to believe," stated the Rev. Marmaduke Prichett of Trinity College, Cambridge, in 1838, "that the order of human society is established by God." "Inequality of rank and condition," agreed Canon Richard Parkinson, was "an ordination of providence." In the early 1840s Ashurst Turner Gilbert, recently installed as bishop of Chichester, spoke of "the mysterious chain of mutual dependency in which human beings are bound to each other." "The Book of Providence," agreed the Rev. Francis Close, perpetual curate of Cheltenham, "is one grand scheme of subordination," which meant the "gradations of society" had to be kept up for the good of everyone. For most clergymen—and early Victorian Britain was still predominantly a religious nation—the social ideal and the social reality remained a hierarchical yet harmonious world, where there was a general acceptance of inequality and the station in life to which one was born.[113]

At the same time, Tory periodicals such as *Blackwoods* were full of similar sentiments, as when the young W. H. Smith stressed the importance of "obedience and reverence" to the "unalterable nature of our social pyramid." Inequality was the divinely ordained nature of society, and submission to it was the only possible response. "Without a social hierarchy," *Fraser's Magazine* agreed, "organised and organising, without authority to uphold the same, without submission thereto, no complete organism can exist." "Everyman," added the *English Review*, "should cultivate the region which Providence has assigned him." Even more vigorous were those members of the Young England group, of which Disraeli was the most famous. For them, as in *Sybil*, the cure for the widening social divide was the reassertion of the organic social order under traditional aristocratic leadership, which would bridge the gap that should never have opened up in the first place. In 1841, in a poem entitled "England's Trust," Lord John Manners, the second son of the fifth duke of Rutland and a friend of Disraeli's, urged a return to a world where

> Each knew his place—king, peasant, peer or priest,
> The greatest owed connection with the least.[114]

As this example implies, the connection between the Gothic and the reassertion of hierarchy was as strong during the 1830s and 1840s as in the 1790s and 1800s. Then, it had been the expression of tradition, order, and continuity against the leveling, revolutionary, republican ideas of the time. Now the same values were being asserted against the liberal, materialist, utilitarian spirit of the age, especially as embodied in the middle-class, money-grubbing factory masters, who were much criticized (and caricatured) by landowners during the debates on the Factory Acts in the 1840s.[115] Great houses were still being gothicized: Charles Tennyson's Bayon's Manor in Lincolnshire, Lord Harrington's Elvaston Castle in Derbyshire, Lord Breadalbane's Taymouth Castle in Perthshire, and Peckforton Castle in Cheshire by Anthony Slavin. The Eglinton Tournament of 1839; the medieval garments of Queen Victoria and Prince Albert at their costume ball three years later; the historic frescoes, Gothic decorations, and chivalric motifs of the new palace of Westminster: all these asserted a social vision of feudalism and hierarchy in which there was an organic link between past and present and among the different ranks of society. This was a very different vision of the British social order from that envisaged by Chartism, with its monster meetings, or by the Anti–Corn Law League, with its middle-class self-promotion and self-mythologizing.[116]

Most members of the governing elite still believed that society was hierarchical and that hierarchy had to be defended and asserted. Among the Whigs, Earl Grey remained committed to preserving aristocracy and safeguarding the "gradation of ranks" and "property and station." Lord Melbourne liked a "tranquil and stable" society and opposed educational reform on the grounds that it would disturb the established ordering of things.[117] And Lord John Russell believed that "religious and moral instruction" were needed to "knit together the inhabitants and classes" and to ensure "a fair and gradual subordination of ranks."[118] Elderly Tories such as the duke of Wellington remained convinced of the virtues and necessity of "hierarchical discipline," and this was no less true of Sir Robert Peel. As befitted someone born in 1788, who had entered politics six years before Waterloo, Peel never accepted the binary or triadic models of society, however much he might on occasion boast of his middle-class origins and seek to woo middle-class voters after 1832. He preferred the idea of society based on rank, degree, and a long chain of social connection, as on his estate at Drayton.[119] Throughout his public life, his first priority was to maintain what he saw as the established order against subversion. Thus understood, repealing the Corn Laws was intended to relegitimate the traditional aristocratic hierarchy rather than to represent the final surrender of patrician power to the middle classes. In this sense, 1846 was 1832 all over again.[120]

So, in some ways, was 1848. As *The Times* made plain on the eve of the last great Chartist demonstration to be held in London, which was intended to assert in dramatic form a mass vision of a deeply divided society and polity, the preservation of "the peace, order and stability" of "this majestic fabric" should be the primary care, interest, and duty of every Englishman.[121] Once more, the image of an integrated social structure was held up as the ideal version of British society, and once again this commonplace image caught, articulated, and reinforced the general view. For the special constables, drawn from all ranks and levels, did indeed prevail against the limited social vision and social understanding of the Chartists. Nor should this have occasioned much surprise. In the dark days of 1840, George Cruickshank had represented British society as a beehive with many ranks and gradations extending from the royal family, the Lords, and the Commons, via the educated, professional, and entrepreneurial middle classes, to the butchers, bootmakers, weavers, carpenters, and sweeps. It was a less powerful, less sensational, less menacing vision of British society than that projected by the Chartists or the supporters of the Anti–Corn Law league. But even in the troubled, disturbed 1830s and 1840s, it was also more accurate, more resonant, more convincing.[122]

The "Politics of Class" Denied

The mid-Victorian British world was more tranquil than its early-Victorian predecessor, although just how much more tranquil remains matter of scholarly debate. As in the eighteenth century, social consensus did not mean consensus about the way society was seen or about the language in which the models of society were described and articulated. In the era of the Great Exhibition and the mid-Victorian boom, when Britain proclaimed itself as the "workshop of the world," there were many who continued to believe that the three-stage model most accurately reflected the social structure of the time. The eminent judge Lord Bramwell took for granted the "permanent existence of three classes," which he described as the "privileged" (the aristocrats and landowners), the "enlightened" (the well-educated members of the middle class), and the "inferior" (who were the "shopkeeping and working classes").[123] Matthew Arnold famously divided society into "three great classes" in *Culture and Anarchy*: aristocratic "barbarians," middle class "philistines," and a working-class "populace." Nor was this commonplace categorization confined to those in the higher echelons:

the trade unionist George Howell divided society into the aristocracy, the middle classes, and the working classes, while Leone Levi, deploying slightly different terminology, wrote of the "working classes" and "the middle and higher ranks of society."[124]

The figure in whose person and attitudes this triadic model of mid-Victorian society was in some ways most vividly embodied and projected was Mr. Gladstone. His father was a self-made entrepreneur who established a fortune from trade, property, and shipping. He was based in Liverpool, it was there that the son was born, and for all his Eton and Christ Church education, Gladstone remained "Liverpool underneath." He was never at ease personally with the working classes, and he "had a habit of entering a room" that was not quite aristocratic. Neither patrician nor pleb, he was very much a man of the middle, and part of him always regarded British society from that perspective. "With the family of which I am a member," he had told the citizens of Liverpool in 1843, "I . . . still claim to belong to that middle class." Thirty years later, he spoke again in the same city, lamenting the practice whereby "those families which have either acquired or received station and opulence from commerce turn their backs upon it and seem to be ashamed of it." "It is not so," he concluded, "with my brother or with me." Much of Gladstone's mid-Victorian politics stemmed from this social perception, especially his wish, when chancellor of the exchequer, to act as a fiscal broker for the upper, the middle, and the lower classes.[125]

The tripartite view of society was reflected and reinforced by that quintessentially mid-Victorian artifact, the railway, with its first-, second-, and third-class carriages that sorted people out, massed them together, and moved them around. "It was only natural," F. M. L. Thompson reminds us, "that the country which invented the railway should immediately devise three separate classes of passenger compartments, strictly segregated, but each open to anyone who could pay the appropriate fare."[126] Equally important in proclaiming and perpetuating this triadic vision was education. "For each class of society," Sir James Kay-Shuttleworth concluded in 1862, "there is an appropriate education," and this meant separate schooling for "the upper classes," the "middle classes," and "the people." These divisions were further consolidated by the three great school inquiries of the mid-Victorian era. The Newcastle Commission set out to provide "sound and cheap elementary education" for the working class. The Clarendon Commission investigated the public schools, out of fear that their inefficiency placed "the upper class in a state of inferiority to the middle and the lower." And the Taunton Commission dealt with "those large classes of English society which are composed between the humblest and the very highest." Small wonder that Mark Pattison claimed that "class education would seem to be as rooted an idea in the English mind as denominational religion."[127]

As in the mid-eighteenth century, this three-level model coarsened and misrepresented social realities in the mid-nineteenth. One indication of this was that it seemed to furnish no convincing answer to the question: who dominated? There were those like Walter Bagehot who continued to believe that "the middle classes—the ordinary majority of educated men—are in the present day the despotic power in England." "The aristocracy and gentry," he contended, rehearsing a familiar story, "lost their predominance" in 1832, when it "passed to the middle classes."[128] But others maintained that the landowners were still in control, most famously Richard Cobden, who soon abandoned his earlier view that 1832 and 1846 had ushered in a new social and political order. "During my experience," he wrote in 1858, "the higher classes never stood so high in relative social and political rank compared with the other classes as at present. The middle classes have been content with the very crumbs from their table." Aristocracy, he later lamented, was "every day more and more in the ascendant in political and social life."[129]

Significantly, both Marx and Engels came to share this contemporary uncertainty.[130] Was mid-Victorian Britain a two-class society where the conflict was between the proletariat and the bourgeoisie or a three-class society with the aristocracy still in control? In their early years, Marx and Engels were convinced that the patricians had been vanquished in the class wars of the 1830s and 1840s, that the middle class was now emphatically in charge, and that the workers' revolution was the next item on history's inexorable agenda. When Marx reached London in 1850, he discerned a "new, more colossal bourgeoisie" that had forced the landed legislature "to pass laws almost exclusively in its interests and according to its needs." Engels agreed that the aristocracy had been "sacrificed" to the "rising star" of the manufacturing bourgeoisie and that the "industrial and commercial middle class" was now the dominant force in the realm. But in later years, both men were compelled to concede that the middle class had not triumphed after all. As early as 1854, Marx said that "the feudalism of England will not perish beneath the scarcely perceptible dissolving processes of the middle class." Seven years later, he was lamenting that the bourgeoisie were confining "all their energies and mental faculties within the narrow sphere of their mercantile, industrial and professional concerns" and had failed to capture real power in the state. And in a similar vein, Engels also came to deplore "the political decline and abdication of the English bourgeoisie."

Two separate but related questions were being raised here: who was dominant in mid-Victorian Britain? were the upper and middle classes separate collective groups? The answer to the first question is ambiguous. In terms of financial resources, political power, and social status, the traditional landed class remained in the ascendant, not surprisingly, given that the 1830s and 1840s had not witnessed a bourgeois revolution. In this sense, there was no "triumphant" mid-Victorian middle class.[131] On the other hand, Britain *was* the preeminent industrial and commercial power in the world, and that was arguably a bourgeois achievement.[132] But it is difficult to know whether this made the middle classes more important than they had been in the eighteenth century. Once again, the best that historians have been able to do has been to replicate the doubts and confusions of contemporaries. In any case, and as in the eighteenth century, it is misleading to think in terms of a homogeneous middle and upper class, with a clear division between them. Both encompassed great ranges of income, from magnates to lesser gentry, merchant bankers to shopkeepers. As the careers of Peel, Gladstone, and Disraeli remind us, they melded and merged imperceptibly into one another, which explains why neither the Whigs nor the Tories in mid-Victorian Britain were the party-political expressions of exclusive, collective, competing class identities.[133]

The triadic model was further weakened because the boundaries between the middle class and the working class were as difficult to discern and draw as were those between the middle class and the upper class. Here again, they flowed and joined invisibly into one another, which meant that highly skilled artisans and prosperous shopkeepers were particularly hard to place in such crude collective categories. In the same way, the Marxist notion that there was an inevitable gulf and ever-deepening conflict between middle-class employers and working-class employees, based on the irreconcilable division between capital and labor, misunderstands and misdescribes the economic and social relations in the mid-Victorian workplace. Most units of production remained very small, rarely averaging more than ten workers: Britain was the workshop of the world, not the factory. Even where the business was on a larger scale, the capitalist process of production was at least as much about cooperation and community as about conflict and coercion. It was very much a joint enterprise, and masters and men had a shared interest in getting their goods made, without which there could be neither profits nor wages. The age of capital was also an age of collaboration.[134]

But it was not just that relations between the middle class and the workers were neither riven nor confrontational; it was also that there was no more a homogeneous proletariat than there was a homogeneous bourgeoisie or aristocracy. For there was a great range of occupations, levels of skill, types of employment, locations of work. One response was to divide them into horizontally delineated subgroups. Robert Applegarth distinguished between "the better class of working man," who was employed, prosperous, and quiescent, and "the careless and indifferent man." Henry Mayhew began with the same two-level model but modified it into a tripartite one: those who will work, those who cannot work, and those who will not work.[135] There were others who contested the validity of such simple categories, insisting on "the very minute subdivisions of ranks" that existed among the workers, a view that was supported by the elaborate tables drawn up by R. D. Baxter in 1867, in which he listed sixty-nine occupational groups in the hierarchy of labor. As Thomas Wright noted, the working classes "are not a single-acting, single-idea'd body. They are practically and plurally classes, distinct classes, classes between which there are as decisively marked differences as there are between any one of them and the upper or middle classes."[136]

If the three-stage model was a crude guide to the intricacies and complexities of mid-Victorian society, then how much more so was the polarized picture? For, as in earlier periods, the line was drawn in many different and inconsistent places.[137] It was still not clear who was a gentleman and who was not. In the eighteenth century, it had been a subject of debate as to whether merchants and bankers and members of the professional middle classes should or should not be included along with the landed gentry and the titular aristocracy, and by the middle of the nineteenth century, virtually anyone with a public-school education might be described as a gentleman, regardless of his parents' social background. The only sure way of knowing you were a gentleman was to be treated as such. But that was something about which it was often not possible to be sure at all.[138] Another great divide— arguably "the sharpest of all lines of social division"—was between those who were respectable and those who were not. But once again, there were different views. Most thought the line should be drawn somewhere through the working classes. But where? Middle-class observers believed only a minority of the workers were respectable; the workers themselves often thought otherwise.[139] A further complication was that there were some members of the middle and upper classes who were not deemed respectable, Palmerston and Disraeli being two outstanding examples.

If the great divide was gentility, then the line generally went somewhere through the middle classes; if it was respectability, then it usually ran somewhere through the working classes. But these were subjective, inconsistent, and irreconcilable divisions, and in any cases, there were other ways in which British society was envisaged as being fundamentally riven. One such cleavage, which was not quite the same as gentility or respectability but was equally important, was that of speech and accent: who dropped their aitches and who did not; who spoke the Queen's English and who did not. This was partly a matter of family and education, but it was also a matter of self-improvement, as manuals of correct speech were produced in ever-increasing numbers for those of humble background who sought to cross the great pronunciation divide.[140] Nor was this the only way in which the spoken word was a guide to social standing and social identity in a world envisaged in terms of "us" and "them." In the greater British realm, language rather than accent was still the fundamental divide and reinforced the idea of inferior and superior, natives and outsiders, not only in Scotland, Ireland, and Wales but in Canada and India as well.[141]

Coexisting with these cultural, behavioral, and linguistic separations was the continued resonance of the idea of "two nations." The great metropolis was regularly depicted as sundered between "the rich" and "the poor," as when the Rev. John Richardson noted in 1856 that "there was little communication or sympathy between the respective classes by which the two ends of London were occupied." Such opinions were also entertained about the rest of urban Britain. In 1867 *Macmillan's Magazine* lamented that "the wall of moral separation between rich and poor appears to have become broader, higher, more impassable."[142] In the same year, the Liverpool Unitarian William Rathbone described in his tract *Social Duties* how industrialization and class segregation in the towns and cities had replaced personal ties between rich and poor with ignorance and sensualism on both sides. And this picture of a deeply riven urban society was reinforced by middle-class social investigators who "discovered" and "explored" alien peoples from the lower classes. As Patrick Joyce remarks, this simplified contrast between "the rich" and "the poor," which seemed literally grounded in the morphology of the great cities, remained important in the representation of mid-Victorian society.[143]

During the 1830s and 1840s, these triadic and dichotomous visions of the British social order had been strongly politicized. But in the calmer mid-Victorian years, they were less frequently (and less influentially) inflected with adversarial and confrontational content. Because there was no agreement as to whether the middle classes had triumphed in 1832 and 1846, further efforts were made in the decades that followed to reassert their decency, probity, and competence and to gain them a greater influence on government and policy. There were demands for financial reform, for an end to the outdated flummery of royal parades and ceremonials, and for commercial legislation. During the mid-1850s, in response to the bunglings of the Crimean War, the Administrative Reform Association campaigned to bring vigorous managerial efficiency and modern business principles into government.[144] Time and again it was argued—as it had been since the 1790s—that the middle classes were uniquely virtuous and patriotic and that an efficient businessman's government would accomplish more than an effete aristocratic government. "Rank and station" were no longer enough.[145]

These middle-class campaigns achieved very little, and least of all in terms of parliamentary legislation. The bourgeoisie may have dominated the provincial towns and cities, but it did not dominate the House of Commons in terms of personnel or policy. It was also deeply divided by religion and party political affiliation, and especially by varying views on the Crimean War. Even Richard Cobden, the politician most identified with the middle classes, was ejected from his Manchester seat at the general election of 1857 and spent the last years of his life complaining at the way so many businessmen fawned on the aristocracy. Nor, as before, did the middle classes' claim to a monopoly of virtue carry the day uncontested. The least damaging reply was that there was no evidence that someone who was good at business would be good at government, a view to which many businessmen themselves undoubtedly subscribed. More serious was the counterassertion that there was nothing uniquely meritorious about the middle class or its business ethics. At best there was moneygrubbing and self-interest; at worst, there was fraud, inefficiency, and bankruptcy. These were not what was needed to rescue the country from the troubles of the Crimea. As the duke of Bedford put it, "The qualities required are not to be found in the middle class, or if found, they will not leave their profitable trades for the lottery of politics."[146]

In the same way, the elemental contrast between "the rich" and "the poor" retained only a limited political resonance during these years. To be sure, the adversarial politics of "us" and "them" were still preached by the survivors of the 1840s. In 1856 the veteran Chartist leader, Ernest Jones, urged that the working and middle classes should unite to campaign for universal manhood suffrage.[147] But the most vigorous efforts to define a broadly based "us" in righteous opposition to an exclusive, hostile, and corrupt "them" came from John Bright, especially in the years after the Crimean War. Bright hated privileged aristocratic monopoly, along with the social structure that went with it. In the 1840s, this had meant campaigning for Free Trade in corn. In the decade that followed, it meant campaigning against the aristocratic monopoly of landownership, the armed services, diplomacy, Parliament, and government and against what he increasingly came to see as the unacceptable restrictions of the franchise. In this, Bright articulated what John Vincent called "the old opposition between people and privilege." He admitted that "the rich are personally kind enough, but they do not care for the people in the bulk." And he urged the uniting of "all those persons who compose the vast population of the country below the great privileged and titled classes of society."[148]

Beyond doubt, Bright tried hard to create a sense of social inclusion among a virtuous and embattled "people" fighting against a corrupt ruling class, state, and legal system that was kept going by conspiracy.[149] From the standpoint of the eighteenth century or of the decades of Cobbett with his attacks on "Old Corruption," this antithesis is very familiar: the ruled versus the rulers, the many in opposition to the few, the people against the aristocracy. Yet Bright achieved very little. In the calmer climate of the mid-Victorian period, adversarial politics built around hostile collective identities did not resonate in the way they had a generation before, at least in England. But elsewhere in the British Isles, adversarial politics based on one deep division in society did begin to revive, especially at the time of the 1868 general election. In Ireland, there was a strong upsurge of hostility, not only to the alien church that Gladstone promised to disestablish but also to the alien landlords; this was partly expressed through the Fenian movement and partly through the ballot box. And in Wales, there was a no less virulent (and no less appealing) campaign against the landlords, who were depicted as Anglican, English, absentee, and uncaring. Here, at least, the polarized vision was powerfully and (for the Liberals) successfully politicized.[150]

In general, the most that can be said is that the triadic and binary models of British society were still popular during the mid-Victorian years but retained only limited political resonance. This was partly because of the tranquillity and prosperity of the time, partly because both models invariably oversimplified the shapes on the ground and in society, and partly because the dominance of the traditional elite was still considerable, far greater than pessimistic aristocrats or ardent reformers were prepared to allow in the aftermath of 1832 and 1846. It was also because those like Bright who sought to preach and practice adversarial politics failed to ground their campaigns in any convincingly defined or consistently articulated social constituency, instead oscillating between the politics of middle-class consciousness (the triadic model) and the politics of middle-class and working-class populism (the polarized model).[151] More than in the 1830s and 1840s, the coherence and consciousness of these social groups was largely in the mind and eye of the beholder. Even in Ireland, the Fenians failed to mobilize "the masses" as a monolithic constituency against "the landlords."[152]

Put another way, this means that the majority of mid-Victorians did not think of themselves or see their social world in the crude terms of competing and conflicting collectivities. "Who can say," asked the young A. V. Dicey in *Essays on Reform*, "where the upper class ends or where the middle class begins?" "What is 'class,' " G. C. Brodrick inquired in 1867, anticipating in his answer the later views of Margaret Thatcher, "but a purely artificial aggregate, which may consist of hundreds, or thousands, or millions, according to the fancy or design of its framer?" Instead, mid-Victorians saw society in the same way as their forebears: as hierarchical both in its social classifications and in its scale of values.[153] They paid attention not so much to the broad and exaggerated contours of collective identities as to an endless series of much smaller and interconnected social gradations. Geoffrey Best puts this well: "Although," he notes, "men used the conventional terms upper, middle, working or lower class, and their usual variants, they were more acutely aware that men actually thought and acted in terms of a more considerably stratified and confused class structure than the nominally tripartite one." It was, he concludes, "as if the social structure was more like that we commonly ascribe to the eighteenth century, of multiple gradations or ranks in a pyramidal order." Hence Thackeray's description of Britain in 1850 as a "Gothic society, with its ranks and hierarchies, its cumbrous ceremonies, its glittering and antique paraphernalia."[154]

Throughout the mid-Victorian period, this was a widely shared opinion. "There is no country in the world," stated Thornton Hunt of the *Daily Telegraph* in 1866, "where there is so little practical separation between the several classes . . . ; and none where social rank and personal influence enjoy a stronger sway over every class."[155] "From the monarch to the peasant," observed Joseph Rayner Stephens, "gradations are measured, are relative, are reciprocal." "The essential hierarchical plan of English society," agreed Henry James after one of his first visits to Britain, "is the great and ever-present fact to the mind of a stranger; there is hardly a detail of life that does not in some degree betray it." In 1867 George Cruickshank updated and revised his picture, first drawn in 1840, of the "British Bee Hive," leaving essentially unaltered the picture of society as a layered, interlocking hierarchy. Trollope's novels do not only depict a carefully graded social hierarchy; they also portray churchmen and politicians being as concerned to uphold that ordered hierarchy has they had been in the eighteenth century. Nor was this a misleading fictional rendition. As late as the 1920s, Lord Willoughby de Broke recalled the rigid county hierarchy that had existed in his youth in Warwickshire, descending from the Lord Lieutenant and the Master of Fox Hounds.[156]

Like the majority of people they governed, almost all the leading politicians in this period saw British society in these terms. As Jonathan Parry has noted, the Whig-Liberal leaders between 1830 and 1885 "shared the standard nineteenth-century belief that civilization depended on the maintenance of social ranks." Lord John Russell had been defending this view since the days of the Great Reform Bill, as had Lord Palmerston, who had been born before the French Revolution and believed in a traditional social order under traditional landed leadership.[157] He said as much in his famous speech in the "Don Pacifico" debate: "We have shown the example of a nation, in which every class in society accepts with cheerfulness the lot which Providence has assigned to it; while at the same time every individual of each class is constantly striving to raise himself in the social scale." Following his contemporaries, Palmerston was using class not as a collective category but as a way of describing an elaborately layered society; he was not celebrating the new, bourgeois-dominated, tripartite social world but the traditional, divinely sanctioned, hierarchical order: the "national fabric." As George Watson has rightly remarked, in an observation that bears quoting a second time, in its proper place, "much of the profusion of class terms and class discussion in the mid and late Victorian era becomes more intelligible and informative if it is seen as based on a general assumption of rank and hierarchy."[158]

These social visions and social vocabularies were shared by post-Palmerstonian statesmen, both Tory and Whig. Notwithstanding his popularization of the idea of the "two nations," Disraeli's social thought was unwaveringly hierarchical, and he passionately believed in what he called the "aristocratic settlement" and the "territorial constitution." By this he meant "the whole ordered hierarchy of rural England, epitomised in his own county of Buckinghamshire," with its careful social gradations and time-honored inequalities. He saw society as a ladder that should be accessible to men of talent (like himself), but he had no wish to see it undermined, laid flat, broken, or removed.[159] And for all his identification with the triadic model of society, Gladstone possessed an "instinctive sense of hierarchy" and believed that "a state of graduated subordination" was "the natural law of humanity." As a child of the pre–Reform Act world and as a follower of Peel, he acquired a Tory veneration for the traditional, providentially ordained social structure that he never lost. In 1865 he outlined his vision of "classless interdependence": "Society is . . . like a well-built, well-ordered fabric—many stones, many timbers, many doors, many windows, many parts and portions of that fabric, all having their separate offices, some of them above and some of them below, some of them larger, and some smaller, but built and framed by the mind of the builder to serve a common purpose." Like Disraeli, Gladstone believed that a hierarchy based on agriculture was the best of all possible social hierarchies and that it was the task of politicians to labor to preserve and safeguard it.[160]

Yet notwithstanding their hierarchical assumptions and traditional views of society, politicians during this period talked constantly in the language of class. In part this was because they still used the word as a synonym for rank or order, as when they habitually described the functioning hierarchy of their era in terms of "class harmony" and "class interdependence." This was what Macaulay meant when he observed in his *History* that in future generations, Victorian England would appear a golden age, "when all classes were bound together by brotherly sympathy." Edward Baines agreed, noting on the eve of Palmerston's visit to Leeds in 1860 that the "new feature of the age" was the "intercommunication of classes."[161] In their speaking tours, Palmerston and Gladstone regularly extolled "the union of various classes of the community." Both regarded the removal of "any occasion of conflict between classes" as the good news of their time. As Lord Clarendon put it to Lord John Russell in 1864, there was now "that union and fusion of classes which constituted the real power of England."[162]

Thus deployed, the mid-Victorian language of class was synonymous with the language of hierarchy, as it had so often been in the past, and politicians regularly used it in this sense: as the best way to describe the stable and successful social world of their day. But they also talked about "class" in another, less secure, and more fearful sense. For they looked back to the 1830s and 1840s as a period of "class" protest and "class" hostility, by which they meant that the traditional social hierarchy had been threatened by different social groups seeking their own selfish advantage at the expense of the rest of the community. It should scarcely need repeating that this was at best an ignorant exaggeration of the social antagonisms and political events that had occurred an increasingly long time before. But that era remained an unhappy memory, and the self-appointed task of mid-Victorian statesmen was to try to ensure its hazards did not happen again.[163] Thus regarded and understood—as the disruptive politics of collective self-interest—"class" was a terrible, ominous thing it was important to deny or repress. As *The Times* explained in 1861, "the word 'class,'" when used as an adjective, "is too often intended to convey some reproach. We speak of 'class prejudices' and 'class legislation,' and inveigh against the selfishness of 'class interest.'"[164]

This alternative meaning of class was also widely used by politicians during the mid-Victorian period. Described and conceptualized in this way, class society was—or would be—the antithesis of a hierarchical society: it was a society that was not at ease with itself, a society that was not functioning properly, characterized by collective antagonisms rather than individualistic harmony. "We should all march together," C. P. Villiers observed, again anticipating Lady Thatcher, "and not divide society into hostile classes believing that causes for permanent antagonism exist." Russell and Palmerston were united in their desire to prevent the disruption of hierarchy by such displays of class hostility. Gladstone thought the painstakingly built and lovingly maintained hierarchy would be ruined if one class became selfishly dominant, whether the aristocracy or the workingmen. For the same reason, Disraeli loathed the idea of class being set against class, and even Richard Cobden was reluctant to "recognise the necessity of dealing with working men as a class."[165]

With the possible exception of John Bright, mid-Victorian public men feared the "politics of class," rejoiced in their demise, and were anxious to ensure that they did not return. It was against this background that the Second Reform Bill was fought out in 1866 and 1867. The basic issue was clear to all the key participants: how best to preserve and defend a hierarchically conceived society and a hierarchically functioning polity when the task of the time was to debate and decide which new social groups were to be enfranchised? Unlike the eighteenth century, and as in 1830–32, hierarchy could no longer be left to take care of itself. Yet once again, there was disagreement as to how it might best be preserved. Some wanted a reform act because they feared that without it there would be class conflict and the overthrow of hierarchy. But others feared that enfranchising large numbers of the working population would be more likely to *bring about* class war than prevent it, as the legislature would become the focus for the politics of class interest and class conflict. Would giving the vote to a numerical majority of the working classes support hierarchy or undermine it?[166] No one really knew or could possibly have known.

This meant that while almost everybody involved with the events of 1866–67 thought instinctively in hierarchical terms, the discussions and debates mainly took place in crude, oversimplified, dichotomous terms. On the extreme left, Joseph Collett, editor of *Working Man*, spoke of "the people of this country" against "the government," while Reform League propaganda depicted a confrontation between "the ruling classes" and "the people." Likewise, the young James Bryce wrote of the tensions between "the rich" and "the poor," and between "the ruling class" and "the working class." John Bright claimed that Parliament was dominated by the "class prejudices" of the aristocracy, which was why "the people" needed to be given a bigger voice in the nation's affairs. Lord John Russell, the only important surviving veteran of the events of 1830–32, no longer defined "the people," as had been the Whiggish custom then, as the middle classes but as the working classes. Those on the other side of the political spectrum also thought in these polarized terms, though they reached different conclusions. Lord Carnarvon resigned from Disraeli's government because he feared the

Conservative bill would lead to conflict "between two clearly defined and perhaps ultimately hostile classes—a rich upper class on the one hand, and a poor artisan class on the other."[167]

In the light of these shared models of society, the practical political question was this: what was the working class like, and were its members deserving of the vote? Liberals portrayed the respectable artisan as a man of thrift, sobriety, and self-respect, a product of prosperity and the spread of education. Such figures seemed to meet Gladstone's definition of the qualities necessary to exercise the franchise, which he had advanced in 1864: "self-command, self-control, respect for order, patience under suffering, confidence in the law, regard for superiors." Edmund Beales, the president of the Reform League, made the same case, arguing that "the working classes themselves are deeply interested in the preservation of law and order, of the rights of capital and property; of the honour and power and wealth of our country."[168] Gladstone not only shared this view, he also believed that "there is no proof whatever that the working classes, if enfranchised, would act together as a class."[169] Here was the crux of the Liberal case: if given the vote, the workers would not act as a class but in a mature and responsible way; they would reinforce hierarchy not overthrow it. On the other hand, if they were denied the vote, then, as W. E. Forster had earlier predicted, "they will agitate as a class and demand admission as a class." To those who supported it, the extension of the franchise was a way of preventing the politics of class.

The opposition case—and this meant opposition both to Gladstone's initial measure and even more to Disraeli's more radical one—was that this positive stereotyping of the working class and this confident prediction of how they would behave if given the vote were no more than foolish, wishful thinking. Robert Lowe believed that, contrary to the optimistic Liberal view, no confidence could be placed in the workers. He feared that broadening the franchise would give the vote not to the splendid paragons Gladstone had portrayed but to the ignorant and the self-interested, who would be easily swayed by irresponsible demagogues, and the result would be the very opposite of what Gladstone had predicted: a parliament dominated by working-class delegates advancing specific and selfish working-class interests. Far from *preventing* the politics of class and reinforcing hierarchy, the extension of the franchise would thus make *inevitable* the politics of class and bring about the overthrow and ruin of hierarchy.[170] Lowe was not alone in this view. Lord Cranborne, who also resigned from the

Tory government, poured scorn on this "tender trust in the people," and another Conservative MP, Beresford Hope, feared that the bill was encouraging class interests rather than dampening them down.

In 1866–67, as in 1830–32, politicians were talking about social groups whose existence was problematic, were generalizing about behavior patterns that could not possibly be known, and were predicting on the basis of no hard evidence what the working classes would do when they received the vote. They were talking a great deal about "class politics" but, as before, it was not easy for them to describe precisely what these classes were. Liberals thought the workers were good and would not behave as a class; Tories thought the opposite. But these respectable, responsible (or unrespectable, irresponsible) workers were as much imagined communities as the virtuous (or nonvirtuous) middle classes had been over thirty years before. As Brian Harrison observes, "Victorian franchise reform was often implemented amid remarkable ignorance of the classes destined for enfranchisement," and in this regard the Second Reform Act was no different from the First. Gladstone had no satisfactory definition of the "working class"; neither did anyone else. As the Tory H. L. Mansel asked Lord Carnarvon in October 1866, "Is Bright's portrait of the lower classes or Lowe's the better likeness?" "I wish," Carnarvon wrote soon after, "we could get information on the component parts and proportion of the 'working class.'"[171]

This led to a further problem. While the bill could only be passed by giving the vote to *some* members of the working class, no one wanted to give the vote to *all* members of the working class. Put another way, this meant that everyone wanted to exclude what they called "the residuum." Gladstone wanted to keep out "the poorest, the least instructed and the most dependent members of the community," while enfranchising "the most skilled and most instructed of our working men." This was the generally held view. But the idea that any firm line could be drawn separating the respectable and responsible from the unrespectable and irresponsible assumed that the working class was more easily divided into two homogeneous categories than in fact it was. As A. H. Layard pointed out to the Commons in April 1866, corroborating the remarks of Thomas Wright and the statistics of Dudley Baxter, there were "as many divisions and sub-divisions" among workingmen as in any section of the community.[172]

In the end, the drawing of the line was largely determined not by careful or empirically supported social observation (how, indeed, could it have been?) but by the exigencies of the political process. When Disraeli unexpectedly accepted Hodgkinson's amendment, this meant that far more members of the working class were enfranchised than Gladstone had ever intended or, at the outset, Disraeli himself had planned: at a conservative estimate, more than three hundred thousand voters were added to the electoral register at a stroke. Nevertheless, Disraeli does seem to have believed that extending the vote and linking it to a redistribution scheme that favored the traditional territorial interest would hold back class politics and class conflict, reinforce hierarchy, and thereby strengthen the natural institutions of the country: "the wider the popular suffrage, the more powerful would be the natural aristocracy."[173] But High Tory critics like Carnarvon, Shaftesbury, Lowe, and Cranborne believed that the passing of this bill meant precisely the opposite: namely, that the class war had been fought and lost. The result of the "leap in the dark" was that power had been transferred "tamely and miserably" from the middle classes to the working classes, from the elite to "the rabble." It was worse than 1832. "Farewell," mourned Beresford Hope, "to the old halls rising over tall trees, and the spacious deer parks." Hierarchy was dead, and the Conservative measure of 1867 had killed it.[174]

The Way They Saw Things Then

Their gloomy Conservative forebears had felt and feared the same in 1832, when they claimed that the middle classes had taken over and the traditional, aristocrat-led hierarchy was ended. But those forebears had been wrong then, and their successors were wrong now. This was partly the result of their pessimistic political inclination, but it was also a matter of ignorance. In 1867 as in 1832, social descriptions and social predictions were far in advance of "real social knowledge". For it was not just the working classes about whom the politicians were ignorant; it was the structure of society as a whole, right to its apex. In the aftermath of the census of 1861, John Bright had argued that there were no more than thirty thousand landowners and that fewer than one hundred and fifty men owned half the land of England. Lord Derby thought that three hundred thousand landowners was a more accurate figure and disputed the existence of a small number of great estates, even though he owned one himself. No one knew the facts about the landowning pattern in general or about the elite at the top of the hierarchy. And so an inquiry was launched, which revealed as never before the extent of aristocratic power and possession. If not as great as Bright had insisted, it was certainly more than Derby had claimed: 710 individuals owned a quarter of the soil of England and Wales.[175]

No wonder the pessimists in 1867 had been confounded: the landed underpinnings of hierarchy were stronger than most of them had known. These facts provided corroboration for those who insisted that, despite or because of the extension of the franchise, hierarchy and deference were still strong. As Leslie Stephen noted in his contribution to *Essays on Reform*, the majority of the British people still had "an instinctive liking for the established order of things," and there were still "innumerable social ties that bind us together spontaneously."[176] These words could as easily have been written in 1832 or in 1789. To be sure, the combined impact of the American, industrial, and French revolutions, the popular disturbances and reforming legislation of the 1820s and 1830s, and the subsequent mid-Victorian boom had in many ways changed the world beyond recognition. England, Great Britain, the British Isles, and the British Empire were very different places in the late 1870s than they had been one hundred years before. Contemporaries were in no doubt that their society was changing at an unprecedented rate.

Nevertheless, the most outstanding theme in the history of social structures and social perceptions during the century from 1776 was not the making of a new society in Britain, whether divided into two or three collective groups. Rather, it was the survival of traditional hierarchical distinctions and attitudes: sometimes (as before) articulated in terms of rank, order, station, and degree; sometimes (as also before) expressed in terms of class. But hierarchy did not merely survive; it flourished and flowered. The industrial revolution did not destroy the old hierarchy but "created hierarchies of its own" with which to reinforce it.[177] The monarchy, Parliament, the law, the armed services, education remained organized around the social principles of assumed inequality, order and station, deference and subordination. And the reform of Parliament, the civil service, and the military had done little to change that, not least because those who were responsible for the reforms did not want to change it. Seeing society hierarchically, and keeping hierarchy going, was the one view that united most politicians, and most people, in this period. When, in the pages of *Pride and Prejudice*, Lady Catherine de Burgh remarks that she liked to have "the distinctions of rank preserved," she spoke not only for her order and her generation but for the majority of Britons during the first three-quarters of the nineteenth century. This was how they saw their society and, in part for this reason, this was how their society was. Small wonder that in 1873, James Fitzjames Stephen dismissed talk of group identity or collective political action as bogus rhetoric, a mere "bag of words." It was a very revealing remark.[178]

For good or ill, with enthusiasm or regret, most Victorians believed that theirs was a viable hierarchical society, that individual identities based on superiority and subordination were a better guide than collective identities based on conflict or accommodation. This perception was increasingly reinforced from the Empire. In the aftermath of the Mutiny of 1857, the British government assumed direct responsibility for Indian affairs and began the active promotion and encouragement of hierarchy. A succession of censuses enabled the British to categorize every person in India on the layered basis of caste. At the same time, the government agreed "to respect the rights, dignity and honour of the native princes as our own." One indication of this was that a new order of chivalry, the Star of India, was introduced in 1861.[179] Another was the proclamation of Queen Victoria as Empress of India, which not only completed this new version of the social order but also led to the imperial durbar of 1877, an invented, pseudomedieval spectacular of rank and inequality. The British were developing in India "a more closely defined honorific hierarchy" and were increasingly concerned with projecting an image of their empire there as a "feudal order."[180] It was a portent of things to come.

CHAPTER FOUR

THE TWENTIETH CENTURY

Social Identities and
Political Identities

During the last quarter of the nineteenth century, Britain entered the age of mass democratic politics, and it was long believed that this witnessed the consolidation, or the triumph, of the polarized model of society, in which two collective, conflicting classes provided "the basis of British party politics," as social identities directly formed and informed political identities.[1] According to this interpretation, the Third Reform Act of 1885 gave the majority of men the vote, which meant that when Liberals fought Conservatives before the First World War, the former represented the hopes and fears of the middle and working classes, while the latter defended the interests of the rich and the aristocracy. By the same token, the Fourth Reform Act of 1918 having enfranchised most adults, when Labour battled the Tories after the First World War, it was an equally clear-cut contest between the workers on the one side and the employers on the other, a contest that made the demise of the Liberal Party inevitable because of its failure to retain and consolidate the necessary class-based support.[2] As the majority of the population was encompassed within the formal bounds of the political nation and as social identities were brought inside the electoral system to an extent that had never been true before, class conflict came to dominate the political process, and class battles were extended from the workplace to Westminster, where they have been waged ever since.

Such, in the Marxist and Marxisant heyday, was the view of many historians and political scientists: the dichotomous model was the most accurate and convincing version of modern British society; democratic politics were the result of this collective conflict and the reflection of these competing class identities; the two political parties represented two very different class constituencies; and these class constituencies were monolithic and antagonistic and could be taken for granted. But in recent years, these views have been criticized for being too naive, as the direct, one-way connections posited between social and political identities and between social and political conflicts now seem too crude and too reductionist.[3] In our post-Marxist, postmodern era, it is more plausible to suggest that mass party politics are as much about the attempt to create, manage, and manipulate social identities as they are the direct expression of them. "Political rhetoric," Jose Harris has rightly argued for this period, "tended to shape as well as reflect social facts," and the social facts and social models that it both shaped and reflected were not one but three: the dichotomous model was there, to be sure, but so also were the triadic and the hierarchical. And all of them were often, but not always, articulated in the language of class.[4]

The "Politics of Class" Propounded Again

"I assert with some confidence," the young R. H. Tawney confided to his commonplace book in June 1912, "that there has rarely been a period when the existing social order was regarded with so much dissatisfaction by so many intelligent and respectable citizens as it is at the present day."[5] As a comment on the period from the 1880s to the First World War, Tawney's remark has much to recommend it. Once again, there was widespread dissatisfaction (and bewilderment) about the social order, which seemed to be changing in many ways, of which the extension of the franchise was only one indication. By 1900 more than three-quarters of the population lived in towns, and three-quarters of those employed were manual workers, making Britain the most urbanized and industrialized nation in the world.[6] There was large-scale labor unrest in Britain during the 1880s and again in the early 1910s, while in Ireland (and to a lesser extent Wales and Scotland) there was unprecedented agrarian and nationalist agitation. The agricultural depression combined with the reform of local government, the threat of Home Rule for Ireland, and the passing of the Parliament Act in 1911 undermined the aristocracy as the economic, social, and political elite. At the same time, the hold and appeal of established religion markedly weakened, and the growth of imperial dominion and the raising of imperial consciousness further differentiated the late Victorian and Edwardian era from the mid-Victorian period.

As in the 1830s and 1840s, these disruptive developments meant that Britons thought about, talked about, and wrote about their social order with a renewed urgency and contentiousness. In Ireland, the polarized model of society was vividly and violently dramatized as the combination of bad weather, bad harvests, falling prices, and falling output led to the most widespread agitation of the century: the "Land War" and the "Plan of Campaign" of the late 1870s and 1880s. On the one side were Michael Davitt's Land League and Charles Stewart Parnell's Irish National League; on the other the Anglo-Irish landlords and the British state. For much of this period, these two monolithic collectivities seemed to be permanently at war, as tenants refused to pay rents, resorted to physical intimidation, and sabotaged the local hunts.[7] From one perspective, this was a battle between virtuous, repressed, exploited, impoverished Catholic tenants ("the people") and parasitic, oppressive, exploitative Protestant owners ("the landlords"). From another, the confrontation was between brutal, ungrateful, rebellious tenants and generous, considerate, long-suffering notables. It all depended which side you were on. Either way, this confrontation provided the most emphatic corroboration of the view so widely held throughout the nineteenth century that Ireland was irrevocably divided and its social fabric was being rent asunder, an impression vividly conveyed by Anthony Trollope in his last novel, *The Land-Leaguers* (1883), in which he "painted a dark and gloomy picture of rural society caught in the throes of class war."[8]

This violently articulated image of Ireland as a bitterly polarized society convinced Gladstone that it was indeed thus divided, and his acceptance of this model, combined with his belief that superior virtue lay with the tenants rather than the landlords, led him down the path to land reform and ultimately to Home Rule itself.[9] But these perceptions of the structure of Irish society and the policies that resulted from them also had a profound effect on Gladstone's perceptions of British society and on the policies he came to advocate there. For in taking the side of the Irish tenants against their landlords, he inevitably incurred the wrath of the propertied classes in Britain, who disliked what they saw as his hostile and interventionist Land Acts, rejoiced at the defeat of Home Rule in the Commons in 1886, and themselves threw it out of the Lords in 1893. Thus repeatedly rebuffed, Gladstone concluded that the British aristocracy was no longer behaving as the disinterested trustees of the whole nation but had become motivated by the narrow, selfish spirit of its own "class" interest. Instead of ameliorating the politics of "class," they were now practicing them.[10]

The result was that during the 1880s Gladstone abandoned his self-appointed role as the champion of the traditional hierarchy and reinvented himself as a crusading moral populist on the side of "the people," and in doing this he repoliticized and reactivated the traditional model of British society as being irrevocably divided between "us" and "them." Hence his famous remark in Liverpool in June 1886 that when it came to matters of "truth, justice and humanity, . . . all the world over, I will back the masses against the classes."[11] For all his qualifications, this was an exceptionally subversive observation, as Gladstone threw his substantial political weight behind those whom he praised (and flattered) as the virtuous majority and contrasted to "class and the dependents of class," by which he meant "station, title, wealth, social influence, the professions." For the rest of his public life, Gladstone's Liberal Party seemed to many to be not so much the traditional cross-class coalition actively working to prevent class war but a newly energized, single-class communion intensifying class antagonisms. Hence, at the end of his career, after the Lords had rejected his second Home Rule Bill, his wish to fight a general election on the polarizing, populist issue of "peers versus people."[12]

Strange though it may superficially seem, this was also the view of Britain's social structure that Lord Salisbury came to share, though he got to it by a different route and drew very different conclusions from it. Like Gladstone, Salisbury was an "out and out inequalitarian" who venerated the traditional, divinely sanctioned hierarchy that was as much on display on his estate at Hatfield as on Gladstone's at Hawarden. But he was convinced that the Reform Act of 1867 had dealt this world a mortal blow, and he was becoming increasingly "apprehensive about the social viability of hierarchy." Indeed, by the 1880s he feared this traditional order was "disintegrating." "Things that have been secure for centuries," he observed, "are secure no longer."[13] For he now believed that society was unhappily but unavoidably divided between "the masses" and "the classes and dependents of class." But while he deliberately used Gladstone's phraseology, he lined up the Tories on the side of the classes. And during the 1880 and 1890s, there were many who shared Salisbury's view, including organizations such as the Liberty and Property Defence League (founded 1882) and writers such as W. H. Mallock, another believer in time-honored and providentially ordained hierarchy who recognized that Britain was now irrevocably split between the few and the many.[14]

In the hands of Gladstone and Salisbury, these revived visions of Britain's deeply riven social order were not just politicized; they were *party* politicized. Indeed, this picture of Britain divided "horizontally" between a Liberal Party representing the masses and a Conservative Party representing the classes resonated well beyond the lives of the two leaders who had created it, reaching its climax in the years before the First World War.[15] For twenty years, it looked as though the Conservatives were winning this class war, but after the general election of 1906, the terms of the engagement shifted, as the obstructionism of the House of Lords increasingly tilted the balance of opinion away from the peers, especially after their rejection of "the People's Budget" in 1909. "Savage strife between class and class" was what Winston Churchill predicted, fearing yet welcoming the prospect. But it was Lloyd George who most effectively took up Gladstone's mantle of the crusading populist, widening the division between the peers, whom he denounced as "five hundred men chosen randomly from among the ranks of the unemployed," and the "millions of people" who, by contrast, were "engaged in the industry which makes the wealth of the country." Here was a vision of a divided society harking back to Paine and Cobbett: virtuous producers versus idle parasites. "The Lords," Lloyd George declared, "shall decree a revolution; but the people shall direct it."[16]

But like the Irish landowners, the defenders of the Lords took the same polarized model of British society and inverted it, offering alternative stereotypes of their own. As they saw it, the battle was not between a parasitical elite and a virtuous people but between a virtuous aristocracy and the swinish multitude. Egged on by Lloyd George, the people were behaving in a self-interested and predatory way, singling out a beleaguered, patriotic nobility for "special and unfair persecution." According to Fabian Ware, editor of the *Morning Post*, the government was appealing to "the worst and most dangerous class prejudices." Contrary to ministers' opinions, the Lords was a "strong, competent, disinterested and impartial body."[17] Unsurprisingly, the monarchs were especially upset at what they regarded as this sudden, ominous polarization of the social and political order. Edward VII thought Lloyd George's speeches were "calculated to set class against class, and to inflame the passions of the working and lower orders against people who happened to be owners of property." But Lloyd George gave as good as he got, both to King Edward and his successor. The trouble with George V, he complained, was that "all his sympathy is with the rich—very little pity for the poor." Here was a deep divide. "Never before," noted Ramsay MacDonald, "have the rich as a class ranged themselves so completely on one side as they have done this time. Loafing and industry were never so well divided."[18]

But this was not the only way in which late Victorian and Edwardian Britons came to regard their society as polarized. One alternative vision was the growing enmity between capital and labor. Between 1888 and 1914 the number of workers organized in trade unions increased from 759,000 to 4.1 million. At the same time, there was a parallel growth in employers' organizations, and a succession of legal judgments went against trade unions, most notably Taff Vale (1901) and Osborne (1909). Part cause, part effect, was the unprecedented growth of industrial unrest, culminating in the wave of strikes in the late 1880s and again in the early 1910s. The first centered around the London match girls, the gas stokers, and the London dockers. "From present appearances," wrote Thomas Lewis in 1890, "we are on the eve of a very serious crisis between Capital and Labour in pretty well every trade in the kingdom."[19] The second centered around the railways and docks, coal miners, and textile workers. In 1912 there were 1,459 strikes, and 40.9 million working days were lost. At the beginning of that year, *The Times* warned that "the public must be prepared for a conflict between Labour and Capital, or between employers and employed, upon a scale as has never occurred before."[20]

This view that the nation was sundered between workers and employers was further intensified by the rise in the 1900s of the Labour Party, which was based on the idea of "class allegiance" and sought to give the workers an enhanced sense of class consciousness and class identity. Labour encouraged all workers to think of themselves as belonging to a single class with a set of common interests that could best be served by direct representation in the House of Commons, where the party numbered twenty-nine MPs in 1906, and forty-two in 1910. As such, Labour was the real class-based party of the Edwardian era, and its very existence intensified the view that Britain was a deeply riven society.[21] Party leaders such as MacDonald and Kier Hardy might declare themselves opposed to the violent, revolutionary concept of a class war, but they had no doubt that Britain was divided between capital and labor and that labor needed all the help it could get. Their aim, as MacDonald put it in the mid-1890s, was to "arouse the labouring classes" to "a knowledge of their power" and to promote "the welfare and improvement of the condition of the working classes."[22]

It was not only employers and employees who saw British society as divided in this way. Fabians such as Beatrice Webb shared the Labour view that there was a fundamental gulf between capital and labor, although they rejected the idea of class war because they thought capitalism would gradually and peacefully evolve into socialism.[23] But the teachings of Karl Marx urged a more adversarial and apocalyptic view of social divisions. His works were becoming increasingly available in English translation, with the first volume of *Capital* appearing in 1887 and the authorized edition of the *Communist Manifesto* in the following year. They offered powerful historical validation of the claim that in modern society there was inevitable conflict between capital and labor. But they also insisted that it was only by revolutionary means that the proletariat could overthrow the capitalists and usher in the classless society. Among Marx's British followers was H. M. Hyndman, leader of the Social Democratic Federation, who believed he was witnessing class war between "the toilers and the spoilers," although he could not bring himself to give history a helping hand in the direction of the proletarian revolution. Very different was the dockers' leader Ben Tillett, who insisted that "there is no peace, because industrial war is permanent under capitalism. The capitalist must fight us, for his interests are antagonistic to ours as a class."[24]

There was yet a third way in which British society was seen as divided: between those who were sunk in poverty and those who were not. In the 1880s the "Condition of England" question became a matter of public concern in a way it had not been since the 1840s. This was partly because a mass of new investigative literature brought to light for a later generation a separate, segregated world of urban squalor and deprivation: "outcast London," "darkest England," a "terra incognita" beyond "the abyss."[25] Many of these accounts of working-class life were highly impressionistic, but at the end of the decade Charles Booth set out to survey the conditions of life and labor in London so as to focus attention on "the problem of poverty in the midst of wealth." Eventually, Booth concluded that 30.7 percent of the population of London were in poverty, a figure substantially corroborated by Seebohm Rowntree in 1901 in his study of York. Here was the most detailed and authoritative evidence yet provided of the continued existence of the "two nations." A century after the industrial revolution, Britain remained a $^2/_3$-$^1/_3$ society.

This Manichaean contrast of misery in the midst of plenty was very much a trope of the times. In 1883 Henry George coined the phrase "progress and poverty" to describe the contrast between "the House of Have and the House of Want." A year later, the Rev. Samuel Barnett founded Toynbee Hall as a missionary settlement in east London, to "bridge the gulf that industrialism has created between rich and poor, to reduce the mutual suspicion and ignorance of one class for the other." After working for Charles Booth, Beatrice Webb came to recognize that Britain was "a community permanently divided into a nation of the rich and a nation of the poor."[26] These social perceptions were vividly underscored by the riots of February 1886 and November 1887 in the West End that dramatized the division between the impoverished "barbarians" in the slums and the comfortable rich who seemed increasingly threatened. There was, Samuel Barnett felt, a "growth of a conscious class hatred," a "growing animosity of the poor against the rich." On into the next century, this remained a familiar formulation, as when L. G. Chiozza Money entitled his 1905 social investigation *Riches and Poverty*.[27] And one of Lloyd George's particular skills was the ease with which, during the battle over the "People's Budget," he was able to elide "peers versus people" into "rich versus poor."

It is, then, not surprising that Lord Rosebery described the late Victorian and Edwardian period as witnessing the "cleavage of classes." But several qualifications have to be entered. For all the use of phrases such as "the classes and the masses" and "class war," much of this polarizing discussion was not carried on in the language of class. There were many other formulations of these conflicting collective identities: landlords versus tenants, peers versus people, aristocracy versus democracy, idle versus industrious, capital versus labor, the few versus the many, the rich versus the poor.[28] And there was also considerable disagreement as to what these polarities actually were. As Charles Booth explained, the division in society between "labour and capital" was not the same thing as the division between "poverty and wealth," and neither of these was the same as "peers versus people."[29] But these conflicting collectivities were not only defining and articulating contradictory and inconsistent social visions and divisions. They were also rhetorical representations, attempts to create coherent, collective, adversarial identities when, as always, society was much more complicated.

Consider the ways in which Irish society was envisaged by nationalists, landlords, and British politicians. The crude confrontational simplicities of landlord versus tenant were rhetorically and politically resonant, but Irish society had always been more elaborately structured than that, and during the last quarter of the nineteenth century, it was becoming more elaborate still. In Ulster there was a growing Protestant middle and working class: the best model of late-nineteenth-century Belfast was the tripartite rather than the dichotomous. As for rural Ireland, "the landlords" were a far more diverse and vulnerable group than nationalist propaganda suggested, while the massed protest movement included greater, middling, and lesser farmers, shopkeepers and priests, publicans and glaziers, smallholders and laborers, who were further divided between north and south, east and west, highland and lowland and who had different economic interests and political ambitions.[30] As a result, the Land League was neither stable nor monolithic. "Unity," Roy Foster points out, "was precariously preserved through rhetoric": the demonizing demagoguery of antilandlordism. No wonder the agitation did not last long and that Anna Parnell called it "a great sham."[31]

In the same way, the equation of the Tory Party with the "classes" and the Liberal Party with the "masses" was largely created by political propoganda. On the Conservative side, the "classes" that they claimed to represent were a varied constituency, ranging from the peerage, via businessmen, to all property owners. And notwithstanding these claims to social exclusivity, there was a great deal of popular Toryism (and Unionism) in Lancashire, the West Midlands, London, and Glasgow; so much so that during the Edwardian era, the Conservatives regularly secured between one-third and one-half of the working-class vote, in large part because of the campaign for Tariff Reform, which was explicitly aimed (among other things) at tying the middle and working classes together.[32] Nor were the Liberals exclusively the party of the masses, for they were supported by businessmen, professionals, and millionaires. Small wonder that in 1912 the Conservatives set up a "Radical Plutocrats Inquiry" to "destroy the dangerous legend . . . that Unionism is the Party of the Rich, and Radicalism the Party of the Poor." When led by Gladstone, Rosebery, Harcourt, Campbell-Bannerman, and Asquith, the Liberals were scarcely in the vanguard of proletarian revolution. Both parties drew supporters from all levels and layers of society: they were class inclusive, even as they projected images of being class exclusive.[33]

The so-called great divide between capital and labor was equally oversimplified. On the one side, capital was not monolithic but split between industry and finance, goods and services, a few large-scale companies and many small-scale operations. In 1898–99, the average British workshop employed less than thirty male workers, and in the

Edwardian period, there were a mere one hundred firms employing three thousand people each, scarcely 5 percent of the total labor force.[34] The massive shipyards of Barrow and Clydeside, the locomotive- and coach-building works at Crewe and Swindon, the large steel works at Middlesborough were very exceptional in a British context and very small scale compared with Pittsburgh or Philadelphia, St. Petersburg or Turin. Even in these large factories, there was an elaborate, carefully differentiated hierarchy from senior managers to the humblest employee, and in the smaller workshops, managers and owners made it a point of pride to be on first-name terms with their employees and to know them personally. When Stanley Baldwin told the Commons in 1925 that as a boy he had known the names of all the workers in the family ironworks at Bewdley, he was describing what had then been a commonplace state of affairs.[35]

Like capital, late Victorian and Edwardian labor was only monolithic in the realm of rhetoric; in practice it was far from homogeneous. The working class was no more "remade" during the last quarter of the nineteenth century than it had been "made" during the first quarter. In terms of skills, status, and income, there were still complex gradations, hierarchies, and divisions, which carried over from the mid-Victorian era. Many industrial workers saw themselves as belonging to a factory community that also encompassed their employers rather than to a class community that encompassed all workers. Many others were not involved in industry at all, especially servants and those in the service sector. These heterogeneous millions did not approximate to a Marxist proletariat.[36] Indeed, in the early 1870s, only 4 percent of the labor force belonged to trade unions, and in 1911 less than one-quarter did. Most employees—and most employers—believed that production was about compromise, consensus, and cooperation, and in this context, strikes were seen as domestic quarrels over specific issues that were local disagreements rather than revolutionary upheavals. The majority of workers were socially conservative, and many were politically conservative as well. Only a minority voted for Labour, which was ostensibly the party of their class: the majority preferred the Liberals or Conservatives, the parties for which their employers voted.[37]

Not surprisingly, "the overwhelming majority" of Britons, "whether economists, labour leaders, workers, politicians or intellectuals," rejected Marx's claim that the division between capital and labor was deep, irreconcilable, and getting deeper. The publication of his works was met with a barrage of criticism from across the political spectrum:

W. H. Mallock, Alice Oldham, James Brodrick, and Bertrand Russell. To talk, Goldwin Smith claimed, "of a war of labour against capital generally" was "absurd." On the contrary, as T. H. Huxley insisted, they were "necessarily close allies." This view that "the middle and working classes are on very friendly terms" was widely held.[38] Before 1914 Labour leaders such as Kier Hardy and Ramsay MacDonald rejected Marxist analysis; they were more interested in "the growth of society" than "the uprising of class." In any case, as J. A. Hobson admitted in 1914, "the number of actual conflicts between capital and labour" was "constantly diminishing": there was "a harmony of interest between the two groups." Thus understood, the labor unrest of 1911–14 did not portend proletarian revolution, in which the social fabric would be rent in twain. As Ben Tillett admitted, there was "a lack of class loyalty and class-conscience" on the part of the workers.[39]

The idea that British society was irrevocably sundered between capital and labor was too crude, and so was the idea that there was one great dividing line between those in poverty and those who were not. For where, exactly, should—or could—the line be drawn? Booth was notoriously vague as to whether the whole of his 30.7 percent who belonged to "the poor" or worse were actually in poverty or merely "in want," and he doubted whether British society could be precisely and authoritatively divided between those who were poor and those who were not.[40] Moreover, much poverty was seasonal or more likely to occur at some stages of the life cycle than others, which meant that many families and individuals were constantly moving into poverty, out of it, and back in again. They did not spend all their lives on one side of a divide that they never crossed. Booth's successors found it no easier to draw a single, definitive "poverty line" across Britain's social fabric, least of all Seebohm Rowntree, who was involved in a protracted controversy with Helen Bosanquet over just this matter. Was this great divide based on statistical measurement of income and expenditure or on a more impressionistic sense of whether a family was living in poverty? It was difficult to know and hard to agree.[41]

Although they were the most explicitly, vociferously, and adversarially politicized, these polarized versions of British society were not the only way it was seen during the late Victorian and Edwardian eras. As in past periods, the three-stage alternative remained much in vogue, and it expressed a very different view from the apocalyptic vision of two interminably warring adversaries. Grace Fulford, whose parents were comfortably off, recalled of the Edwardian era, "There was a class distinction. Definitely. There was the working class, and middle class and the aristocrats." Lord Meath agreed, observing in the upper house in 1909 that what the country now needed was "discipline in the upper classes, discipline in the middle classes, and discipline in the lower classes."[42] But, as before, this triadic vision of society was not always articulated in the language of class. Although L. G. Chiozza Money had entitled his study of British society *Riches and Poverty*, he had actually analyzed it in terms of "the rich," "the comfortable," and "the poor." And when C. F. G. Masterman published *The Condition of England* later in the same decade, he wrote of "the rich," "the middle classes," and "the working people."[43]

Although articulated in different languages, these three-level accounts of late Victorian and Edwardian social structure seem generally to agree. But on closer inspection, they were often describing very different societies—or, rather, very different parts of the same society. Here are two examples. Dispensing with the language of class, Allen Clarke, who worked in the Lancashire cotton textile industry, divided society in Bolton and Oldham in the 1890s as follows. The "first caste" consisted of "employers, clergymen, solicitors, physicians, tradesmen on a large scale," the "second caste" was "composed of the best-paid clerks, book-keepers, managers, and the better sort of working folks," and the "third caste" was "made up of 'labourers' and poorer workmen."[44] But the social world as envisioned by an Essex farmworker's boy was very different. He agreed that Edwardian Britain was "something like the railway carriages were at one time," with "first, second and third class," and he illustrated this with reference to the seating patterns in his local church. His mother, who was poor, sat at the back; in the middle were "the local shopkeepers and people who were considered to be a little bit superior to the others"; at the front were "the local farmers, the local bigwigs, . . . posh people."[45]

In part, these were different visions of the social structure because the social structures of industrial Lancashire and agricultural Essex *were* different: the apparently uniform three-stage model encompassed (and also concealed) a wide variety of local variations. But it was also during this period that "the middle class" expanded in three significant ways that Marx had not foreseen. There was a noticeable proliferation of the "lower middle class": that army of clerks and office workers who were neither factory laborers nor factory owners but who merged into the working class beneath and the prosperous middle class above.[46] There was a pronounced growth of the professions: those lawyers, doctors, teachers, and civil servants whose numbers, qualifications, and incomes were all expanding rapidly at this time.[47] And there was a new plutocracy of superrich bankers, financiers, and businessmen that merged (or bought its way) into the traditional aristocracy.[48] In terms of income, expenditure, occupation, and way of life, this was a huge swathe of British society to encompass within the misleadingly homogenized category "middle class." Here is one example of contemporary misunderstanding. The Edwardian middle class, G. K. Chesterton claimed, "really was a class and it really was in the middle. . . . It was separated from the class above and the class below." But it was too big and too varied to be "really" a class, and it was not "separated" from its superiors and inferiors.[49]

This triadic view of society, which gave special attention to the middle class, was not only less well founded than in any previous period; it was also much less resonant politically than it had been one hundred years before and far less appealing politically than was the polarized, confrontational model. During the late eighteenth and early nineteenth centuries, members of the middle class had asserted that theirs was a uniquely virtuous group that accordingly deserved political rights. Now, by contrast, many argued that their brief era of political dominance had come and gone. By the end of the nineteenth century, it was widely believed that the mid-Victorian period had witnessed the zenith of middle-class political power, sandwiched between the rule of the patricians and the rule of the people. As the duke of Westminster told Gladstone, "The Reform Bills of 1832, of 1867, and of 1885 have in the main removed the preponderance of electoral power from the aristocracy and from the middle classes, and have placed it in the hands of the masses."[50] Or, as the young Winston Churchill put it, the years 1832 to 1885–86 had witnessed "the long dominion of the middle classes." But that was now over, and "the people" were in charge.[51] This was exaggerated on both counts, and it was not how the majority of mid-Victorians had viewed their social and political world. But it was the conventional wisdom of the generation that came after.

One reason for this was that between the 1880s and the First World War historical accounts stressing the earlier importance of the middle class became commonplace. Part of the explanation was deemed to lie with the industrial revolution, which in Alice Green's words "created a society unknown before—a middle class of prodigious wealth and activity" whose entrepreneurial endeavors were now being extensively written about by the Webbs and the Hammonds. The arrival of this new class soon received appropriate political recognition in what Sidney Webb described as "the Great Reform Bill of 1832, by which the reign of the middle class superseded aristocratic rule," an analysis repeated in almost every historical work of the period, from A. V. Dicey among an older generation to G. M. Trevelyan among the younger.[52] Thus was ushered in what Walter Lyon Blease described in 1913 as "The Middle Class Supremacy," a supremacy that was ended with the Second and Third Reform Acts, which created a preponderantly working-class electorate. It should be clear that as an account of economic, social, and political development from the 1780s to the 1880s, this leaves much to be desired. But there can be no doubting how powerful and pervasive an interpretation it became in late Victorian and Edwardian Britain.[53]

According to this interpretation, the late Victorian and Edwardian middle class was on the wane. Its rule was over, and it was increasingly beleaguered, caught between a hostile working class and Liberal governments ever more inclined to increase taxation. To the extent that the triadic image of society was politicized, it was in a very different way from how it had been one hundred years before. For this was the politics of middle-class defense, not of assertiveness. Just as the late-eighteenth- and early-nineteenth-century accounts exaggerated middle-class strength, so these subsequent accounts exaggerated middle-class weakness. Hence the evolution of a right-wing Middle Class Defence Organisation and George Sims's articles in the nominally Liberal *Tribune* entitled "The Bitter Cry of the Middle Classes," which were widely read and applauded. Hence, too, these lines of Hilaire Belloc:

> The people inbetween
> Looked underdone and harassed
> And out of place and mean
> And horribly embarrassed.[54]

The fact that all members of the Edwardian middle class were feeling beleaguered was no more true than that all their forbears in 1810 had been feeling assertive: these were (as usual) sociological simplifications for political (and poetical) purposes. Nor were they the only ones. For while some believed the Edwardian middle class was predominantly beleaguered, others insisted that its defining characteristic was guilt: guilt over the exploitative, selfish part it had played in the industrial revolution. According to Beatrice Webb, the last quarter of the nineteenth century saw a growing "consciousness of sin" that was "a collective class consciousness" on the part of the middle classes, a consciousness reinforced by the hostile accounts of the entrepreneurs in the industrial revolution that the Webbs and the Hammonds provided.[55] And this consciousness was most memorably articulated by Arnold Toynbee in his anguished lament to the workers, expressed in the conventional, three-layer model of society: "We—the middle classes, I mean, not merely the very rich—we have neglected you . . . we have sinned against you grievously . . . but if you will forgive us . . . we will devote our lives to your service."[56]

Of course, there were many among the middle classes who were wholly devoid of this sense of guilt; once again, ideological stereotypes were being imposed on a bourgeoisie whose range and diversity defied any such monolithic characterization. And many such identities were foisted on them. One of these was that they were increasingly plutocratic, vulgar, and immoral. Just as Lloyd George attacked the aristocracy as effete, self-interested parasites, so there were Tory peers who retaliated by disparaging the superrich as greedy, rootless, unpatriotic, self-indulgent, hypocritical, unscrupulous adventurers. This not only included Liberals such as Cadbury and Rowntree, Brunner and Mond; it even, on occasion, encompassed those within their own party.[57] "Their whole method of looking at politics," observed Lord Robert Cecil about the Tariff Reform League, run by that Birmingham businessman Joseph Chamberlain, "appears to me utterly sordid and materialistic, not yet corrupt, but on the high road to corruption." It seems unlikely that the middle class was intrinsically any more corrupt than the aristocracy. But this scandalmongering stereotyping of the middle class—insisting that an entire social group was behaving in a corrupt way—was a pronounced feature of Edwardian political rhetoric.[58]

A different identity again was that the middle class was feeble, complacent, and defeated and that the vigor, energy, and inventiveness that had characterized them in their halcyon days of entrepreneurial success had now deserted them. The late nineteenth century saw the first "great depression": in trade and industry, in prices, profits, and interests. It also saw the gradual overtaking of Britain by Germany and the United States as the foremost industrial and manufacturing powers. Hence the "Made in Germany" scare of the 1880s and the "American Invasion" scare of the 1900s. As early as 1884 Lord Randolph Churchill pronounced the iron industry to be "dead as mutton," coal to be "languishing," and cotton to be "seriously sick." "In the age of steam," one factory inspector observed in 1901, "this country led the way, whereas in the age of electricity, we seem to follow America and other countries."[59] And who was to blame for this lamentable state of affairs? Those middle class entrepreneurs who so conspicuously lacked the vigor of their heroic predecessors and had succumbed to what Alfred Marshall described as the "easy self-complacency engendered by the abnormal prosperity in the third quarter of the nineteenth century."[60]

The varied collective identities that were so inventively wished on the Edwardian middle classes were little more than rhetorical imaginings. A great deal that was said about them, or that they said about themselves, was wrong or contradictory or both. The idea that they had attained power, wielded power, and lost power between 1832 and 1885 was a very simplistic account of the economic, social, and political history of the nineteenth century. Some members of the middle class may have felt guilty or beleaguered, but this plainly did not apply to everyone. Nor was it easy to reconcile one view that they were pushy and thrusting with another claiming they were weak and feeble. In truth, there was no such thing as *the* late Victorian and Edwardian middle class; it was far too protean, varied, and amorphous for that. But there *was* something that these varied, inaccurate, and contradictory images of the middle class did have in common: they all began with the triadic vision of society, and they gave the most attention to those in the middle. Hence C. F. G. Masterman's remark that "it was the middle class which stands for England in most modern analysis" and that they felt "contempt for the classes below it, and envy of the classes above": a standard three-stage formulation, with the weight in the middle.[61]

The belief that late Victorian and Edwardian society was divided into three distinct social groups and that the whole of the middle class could be described in terms of one defining and characteristic mode of behavior lay predominantly in the eyes of the beholder. Even Masterman, who had built his analysis in *The Condition of England* around this model and given most emphasis to a monolithic suburban middle class, recognized its limitations. For he also divided British society into four layers or alternatively into two. Another writer, who was much interested in the Edwardian middle classes from which he sprang, was George Orwell. He, too, recognized that there was no such thing as one middle class but instead a series of overlapping layers, which was why he described himself as being a product of the "lower-upper-middle class."[62] From this perspective, British society was much more complex than the three-stage (let alone the two-stage) model would suggest, a conclusion Charles Booth had already reached a generation before Orwell. For Booth was happy neither with his two-layer model of those in poverty and those who were not nor with the more elaborate eight-class taxonomy that he had also devised. "It is to be remembered," he wrote, "that the dividing lines between all these classes are indistinct; each has, so to speak, a fringe of those who ought to be placed within the next division above or below; nor are the classes, as given, homogeneous by any means. Room may be found in each for many grades of social rank."[63]

In thus qualifying his findings, Booth was not only mixing up the languages of class and rank in a way that was still commonplace in his time; he was also recognizing that British society was not best seen in terms of collective classes but rather as a more complex, layered, hierarchical world. To be sure, there were many who shared Lord Salisbury's fear that hierarchy was collapsing and social disintegration was nigh. Viscount Halifax thought "the foundations are being shaken everywhere," Lord Selborne believed "the social system is out of joint," and Masterman lamented that the "one single system of traditional hierarchy has fissured into a thousand diversified channels."[64] Yet even as the aristocracy began to decline, hierarchical perceptions lived on. As Engels observed in 1889, the "old and established" custom of "the division of society into a scale of innumerable degrees, each recognised without question," persisted. And Patrick Joyce has recently urged that in the factory towns of late-nineteenth- and early-twentieth-century Lancashire were to be found "conceptions of the social order" emphasizing "the inevitability and even the necessity of prevailing social hierarchies," which were regarded as "well-nigh immovable and . . . preordained and natural."[65] But it was not just that the hierarchical vision of British society survived: during these years it was successfully refurbished, reconstructed, and reinvented. How did this happen?

An important part of the explanation lies with the Conservatives. They may have claimed they were waging war on behalf of the classes against the masses, but the most effective way they did so was by reviving hierarchy. Crucial to this endeavor was the Primrose League, which was founded in 1883 and which in its heyday during the 1890s was the largest political organization in Britain, with a membership of more than a million. Its recruits came from the country as well as the town, from all social levels, and were women as well as men. Martin Pugh has recently drawn attention to its "deferential and hierarchical character," as its mass membership was sorted according to an elaborately graded ladder, modeled on and mimicking the official honors stem and extending upward from "Associates," via several ranks of knights and dames, to the "Grand Master" or party leader. Its branches were called habitations; its upper echelons groaned with aristocratic grandees; and it was run by a Grand Council. In its ethos and style, its badges and decorations, its titles and orders, its ritual and ceremonial, the Primrose League was by turns antiquarian, chivalric, Gothic, and medieval. Thus regarded, it was a most successful instrument in promoting, among its million-odd members, a hierarchical cast of mind and a hierarchical view of the British world.[66]

At the same time, the honors system on which the Primrose League was based was itself being changed. Honors were not just about rewarding people in a way that was appropriate to their achievement; they were also about rewarding people in a way that was appropriate to their social rank. Until the last quarter of the nineteenth century, they had been generally confined to those at the summit of the traditional landed hierarchy. But from the 1870s onward peerages were given out in greater numbers, and to people of more humble background, especially to plutocrats like Iveagh, Leverhulme, Northcliffe, and Cowdray. At the same time, traditional orders of knighthood were amplified and extended (such as the Order of St. Michael and St. George), new orders were created (such as the Royal Victorian Order), and many more knights bachelor were dubbed. The result was an increasingly elaborate order of honorific precedence, extending from the peerage, via knights grand cross and knights commander, to commanders and members. Lord Curzon was not alone in lamenting that honors were "no longer confined to any one class or caste in this country." But the recruitment of so many more people into the honors system also served to strengthen hierarchical perceptions, as provincial outsiders such as Edward Elgar sought to rise from a knighthood, to a GCVO, to a baronetcy, and even, perhaps, to the peerage.[67]

These revived and elaborated honorific hierarchies were extended more broadly to the British Empire, which in the late Victorian and Edwardian heyday of the "new imperialism" was a major component in this renewed "instinct for hierarchy."[68] The creation of the Order of the Indian Empire, the imperial durbars of 1902 and 1911, and the increasing esteem accorded to the native Indian princes meant that by the time Lord Curzon became viceroy, "hierarchy was the axis around which everything turned" in the Indian Empire. At Calcutta and Simla, the choreographed viceregal rituals of rank and status were more elaborate than at Windsor or Buckingham Palace. Throughout the Raj, protocol was strictly governed by the "warrant of precedence," which gave essential advice as to whether the superintendent of the opium factory at Ghazipur was to be seated ahead of the general manager of the Rajputana Salt Resources at dinner.[69] As David Washbrook has pointed out, "in social terms, the British Raj was happiest dealing with what it conceived to be a feudal social order . . . of inherited social hierarchy." And where such a feudal hierarchy did not exist the British were endlessly inventive in creating one.[70]

In the four great imperial dominions of settlement, the hierarchical view of social structure was nowhere as fully elaborated as in India, not least because there was no indigenous ranked society out of which it could be developed and on to which it could be grafted. But by the late nineteenth century, these settler societies were stabilizing and gradually developing their own local elites, which became increasingly attracted to British "hierarchical attitudes." In 1891 and 1895 Sir Bernard Burke collected and codified these families in his *Colonial Gentry*, emphatic evidence that hierarchy was alive and well and visible in New South Wales. And it can hardly be coincidence that during the last quarter of the nineteenth century these local settler hierarchies were legitimated and completed by grand viceregal courts, presided over by junior members of the royal family or British aristocrats, that in their ceremony and protocol owed much to India. Invitations to Government House were highly prized and so, too, were the imperial honors that now tied the most distant province of the most far-flung dominion to this greater, imperial British hierarchy, as peerages, knighthoods, and lesser orders were given out in increasing abundance from the 1880s onward: to businessmen, prime ministers, and other important figures.[71]

This renewed hierarchical vision was further strengthened by the revived cult of royalty, as the imperial monarchy was caparisoned with unprecedented pomp from the time of Queen Victoria's jubilees onward and reinvented itself as the elevated symbol of "authority, hierarchy and duty."[72] For this was the vision of British society that was put on display at the jubilees, funerals, and coronations that were staged with such imaginative splendor during this period, as all the resources of visual rhetoric were mobilized to demonstrate that order, rank, and station were the only ways in which it could be conceived and that any alternative model was literally unimaginable. Hence the claim of the archbishop of Canterbury that socialism had "had a check" after the Golden Jubilee celebrations, which projected a very different (and more persuasive) version of the social order from that articulated by the rioters in the West End. Likewise, the coronation of George V displayed an ordered British world extending down from the king-emperor to his humblest subject and out from Westminster Abbey to far beyond the seas that was far more resonant than the competing visions of a society deeply riven between peers and people, or capital and labor, or rich and poor.[73]

These ritualized public occasions centering on the sovereign put hierarchy on display with unprecedented vividness and immediacy, and stately pageants proliferated, not just in London but throughout Britain and the empire, as villages, towns, and cities vied with each other to mark royal rites of passage in appropriately celebratory or funereal style.[74] Many towns also evolved their own festivities, centered on the mayor or other local celebrities: the Lord Mayor's Show in London, the Oyster Feast in Colchester, the inauguration of the lord warden of the Cinque Ports in Dover, and the installation of chancellors at Oxford and Cambridge and the new provincial universities.[75] It became the fashion to seek aristocratic mayors—Lord Shaftesbury in Belfast, the duke of Norfolk and Lord Fitzwilliam in Sheffield, and Lords Bute and Windsor at Cardiff—who embodied local tradition, completed the civic hierarchy, and incorporated it by their titled rank into the national order. At the same time, there was a renewed interest in the physical artifacts of hierarchy and antiquity: town halls ornamented with statues of historic figures and local worthies, maces, regalia, and armorial bearings. Among such objects and against such backgrounds, hierarchy flourished.[76]

Underpinning these developments, domestic and imperial, political and ceremonial, was a new ideology, much more plausible and pervasive than Marxism, that relegitimated the idea that society was providentially ordered at the very time when, in an increasingly secular age, traditional religious sanction for this view was weakening. For while God no longer preordained hierarchy theologically, it seemed that evolution preordained it scientifically.[77] This was the legacy of Charles Darwin and Francis Dalton to vernacular visions of society: they secularized and temporalized what had previously been the religiously sanctioned linear hierarchy of the Great Chain of Being.[78] Inequality, so this argument ran, was the natural result of natural selection: men, like animals, were not born equal, nor could they be made equal. Not surprisingly, conservative apologists such as Mallock and Lord Hugh Cecil, who sought to declare war on socialism, Lloyd George, and Marx and to defend hierarchy as the inevitable order of society, found in evolution a new doctrine with which to support their claims concerning "the variety and degree of inequality which is inherent in mankind" as a "natural tendency."[79] This explains why many conservatives still believe freedom must mean freedom to be unequal and thus for hierarchy to continue. Hence their belief that liberty and equality are not compatible. Liberty, freedom, and hierarchy, yes; liberty, freedom, and equality, no.

This is a very different picture of late Victorian and Edwardian society from that put forward by Gladstone or Lloyd George, by Hyndman or Masterman, and it is important to emphasize that it was still articulated as much in the language of ranks, orders, and degrees as in the language of class. Indeed, across all three models of British society, these varied vocabularies persisted into the twentieth century; even those regarded as raising the temperature of class war did not necessarily do so in the language of class. Churchill did, but Lloyd George preferred to speak of a virtuous "people" against a corrupt elite: the language of Paine, Cobbett, John Bright, and Gladstone—and later of Thatcher.[80] It is, then, an exaggeration to say that from the 1880s, "one development is incontrovertible," namely, that "the language of 'ranks,' 'orders' and 'degrees,' which had survived the Industrial Revolution, had finally been cast into limbo. The language of class like the facts of class, remained."[81]

Consider, in this regard, Robert Roberts's recollections of life in early twentieth century Salford. Two important points emerge from his account. One is the range and richness of his vocabulary as he described the "social ladder" or "social pyramid" in terms of ranks and orders, gradations and degrees, layers and strata, classes and caste. The second is the familiarity of the models this varied vocabulary described. There was the layered hierarchy, extending "from an elite at the peak, composed of the leading families, through recognized strata to a social base whose members one damned as the 'lowest of the low' or simply 'no class.'" There was the tripartite model, sometimes the "upper classes," the "bourgeoisie," and "manual workers"; sometimes the "middle and upper orders" and the "working class." And there was the polarized model, divided between "the rich and the poor" or "upper class families and working class households."[82] His overriding impression was of a complex, finely graded hierarchy, in which people were deeply sensitive to the smallest nuances of status. They did not think in terms of collective identities locked in bitter, permanent, inevitable struggle, and their battles with employers were more for survival than part of a great class war against capital. "The problem of the 'proletariat,' they felt, had little to do with them."[83] In envisaging British society as he did, there seems little doubt that Roberts was a better guide than Marx.

The "Politics of Class" Denied Again

The widespread "dissatisfaction" with "the existing social order" that R. H. Tawney had discerned in Britain on the eve of the First World War was nothing compared with the greater anxieties that resulted from the wrenching disruptions of the conflict itself and the troubled and uncertain aftermath of the Allied victory.[84] To be sure, the king's speech to the first postwar parliament held out the hopeful prospect of "a better social order": a world safe for democracy and a land fit for heroes. The extension of the franchise to all adult males and to women above the age of thirty under the Fourth Reform Act of 1918 brought full-scale democracy into being in Britain for the first time. But whether this was a safe or stable democratic world was less certain. Far from portending a "better social order," there were many who shared the fears of the Hon. William Ormsby Gore that the aftermath of war would bring the "overthrow" of the "existing social and economic order" by the "direct action" of militant revolutionaries who were part of a worldwide conspiracy extending from Chicago to Clydeside, from Petrograd to the West Riding.[85] There were good grounds for such concerns.

To begin with, it seemed that a world that was safe for democracy was not a world that was still safe for hierarchy. As Winston Churchill recalled, with a nostalgia that many of his generation came to share, the pre-1914 era had seemed in retrospect so stable and so secure, but now it had vanished forever. The great royal dynasties that had been at the apex of an interconnected European hierarchy had been overthrown in Russia and deposed in Germany and Austria-Hungary. Across the continent, crowns and thrones had perished, aristocracies had been vanquished, great estates and splendid possessions had been confiscated, and venerable titles abolished.[86] Compared with the revolutions of 1917–19, those of 1789 and 1848 had scarcely signified. Ordered, stable, traditional societies had been uprooted and torn apart as revolution was followed by civil war and anarchy and then by the tyranny of fascism or communism. The creators of these brave new worlds took pride in the fact that they were a complete break with the regimes they replaced and owed nothing to precedent, tradition, or religion. But this wide-scale collapse of settled values and historic institutions caused interwar traditionalists great anxiety and unease.[87]

In this disruptive continental context, the demise of hierarchy in Britain seemed scarcely less pronounced. The war itself, by discrediting much of the military caste, "discredited also the pre-war social hierarchy to which it was attached." The House of Lords had lost its powers of veto under the Parliament Act of 1911, and the rise of Labour as the second party in the state meant it became increasingly marginalized, which in turn meant politics and government no longer functioned hierarchically: it was now impossible in practice for peers to be prime ministers. At the same time, the massive sales of land, houses, and works of art in the aftermath of the First World War portended the end of the traditional, ordered, stable rural world in Great Britain.[88] But this was nothing compared with the ending of hierarchy in southern Ireland. The combined effect of the Land Purchase Acts and the abolition of the Senate meant that "landlordism" virtually disappeared, and in de Valera's new Irish nation it was impossible to conceive of the social order in a hierarchical way. This was symbolized by the disappearance of the viceregal court in Dublin and the ending of appointments to the Order of St. Patrick. The creation of this egalitarian Irish nation was the most serious disruption to the social order in the greater British world since the American revolution, and these antihierarchical changes closely paralleled those taking place in other European countries during the 1920s and 1930s.[89]

Along with the undermining of hierarchy in the British Isles went a corresponding undermining of the obsequious states of mind on which hierarchy had depended and served to inculcate. Indeed, this change in attitudes was the most pronounced consequence of the First World War, as ordinary people no longer saw their society hierarchically or their place within it deferentially. As early as 1920, A. L. Gleason noted that workingmen were "beginning to use a manner of jaunty equality" in their dealings with their social superiors that had not been present before the war. Robert Roberts agreed that there was a "blurring of the social layers," as those who "only a few years before had 'known their place' and kept to it" now "seemed no longer willing to return to the ranks of servility." As a result, there was "a weakening of class distinctions," and "old deference died." "No longer did the lower orders believe en masse that 'class' came as natural 'as knots in wood.' "[90] Once again, the variety of social vocabularies on display is worth noting. But they all sent out the same message: in housing, transport, morals, leisure, and dress, society was become more equal and more homogeneous. No wonder J. B. Priestley later wrote that interwar Britain was a society "without privilege" and "as near to a classless society as we have yet got," by which it is clear he meant a society without hierarchy.[91]

This belief that the traditional model no longer applied reinforced the alternative view that interwar Britain should best be understood as the three-layered society many thought it had been before 1914, though there was the usual disagreement as to what, exactly, the three layers were and about the language in which they ought to be described. In *England After War*, a sequel to his earlier survey, C. F. G. Masterman opted for "aristocracy," "middle class," and "workmen" or, alternatively, for "feudalism," "bourgeoisie," and "plebeians." A decade later, in *Brave New World*, Aldous Huxley thought society was evolving into a meritocratic, materialistic, Ford-worshiping order, which he fancifully classified into clever, professional "alphas," obedient executive "betas," and hard-working "gammas."[92] But when G. D. H. and Margaret Cole surveyed the condition of Britain in 1936, they divided the social order, less imaginatively and more conventionally, into "the rich, the comfortable and the poor," which meant that Disraeli's dichotomous description needed modifying, as they felt that "in some connections, it is more realistic nowadays to speak of 'three nations' than of two."[93]

As usual, this model was most attractive to those in the middle. According to A. J. P. Taylor, the middle classes "set the standards of the community" and "were its conscience and did its routine work." They were still expanding, as evidenced by the mushrooming of suburbia, especially on the outskirts of prosperous towns in the Midlands and the southeast. It was this growth in "the middle groups lying between the rich and the poor," who had "increased considerably both in relative numbers and in social importance," that persuaded the Coles that Disraeli's account of the "two nations" needed serious modification.[94] So did Karl Marx's. Writing in 1941, George Orwell noted that "one of the most important developments in England during the past twenty years has been the upward and downward extension of the middle class": those connected with "modern industry" who were "managers, salesmen, engineers, chemists and technicians of all kinds" and the "professional class of doctors, lawyers, teachers, artists, etc." As a result, Orwell concluded, "the tendency of advanced capitalism has ... been to enlarge the middle class and not to wipe it out as it once seemed likely to do."[95]

From this perspective, interwar Britain was a quintessentially middle-class society, and one sign of this was that politics was dominated by them as never before. The electorate might be unprecedentedly plebeian, but Parliament and government were unprecedentedly bourgeois. In order to inject some dynamism into his flagging wartime coalition, Lloyd George brought in business-men in large numbers (Devonport, Rhondda, Beaverbrook, and Geddes among them). Stanley Baldwin memorably described the House of Commons returned in 1919 as full of "hard faced men who looked as though they had done well out of the war," and during the 1920s and 1930s businessmen and professionals formed the two largest categories of MPs.[96] All the interwar Conservative prime ministers were drawn from this group. Bonar Law was a Glasgow-born steel manufacturer who had emigrated to Canada but later returned to Britain. Baldwin was a Midlands ironmaster who also acquired a clutch of company directorships. And Neville Chamber-lain was a scion of one of Birmingham's great industrial dynasties, had spent the first half of his life in business in the city, and was proud of it. "I come," he once observed, "from the middle classes, and I am proud of the ability, the shrewdness, the industry and provi-dence, the thrift by which they are distinguished."[97]

But there were others who, while sharing this triadic perception of British society, took a very different view of middle-class prospects: far from being unprecedentedly dominant, the middle classes were un-precedentedly on the defensive. They were regularly referred to as the "new poor," and in *England after War*, C. F. G. Masterman devoted a chapter to "the Plight of the Middle Class." Among them were many ex-officers who could find no work on returning from the trenches or had had to take menial employment and become submerged in the working class, a predicament caught in Warwick Deeping's best-selling novel *Sorrel and Son* (1925).[98] More generally, in the inflationary after-math of the war the middle classes felt threatened on all sides: by high-taxing governments, by militant trade unionists, and by Bolsheviks abroad and communist agitators at home. Hence the formation in 1919 of the "Middle Class Union," which appealed to "all unorganised citizens who come between the federated manual worker on the one hand, and the smaller but almost equally powerful class who stand for organised capital." Finally, there was the *Daily Mail*, which throughout the 1920s catered to (and helped reinforce) this sense of middle-class identity and concern, while at the same time flattering them that they were the "people of this country" and which was joined and surpassed in this endeavor during the 1930s by the *Express*, the *Telegraph*, and the *Mirror*.[99]

Alternatively, the middle classes were described not as threatened and weak but as incompetent, vulgar, and unpleasant. The patrician Willie Bridgeman scorned the businessmen Lloyd George appointed to his government as "narrow in their outlook, bad at working together, and generally ignorant of matters outside their own particular sphere." Tory grandees like the Cecils dismissed the "middle class monsters" in the cabinets of Stanley Baldwin, appeasement was denounced as the sort of spineless foreign policy that had to be expected once the middle classes had taken over, and Neville Chamberlain was disparaged on account of his Brummagem origins.[100] But there was also negative stereotyping from within the middle class itself. In his novel *Riceyman Steps* (1923), Arnold Bennett explored lower-middle-class meanness and its consequences: matters he knew well, because this was his own class. George Orwell came from a higher social stratum, but he also concluded that the middle classes were unimaginative and callous, themes he explored in *Keep the Aspidistra Flying*, *A Clergyman's Daughter*, and *Coming Up For Air*.[101]

But there were others who claimed that no single middle class existed and that it was as wrong to see interwar Britain as a triadic society as to see it as hierarchical. This was the conclusion of A. M. Carr-Saunders and D. Caradog Jones in their *Survey of the Social Structure of England and Wales*, first published in 1927. "Do social classes exist?" they asked. "We hear less than formerly of the 'upper,' 'middle' and 'lower' social classes," and their view was that this was right. "There is," they argued, "no longer any recognisable 'upper' class." As for the "middle class," "it never was anything more than a heterogeneous assemblage of very diverse and non-cohesive elements." And what they called "the wage-earning element" was on many issues "divided against itself." This meant it was "a mistake to speak of class divisions and class distinctions today." The belief in three social classes was "the result of studying social theory of doubtful value and of neglecting social facts," for such social classes were "a sheer figment of the imagination." A decade on, they reiterated this conclusion: "Is it not a misreading of the social structure of this country to dwell on class divisions when, in respect of dress, speech, and use of leisure, all members of the community are obviously coming to resemble one another?"[102]

This question clearly expected an answer in the affirmative. But not all interwar Britons gave it. For others believed that the reason for the decline of hierarchy and the obsolescence of the three-stage model was that society was unprecedentedly riven, the inevitable result of those pre-1914 trends toward economic and social polarization between capital and labor that the war and postwar years intensified.[103] On the one side, there was a continued decline in the number of small workshops and an unprecedented growth in large-scale factories, often associated with new industries, such as the motorcar production lines at Longbridge and Cowley. The 1920s also witnessed a succession of mergers and consolidations that meant the formation of giant new businesses, such as the "big four" railway companies were created in the aftermath of the First World War and ICI in 1926. This simultaneous expansion in the scale of production and business organization inevitably undermined the localized, paternal world where owners, managers, and workers had been part of the same close-knit factory communities.[104] No wonder Stanley Baldwin—whose family ironworks was absorbed into a larger conglomerate at just this time—lamented its passing.

On the other side, and partly in response to these developments, there was a further upsurge in trade-union membership and militancy. In 1914 there were 4.1 million members; by 1920 there were 8.3 million, representing almost half the total workforce. Part cause, part effect, was a massive increase in industrial disputes. Between 1911 and 1913 twenty million working days a year had been lost in strikes, but between the beginning of 1919 and the end of 1921 the figure was forty million.[105] Here was society riven between consolidated capitalism and organized labor as never before, a division that was provocatively proclaimed on "Red Clydeside" in 1916 and 1919 and in the general strike of 1926, when trade unionists confronted Oxbridge undergraduates, aristocratic volunteers, and society ladies staffing essential services. The result, according to A. J. P. Taylor, was "class war, in polite form." But for many, it was too serious to be polite. As Walter Barber told a mass meeting in Bradford, Britain was polarized between "the workers" and "the government and the ruling class." This was the standard formulation: "the working class" against "the capitalists." "It was more than a battle for the miners," Bill Ballantyne recalled. "This was a class war issue."[106]

Under these circumstances, it is hardly surprising that the Labour Party, the political representative of workingmen and financed by the trade-union movement, increased its share of the vote in 1918 from less than 8 percent to nearly 24 percent and thereafter superseded the Liberals as the second party in the state. This both expressed and enhanced a sense of working-class solidarity much more powerful than before the First World War, which meant that during the 1920s Ramsay MacDonald and his colleagues became "the focus of the mute hopes of a whole class" in a way that had never previously been true of politicians or classes.[107] And the party they led projected a vision of society divided between what Philip Snowden called "two distinct and antagonistic classes." Ramsay MacDonald agreed. "The true separation in society," he argued, "is the moral and economic division between the producer and the non producer," and this "moral and economic" vision lay behind clause four of the constitution the party adopted in 1918. For in declaring that its aim was to "secure for the producers by hand or by brain the full fruits of their industry" by bringing about "the common ownership of the means of production," Labour was throwing down the gauntlet from the workers to the capitalists.[108]

Indeed, the party's most militant members went further in their analysis of interwar British society as deeply divided. They did not accept their leaders' view that social change should be gradual because socialism was inevitable. During the early 1920s "Red Clydeside" MPs such as James Maxton and John Wheatley believed it was their duty to articulate, as loudly as possible, the grievances and aspirations of the class they were there to represent against selfish managers and bloated capitalists. For them, and for members of the Independent Labour Party (ILP) later in the decade, debates in the Commons were merely skirmishes in the class war, a war that had to be fought outside the Commons chamber as well as within. They were convinced that Marx's analysis of industrial society was right, that the struggle between labor and capital was reaching a more bitter phase, and that the proletarian revolution was soon coming.[109] After the "betrayal" of 1931, when it seemed as though the workers had been defeated by the capitalists once again, a new generation on the Far Left, which included Harold Laski, Stafford Cripps, and Aneurin Bevan, insisted that society was "a theatre of conflict between economic classes."[110]

Although Bevan was convinced capitalism was doomed and impatient for the proletarian revolution, he continued to believe that in Britain the class war between labor and capital could best be fought (and won) through Parliament. But there were others whose analyses of social structure and social processes were, under the combined influence of Marx and Moscow, more apocalyptically extreme. The

British Communist Party was founded in 1920 and enjoyed a certain amount of militant support, especially in Scotland and the south Wales coalfields. They rejected the gradualist approach of the Labor leadership and regarded the more left-wing Clydesiders and the ILP as exhibitionists and agitators with no clear revolutionary strategy. Following Lenin as well as Marx, the Communists believed that class interests were clear, unified, and incompatible and that the working class must seize power for itself as the necessary precondition for abolishing class divisions between labor and capital. To this end, they established the Plebs League "to develop and increase the class-consciousness of the workers" and Proletarian Schools, where children were taught ten "proletarian maxims," including the injunction "thou shalt wage class war."[111]

Whatever their internal disagreements, the trade unions, the Labour leadership, the "Red Clydesiders" and the Communists were at one in their perception of interwar Britain as deeply riven. This division between labor and capital was reinforced by education, for, as A. J. P. Taylor recalled, "the children of the masses went to free day schools until the age of fourteen; the children of the privileged went to expensive boarding schools until eighteen. The dividing line between them was as hard as Hindu castes. No child ever crossed it." In the postwar years, this state of affairs was constantly criticized by the Labour Party, which deplored "the organisation of education on the lines of class" that divided society into "the mass of men and women" and "a privileged minority."[112] But nothing was accomplished, and the divisiveness of the education system was taken by many to be both a cause and a symbol of the divisions in society. Despite their claim that Disraeli's "two nations" model was obsolete, G. D. H. and Margaret Cole sometimes had second thoughts and admitted that "the rich and the poor confront each other pretty much as they did before the war," a picture corroborated by John Hilton's book published in 1938, entitled *Rich Man, Poor Man*.[113]

This was not the opinion only of political activists and left-wing intellectuals; it was also how many people understood their society and their place within it, as Richard Hoggart recalled in *The Uses of Literacy*, his account of interwar life in Leeds written in 1957. The working classes, like their forebears in the age of Gladstone, had a strong sense that "the world is divided into 'Them' and 'Us,'" which he claimed was the urban version of the rural divide between landlord and peasant. From this perspective, "Them" were "a shadowy but numerous and powerful group, affecting their lives at almost every point": they were "'the people at the top,' 'the higher ups,' the people who give you your dole, call you up, tell you to go to war, fine you, make you split the family in the 'thirties to avoid a reduction in the Means test allowance, 'get yer in the end,' 'aren't really to be trusted,' etc." "On the whole," Hoggart concluded, "and particularly this century, the sense of 'Them' among working-class people is not of a violent or harsh thing"; the main attitude was of distrust rather than fear. But he also noted that "the 'Them/Us' attitudes seem to me strongest in . . . those with memories of unemployment in the 'thirties, and of all of the 'Thems' of those days." To whom he might have added those with memories of the general strike and all the "thems" of 1926.[114]

As in previous periods, this view that British society was polarized was shared by those who placed themselves on the other side of the great divide, many of whom wished to consolidate property and privilege against what they saw as the revolutionary threat mounted by the organized working class. In the aftermath of the First World War and again following the formation of the National Government in 1931, many Conservatives and Liberals thought the only hope was to put together an antilabor coalition and find common political ground on which the classes could fight to defend themselves against the masses.[115] One figure who took up this cry was Winston Churchill. Before 1914 he had been on the side of "the people" in the great political, social, and rhetorical divide of the New Liberal years. But by the interwar years he had changed parties and denounced Labour as a class party exclusively fighting the battle of workers' interests. For all their disagreement over economic policy, this was a view Churchill shared with John Maynard Keynes, who refused to join the Labour Party because it was "a class party, and the class is not my class." If and when it came, "the class war" would find Keynes "on the side of the educated bourgeoisie."[116]

This was the alternative model of interwar Britain as a riven society: instead of virtuous workers facing exploitative capitalists, the respectable and responsible were being threatened by those who were not. From this perspective, the Conservative Party was especially successful in presenting itself as the party of order and patriotism, while Labour was denounced for "acting purely selfishly, and for their own class only." In the same way, the trade unions were dismissed as militant and aggressive, with Bolshevik and Communist ambitions, constantly disputing with their employees, as in 1926, and putting their sectional demands before the good of the nation as a whole. By these means, much interwar Tory propaganda was devoted to stigmatizing and demonizing the working class, or at least the trade-union and industrialized section of it. Here was a new edition of the dichotomous version of society, with new social identities being constructed and new languages in which to articulate them: on the one side was the virtuous, patriotic "public"; on the other was an alien, unpatriotic, homogeneous "proletariat," unionized, factory based, or unemployed and "fertile soil for agitators and propagandists." This was the Tory vision of interwar society, and as its success at the polls showed, it worked very well to mobilize this "not-working class, who behave differently from the working class."[117]

This was the "classes versus the masses" model of British society and politics that Salisbury had projected and party politicized nearly half a century before but now was given a new potency and relevance by democracy, the collapse of the Liberals, the rise of Labour, and unemployment. The hostile characterization of the industrial working class by a Conservative Party claiming to stand for "the public" was as much an "ideologically determined class stereotype" as the hostile characterization of capitalists by the workers. But as C. F. G. Masterman explained, it resonated with the "fear" and "contempt" for organized labor that was widespread among those of superior position.[118] Like many people from his social background, George Orwell had been brought up to believe that the working classes were "stupid, coarse, crude, violent"—and that they smelt. During the interwar years, it was widely believed that they drank and gambled, which pauperized families, reduced working hours, and corrupted a whole class; that they were incompetent in the management of their own interests; and that they were easily demoralized by unemployment.[119] As in the 1880s, this working class constituted a separate, alien world that was generally believed to be inhospitable and physically dangerous: the two nations still lived—and lived apart.

Yet for all the resonance of the politically polarized vision of society, this remained a grossly exaggerated picture. Most people recognized that British society was still very "finely graded" into "discrete social layers" that comprised "an impossibly complex series of steps."[120] Perceptive contemporaries noticed this and drew the right political conclusions. "Don't delude yourselves," J. R. Clynes of the National Union of General Workers told the Trade Unions Congress (TUC) in 1919, "with the conviction that your class is united." These were wise words, and they retained their force even in 1926, when the majority of workers stayed at work and the majority of strikebreakers were not from the other side of the great social divide but were other workers or came from among the ranks of the unemployed.[121] And the workers were not only not united; they were not revolutionary. "Red Clydeside" was largely a myth, and the General Strike was about wages, not about the overthrow of the capitalist order or the British constitution. Part of the working class might be unionized, but there was a large section that was not: by 1933 trade-union membership was scarcely above what it had been in 1914 and less than half the total workforce. The homogeneous proletariat with common economic interests and revolutionary political ambitions was a figment of the deluded hopes and excessive fears of the Far Left and the Far Right.[122]

Nor was there any homogeneous capitalist class. There were wartime profiteers and those living on fixed-interest government stock; those who ran declining industries in the north and those who ran the new industries in the south; those concerned with overseas markets and those preoccupied with domestic markets. And as Winston Churchill discovered as chancellor of the exchequer, there were the bankers and the City on one side and businessmen and manufacturers on the other. When he observed that he would "rather see finance less proud, and industry more content," he was drawing attention to one essential division in what was too readily assumed to be a monolithic "capital."[123] It was no easier for the second Labour government to deal with what was too easily supposed to be a monolithic working class, because it "was a collection of groups whose interests often seemed to be in conflict": farm workers versus industrial workers; miners versus other workers; unemployed versus employed. In any case, throughout the interwar period, Labour failed to gain even 50 percent of the working-class vote: many refused to regard themselves as working class or to recognize Labour as their political vehicle, and one-third of them voted Conservative, including many trade unionists.[124]

This means that throughout the interwar years, there was no direct elision of an economically and socially polarized conflict between workers and management into a politically polarized conflict between Labour and Conservatives. On the contrary, there was an unprecedentedly large and heterogeneous electorate, for whom "class did not guarantee opinion."[125] Even as some politicians tried to create such collective, adversarial identities, others were simultaneously and more successfully denying these polarized politics of class. Indeed, this process of denial was more ardently and resourcefully carried on by political leaders in interwar Britain than it had been by their forebears in the mid-Victorian era. With full adult suffrage, those who wished to damp down the "politics of class" thought they had to work very hard at it. And they did. Among the Conservatives—and among Labour, too—there were men who insisted that society was not about class identity, class consciousness, and class conflict and who offered an alternative vision based on reconciliation, community, and hierarchy. And they were helped, as in the late Victorian and Edwardian periods, by the reinforcing agencies of honor and empire, sovereign and ceremony. The result, as commentators noticed, was that hierarchy survived and flourished as the most plausible way of seeing interwar Britain: to the delight of some and the despair of others.

Like its prewar predecessor, the interwar Tory Party sent out ambiguous signals when proclaiming its own social identity, or describing the identities of the people whose votes it wished to get, or giving an account of the social structure of the nation as a whole. In one guise, it presented itself as the party of the middle classes, of property, of the public: collective identities opposed to the industrialized workers. But as before and after, many Tories during the twenties and thirties thought of British society in terms of individuals rather than conflicting social groups. "Toryism," Duff Cooper noted, "hates the division of Englishmen into classes." "The Socialist," agreed the Hon. Edward Wood, anticipating Margaret Thatcher, "advocates the class-conscious solidarity of a section, and forgets that class distinction is an artificial creation, which flies before any of the elemental emotions." John Buchan agreed. He disliked the fashion for thinking (like old Lord Salisbury!) in such abstractions as "masses" and "classes" instead of individuals. This, he believed, was the result of "shallow Marxian materialism," which mistakenly envisaged the workers in impersonal collective terms.[126]

The most influential and articulate purveyor of this brand of interwar Conservatism was Stanley Baldwin, who devoted his main efforts as party leader and prime minister to delivering a succession of much-praised and widely publicized speeches in which he talked to the British about how they ought to see themselves and the society to which they belonged.[127] He began with the Tory platitude that people were varied and independent individuals and not collective or impersonal abstractions. This meant he rejected the three-layer model of society consisting of "the gentry . . . , the middle classes . . . , the lower classes," for these were "old invidious expressions." And he rejected the two-stage model, which divided the nation between "labour and capital" or "the employers and the employed." These descriptions were unacceptable because they put individual people into collective classes and presumed (and incited) conflict between them. For Baldwin, the Unionist party was "unionist in the sense that we stand for the union of those two nations of which Disraeli spoke two generations ago; union among our own people to make one nation of our own people at home."[128]

Baldwin's aim was thus to dampen down the dangerous fires of class consciousness and class hatred that he feared had burned up before the First World War and again at the time of the General Strike. "There is," he remarked, early on in his years of power, "only one thing which I feel it is worth giving one's whole strength to, and that is the binding together of all classes of people in an effort to make life in this country better in every sense of the word."[129] He was convinced that "class hatred" was not "indigenous to English soil," and he was hostile to Bolshevism and those who are "preaching class war and hatred where we preach peace and a united people." And peace and unity were possible because there was "a brotherly and neighbourly feeling which we see to a remarkable extent through all classes." Baldwin's message was that individual cooperation, not collective conflict, was the British way, and by the end of his public life he felt sure he had got this message across. "I think," he concluded in 1937, "that in recent years, in spite of all the troubles we have had, there has been a much better understanding among all classes in the country of each other's lives and methods of thought."[130]

This was the negative side of Baldwin's rhetoric about the social order: persuading people to stop thinking of themselves in terms of collective categories and conflicting classes. Class, the politics of class, and politics *as* class were languages and identities and activities he sought to drive off the agenda of public discussion. Indeed, Baldwin only used the language of class to describe the social identities he wanted people to *stop* thinking about. But he was also clear about what he wanted to put in their place. Instead of the conflicting collectivities of the three- or two-stage model of society, Baldwin urged and commended the consensual, individualist, inegalitarian, hierarchical model, though he never actually used this latter word, preferring instead to sketch out his alternative visions of society more evocatively and allusively. One such vision was the countryside: a place of order, simplicity, and nobility, where everyone knew his or her place and which functioned and cohered on the basis of reciprocal rights and obligations. The other was the factory culture of his youth, where again relations were individual rather than collective, built around friendliness and reconciliation.[131]

Thus described and evoked by Baldwin, the countryside and the factory were stable, organic, harmonious Burkeian communities in which identities were individual and personal, reinforced by a shared sense of ancestral roots and historic associations. Ideally, as in the past, this added up to a society that was well balanced between the country and the town and well ordered in its "cohesive inequality." But Baldwin quietly and constantly insisted that this was not merely an anachronistic or irrelevant or nostalgic vision of British society. On the contrary, he believed that the best antidote to the unnatural, shallow, and transient divisions in the modern world was to turn again to these more wholesome, consensual, and hierarchical identities. As a politician and a public teacher, Baldwin's main concern was to change the way the British looked and thought and felt about their society and themselves, by reminding them of the continued appropriateness and relevance of "traditional hierarchical ideas." This was his social vision, and he reasserted it as the social vision of many millions of other Britons, too.[132]

For Baldwin and his Conservative followers, interwar politics was primarily about the re-creation of traditional social identities in a nontraditional world, and in this endeavor he was tacitly assisted by the Labour Party leadership. Those on the Left believed it existed to promote class war in the interests of the workers, but those on the Right rejected the idea that Labour represented only one class and discounted the Marxist theory of class war and class struggle. As Arthur Henderson put it in 1919, "Labour is in politics, not in the interests of a class, but to further the interests of the community as a whole." During the 1922 election, Philip Snowden rebutted the widespread accusation that "the Labour Party exists for the benefit of one class." It was "the very opposite of a class party," he insisted, for its objective was "justice for all men and women of every class who live by honest and useful work."[133] A generation later, Evan Durbin argued that "the economic life of an advanced society is peculiarly the sphere of the most complex and successful kinds of co-operation." Far from polarizing society between warring classes, the development of the economy had made the social structure more complex and more integrated. Hence Labour's alternative vision of British society, built around cooperation and social harmony.[134]

As the dominant figure in the party for much of this period, Ramsay MacDonald shared these gradualist, organic, evolutionary views; indeed, he was at one with Baldwin in not envisaging British politics or society in terms of collective identities and class conflict.[135] He, too, possessed what David Marquand describes as an "almost Burkeian sense" of the importance of tradition and convention in binding the nation together. After the disruptions of the First World War, he had no wish "to defy or even to subvert the established order," or "to sweep away the elaborate gradations of status and position so characteristic of the British social system, or to abolish the traditional protocol of British public life." Hence his veneration for monarchy, for King George V, for "the spirit of ceremony," and for the substance, too. Hence his "obvious delight" in living at Chequers and visiting great houses, his friendship with Lady Londonderry, and his sensitivity to "the traditions of the countryside." These were the outward and visible signs of the hierarchical society MacDonald sought to preserve. In his own way, he "fought against a class view of politics" as much as Baldwin, and this was his justification for leading a "National Government" against the "petty and passionate class movement" of those in the Labour Party who deserted him.[136]

During the interwar years, both Baldwin and MacDonald were actively engaged in recasting and reviving hierarchical Britain, and they could turn to powerful allies in this endeavor. One was the honors system. As a consequence of the First World War, its hierarchical reach was extended throughout the nation with the creation of the Order of the British Empire, which was the order of chivalry of British democracy, as everyone was eligible for it. This was an unprecedented innovation. But everyone was eligible only according to their social standing. It extended from knights and dames grand cross, via knights and dames commander, to commanders, officers, and members. The rich, the powerful, and the famous got the knighthoods; those beneath became commanders; and those at the bottom became officers and members.[137] Here were hierarchical honors for a hierarchically conceived society. And it worked, connecting the craving for recognition with the acceptance and reinforcement of social hierarchy, a connection that has remained indissoluble in Britain ever since. Witness, for example, the enthusiasm with which trade unionists and Labour politicians came to embrace it.[138]

Behind this lay the British monarchy itself: the fountain of honor and the apex of traditional society, and the one European great-power royalty that successfully survived the cataclysms of 1914–18. This, in turn, was crucial to the survival of hierarchy as a way of seeing interwar Britain. It was partly a matter of contrast. The upstart Communist and Fascist dictatorships put on new, high-tech spectaculars at Nuremberg and in Red Square that were appropriately modernistic displays for societies that had rejected any historic continuity with the past. But the ceremonial associated with the British throne expressed and articulated a view of the world in which continuity and stability, rank and order were maintained against the disruptive and leveling social regimes that seemed in power everywhere else. It was also a matter of creativity, as new-old royal ceremonials were invented to augment the "traditional" dramatic representations of the social hierarchy. For in addition to the funeral of George V and the coronation of George VI, there were the invented spectaculars of Queen Alexandra's funeral and King George V's Silver Jubilee, and there were the public royal weddings, beginning with the duke of York's in 1923. Royalty and hierarchy might have collapsed elsewhere in Europe, but in interwar Britain, they both adapted and thrived.[139]

At the same time, nonroyal public life remained built around hierarchy. Labour mayors embraced the ornamental trappings of civic office as enthusiastically as did local aristocrats or such petty-bourgeois worthies as Alderman Roberts in Grantham.[140] There were also two ceremonial innovations that projected and consolidated the traditional view of an ordered, stable society. The first was the Remembrance Day observances held each November 11, in London at the Cenotaph and at war memorials throughout Britain and the empire. In Whitehall, wreaths were laid by representatives of the imperial hierarchy, from the king-emperor down; elsewhere, by representatives of the local community, led by the mayor. The second was the practice of celebrating the Festival of Nine Lessons and Carols on Christmas Eve, following its adoption by the chapel of King's College, Cambridge, in 1919. Once again, it was a display of community-as-hierarchy, with the lessons being read in ascending order of status and seniority, from a junior choirboy to the senior ecclesiastical or civic dignitary. On November 11 and December 24 every year, this homely, Baldwinite version of social hierarchy was put on display.[141]

As this suggests, the empire still mattered (it was, indeed, at its greatest territorial extent) as an agent and expression of stable order. To be sure, there were "troubles" in Ireland, Egypt, and India, and the dominions were no longer subordinated to the mother country and prided themselves on being more open societies. But hierarchy was reinforced in the empire, and the empire still reinforced hierarchy. In northern Ireland, a new proconsular court, centering on the governor, was created at Stormont as a deliberate counterpoise to the nonhierarchical society south of the border. In Canada, New Zealand, and Australia, the elaborate rituals of the viceregal regimes were still based on rank and station, and the governors-general remained overwhelmingly aristocratic or royal in background.[142] And in India, King George V pledged his "inviolate and inviolable" support for the native princes, while the inauguration of Lutyens's capital at New Delhi set the hierarchy of the Raj in stone, the residential layout corresponding to the careful gradations of the imperial administration. As Lucy Smalley recalled in Paul Scott's *Staying On*, "a hierarchy was a hierarchy, and a society without a clear stratification of duties and responsibilities was no society at all, which the Indians knew as well as anyone, let alone the British." Indeed, the reason the High Tory diehards (many of them aristocrats) were so opposed to constitutional reform in India during the 1930s was that they feared the traditional hierarchy of the Raj and the maharajas would collapse as a result.[143]

Not surprisingly, the social order as a surviving hierarchical order was much discussed (and defended) in this period. High Tories such as Lord Hugh Cecil reiterated the view that it was providentially ordained, that inequality was the inevitable human condition, and that this was the proper basis on which to construct societies.[144] In 1923 Hilaire Belloc wrote approvingly of "the old, hieratic society of Britain" and insisted that "the texture of society demands stratification," the key to which was "personal not official relations of superior and inferior." Britain, he believed, was "a kind of society naturally arranged by the instinct of all its parts," the implication of which was that the new nations created in 1919 were unnatural. It was, he later insisted, the only surviving aristocratic state, its class system and its hierarchy intact. For Belloc, class did not mean warring collectivities but a diverse, organic, unequal, layered society. And one of the essential supports of this hierarchical society was "the complicated system of titles." "The whole of this remarkable complex of honorific labels," he went on, "is worthy of note by any who would seek to understand modern England, because it testifies to an appetite for diversity in unity, or (as some would call it), for inequality, which marks the English people."[145]

On the other side was R. H. Tawney, who (unlike Belloc) disliked hierarchy very much but agreed that it did exist. Despite the decline of "aristocratic society," he believed the "cult of inequality" remained as strong as ever.[146] The British saw their society as "a hierarchical social order" "so venerable and all-pervading, so hallowed by tradition and permeated with pious emotion" that "it seems inconceivable to its adherents that any other system should exist," and "until attention is called to it by the irreverent curiosity of strangers, they are not even conscious of the facts of its existence." But outsiders "come to the conclusion that Englishmen are born with *la mentalité hiérarchique*," an outlook that "determines all the time their outlook on society," in part because they took for granted the "curious rituals" by which "the gradations of the social hierarchy are preserved and emphasised." "The predominant characteristic of the English social system," Tawney concluded, "is its hierarchical quality," by which he did not mean occupational hierarchies, based on function and office and a capacity to do a job, but social hierarchies, where differences were based on wealth, birth, and position and were about circumstance rather than capacity.[147]

Hierarchy, it bears repeating, probably remained the most appealing way in which British interwar society was seen, as the visions and representations of hierarchy were reconstructed to reestablish it in an era when the traditional ordering of society seemed under unprecedented attack. But as Baldwin's use of the rhetoric of social perceptions made plain, social structure remained as much in the eye of the beholder as in the nature of society itself. And the perceptions of interwar British society may best be understood as a continuation of the three traditional models, suitably refashioned for the 1920s and 1930s. Some believed hierarchy was collapsing; others that it needed relegitimating; others that Baldwin was firm about hierarchy in Britain but weak about it in India. Then again, there were those who insisted the three-layered view of society was the most accurate, although there was serious disagreement as to whether the middle class was suffering or expanding. But this emphasis on the importance of those in the middle was not easily reconciled with the view that interwar Britain was polarized as never before between capital and labor. It was confusing—but in a familiar and functioning way.

These ambiguities and contradictions in social perceptions were vividly displayed in a series of programs transmitted on the BBC late in 1938. Chaired by the sociologist T. H. Marshall, they began with the question "What do we mean by class?" and surveyed class in primitive societies, medieval England, India, New Zealand, Norway, and the

United States.[148] They looked at class and education, occupation, wealth, and manners.[149] And the participants concluded that class was very important in Britain, but they could not agree what it was or what the class profile of British society looked like, except that it was "extremely complicated." Unsurprisingly, they came up with the usual three models. Some argued that Britain was deeply riven between those who worked and those who did not. Some claimed that it was divided into three on the basis of education, among those who left school at fourteen or eighteen or university at twenty-two. And others thought it was a layered fabric with no clear-cut distinctions, where "almost everything that is lovely and old and traditional is part of a social system where privilege is buttressed by pageantry."[150]

Inevitably, these disagreements about the social structure in Britain led to controversy about the nature of social relations, the climax of which was a debate on "the class struggle" between the Marxist Arthur Horner and the economic historian M. M. Postan. Horner asserted that collective classes were the essential mode of social identities, that class cleavage and class war were the inevitable state of capitalist society, and that the class war had been won by the workers in Russia but was still being fought in England. Postan replied that the idea of class war as "the one predominant influence in history" was much exaggerated, that classes cooperated with each other more than they battled against each other, and that there were many other forms of social identity (among them national, religious, and economic) that cut across class lines and class categories.[151] The fact that a Marxist could talk on the BBC was evidence that such views of British society were taken more seriously by the generation of post-1917 than by the generation before, although Postan clearly had the better of the argument. Be that as it may, the society that he and his cobroadcasters analyzed was once again on the brink of massive change, this time to be wrought by the Second World War. Again, however, they were changes in perceptions more than in substance.

Class Acts and Class Facts

In 1940, as if in inadvertent corroboration of these recent BBC broadcasts, George Orwell composed his patriotic-cum-revolutionary polemic *The Lion and the Unicorn*, in which he memorably described England as "the most class-ridden country under the sun."[152] Orwell was obsessed with class, but when he tried to describe the social structure of his native land, his efforts were disappointingly confused and dismally commonplace. From one perspective, wearing his Tory hat, he saw England in traditional, hierarchical terms, as a layered society of exceptional complexity, "bound together by an invisible chain" and "stretching into the future and the past." From another standpoint and as befitted the offspring of an imperial and professional family, he divided English society into upper, middle, and lower classes, with himself very much part of the "middling people." From yet a third vantage point, that of a socialist revolutionary, he saw England as fundamentally riven between "two nations": on the one side, "the moneyed classes," "the ruling classes," and "the reactionary classes" and, on the other, "the poor," "the common people," and "the mass of the people," who, he hoped, would soon rise up against their masters in an "English revolution."[153]

Beyond any doubt, Orwell was astonishingly sensitive to (and guilty about) the elaborate nuances of social status and social identity; indeed, he once described himself as "both a snob and a revolutionary." But his knowledge of everyday social conditions was much less accurate than some have supposed and, as must be plain to anyone who has persevered with this book, his analysis of social identities is wearyingly familiar, in both its categories and its contradictions.[154] Nor was there much evidence during his own lifetime to support his confident assertion that the "older class distinctions are beginning to break down." For not only does this go against his much-quoted claim to the contrary, it was hardly borne out by the history of social structures and social perceptions in Britain from the 1880s to the late 1930s that has been unfolded thus far, nor indeed by subsequent developments from the 1940s to the 1990s. As for his belief that there would be a people's revolution that might bring with it a "classless society," he was no more correct in this prediction than Thomas Paine or the Chartists or Karl Marx had been before him or than Aneurin Bevan or John Major would be after him.[155]

It is a cliché that the years between 1940 and 1979 witnessed change in Britain on a massive scale. The Second World War was the defining experience of more than one generation, whether in the blitz, or because of evacuation, or on account of military service. Thereafter the pace of change never let up. Domestically, there was the creation of the welfare state, the nationalization of industry, the success of the postwar mixed economy, the unprecedented prosperity of the affluent society, the decline of the traditional working class, the marginalization of the traditional aristocracy, the moral and behavioral revolutions of the

1960s, and the recurrent financial crises of the Wilson-Heath-Callaghan years. Internationally, Britain gradually but inexorably declined from being a first-ranking world power, the empire was dismantled with astonishing rapidity between 1947 and 1968, and the pound sterling was twice devalued.[156] That British society changed cannot be contested, but how far the popular ways of looking at it and thinking about it changed is, once more, open to question. For the three models of society that Orwell had so artlessly and contradictorily summarized remained as much in evidence as before. Indeed, thanks to the unprecedented proliferation of sociological surveys, we know about them with greater accuracy than had hitherto been possible.

It was widely believed during the Second World War that the unified and resolute response to Nazi Germany had rendered all three models of British society obsolete. "There is," observed Vivienne Hall in September 1939, "one thing, and one only, about this war—it is an instant and complete leveller of classes." A year later, the London correspondent of the *New York Herald Tribune* made the same point. "Hitler," he claimed, "is doing what centuries of English history have not accomplished—he is breaking down the class structure of England." Winston Churchill agreed. "There is," he told the boys of Harrow School in December 1940, "no change which is more marked in our country than the continual and rapid effacement of class differences."[157] That this was how many Britons came to see their society between 1939 and 1945 cannot be denied. Greater social mixing went on, and there was more sympathy between those of different social position. But for all the feeling that Britain was a united nation, this was in many ways only that: a feeling, a mood, a vision. For the old views of Britain's unequal and divided social structure constantly recurred. "The belief," Kenneth Morgan notes, "that the British class system dissolved or was basically modified during the war is a total myth."[158]

Notwithstanding the wartime camaraderie, there were many who maintained, like Orwell, that British society remained fundamentally divided between "us" and "them"; indeed, it seemed to many that the war merely drew attention to this basic division and intensified it. Despite the talk of a "people's war" and equality of sacrifice, it was widely (and rightly) believed that "the rich" suffered less under rationing than "the ordinary people." There was also noticeable hostility, depicted and promoted in such populist newspapers as the *Daily Mirror*, to those in authority, described and demonized in a Cobbett-like idiom as a latter-day "Thing" consisting of "Colonel Blimp, the old school tie, and vested interests." Indeed, the responsibility of "men in high places" for causing the war and the unmerited privileges they retained during it were a major source of grumbling. "We were anti 'They,' " Allen Lane recalled of these years. "We were against the privileged classes."[159] And this was as true of those Britons who served on the battlefields as those who endured the blitz. On the basis of his military experience, a British Eighth Army infantryman offered his own earthy formulation of the basic divide in British society: "one class gets the sugar and the other class gets the shit." Even Churchill recognized the truth of this when he went on to tell the boys of Harrow School that in future "the advantages and privileges which have hitherto been enjoyed by the few shall be far more widely shared by the many."[160]

Not surprisingly, postwar Britain was seen by many as a polarized society, and that perception of the social structure remained strong in subsequent decades. The working-class belief that there remained an essential division between "us" and "them" was memorably caught by Richard Hoggart in *The Uses of Literacy*, written during the 1950s, and many accounts of British working-class life at this time also played on this basic social dichotomy. And although "vested interests" and "Colonel Blimp" had largely had their day, a new version of "The Thing" attained great popularity in these years: "The Establishment," a concept first made famous by A. J. Taylor and Henry Fairlie and later used as the title for a book edited by Hugh Thomas.[161] The concept, like the book, summoned up the image of an interlocking old-boy network, which was later laid bare by Anthony Sampson in *The Anatomy of Britain* and was deemed to be privileged, nepotistic, out-of-date, inefficient, and corrupt. Indeed, it was widely believed that Britain was divided between incompetent, amateur management and incorrigibly hidebound workers, as in Michael Shanks's account of *The Stagnant Society* or in the Boulting brothers film "I'm All Right, Jack." In yet another idiom, Nancy Mitford offered yet another version of Britain as a divided society, in which the upper and upper middle class were designated as U speakers while everyone else was non-U.[162]

These binary, polarized social perceptions received scholarly corroboration at the hands of three Oxford academics who in 1966 published an article entitled "On the Analytical Division of Social Classes," in which, on the basis of a wide sampling survey, they expressed their conviction that the "two class formulation" of working class and middle class was "much more than an analytical simplification of those who have studied social class in Britain." On the contrary, it was, they were sure, "a simplification which has a profound hold on the perceptions of class found in British society." Of their questioned sample, 29 percent allocated themselves to the middle class, and 67 percent to the working class, leaving a mere 4 percent unaccounted for. This was, they concluded, "a testament to the popular acceptability of the two class formulation" of British society and to the "psychological validity of treating social stratification in terms of two main classes."[163] A later survey merely confirmed the widespread "acceptance of the view that British society is divided into two primary classes." This was, they insisted, "much more than a sociologist's simplification": the "extraordinary hold of this dichotomy" was "deeply rooted in the mind of the ordinary British citizen."[164]

From the 1940s to the 1970s, these binary social visions were regularly and repeatedly politicized. For all the talk of unity and consensus, the wartime Labour Party intensified the popular mood of dissatisfaction with the elite. There was opposition to the Butler Education Act because, in preserving public schools, it was perpetuating the very social division to which Labour most objected. The 1945 election was widely seen as a contest between "the people" on the one side and the "old gang" on the other. In the *Daily Herald*, a cartoon depicted Churchill not as the great war leader but as the creature of vested interests, monopolies, and privilege. As Harold Nicolson noted, "people" felt in a "vague and muddled way" that it was all the fault of "them"; "class feeling and class resentment" were "very strong."[165] They remained so thereafter. Attlee's government, by raising taxation, nationalizing industries, setting up the welfare state, and reducing the delaying powers of the House of Lords, attacked aristocrats, the rich, bankers, doctors, newspaper owners, and shareholders, and these measures were accompanied by extravagantly denunciatory language from ministers such as Bevan, Shinwell, and Dalton. The Tories saw these as "monstrous and quite unnecessary" pieces of "class legislation," the inevitable product of a "class party" preaching the "gospel of class war."[166]

But this was, of course, a game at which two parties could—and did—play. For in reply, it was easy for Labour to present, and to denounce, the Tories as being the representatives of "vested interests" and thus the makers, not the victims, of the class war. "The Conservative Party," Attlee insisted in 1945, "remains as always a class party . . . but represents today, as in the past, the forces of property and privilege."[167]

This accusation was regularly repeated, and there was something to it. Throughout this period, as in the 1880s and 1890s and again during the interwar years, the Tories *did* seek to attract the support of the propertied and the privileged. This meant assembling, as in the days of the great Lord Salisbury, a broad coalition of the "haves" in society: the traditionally wealthy, the middle classes, and the new "embourgeoisified" rich from among the workers, those whose growing affluence in the 1950s and early 1960s enabled them to buy houses and own cars and washing machines. Indeed, as more and more people became affluent, the Tory Party, as their representative, seemed destined to do better and better at the polls. "The class war is over," Harold Macmillan announced after his triumph in the 1959 general election, "and we have won it." Labour largely agreed.[168]

But this Conservative rejoicing turned out to be decidedly premature. For in the early 1960s Harold Wilson brilliantly redefined the popular vision of Britain as a divided society and did so greatly to Labour's advantage. Drawing on recent writing about an out-of-date and essentially Conservative establishment, aided by the seediness, enfeeblement, and mediocrity revealed at the top by Profumo, Macmillan, and Douglas-Home, and supported by *Private Eye* and "That Was The Week That Was," he depicted a nation dangerously riven between players and gentlemen, innovators and traditionalists, technocrats and territorial magnates. In the language of Cobbett and Lloyd George, he railed against "the grouse moor image," "aristocratic connection," "inherited wealth," "speculative finance," "lordly amateurs," and "gentlemen."[169] In the 1970s it looked as though these social divisions were deepening still further, as Tony Benn embraced a new form of radical populism directed against the establishment in all its forms, as Arthur Scargill took on the leadership of the National Union of Mineworkers, as the strike of 1974 seemed the most threatening challenge of the century to the government and the propertied, and as class antagonism reached unprecedented levels. "We took the view," noted Scargill, "that we were in a class war. We were not playing cricket on the village green like they did in 'twenty six."[170]

This was powerful rhetoric, but was it any more than that? Was British society genuinely thus split between the party of the workers and the party of capitalists, each one as much a "class" party as the other? To the extent that workers were more likely to vote Labour and the middle classes to vote Conservative, there was truth in this. Here was "the classes" versus "the masses" 1950s and 1960s style. But as in the

1880s and 1890s and again in the interwar years, this was only a partial (and in some ways misleading) truth. For the picture of two homogeneous classes locked in perpetual conflict and elided into two homogeneous political parties of which the same was true was, as before, a massive oversimplification. As Donald Chapman wrote to G. D. H. Cole in 1947, "modern British society" was just "too complex a structure" to be cut down the middle in this single, simple way.[171] And politicians seem to have been as ignorant of the social groups they were describing (or trying to call into being) as their forebears had been in 1830–32 or 1866–67. Although the Tories delighted in working-class embourgeoisement, and although Labour feared it, this turned out to be no more than another ideological stereotype: there was very little evidence that prosperous members of the working class crossed a great social (and political) divide and became middle-class Tories.[172]

In fact, and as before, parties were as much about the creation of social identities as they were a reflection of them and, as before, the identities they projected and helped to create were ambiguous. To be sure, there were those who believed that Labour represented "the workers" and the Tories "the privileged." But both parties generally sought to project an inclusive rather than exclusive image, stressing the diversity of their support rather than its homogeneity. On the Labour side, integration and gradualism remained the goal of the leadership, from Attlee and Bevin to Wilson and Callaghan: all of them rejected Marxist notions of class conflict. Developing the interwar revisionism of Evan Durbin, Anthony Crosland's *The Future of Socialism* declared that Marx had "little or nothing to offer" in terms of "the correct analysis of our society" or "in respect of practical policy."[173] Appropriately enough, the nationalization measures passed between 1945 and 1951 were more concerned with planning and investment than they were skirmishes in the class war. Labour, Attlee explained in 1967, was "more and more a national party and not mere section. . . . It is not in the least a class party today."[174]

It was the same on the Conservatives side. Ever since Disraeli, much of their rhetoric had stressed that theirs was the "national party," uniting the classes rather than setting them against each other, and this remained the case during the postwar period. After all, one-half of their votes came from the working class. "The Conservative Party," observed one delegate at the 1956 conference, "is a classless party, and will not pander to any one class as the Labour Party does." Harold Macmillan agreed. As long as he was their leader, he told the Tories, they would never be "a party of any class or sectional interest."[175] Nor was Edward Heath a class warrior: quite the reverse. At the height of the miners' strike in 1974, he told the nation: "There could not be any 'we' or 'they.' There was only 'us'—all of us." In short, both major parties sought to present their opponents as class based and sectional, while claiming that they themselves stood for something more broadly based, inclusive and patriotic. The identities they constructed and proclaimed remained ambiguous, transcending the division of society, even as in other ways they embodied it and projected it. As A. J. Davies remarks, "any simplistic assumption that each of the two major political parties is purely a class party is wrong."[176]

In any case, and as usual, the lines that were drawn across British society were vague, malleable, and contradictory. Aneurin Bevan may have believed in the Marxist division between labor and capital, but that was not the same as the distinction Harold Wilson made between gentlemen amateurs and expert players. In the same way, the oft-mentioned division between "The Establishment" and the rest was almost impossible to sustain in detail because much of the attractiveness of the idea of "The Establishment" lay in its very vagueness. Even Henry Fairlie admitted that "it has its roots in no class and no interest," which meant it was no easier to discern or define in Macmillan's day than it had been in Cobbett's.[177] As for Nancy Mitford's division of British society into U and non-U speakers, for all its whimsical popularity and appealing simplicity, it hardly made much sense in (or of) reality. In 1958 Harold Macmillan claimed that his Conservative cabinet was "probably more non-U than the Socialists were." Even academic sociologists admitted that it was in practice extremely difficult to agree on, let alone draw, one single, simple line through the whole of British society. And while Michael Shanks thought a new division between a meritocratic elite and the rest was a good idea, Michael Young warned instead of its dire consequences.[178]

Many Britons rejected this polarized vision and believed that the most plausible way of thinking about and seeing their society remained the triadic division. Between 1948 and 1951 Margaret Stacey undertook a detailed study of Banbury and concluded that there were three such classes: "upper, middle and working." At almost the same time, F. M. Martin conducted a survey of Greenwich and Hertford and reached an identical conclusion. "The great majority of our subjects," he observed, "thought in terms of a three-class system, and most of them described these classes by the same set of names—upper, middle and working."[179] And these local studies were corroborated by national investigations. When Carr-Saunders and Caradog Jones made their third and final survey of British society in the mid-1950s, they were more inclined to believe in classes than they had been before and concluded that a "threefold division probably does less violence to reality than any other." This was also the opinion of Professor A. S. C. Ross, whose writings had been cited by Nancy Mitford when she divided British society into U and non-U speakers. This was, he insisted, the wrong way to see things. "Today, in 1955," he urged "the English class system is essentially tripartite—there exist an upper, a middle and a lower class."[180]

As before, this three-layered division tended to appeal to those who were in the middle, and, again as before, they tended to regard themselves in one of two ways: either as better than those above and beneath or as threatened by those above and beneath. Here is Mrs. Brinton Lee writing in 1941 and putting forward a different view of wartime British society from those who thought it unprecedentedly united (or divided). "I believe," she observed, "the strength and civilisation of a nation is shown by the growth of its 'middle classes,' that is the number of people who are neither poor and oppressed or rich and idle": positive stereotyping that might have come straight from the 1790s or the 1830s. The young Robert Carr took the same view, describing the middle class as being "rich in a spirit of independence, of responsibility for themselves and their families."[181] "The English middle classes," Lewis and Maude wrote in 1950, "perform the same functions as their American counterparts: they provide most of their nation's brains, leadership and organising ability, and they are the main vehicle for the transmission of the essential national culture." And they quoted with approval Herbert Morrison's remark of 1948: "The middle classes, whose energies helped to make Britain great during the nineteenth century, can look forward with confidence to an important and prosperous future."[182]

But could they? Throughout this period, there were many who thought otherwise and believed that the British middle classes were being crushed between an increasingly militant working class and a dominant, intrusive, and parasitic establishment, which by this time was governmental rather than aristocratic. Lewis and Maude argued that this "plight" was the consequence of the vindictive Labour administration, which squeezed the middle classes economically and undermined their standard of living by increasing taxes and prices.

Deprived of their prewar domestic servants and with less leisure time than ever before, they were "beset with worries" on all sides.[183] Even under the Tories, in the era of "you've never had it so good," this embattled perception remained. Although the party claimed to "stand for the middle classes," many of its supporters were alienated by its refusal to reduce taxes and roll back the welfare state. During his brief spell as prime minister, the Tory central office told Sir Anthony Eden that "the middle classes feel that they have not had a square deal and are looking for somewhere else to go." And when the Tories lost the Orpington by-election in 1961, Macmillan described the loss as "a revolt of the middle class or lower middle class, who resent the vastly improved conditions of the working classes and are envious of the apparent prosperity and luxury of the rich." By then, indeed, the phrase "middle class revolt" was widely in use in Tory circles.[184]

There was something in this, especially during the Macmillan years. In theory and practice, he should have been a leader unusually sensitive to the triadic view of British society and the particular importance and anxieties of the middle classes. He was, after all, the grandson of a Scottish crofter, he had married the daughter of a duke, and he was a successful publisher. But the fact of the matter was that Macmillan did not like the middle classes from which he sprang. In 1957 he wrote to a colleague in a tone of Olympian disdain, "I am always hearing about the middle classes. What is it they really want?" The reply was crushing: "Conservative governments, who should understand their problems, have not shown them much sympathy."[185] But Macmillan viewed the middle classes neither with comprehension nor with compassion. He claimed that the Tory Party in the thirties had been "dominated by second-class brewers and company promoters" and that Neville Chamberlain was "very, very middle class, and very, very narrow in view." Indeed, for Macmillan, "middle class" was a term of reproach, as when he described Hugh Gaitskell as "too much the middle-class liberal" and Selwyn Lloyd as "a middle-class lawyer from Liverpool." Nor did he like, or understand, the suburbs. Indeed, just about the politest thing he could bring himself to say about the Tories under Thatcher was that "a great national party has become reduced to a suburban rump."[186]

In fact, of course, the middle classes did very well out of the welfare state, not least because of the universal nature of the benefits it bestowed, designed, in Attlee's words, "not for one class, but for all."[187] Despite their complaints, they got a great deal in exchange for their higher taxes. But throughout the 1960s and on into the 1970s, the complaints continued. As trade-union militancy and membership grew, the middle classes felt ever more threatened by their social inferiors, who it seemed could bring the country to a standstill. And they also felt repressed and let down by successive Tory administrations, which would not stand up to the unions and could not manage the economy but raised taxes on the middle classes higher than ever before. Between 1964 and 1974 the proportion of middle-class Conservative voters steadily fell, as they transferred their loyalties to the Liberals and Labour.[188] It was against this background that Tory radicals such as Enoch Powell and Sir Keith Joseph began to develop new policies: the reduction of taxes and government intervention, the taming of the unions and the toleration of growth in unemployment, and the proclamation of the vigorous values and free-market virtues of the middle class. Truly, it was a synthesis of the traditional rhetoric of middle-class beleaguerment and middle-class self-praise.[189]

In the light of the arguments developed in this book, it should scarcely need saying that this was indeed rhetoric: yet another example of sociological imagining and ideological stereotyping. For who, exactly, made up this British middle class, sandwiched and suffering between the workers and the government? As before, it was in practice extremely difficult to find out. Lewis and Maude admitted that it was virtually impossible to define precisely who the middle classes were, in terms of numbers or occupation or profession: they might be a small or a large band depending on the criteria employed.[190] Indeed, the very idea of dividing British society into three and giving particular attention to those in the middle was fraught with difficulties. For, as F. M. Martin discovered, this tripartite vision of the social order meant very different things, depending on the position, the perspective, and the presuppositions of the beholder. Middle-class people tended to think of their class in terms of respectability and integrity; those beneath were more impressed by their snobbery and pretensions to superiority. From some perspectives, the middle class was a wide social band, ranging from manual workers to professionals; from others, it was much more narrowly conceived.[191]

Not surprisingly, then, many people in Britain during the 1950s and 1960s could not make up their minds whether the two- or the three-stage model best described the social world they inhabited, any more than historians writing in this period could decide whether the two- or three-stage model better characterized the social world they believed the industrial revolution had made.[192] In 1959 Hugh Thomas noted that Britons were "accustomed to think of their society as being organised in three classes—upper, middle and lower." But he also recognized that there was "a more stark division" between 'gentleman" and "the rest." When Margaret Stacey surveyed Banbury for a second time in 1966–68, her conclusions were much less clear-cut than they had been a decade before. She thought that the "social images" of class that Banburians had in their minds were "weak and confused" and that the place was now "composed of two or three social levels."[193] As if in corroboration of these confused and alternative collectivities, a survey of factory workers undertaken soon after concluded that 93 percent believed class existed, 29 percent had an image of a two-class society, and 60 percent an image of a three-class society.[194]

But it was not just that many Britons could not decide whether their society was characterized by two or by three collective groups: many did not envisage it in terms of collective groups at all. When David Butler and Donald Stokes made their inquiries in the early 1960s, over half the people they asked about their social situations did not wish to put themselves in any such categories. That was not where they saw themselves as belonging, and that was not how they envisaged the society to which they belonged.[195] In the same way, although Harold Macmillan might claim that the Conservatives had won "the class war," he preferred to believe that British society should not be envisaged in terms of conflicting collectivities. As he told the queen in the aftermath of his victory at the polls, "the most encouraging feature of the election . . . is the strong impression I have formed that Your Majesty's subjects do not wish to allow themselves to be divided into warring classes or tribes filled with hereditary animosity against each other." Even Lewis and Maude, who wrote about the middle classes, recognized that behind the triadic view of society there lay a "unifying principle," an "older tradition," and that, they believed, was "the idea of hierarchy."[196]

They were right to do so. For notwithstanding all the forebodings in 1939 and again in 1945 that civilization as they knew it was coming to an end and there would be "a decline in the value formerly placed on hierarchy and deference," the fact is that many Britons continued to see their society in this way and from this perspective. "Traditional social values" and traditional ways of seeing society survived both Hitler's bombs and Attlee's bills. "There endured," Kenneth Morgan notes, "after 1945 a powerful civic culture, a commitment to hierarchical and organic values."[197] So there did. Indeed, this power, this commitment, and these ways of seeing society were put literally on parade in 1953 at the coronation of Queen Elizabeth II, a pageant of history, empire, and inequality, described for television in just these terms by Richard Dimbleby. "The old world persists, thank God," rejoiced Henry Channon. Henry Fairlie made the same point, less appreciatively. Alluding specifically to the Dimbleby commentary, he regretted that the BBC had done much "to create and perpetuate reverence for the orders, the privileges and the mysteries of a conservative society."[198]

To outsiders viewing Queen Elizabeth II's coronation, it most successfully projected a sense of order, tradition, and hierarchy. A Frenchmen, Pierre Laroque, described this soon after. Britain, he suggested, was "an old country, attached to her traditions." "The British social hierarchy," he went on, "is to a large extent one of the products of these traditions." It was, he believed, "an accepted hierarchy which is widely recognised and has never been seriously debated." "The majority of the population," he thought, "even show a real attachment to this social hierarchy." And this, he concluded, was the reason why there "had never been deep class antagonism in Great Britain."[199] Several points stand out from this account. The first is his failure to note that many of these "traditions" celebrating and proclaiming hierarchy were, in their 1950s form, little more than half a century old. The second is the similarity between his analysis of British society and that which R. H. Tawney had sketched out, with rather less appreciation and approval, twenty years before. And the third is that as a description of how many—perhaps a majority—Britons saw their society in the years immediately after the Second World War, it was surely right.

This was, after all, how the most moderate and the most powerful Labour leaders saw Britain and wanted Britain to stay. However much they were committed to improving the lot of the workers, neither Attlee nor Wilson nor Callaghan had any wish to overturn what each saw as the established (and unequal) social order. Attlee was a great believer in the fixed world order of his youth and a passionate supporter of monarchy, empire, Haileybury, and the House of Lords, as evidenced by the relish with which he accepted honors, in ascending order of prestige: the CH, the OM, the Garter, and an earldom. It was no less true of Wilson, who shared Attlee's veneration for the crown and the oldest order of chivalry, or of Callaghan, who also accepted both a peerage and the Garter with alacrity.[200] Even Tony Crosland recognized that Britain remained "to an exceptional degree" a "class society," by which he meant a complex, graded, layered, traditional, hierarchical society. Under these circumstances, it was hardly surprising that Marx, with his crude and conflicting collectivities, offered no relevant or reliable guide to it. Slightly more surprising was Crosland's evident attachment to so many of the props of hierarchy, especially the monarchy, the House of Lords, the public schools, London clubs, and the Brigade of Guards.[201]

If this was true of the Labour leaders, then how much more so was it of the Conservatives? Churchill may have been seen as a class warrior, on the side of the people against the peers before 1914 and on the side of the propertied versus the people thereafter, but as the grandson of a duke and a child of Blenheim, he (in the words of Violet Bonham Carter) "accepted class distinctions without thought." As Isaiah Berlin explained, he believed in "a natural, social, almost a metaphysical order—a sacred hierarchy which it was neither possible nor desirable to upset."[202] The same was true of Anthony Eden, whose most agreeable piece of autobiographical writing dwelt on the ordered, finely graded landed estate on which he had been brought up at the turn of the century. Harold Macmillan may have been a product of the middle classes, but as befitted someone who came to dislike the social group from which he sprang, he became increasingly attracted to (or obsessed with) the minute distinctions and gradations of aristocratic rank. And Sir Alec Douglas Home, the "fourteenth earl," was an authentic landed grandee, the visible embodiment of the continuing Conservative commitment to the hierarchical, Christian values of the countryside.[203]

But it was not just Conservative leaders who regarded hierarchy as the ideal vision and version of British society; so did Conservative followers. For them, the appeal of Butler's 1944 Education Act was not that it created more opportunities but that it was concerned with "preserving educational privileges and the belief in hierarchy." For all the talk of fundamental changes in Tory thinking after 1945, it was this belief that remained at the heart of Conservative philosophy for the next twenty years.[204] In numerous pamphlets and publications, Conservatives rejected Marxism and its collective and conflicting classes and reasserted their belief in "the traditions and values of the old world." By these, they meant the inevitability and rightness of inequality, the fundamental unity of society, and the "infinity of gradations" within it. They preferred to see society as composed of individuals who knew their place rather than classes that did not. The ideal images of

British society were still pure Baldwin: the ordered and organic countryside, the paternal factory characterized by partnership between managers and workers, and the church and the empire. Even as late as 1971, Anthony Sampson could claim that "the Conservatives have remained, through all their transformations, associated with the settled, inherited society of the countryside," by which, of course, he meant belief in hierarchy.[205]

This view of how British society was and how it ought to remain was still extremely popular among ordinary people during the late 1940s, 1950s, and early 1960s. As befitted those with a hierarchical and deferential caste of mind, many members of the middle and (especially) the working classes believed in an individualistic and finely graded society. They also regarded the monarchy, the Lords, the empire, and the countryside as the visible, institutional embodiment of these social visions and social arrangements.[206] And so they happily and loyally voted Conservative, partly because the Tories were the party most likely to safeguard this vision of society and the institutions that embodied it and partly because they saw elections not as an arena of class struggle but as the opportunity for people of acknowledged humble social station to accord the party of their social superiors the necessary support it required to govern the country. From this perspective, it was entirely "natural" that deferential voters with traditional hierarchical perceptions of the British nation and the Tory Party should vote Conservative. What needed explaining was the "deviant" behavior of those voters who rejected this vision of British society and supported Labour instead.[207]

These discoveries and explanations came as something of a shock to those many British sociologists who focused their attention during the late 1950s and 1960s on the chimerical "embourgeoisified worker" rather than on the much more real "deference voter." Yet from the long-term perspective that this book opens up on these sociological findings, there is nothing unexpected or unusual about them. The vision of British society as an ordered, integrated, layered hierarchy had almost always been historically the most powerful, the most popular, and the most resonant. The alternative visions of collective identities and conflicting groups certainly existed, but it had often been difficult to persuade people that this was how British society actually was and harder still to persuade them that this was how it might be or ought to be or could be. So it should hardly be surprising that, even as late as the 1950s, at least one-third of the working class continued to see British society and their place within it very much as Robert Roberts had seen it in the 1900s and as Stanley Baldwin had urged them to see it during the interwar years. The "deferential voter" who supported the Conservatives was neither deviant nor novel: he or she was the direct descendant of earlier generations of countless ordinary people who had habitually seen British society in traditional, hierarchical terms.

But during the late 1960s and 1970s, it seemed as though these views of society were changing. In part this was because of changes within the Tory Party, which ceased either to embody or to defend hierarchy. Beginning in 1965 aristocratic and wealthy leaders were replaced by those of a very different social background: Edward Heath and Margaret Thatcher, respectively a carpenter's son and a grocer's daughter. Cabinets and shadow cabinets were no longer dominated by aristocrats or Old Etonians but by self-made men.[208] Under these circumstances, it was no longer possible to argue that the Conservatives should be elected because they were the natural leaders from the top of the social hierarchy. And even those who might still be described in these terms recognized that the suburbanization of the Tory Party meant that it was no longer possible to project it as the embodiment of a hierarchical view of society based on the traditional rural order. Writing in the 1970s, neither Sir Ian Gilmour nor William Waldegrave, both from the liberal, patrician wing of the party, was prepared to defend a graded, unequal social order as the best of all possible social worlds in the way that R. A. Butler had been able to do only twenty years before. The Tories were no longer a party "heavily impregnated with respect for class and rank."[209]

This change in perceptions of the British social order was not only due to changes within the Tory Party. It was also connected with, and a prime consequence of, the simultaneous ending of the British Empire. Despite the well-argued claim that this "left scarcely any visible political traces and cast no serious shadow on the viability of British institutions," there seems good reason for taking an alternative view.[210] For it seems clear that the British did not see themselves—indeed, could not see themselves—in the same way without an empire as they had done when they possessed one. From the late nineteenth century, empire had been an essential element in the British perception that they belonged to a hierarchical society, and when it disappeared, one crucial prop to this self-image was knocked away. The independence of India and the subsequent collapse and integration of the princely states brought to an end the elaborate, ceremonial world of the Raj, the most complex and ornamental hierarchy the British ever created and supported overseas.

And in the old dominions, the disappearance of British aristocrats as governors-general, their replacement by native-born proconsuls, and the subsequent scaling-down of the viceregal regimes were further blows to the traditional hierarchical image of empire.[211]

But these were not the only ways in which empire and hierarchy, having mutually buttressed each other, now faltered and fell together. For the British Empire had not just reinforced ideas and perceptions of hierarchy by exporting it overseas; it had also reinforced these ideas and perceptions at home. As the young Peregrine Worsthorne argued in a powerful and prescient article that appeared in the aftermath of Suez, the hierarchical view of things was closely associated in the public mind with the greatness of the nation, and both of these in turn were closely associated with the Conservative Party. But, he went on, "a social system that seemed right and proper while it produced a nation capable of leading the world will look very different when that nation is in decline." "What," he wanted to know, "is the point of maintaining a Queen Empress without an empire to rule over?" "Everything," he concluded, "about the British class system begins to look foolish and tacky when related to a second-class power on the decline." During the 1960s and 1970s, this prediction was amply borne out: the "decline of deference" and the lessened respect for established institutions were in considerable part a consequence of the loss of empire and the undermining of the establishment and the established way of looking at things that resulted from it.[212]

By the mid-1970s, "the collapse of deference" was a phrase that seemed to be on everyone's lips, sometimes with regret, often with relish. Either way, it seems clear that perceptions of British society as a divinely ordained and successfully functioning hierarchy were much diminished, in part because the party of hierarchy was metamorphosing into something else, in part because the hierarchical empire was unraveling. Not surprisingly, this meant that the other two ways of seeing British society became suddenly much more popular.[213] In the Conservative Party, there was a growing concern for the "plight of the middle classes," sandwiched as they were between an overmighty state and an increasingly militant working class. And as industrial relations worsened and the winter of discontent of 1978–79 approached, when more workers would be on strike than in any year since 1926, this updated triadic model was easily elided into the polarized model, according to which class war was once again on the brink of breaking out, with organized, unionized, militant workers on one side, supported by an ever-more-radical Labour Party, and threatened, beleaguered, demoralized property owners, supported by an ever-more-radical Conservative Party, on the other. It was "the classes" versus "the masses" all over again. At least, that was how it seemed.[214]

New Society, Old Society

Beyond any question, the final extensions of the franchise, beginning in the mid-1880s, had made British politicians more aware of social groupings and social identities than they had ever been before or had ever needed to be. The fact that this chapter is longer than the two that preceded it is evidence that politicians were paying greater attention to these matters than their predecessors had done. Since the 1880s, politics has been more about the discernment of social perceptions and the articulation of social identities than ever before. But two qualifications need to be entered. The first is that the social models that underlay the social identities remained demonstrably the traditional three. The second is that it bears repeating that there was no simple elision from social classes to political parties. As at the time of the First and Second Reform Acts, politicians were vague and unclear as to exactly what the social groups in British society were, and their parties sent out very mixed signals, about both the nature of British society in general and the nature of those voters whose support they sought. And so, while social identities and political identities have been more closely connected during this period than ever before, the nature of those connections remains complex, contingent, contradictory, and confused.

It should also be clear that throughout this period, the vocabulary of social description continued to remain exceptionally varied. The "language of class" had not vanquished all alternative forms by 1900 and, as the rhetoric of Stanley Baldwin eloquently demonstrates, it had still not done so by the interwar years. At the same time, and as in earlier periods, the "language of class" was used as a shorthand term for all three models: class as hierarchy; class as upper, middle, and lower; and class as "us" and "them." For all three vernacular visions of the British social world were still available, even though sociologists working during the 1950s and 1960s tended to deal with class almost exclusively in terms of three or two collective categories. A careful reading of the scholarly literature makes plain that many of them recognized there was an alternative, individualistic, and hierarchical way in which people still saw postwar British society, but they generally lacked the means or the inclination to address it explicitly. Several sociologists also recognized that conceptions of the social order were subjective, varied, and discrepant, but this important insight, too, was lost in much of the detailed analysis of collective classes that followed.[215]

But despite the sociologists' general indifference to hierarchy and notwithstanding the widespread talk of the "end of deference," social perceptions in Britain in 1979 remained tied to the three models that had long been in existence. By convenient coincidence, that year also witnessed the publication of Jilly Cooper's book on class. As a work of social observation and analysis, it was hardly in the league of Gregory King or Adam Smith or Karl Marx or George Orwell. But it was of considerable interest and significance. Its subtitle was "A View from Middle England," and in the years after 1979, "middle England" would be much talked about: what was it, where was it, what did it think, did it exist? When describing "the class system," Cooper found herself sliding among the three familiar models of society: the polarized, the triadic, and the hierarchical. While admitting that class was complicated and confusing, she insisted it pervaded everything: gardens, food, drink, health, the arts, sport, sex, religion, death. But she also recognized that class was "alive and well and living *in people's minds*": it was how they saw and understood their society.[216] So it was. Indeed, during the next decade and a half, the way Britons saw themselves and understood their society was to be subjected to the most sustained and persistent campaign of reeducation since Stanley Baldwin. It is almost, but not quite, time to return to Margaret Thatcher.

CHAPTER FIVE

CONCLUSION

Toward a "Classless Society"?

It is alleged that the French historian Emmanuel Le Roy Ladurie classified his professional colleagues neither in hierarchical nor triadic terms but as forming two distinct categories of scholar: the parachutists, who survey the broad landscape of the past from a great height, and the truffle hunters, who immerse themselves in the dense morass of evidential detail. Both approaches have their advantages and their dangers: the parachutists seek to comprehend the overall picture but at the price of a certain unavoidable superficiality; the truffle hunters know the facts but lack the wider conceptual framework in which to place them.[1] Ideally, and as Leopold von Ranke pointed out well over a century earlier, historians need to move back and forth between the universal and the particular, the telescope and the microscope, and this book has tried to adopt just such an approach, blending general argument with specific detail.[2] But, on balance, it is more about generalities than it is about specifics: it has surveyed a large, complex, much-disputed, and massively researched historical problem and drawn extensively on the detailed writings of other scholars, even as it has developed an argument to which most of the authors cited and thanked would probably not themselves subscribe.

The explanation and resolution of this apparent paradox have been well put by W. H. McNeill, a historian who has always been on the side of the parachutists. "Every increase in historical detail," he rightly notes, in words that apply to both the subject covered in this book and the way it has been treated, "risks losing sight of larger patterns which may be more important for public action and understanding." We must not, he insists, be weighed down by too much erudition; "what matters is perspective and proportion, not detail."[3] Although there is an abundance of detail in these pages, it is only a tiny fraction of the total amount of knowable, available, and pertinent evidence. Inevitably and unapologetically, this book has been primarily concerned with tracing patterns, adopting perspectives, and establishing proportions. But it is now time to turn more directly to those matters of public understanding and public action on which this book also seeks to throw some historical light, partly by drawing together the arguments that have been thus far developed, partly by assessing the impact of Margaret Thatcher on British social perceptions and social attitudes, and partly by considering John Major, Tony Blair, and the idea (and the ideal?) of the "classless society" to which they both seem so attached.

Long-Term Retrospective

The arguments advanced in this book may be easily summarized. During the last three hundred years, British society has been observed and imagined, envisaged and understood, by most of its inhabitants in only three basic ways. Nor should this occasion any surprise, given that these models have been in use at least since the medieval period. The first was hierarchical, which described society individualistically as an interlinked, finely layered, and elaborately graded procession; the second was triadic, which divided it into three collective constituencies, usually upper, middle, and lower; and the third was the dichotomous, which saw society as polarized between the two extremes of "patricians and plebs" or "them and us." Across the centuries, these three models have been astonishingly resonant and appealing, not only at a popular level but also among intellectuals and commentators, from Burke and Paine to Marx and Mallock and beyond. One indication of this is that when A. H. Halsey recently set out to revise his justly famous book on social structures and social change in twentieth-century Britain, he felt obliged to choose among what he described as "the vulgar Marxist theory of two classes at war," "the simplification of three social strata of social classes," and "the vulgar liberal conception of a continuous hierarchy of prestige or status."[4]

It is also clear that at all levels of society, and across the centuries surveyed here, Britons have moved back and forth from one of these models to another. These pages have presented many examples. Edmund Burke was a defender of organic, traditional, individualist hierarchy, but he also regretted the rise of a middle class between those above and below and on other occasions divided society into a virtuous elite confronted by the "swinish multitude." Disraeli and Mallock (and

Winston Churchill) idealized hierarchy, but they also feared Britain was divided into "two nations." As a son of Liverpool, Gladstone saw society triadically; as an "out and out inequalitarian," he envisaged it hierarchically; when backing "the masses" against "the classes," he viewed it adversarially. And from Robert Roberts via George Orwell to Jilly Cooper, many twentieth-century commentators have had recourse to all three models. As such, these visions of British social structure and social identities have coexisted not just within the same society but within people's minds. Small wonder that in 1988 the sociologist Gordon Marshall concluded, in words that merit quoting again and at greater length, that "the 'class consciousness' of the majority of people is characterised by its complexity, ambivalence and occasional contradictions. It does not reflect a rigorously consistent interpretation of the world."[5]

Indeed, it is in part the very vagueness and superficiality of these three models of society that has enabled Britons to live with them for so long and to move so easily from one to the other. For they were and are essentially ideal types, not wholly divorced from social reality but very much simplifying it. British society has never been a single, unitary, integrated hierarchy; it has never been divided into three hermetically sealed and homogeneous collectivities; and for all the exhortations of revolutionaries from Paine to Marx, Orwell to Scargill, it has never been so deeply divided that the masses were likely to rise up and overthrow their betters. All these versions of society were (and are) simplified imaginings or rhetorical constructs. They are not "real social knowledge" so much as "imagined constructions" or "rhetorical devices," what George Eliot once memorably called "picture-writing of the mind."[6] In their purest forms, they are clearly incompatible. But in practice, most Britons have easily moved from one model to another: from individualist, integrated hierarchy to adversarial, collective "us" and "them"; or from a three-stage to a two-stage model, by dividing the middle class into patricians and plebs; or from a three-stage model to hierarchy, by assigning people individual status rankings. When thinking about society and when thinking about themselves, this is what most Britons are constantly doing: silently and easily shifting from one social vision to another.

The simplicity and the stamina of these three descriptions of British society have been insufficiently appreciated and inadequately studied, and the same may be said of the facility and frequency with which Britons have always been able to move from one version to another.

But this is not just because the models can be easily molded and melded and merged; it is also because the same language has often been used to describe all of them. To be sure, there were (and are) vocabularies that are specific to hierarchy or to the three- and two-stage models, and many instances have been given in this book. But there is also language that applies with equal appropriateness to all of them. The vocabulary of rank, station, order, and degree, which is often associated exclusively with hierarchy, turns out on closer inspection to have been used frequently in describing three- or two-layer societies, and that practice is with us still. The same applies to the language of class, which has been exclusively associated by historians and sociologists with collective categories and identities but which has always been commonly applied to all three models of society, as it continues to be today.

This in turn means that the *models* of British society are more important in the constitution of our social understandings and the construction of our social identities than the *language* in which they are expressed and articulated. For the language of ranks or of class cannot by itself create social descriptions or social identities, because it might be referring to any one of the three available models of society and does not by itself make it clear which. Perhaps this was what Paul Fussell meant when he observed that "nobody knows for sure what the word *class* means."[7] Here are two examples by way of illustration. When Britons talk, as they regularly do, of "the class system" that they believe prevails, they might be referring to class as hierarchy, to class as upper, middle, and lower, or to class as "us" and "them." From the language itself, it is impossible to tell. And when John Major spoke of wanting to create a "classless society," did he mean the abolition of hierarchy, or of the distinctions upper, middle, lower, or of the divide between "us" and "them"? Once again, the words cannot tell us.[8] As these examples suggest, the connection between social vocabularies and social identities is more complex and contingent than generally recognized. The "language of class" is not the real issue; the real issue is the models of society that it and other languages articulate, make real, and bring to life.[9]

It is, then, mistaken to suppose that the so-called rise of the language of class in Britain during the late eighteenth and early nineteenth centuries happened because new collective classes were coming into being—perhaps three, perhaps two—that overturned and superseded the old individualist hierarchy. Yet it remains a widely held belief that the period from the 1790s to the 1830s witnessed the origin of contemporary "class distinctions" in Britain.[10] But class, like rank, often meant hierarchy, and it is the failure to recognize this that helps explain one of the greatest gaps in modern British historical writing: the lack of due attention to hierarchy as a way of seeing society and as a system of social belief. It has been ignored by historians of the Right, who tend to take its continued existence for granted, and by historians of the Left (and most sociologists), because they take its disappearance no less for granted.[11] Yet as E. M. W. Tillyard pointed out two generations ago, the Elizabethan world picture did not die with the Elizabethans. "We shall err grievously," he noted, "if we imagine that the Elizabethan habit of mind [seeing the world hierarchically] is done with once and for all. If we are sincere with ourselves, we must know that we have that habit in our own bosoms somewhere." One of the purposes of this book has been to urge that we cannot understand the history of modern British society unless we recognize the continued existence of hierarchy as a way of seeing and making sense it.[12]

Marxists and Marxisant historians (to say nothing of sociologists) have not generally been at ease with hierarchy, and in largely ignoring it, they have been much in error. But non-Marxists, and anti-Marxists are no less in error in asserting, along with Margaret Thatcher, that class is exclusively "a communist concept" that "groups people as bundles and sets them against one another."[13] Class, as this book has sought to show, has not only meant three different ways of looking at British social structure, one of which is very strongly individualist and consensual rather than collective and conflictual. Class—in all its three guises—was alive and around in Britain for more than half a century before Marx, and—again in all its three guises—it is clearly going to survive in Britain long after Marxism's day is done. Since Marxism's day does seem to be done, this is an appropriate point to add two final observations on this subject. The first is that, in asserting in *The Communist Manifesto* that "society as a whole is more and more splitting into two great hostile camps, into two great classes directly facing each other: bourgeoisie and proletariat," Marx was wrong in his own day and has become even more wrong since his death.[14] The second is that, in describing society as deeply riven, he was merely offering the most elaborately worked out (and generalized) version of a very commonplace (yet specific) model.[15]

One purpose of this book has been to argue that three models of British society have been continuously present during the last three hundred years, that for much of the time they have easily coexisted in people's minds and imaginations, and that the hierarchical vision of British society has been the most pervasive and persuasive. But it has also been concerned to describe and explain how at different times hierarchy became less appealing to some people, who instead embraced one or both of the alternative ways of seeing their society and did so in a more adversarial frame of mind, envisaging their social existence in collective and confrontational terms rather than consensually and individualistically. This, it bears repeating, now seems a more appropriate way to approach the problem of class than to suggest that classes were coming into being, did battle, won or lost, rose and fell. No doubt part of the explanation for changes in the appeal of visions of society lies in the changes in society themselves: social reality *does* influence and inform social perceptions. But as has been regularly demonstrated, changes in the ways in which people saw society—or came to see society—were often more rapid than changes in society themselves. And while many developments (growth in population, urbanization, secularization) have been in one direction only, the ways in which people have seen their society have gone back and forth, from one model to another, across the decades. How, then, is this to be explained?

Part of the answer to this question must have to do with discontent, not in the sense that discontent results in fundamental changes in the social structure, which has not been the case in Britain during the last three hundred years, but rather in the sense that it is discontent that causes some people to see their society in an alternative way. For dissatisfaction means they discover new friends, make new enemies, and establish (for a time) new identities; it means that riots and protests project and render credible what is literally a dramatically different version of their society from that proclaimed by elaborately staged and carefully ranked official processions; and it means that the three- or two-stage models of their society thus come, for a time, to have more appeal than the traditional hierarchical picture. But if this is right, then we ought to be looking at the ways in which social description becomes explicitly politicized. For most politicians, from Wilkes to Cobbett, Cobden to Gladstone, Lloyd George to Baldwin, Thatcher to Major, one of the most important tasks has been to persuade people to see their society differently, and to persuade them to see themselves differently: in short, to change people's sense of identity, which in practice meant moving them from accepting one vision of British society to embracing another.

Consider, in this light, the following examples. When Wilkes invoked "the common people" against the Hanoverian oligarchy, when the Whigs in the 1820s lamented that the social fabric was being rent in twain, when the Anti–Corn Law League described themselves as a "middle-class set of agitators" railing against "aristocratic tyranny," when the great Lord Salisbury feared the "disintegration" of hierarchy, when Lloyd George attacked "the peers" in the name of "the people," when Stanley Baldwin tried to heal class divisions, and when Aneurin Bevan sought to widen them, people *did* come to believe that these arresting but oversimplified descriptions were genuine, truthful accounts of how British society actually was or was actually in the process of becoming. But in fact they were no such thing: they were not objective descriptions of the British society of their day, and neither were they evidence that old social formations were dying or new social formations were coming into existence. They were merely evidence that politicians were trying to change the way ordinary people looked at their social worlds.

This has involved politicians in two related and complementary activities. The first consists of providing the collective social categories through which people can understand society as a whole. The second consists of trying to persuade them that they belong to one collective category rather than another by extolling the merits of one group while denouncing the other group (or groups) as being wholly without virtue. Much political endeavor in Britain, from the time of Wilkes to our own day, should be understood in this light: as the attempted creation of alternative social identities that are endowed, as appropriate, with either good or bad qualities. "Ideological stereotyping" is the name rightly given to this activity.[16] And the measure of a politician's success is the extent to which he (or she) succeeds in persuading a significant proportion of the public to accept these oversimplified collective categories as authoritative accounts of how society is and these oversimplified moral evaluations as authoritative accounts of how these different collective groups behave (or misbehave). Thus regarded, the task of politicians is the creation and manipulation of social identities, sometimes articulated in the language of class, sometimes not. It is not so much that "real" social identities directly inform and animate party politics; it is that party politics is concerned with creating social identities.

Of course, and as the examples just noted suggest, only a limited number of such identities are available in practice: decent middle classes against a corrupt elite and idle laborers, the virtuous many against a selfish and irresponsible few, the virtuous few against a selfish and irresponsible many. Along with stable, venerable, time-honored hierarchy, these constitute just about the full repertoire of sociological and rhetorical options, and the social identities articulated and projected by British politicians generally conform to one or another of them. Most are concerned to define, homogenize, and praise certain numbers of people (who are occupationally, sociologically, and behaviorally very diverse) and to define, homogenize, and demonize others (of whom the same may be said). This is what politicians always do when they seek to create social identities and transform social understandings. How successful they are in these endeavors depends on the extent to which their images resonate and the number of people with whom they resonate. Politics does shape perceptions of social structure, but these perceptual options are distinctly limited in their number, because all of them are ultimately derived from the same three basic, enduring models of British society.

But this book has not been entirely about unchangingness. One reason for this is that each of the three models of British society that I have discussed carry with them an implicit temporal dynamic and perspective that is part of their appeal. Hierarchy is generally about how society *was*, a backward-looking picture of an ideal way of ordering the world that needs to be preserved or restored. The three-stage model tends to be about how society *is*, especially when viewed, as is usual, from the vantage point of those in the middle. And the two-stage model is often concerned with how society *might be*, perhaps for good (if you are a would-be revolutionary), perhaps for ill (if you are not). A second reason for stressing change is that the relationship between politicians and social identities during each of the three centuries that have been surveyed is in some ways significantly different. Before 1776 politicians (with the exception of John Wilkes) did not talk about social structures or social identities, and they took hierarchy for granted. Between the 1780s and the 1870s, they no longer felt they could take hierarchy for granted, and they worked hard to preserve it and to dampen down alternative, collective social identities. And after the Third Reform Act, social identities were brought inside the electoral system, which meant that politicians became more active than ever before in trying to mold and manipulate them.

But notwithstanding these significant changes over time, it *is* the enduringness of these three basic ways of seeing British society that most stands out. Although they do not realize it, this is probably what most outsiders mean when they remark—as they regularly and repeatedly do—that the British are more obsessed with class than any other nation.[17] For it is *not* that Britain is the most unequal society in the world: the rich are not as rich as those in the United States, nor the poor as poor. Nor is it that social mobility is uniquely restricted: it is in fact, comparable with most countries in Western Europe. Rather, it is that the British think and talk about their inequality and immobility more, and that is because, for good historical reasons, they have a larger repertoire of surviving vernacular models in which to describe and discuss them than do most nations.[18] When Orwell remarked that Britain was the "most class-ridden country under the sun," this is surely what he meant—or what he ought to have meant. For there *is* something unusual about the history of social structures and social perceptions in Britain and also about the interconnections between them. Britain has had no 1776, no 1789, no 1917, no 1921, no 1947: hierarchy has not been forcibly abolished; society has not been revolutionarily changed; and neither have the three different ways in which people look at it.

This, in turn, explains why the history of class in Britain should only be written, and can only be written, as the history of multiple identities. Such a conclusion brings us a long way from the single master narrative built around class formation, class consciousness, class war, and class dominance with which this book began. This may have been the way historians saw the British past a generation ago, but it is not the way they see it now. In the postmodern world we inhabit today, this seems a necessary and healthy development. But postmodernism should not be taken to extremes: multiplicity is not the same as incoherence and should be made neither the excuse nor the justification for it. What has been offered here instead is an alternative master narrative built around a very different notion of class: class as social description, social perception, social identities, and political creation. This history of class is as much about the history of *ideas* about society as it is about society itself. Thus properly regarded and understood, class remains an essential element in the British past and in British life, and there is no one whose attitudes and accomplishments provide more emphatic proof of that than Margaret Thatcher.

The Impact of Thatcher

Throughout her years in power, Margaret Thatcher was determined to "change the way we look at things, to create a wholly new attitude of mind," and in this messianic endeavor, the transformation of social visions and the social attitudes that went with them was as important to her as it had previously been to Stanley Baldwin, though in a very different way.[19] The essential starting point for any investigation into Thatcher's conceptions of Britain's social structure is Grantham: the place where she was born and that she vividly recalls in her memoirs. Her most expansive recollections are of the town on display in the civic processions associated with Remembrance Day and King George V's Silver Jubilee in 1935: the "mayor, aldermen and councillors with robes and regalia," followed by the "Brownies, Cubs, Boys' Brigade, Boy Scouts, Girl Guides, Freemasons, Rotary, Chamber of Commerce, Working Men's Clubs, trade unions, British Legion, soldiers, airmen, the Red Cross, the St John's Ambulance," and then the "representatives of every organisation which made up our rich civic life." All these, she recalls, "filed past." This, for her, was the outward and visible expression of a layered, hierarchical society, held together by loyalty to monarchy and empire. In such a community, she "did not grow up with the sense of division and conflict between classes." Indeed, she did "not see that class was important."[20]

This was not the only way in which Thatcher recalls the social order of her youth in Grantham, though it is certainly the one on which she dwells most vividly, evocatively, and affectionately. She also remembers that she was born and brought up, "neither poor nor rich," in the middle-class world of prosperous shopkeepers and small-town businessmen, who formed the solid backbone of local society. Some distance above, there was the aristocratic splendor of such local landed notables as the earls of Brownlow and the dukes of Rutland. Some distance beneath, there was another and very different world of unemployed workers queueing up for the dole at the Grantham Labour Exchange. And finally, seeing Grantham yet a third way, Lady Thatcher remembers one deep, fundamental social divide: "the real distinction in the town," she thinks, "was between those who drew salaries for what today would be called 'white collar' employment, and those who did not."[21] Taken together, these recollections add up to the three familiar modes of social description: the hierarchical, the triadic, and the dichotomous. Thus described, Grantham in 1935 bears a striking resemblance to

Montpellier in 1768 and to the stock pictures of British society across the centuries.

In other ways, Thatcher's original social vision was even more localized. Her father kept a grocer's shop, and this meant that in her formative years, she got to know about people not as manufacturing producers or as collective aggregates but as individual consumers. "We lived," she recalls, "by serving the customer."[22] This in turn meant that she did not share the view of Adam Smith (or Karl Marx) that social identities were fundamentally fashioned by a person's relationship to the means of production and that as a result they were primarily shared, group identities. This preference for individual consumers over collective producers was further reinforced by the fact that Grantham provided her with no first hand experience of the factory-based, traditional working class as a sociological entity. Apart from a light engineering works, there was no heavy industry in the town and no large-scale, segregated industrial workforce. To be sure, Thatcher's Grantham was not Trollope's Barchester but neither was it Dickens's Coketown. And although she went away to Oxford, qualified as a lawyer, married a businessman, and lived in London, she never achieved first-hand knowledge of the industrial working classes or of manufacturing industry.[23] Nor, having entered politics and risen to the top, did she much modify the three visions of society she had formed while living above the corner shop.

Indeed, as prime minister, Thatcher's social vision of Britain and for Britain was in many ways Grantham writ large. She continued to believe in ordered hierarchy, and she felt an almost Burkeian reverence for "a great chain of people, stretching back into the past and forwards into the future," just like those civic processions from the days of her youth. To begin with, she had a deep respect for the institution of monarchy as the apex and epitome of an established society: nobody would curtsy to the queen lower than she.[24] Nor was this obsequiousness confined to the crown. As one contemporary noted, "She still actually has a sort of reverence for the Archbishop This and the Lord That and the Duke of Whatever. She really does. She actually still slightly bends the knee. It's not as if she thinks it: she was brought up to it." The hierarchical outlook of her youth, epitomized by the Brownlow family silver and her father's mayoral chain and aldermanic robes, accompanied her to 10 Downing Street. And so did her belief in the permanence of social inequality and the importance of social subordination. Like Disraeli and Churchill before her, she saw society as a ladder, with "differentials at every level," and she was deeply opposed to any government intervention intended to undermine it, or lay it flat, or break it, or remove it.[25]

But as befitted someone who had been born in the lower middle class and risen by marriage and merit within the same class, Thatcher also remained wedded to the three-layered model of society. For she genuinely believed that "the great middle mass of the British" were the repository of all the virtues she most admired. Among them were thrift, hard work, self-reliance, independence, and responsibility: qualities she once described as "Victorian values" but that were in fact the values of her father's Grantham shopocracy.[26] Put more positively, this meant that she regarded the middle classes as the backbone of the enterprise economy she sought to promote and as the most important wealth creators of the nation, epitomized by men such as Lords Taylor, White, Hanson, and King, whom she delighted to ennoble. And she took pleasure and pride in contrasting these vigorous middle-class attributes and these exemplary middle-class entrepreneurs to the languid, appeasing, privileged aristocracy and to a working class easily swayed by the propaganda of trade-union leaders. For Thatcher was in no doubt that it was "the interests of the middle class of a country" on which "future prosperity largely depends."[27] She was herself indebted to Enoch Powell and Sir Keith Joseph for these views. But in a longer perspective, she was merely resorting to a rhetoric that had been commonplace in Britain since at least the late eighteenth century. All that was unusual was that she asserted it with a conviction that had not been heard in a hundred years.

At the same time, Thatcher continued to believe that British society was riven by one great, single divide, though it was not primarily the line that she had earlier discerned in Grantham. For now the starting point was Communism, which she claimed "gives privileges to the few at the top, and none to the many" below. Nor was Socialism any better. It resulted in "two nations: the privileged rulers and everyone else." And it produced "the most stratified of all societies, divided into two classes, the powerful and the powerless, the party-bureaucratic elite and the manipulated masses."[28] In Britain, this had given rise, since the Second World War, to a self-interested, self-perpetuating, and unaccountable elite, contemptuous of "the people," that occupied entrenched positions in the BBC, the Foreign Office, the universities, and the Church of England. It was against this new form of "Old Corruption"—and its 1980s characterization as the "chattering classes"—that Thatcher presented herself as an antiestablishment crusader, a Tory who was on the side of the plebs against the patricians, the producers against the parasites.[29] Here was a new-style populism, with Thatcher as a latter-day Cobbett claiming "it is our policies which are in tune with the deepest instincts of the British people." And it was on the basis of this adversarial vision of society that she campaigned for "an irreversible shift of power [in Britain] in favour of working people and their families."[30]

As the foregoing quotations frequently serve to show, Thatcher expressed her views on Britain's social structure with characteristic force and candor. But for all their inimitable articulation, the models that she used were commonplace—indeed, so commonplace that they may be closely compared to those Gladstone had used a century before. Like Gladstone, Thatcher was an "out and out inequalitarian" pledged to protect and preserve hierarchy. Like Gladstone, Thatcher came from the upwardly mobile middle classes, and she was very conscious that society was divided into three basic groups. And like Gladstone, Thatcher was a moral populist on the side of "the people" against the "upper ten" and would back "the masses" against "the classes" anytime.[31] Nor are these the only similarities. For like Gladstone again, she moved easily from one of these models to another. In one guise, she was a neoconservative, believing society was a Burkeian hierarchy of disciplined authoritarianism and ordered subordination. In another, she took a neoliberal view that society was a tripartite construct, dominated by the laissez-faire ideology and entrepreneurial ethos of the middle classes. From yet a third perspective, she was a neopopulist confrontationalist leading what was often described as "the peasants' revolt" against established and entrenched elites. Here were contradictions aplenty. But such was the force of her personality and the extent of her dominance that in her years of power, they were rarely remarked upon.[32]

In any case, whatever the commonplace contradictions of her social visions, Thatcher was extremely accomplished at turning these vague and contradictory rhetorical imperatives into vigorous political programs. To begin with, she was determined to drive the language of class—and the idea of class conflict—off the agenda of public discussion, and this was something she very successfully accomplished.[33] The word "class" hardly ever appeared in her speeches, except when she was denouncing Communists or Socialists or the Labour Party or the trade unions. Politics, she insisted, was not "a matter of social class," and "class warfare" was an "outmoded Marxist doctrine" that had incited social conflict where it would not otherwise have existed. At every opportunity, she berated Marxists as believers in false laws of history and of human behavior based on the misleading categories of class and the concept of class struggle. Marx had been wrong to claim that class was the key to the politics of the mid-nineteenth century, and his prescriptions for the future were as mistaken as his contemporary analysis. For there was not now and there had never been such a thing as "an underprivileged and internationally recognisable" working class. Indeed, the very idea that history—or society—was fundamentally about "one class against another" was to her a perversion of the truth.[34]

Thatcher's constantly and determinedly negative rhetoric was very successful in discrediting class and class conflict as the languages and concepts of political discussion, and it is not coincidence that it was also in these years that they disappeared as the languages and concepts of historical inquiry.[35] She did not accept collective social categories based on mutually hostile relations to the means of production. Instead, and more positively and predictably, she talked about individuals and consumers. The purpose of production, she insisted, was "to discover what the customer will buy and to produce it." "People must be free to choose," she went on, "what they consume in goods and services." The market economy was not about collective groups of producers: instead, it devolved "the power of consumer choice to customers." Here were her childhood memories of Grantham elevated into social taxonomies for the country as a whole. In the same way, she repeatedly spoke of "the nation," or "the people," or "the working people," or "the British people," or "the working population." Indeed, she even coined the phrase the "classless society" long before her successor, John Major, made it his own. "It was not so much," she was later to write, "that I wanted a classless society, as the socialists (somewhat disingenuously) said they did, but that I could not see that class was important."[36] We are back to her father's shop: class had not signified in the Grantham of her youth, and she was resolved it should not signify in the Britain of her prime.

But for all Thatcher's hostility to Marxism, Communism, and Socialism and notwithstanding her resulting determination to stamp out the language of class and the substance of class conflict, Hugo Young is surely correct when he notes that she was in practice "acutely sensitive to class." Despite her veneration for the traditional Burkeian hierarchy, she was "remarkably indifferent" to those who personified that hierarchy at its apex: royalty, aristocracy, and landed gentry. Both ideologically and socially, she was ill at ease with the old-style paternalism of the queen and the Prince of Wales; the snobbish, self-perpetuating royal court was just the sort of elite vested interest that radical Thatcherites wanted to sweep away, and she herself had no more regard for royal audiences at Buckingham Palace than for country pursuits at Balmoral.[37] She was equally suspicious of the traditional Tory patricians: she had no time for "the agonised social conscience of the English upper classes", and hated their condescension, their patronizing attitudes, and their concern for an idealized poor from a position of inherited privilege. It is easy to see why. To read the memoirs of such ministers as Lord Carrington or Lord Whitelaw is to encounter an alternative social world: rural, privileged, secure, centered on the paternal family estate and the ordered ranks of the regiment. It is, in short, a very different version of the local hierarchy from that which Thatcher recalled in small-town Grantham.[38]

Here was the basis for a conflict of social perceptions and political attitudes within Thatcher's cabinets that amounted to a kind of class war. For she knew she was "of a different class" from them, and they knew it, too. As a result, she was the target of a great deal of social disparagement. There were whispers at court, Willie Whitelaw thought her "governessy," Francis Pym claimed she was "a corporal" rather than a "cavalry officer," and Sir Ian Gilmour warned against "retreat behind the privet hedge into a world of narrow class interests and selfish concerns."[39] She was clearly enraged by this patrician condescension, and her memoirs record not only her resentment but also her scarcely concealed delight in getting rid of these privileged notables. She had no time for Lord Carrington's notions of "dignity." She described Jim Prior as a "false squire," a phrase that clearly ranked high in her lexicon of personal and political abuse. And when she sacked Lord Soames, he gave her the impression that "the natural order of things was being violated and that he, a "dispossessed grandee," had been "dismissed by his housemaid."[40] The metaphor is as revealing as the phraseology. For all her attachment to traditional order and inequality, Thatcherism did portend "the end of deference" and the erosion of respect for an ordered vision of society. It was, after all, during the 1980s that Thatcherite newspapers toppled the monarchy from its revered place at the summit of the social hierarchy.

Thatcher's deep-rooted dislike of the traditional aristocracy was matched by her equal dislike of the traditional working class, especially organized labor, about which she had never known (or cared) all that much and about which she had unthinkingly absorbed the powerful Tory negative stereotypes of the interwar years. Unlike the grandees in her party, she neither romanticized nor sentimentalized the workers. On the contrary, she regarded them as "idle, deceitful, inferior and bloody minded," a catalog of behavioral failings no less selective than the moral approbation she simultaneously lavishedon the middle class.[41] She was widely criticized for her lack of public compassion for those less well off and less fortunate and her hostility to the traditional paternalist concern for them. She did not like the culture of dependency, regarded the rise in unemployment during the early 1980s with an equanimity bordering on indifference, and believed (along with Norman Tebbit) that out-of-work people should stop complaining, get on their bikes, and go out to look for jobs.[42] Here was another binary Thatcherite social vision, but a very different one from that in which she was on the side of "the people" against a corrupt establishment. For now, in a manner reminiscent of her sense of the great Grantham social divide, she presented herself as being on the side of the majority of the decent, respectable population against the most unsavory and wayward elements of the working class.

It was this confrontationalist vision of society that reinforced Thatcher's determination in 1984–85 to take on Arthur Scargill and what she termed the miners' "insurrection." Unlike Harold Macmillan, she did not think these people were "the best men in the world," who had beaten the armies of the Kaiser and Hitler and who "never gave in."[43] On the contrary, she thought they were revolutionaries, "the crack division of the working class," and that they had to be defeated. This was a class war Thatcher was determined to fight—and to win. So was Arthur Scargill. He was a Marxist-Leninist who believed in "pure class struggle," he thought the miners were the vanguard of the working-class revolution, and he was determined to secure "victory" for the proletariat.[44] But his lurid rhetoric and apocalyptic social vision never shaped any social reality except that existing inside his own head, for the miners' struggle was not synonymous with the struggle of the working class, and there was nothing he could say or do that would have made it so. In beating Scargill and the miners, Thatcher scored a political and rhetorical victory against the Marxist vision of society, which in defeat looked increasingly outmoded and irrelevant. It was, she claimed, a triumph for "the whole working people of Britain" over "the rule of the mob."[45] The words, as usual, were carefully chosen: class war, yes; the language of class, no.

All this suggests that Thatcher's notion of Britain as a "classless society" was one where she had won the class war, where there were no collective class identities or class enemies left, and where she had driven class off the agenda of public perceptions and discussion. Yet to do this she herself had to be obsessed with class, and that she seems to have been. Nor was this the only irony and contradiction in her position. For while she had driven the language of class off the agenda, the three basic models of British society, which were frequently but not exclusively articulated in the language of class, remained essentially unchanged, and most of all at 10 Downing Street itself. The vocabularies in which social perceptions were described had altered; the social perceptions themselves continued largely unaltered. Although she did not use the words or concepts, she still envisaged the British social structure in terms of traditional hierarchies, or as three collective groupings, or as fissured by one great divide that was drawn at different levels for different political purposes. Small wonder that Thatcher never projected a fully coherent social vision. Perhaps this was what she meant when she famously remarked that "there is no such thing as society. There are only individual men and women, and there are families."[46]

Nor did Thatcher succeed in pinning behavioral characteristics on particular social groups in the way that she wished. She hated the patrician "wets" for their weakness, disloyalty, condescension, and vacillation. But two of her most fervent supporters in cabinet came from just that much-despised social group—Willie Whitelaw and Nicholas Ridley—and displayed no such incontinent tendencies. She celebrated the entrepreneurial and money-making virtues to such an extent that she was rightly accused of "bourgeois triumphalism."[47] But she alienated many, many members of the professional, university-educated middle class, who (like Jonathan Miller and Mary Warnock) rejected her celebration of business attitudes and wealth creation, found her incorrigibly strident and suburban, and increasingly moved to the center parties and modernizing Labour. And she attacked organized labor with unsympathetic ferocity and was icily compassionless to the underprivileged. But she won the votes of many trade unionists, upwardly mobile workers, and first-time owner-occupiers for whom voting Tory had previously been unthinkable.[48]

It is difficult to avoid the conclusion that Thatcher brought about a revolution neither in social perceptions nor in social attitudes, though she clearly tried very hard to achieve both. To be sure, she made the language of the customer and the consumer more pervasive than the language of class or that of the producer, and she was very determined to accomplish this. But this change in people's thinking would probably have happened sooner or later in any case, given the long-term decline in traditional manufacturing in Britain and the rise of many new service industries. Moreover, she offered no new vision of social structure as a whole, and her attempts to come up with a new moral sociology also made little progress. Even more interestingly, the relationship between what she said about society and the way voting habits actually changed owed little to her. For as Daniel Bell pointed out some time ago, these developments—an increasingly radical middle class and an increasingly conservative working class—have been commonplace in most postindustrial societies.[49] All that can be said is that she politicized social categories and social models in an adversarial way as no British political leader had done since Lloyd George, a figure whom in many ways she markedly resembles.

Nevertheless, it is arguable that the most resonant and abiding descriptions of British society during the Thatcher years were not in the end those of her own choosing or articulation. The massive rise in unemployment during the early 1980s and the evidence that poverty and inequality were increasing during the later part of the decade led many to believe that the fabric of British society was once again being rent asunder, and the language of the "two nations" duly came back on the agenda of public discussion. It was clear, according to the archbishop of Canterbury, "that rich and poor, suburb and inner city, privileged and deprived, have been becoming more sharply separate from each other." The sociologist A. H. Halsey agreed, arguing that there had been a polarization between "a majority in secure attachment to a still-prosperous country, and a minority in marginal social and economic conditions," a new underclass of poor and unemployed and black youngsters in inner cities who were turning to crime and drugs. It was not only "one nation" Tories who increasingly believed (and feared) that Britain was becoming $^2/_3$-$^1/_3$ society of winners and losers, where the latter could expect nothing from the former. Combined with the early riots at Toxteth and Brixton and those that came later over the poll tax, this projected an image of a deeply divided British society under Thatcher that was very different from that she had hoped to impose.

Major, Blair, and Beyond

In any case, Thatcher has been gone a long time. How, then, have and do those politicians who have come after her conceive of contemporary

British society? What sense of its overall shape and form and structure do Major, Clarke, and Heseltine, or Hague, Redwood, and Howard, or Blair, Brown, and Prescott, or Cook, Harman, and Ashdown actually have? In what words and categories do they conceive and describe the social world around them? How do they think British society has evolved across the centuries to get the way they think it is now? These questions are rarely asked of British politicians. But because they have been, are now, or wish to be responsible for conducting the nation's affairs, it does not seem unreasonable to inquire what social vision they have of the aggregate of people over whom they have governed, are governing, or wish to govern. Do they think there is such a thing as society? Does it consist of two or three collective groups? Or is it best envisaged in another way? And in what language do they think about British society and describe it? Such questions might be asked of politicians every time there is a general election, and they might be regularly and insistently repeated in between elections. But even without explicit answers, it is possible to give some idea of what British politicians have been thinking and saying about British society in the aftermath of the collapse of Communism and Thatcherism.

When Margaret Thatcher left office reluctantly in November 1990, she was followed by someone who also made much of politicizing social descriptions and owed his election as leader of the Conservative Party to his repeated identification with a Thatcher phrase he had made even more his own: the "classless society."[50] But whereas Thatcher meant by this that she had won the class war against the unionized workers and had driven class off the agenda of public and political discussion, John Major meant something very different: a society that was "at ease with itself," that was not fissured by any great divide, and where people were not looked down on because of their lowly social origins. Thatcher's "classless society" was the product of confrontation and struggle and victory; Major's "classless society" was one where everybody would try to be nicer to each other. In the manner of his hero, Stanley Baldwin, he presented himself as a class conciliator rather than a class warrior.[51] This may explain why the phrase became much more associated with him than with her and why it has taken on a life of its own during the 1990s. Yet on closer inspection, Major's vision—or, rather, visions—of British society turn out to have been very familiar.

Like Thatcher, Major envisaged people as disaggregated consumers rather than collective producers: hence his attacks on Labour for treating them "as blocks and groups" but never "as individuals" and his belief in the importance of customer choice. But he was less successful than Thatcher in disguising the inherent (and inherited) contradictions of the modern Tory social vision: was Britain a Burkeian hierarchy, or a three-level society with a dominant middle class, or "two nations" divided between us and them? In one guise, Major was a Trollope-reading social traditionalist wedded to "the vivid tapestry of distinctions that we have in this country," exemplified by the royal yacht and the hereditary peerage, both of which he defended with a reactionary vehemency that would have done credit to the duke of Wellington.[52] In another, he saw Britain from a middle-class perspective, as evidenced in his suburban liking for school uniforms and the Great Western Railway, John Arlott and Brian Johnston, and his love of Surrey cricket and Chelsea football. But he was also a Tory populist: the self-made man from Brixton battling against the condescending establishment of the "chattering classes," supporting the "Citizen's Charter" for ordinary people, and attacking Tony Blair for his elitist education: "New Labour, old school tie."[53]

Since Major's departure, Tory visions of British society have been much less in evidence. But some indications of what Hague's party thinks may be gleaned from the words of Michael Portillo. From one perspective, he is a crusading populist, railing against sick, corrupt, unpatriotic, self-perpetuating elites in Britain and Brussels: "the people who think they know what's best for us." From another, he is the standard bearer of the free-marketeer hard Right, stressing the importance of "entrepreneurial flair" and the middle classes. But as befits a product of Maurice Cowling's Peterhouse,[54] he has also embraced traditional hierarchy, urging the need for "order in society" and "respect and duty from top to bottom" and quoting these familiar lines from Shakespeare's *Troilus and Cressida*, which remain central to one strand of Conservative social philosophy:

> O, when degree is shak'd,
> Which is the ladder of all high designs,
> The enterprise is sick! How could communities,
> Degrees in schools and brotherhoods in cities,
> Peaceful commerce from dividable shores,
> The primogenitive and due of birth,
> Prerogative of age, crowns, sceptres, laurels,
> But by degree, stand in authentic place?

Take but degree away, untune that string,
And, hark, what discord follows![55]

As these examples suggest, the same deep contradictions remain at
the heart of the Tory social vision that emerged in Margaret Thatcher's
day, between the neoconservatives who see Britain in terms of hierarchy
and history, order and subordination, the neoliberals who embrace the
three-layered, middle-class, free-market option, and the neopopulists
who draw one great divide between "the people" (who are good) and "the
elite" (who are bad).[56] Whether it will be possible for the Tories to
contain and fudge these divergent models of society indefinitely, only
time will tell. It is one thing for ordinary people to live with these different visions and to move from one to another as they navigate their way
through their social life. It is quite another for a political party to espouse
all three of them when they carry such very different, very potent ideologies and such very different views of the nation's past, present, and future. During the course of the twentieth century, the Tory Party has
moved from patrician to middle class to petty-bourgeois leadership, and
during that time, its traditional hierarchical social vision has been joined
by the middle-class triadic and the populist-confrontational models. Indeed, it has been the party's capacity simultaneously to broaden its personnel and widen its social vision that goes a long way toward explaining
its unique electoral success.[57] But for how much longer? Who can say?

Like the Conservatives, New Labour nowadays talks the language
of individual "consumers" and "citizens" rather than that of collective
"workers" or "producers" or "classes."[58] And like the Tories again, it has
embraced the three conventional models of society, though not always
with the same attitudes to them. When Tony Blair attacks "a class
system unequal and antiquated," and when he laments that "Britain is
still, after all these years, a place where class counts," he is insisting that
the "old hierarchy of deference" remains and that it has to be "dismantled."[59] He agrees with the Tories that it exists; unlike some of them,
he wants it to go. But when he says that "between the underclass and
the overclass is a new and growing anxious class," he embraces
the three-layered model of British society, appealing to those in the
middle, including businessmen and entrepreneurs, whose anxieties he
promises to allay more effectively than the Conservatives. And when
he attacks the Tories as "the party of privilege," governing in the interests of "the elite at the top," or when he urges that "wealth, power and
opportunity" should be "in the hands of the many, not the few,"

or when he mourns Diana as "the people's princess," he is resorting to the binary model, with New Labour as the party of "the anti-establishment" and ordinary men and women.[60]

The similarities between the social visions of the Conservatives under Major and Labour under Blair are thus very marked, and their triadic images are especially alike in all except their vocabulary. In the case of the Tories, the images have been built around the idea of "Middle England", a phrase apparently derived by Margaret Thatcher from Richard Nixon's idea of "Middle America".[61] But it has been especially associated with John Major ("the personification of middle England") and also with Kenneth Clarke (born in "the unchanging world of middle England"). For them, middle England means "the long shadows falling across the county ground . . . the invincible green suburbs . . . old maids bicycling to Holy Communion."[62] This is emphatically England, not Britain, and the "middle" being referred to is neither geographical nor sociological but essentially rhetorical. As Martin Jacques recently explained, "Middle England is primarily a political invention . . . a metaphor for respectability, the nuclear family, heterosexuality, conservatism, whiteness, middle age and the status quo."[63] It is, in short, the latest version of the traditional three-layer model of society—which has always privileged those in the center—with a contemporary, sub-Baldwinian, sub-Orwellian spin.

Tony Blair's equivalent social image was that of "community," which was intended as a retort to Thatcher's claim that there is no such thing as society.[64] But like "Middle England," "community" is a term at once comforting and vague. It is comforting because it disregards social inequality or class conflict and because communities are depicted as inclusive congregations of the virtuous: no one speaks of the "gun-owning community" or the "fox-hunting community," or the "smoking community": they are "lobbies" or special-interest groups, with selfish and sectional agendas. By contrast, a recent list of "communities" by a well-disposed commentator enumerates "trade unions, business associations, co-operatives, universities, cricket clubs, churches, Rotary Clubs, the Women's Institute, local councils and the BBC," most of which are as middle class (and as Middle England) as Major's bicycling old maids. Beyond that, and like Middle England again, there is no real sociological or geographical substance to the notion of "community," and in the postmodern era of shifting and multiple identities, it is difficult to see how there can be. Like Middle England, "community" is an unspecific rhetorical construct, and as Benedict Anderson noted some years ago, all communities are by definition to some degree "imagined."[65] Thus regarded, Blair's "community" was virtually identical to Major's "Middle England," though of a slightly pinker hue, appealing to readers of *The Independent* rather than *The Daily Telegraph*.[66] Indeed, as the 1997 general election drew nearer, Blair and his supporters became more interested in defining and seeking the votes of "Middle Britain" than in defining or talking about community. The broader geographical range was appropriate (indeed, essential) for a party heavily dependent on Welsh and Scottish votes. But like "Middle England", "Middle Britain" was largely a rhetorical construct, based on imaginative and collective behavioral stereotyping. The result was two different versions of "the middle" that were offered to the electorate by the party leaders. According to Labour, it was a "constituency of enlightened self-interest, perhaps even altruism, where voters would happily pay more taxes for better schools, hospitals and transport, and more social justice." But according to the Conservatives, Middle Englanders preferred "tax cuts and people to stand on their own two feet." They "looked back fondly on Margaret Thatcher, loathed trades unions, wanted to be tough on crime."[67]

Here were two mutually exclusive versions of what was supposed to be the same social group. But they also had much in common. Both assumed the three-stage model of British society, with "the middle" as the most important. Both were post-Thatcher attempts to talk to and about what they believed to be the middle class, without actually using the dreaded word "class" as a collective social category. And both sought to convey an impression of concern for the middle-class feelings of insecurity and marginalization that had come to the fore during the 1970s and 1980s: the old beleaguered refrain once again.[68] Thus understood, "Middle England," "community," and "Middle Britain" are merely the latest attempts by politicians to persuade the British public to look at the social structure in a particular way. They are the venerable triadic model articulated in a 1990s idiom, and they no more constitute "real social knowledge" than do most politicized forms of social description. And as so often in the past, neither of these essentially political formulations could be easily or consistently related to alternative social visions that both party leaders also pledged themselves to realize: in positive terms, the "classless society" Major sought to create; in negative terms, the "class distinctions" that Blair proclaimed his wish to abolish.[69]

Both the present and past prime ministers are prepared to use the language of class to describe something they think to be bad and want to get rid of, namely, the social order as it now is. For however much it is welcomed (or feared) that deference weakened during the 1960s or the 1980s, there are few today who believe that Britain is yet a "classless society." Most people still see Britain as a class-bound society, sometimes as a traditional hierarchy, sometimes in terms of three basic divisions, sometimes in terms of "us" and "them."[70] What, then, would have to be done to persuade Britons to view their class-bound society in a wholly new way, to remodel (literally) their perceptions of the social structure so that they came to believe that it had become classless? It is not clear whether either Major or Blair has posed or addressed this question. But in order to do so, they would need to break it down into three more manageable areas of inquiry. First, what would a "classless" society look like? Second, what steps would have to be taken to make it possible to persuade Britons to see their society in this new (indeed virtually unprecedented) way? Third, is it realistic to suppose that such a "classless society" can in practice be brought about?

Since there have been inequalities of wealth and power in most societies throughout recorded history, it seems unrealistic to define a "classless" society as one in which these inequalities have been abolished. Instead, it is more plausible to define such a society as one in which the majority of people do not think about the social order in terms of a formal or informal hierarchy, in terms of an upper, middle, and lower class, or in terms of a great divide between "us" and "them." In this sense, the pioneering and prototypical classless society remains the United States of America. Undeniably, there are great—and growing—inequalities of wealth and power in the USA.[71] But these do not translate into corresponding inequalities of social prestige or social perceptions. Unlike the British, Americans do *not* conceive of their society hierarchically. Nor do they think of it triadically, as the overwhelming majority regard themselves as middle class. And nor, therefore, do they think of their society as being fissured in one deep, fundamental way. (Or if they do, it is on the grounds of race, not class.) By comparison with the British, Americans are not interested in the language of class or in the models of society that in Britain that language describes. The result, as Lord Beaverbrook once remarked, is that in the new world, unlike the old, the only difference between the rich and the poor is that the rich have more money.[72] This remains a shrewd insight.

Because it was originally a British colony, the classlessness of the United States is also of some relevance to the second question: how might Britain become a classless society? This may be an extreme over-simplification, but the Americans achieved it in part by abolishing all formal titles during the last quarter of the eighteenth century, in part by spreading themselves out in localized settlements across an entire continent during the nineteenth, and in part by creating the world's most successful and democratic capitalist economy during the twentieth century. It is the combination of these historical, geograph-ical, and economic developments that has produced in the United States that nonhierarchical, nondivided, overwhelmingly "middle-class" nation that remains the closest thing we in the West know to be a "classless" society. And the American experience carries with it important implications for the potential creation of a classless society in Britain. In order to render the hierarchical model of class inapplic-able, the visible manifestations of hierarchy would have to go. This would mean doing more than abolishing the rights of hereditary peers to sit or vote in the House of Lords. It would mean the blanket aboli-tion of titles: not just life peerages and knighthoods but also hereditary peerages and baronetcies.[73] It would also imply doing something about the monarchy, not necessarily abolishing it but certainly making it less of a hierarchical institution and legitimator than it still is at present.

On the basis of the precedent afforded by the United States, this would be the minimum that would required to rid the British of their hierarchical view of themselves. How might they be persuaded to give up on the triadic formulation of upper, middle, and lower class and come to see almost everyone in the nation as belonging to the same middle class? The abolition of titles would, of course, go some way toward eliminating the sense of upper-class separateness. The duke of Westminster would still be a very rich man as the nonducal Mr. Gerald Grosvenor, but he would no longer be an aristocrat. Instead, like Rockefeller or Mellon or Gates, he would be a very wealthy mem-ber of the middle class. There would also need to be a greater cult of self-help and the entrepreneurial virtues than even Thatcher was able to achieve in her attempts to turn Britain into a second United States. And it would also be necessary to rid the working class of what Ernest Bevin famously called their "poverty of expectations" and to reduce the number of those who worked with their hands very substantially. Historically, there has always been a bigger lower class in Britain than in America, just as there has always been a bigger upper class. The plebs as well as the patricians would have to be diminished and downsized, and the middle class correspondingly increased in number, size, and self-regard, so as to become, as in the USA, the only serious and substantial part of society.

These developments would render the tripartite model of British society less credible, as everyone increasingly came to see themselves as part of a massively expanded and reconceptualized middle class. This, in turn, would make it less likely that Britons would continue to think of themselves as a deeply divided society, split between "us" and "them," officers and men, U and non-U, those with accents and those without. But this would not of itself be sufficient to bring about a society whose inhabitants believed themselves to belong to a new, non-traditional, classless meritocracy. For something would also have to be done about education. The division between those who enroll in the state system and those who are educated at fee-paying schools is widely thought to perpetuate and intensify the view that Britain is not one but two nations, characterized by what many believe to be social apartheid.[74] There is much to be said for this view. Yet it remains unclear just how education can be reformed so that it is simultaneously meritocratic and classless. No British government this century has been prepared to tackle this exceptionally complex and contentious question with the courage and imagination it requires. But until it is addressed, it seems safe (and sad) to predict that many people in Britain will continue to describe the nation's social structure as being deeply polarized.

These reforms would be the minimum required to persuade the British to stop thinking about themselves and talking about their society in terms of the three models that are all regularly articulated in the language of class. But is such a "classless society" something the British actually want? A nation that was agog over whether the soon-to-be divorced Princess of Wales should be allowed to retain the honorific "Her Royal Highness" is clearly besotted with class as hierarchy.[75] A nation that could not decide whether John Prescott was right to announce he had left the working class for the middle class is no less preoccupied with class as the three-layered model of society.[76] And a nation that was gripped by the courtroom battle between Imran Khan and Ian Botham, a large part of which was devoted to considering and contrasting their social origins, is equally obsessed with class as "gentlemen versus players."[77] None of these episodes suggests a society in which there is any overwhelming desire to be rid of divisive social distinctions, still less to stop talking about them.[78] Nor has a government yet been elected with the will and the knowledge to take the matter up. For all his talk of a "classless society," John Major did little to match his deeds to his words. Tony Blair has promised to do better. Perhaps he will. But as Disraeli once remarked, Britain is a very difficult country to move.[79]

How We See Ourselves

It has recently been argued that landscape is what culture does to nature: investing the wilderness with shape and significance. This is partly a matter of making and remaking the landscaping itself: of preserving the trees, diverting the rivers, planting the flowers. But it is also the process whereby these trees, rivers, and flowers become invested with meanings and morals and myths, and that process is as much a matter of perception and politics, of language and rhetoric, of feeling and sentiment, as it is the result of the conscious acts of landscaping themselves.[80] By the same token, it has been argued in this book that class is best understood as being what culture does to inequality and social structure: investing the many anonymous individuals and unfathomable collectivities in society with shape and significance by molding our perceptions of the unequal social world we live in. As with landscape, this is partly a matter of the social structure itself, which does change and evolve in terms of numbers, occupation, wealth, and location. But it is also a matter of politics and perceptions, rhetoric and language, feeling and sentiment. And just as the meaning of landscape is often contested, so the meaning of social structure is disputed, not so much in terms of language as in terms of the different models of it that different people employ at different times for different purposes.

The way we see ourselves, the way we see ourselves in society, the way we see the society to which we belong, and the way these things interconnect and change over time: these are complex and important issues that have only recently come to the surface of historical consciousness and inquiry. But when the Prince of Wales feels "a nostalgia for forgotten hierarchies" where "everyone knew their place," when Alan Bennett is skeptical about "the conventional three-tier account of social divisions," and when John Kenneth Galbraith tells us that the great divide in the world today is not between labor and capital but between rich and poor, we ought at least to be able to recognize these views for what they are: not original interpretations but accounts with a very long historical pedigree, and not complete visions of society as it is but different, partial visions of society.[81] As these examples serve to remind us, along with the many others that have been provided throughout these pages, we need to think more carefully about how we think about ourselves as social individuals and as social groups, about how our forebears thought about themselves, and about how our successors might think about themselves. Only then shall we better understand the complexities of the class-bound society that Britain was and is and the obstacles that remain to achieving the classless society that Britain might, should—or shouldn't?—become.

LIST OF ABBREVIATIONS

Since the notes to each chapter constitute what is, in effect, a running bibliography, I have dispensed with a separate list of further reading. In each chapter full references are given with every first citation but abbreviated thereafter. The following abbreviations have been used throughout the notes:

AHR	*American Historical Review*
EcHR	*Economic History Review*
EHR	*English Historical Review*
HJ	*Historical Journal*
HW	*History Workshop*
JBS	*Journal of British Studies*
JMH	*Journal of Modern History*
P&P	*Past and Present*
SH	*Social History*
TRHS	*Transactions of the Royal Historical Society*
WMQ	*William and Mary Quarterly*

NOTES

Most of the publishers mentioned in these notes are located in Great Britain. Those located in the United States are generally identified by city and state, except in the case of big cities (such as New York) or notable centers of learning (such as Princeton). The exception to this last is Cambridge, Mass., which is located within a state to differentiate it from its English counterpart.

PREFACE

1. J. Betjeman, "Beside the Seaside," in *Collected Poems* (London, 1979), p. 163.
2. S. Ringen, "The Open Society and the Closed Mind," *Times Literary Supplement*, 24 January 1997, p. 6.
3. P. N. Furbank, *Unholy Pleasure: The Idea of Social Class* (Oxford, 1985), p. 12.
4. K. V. Thomas, "History and Anthropology," *P&P*, no. 24 (1963), p. 18.
5. A Mori opinion poll conducted on 22 August 1991 concluded by a majority of more than five to one that "there will never be a classless society in Britain" (A. Adonis and S. Pollard, *A Class Act: The Myth of Britain's Classless Society* [London, 1997], pp. 3–4). See also S. Hasler, "Britannia Rules—But She's Still Enslaved to Class," *Sunday Times*, 22 December 1991.
6. J. Cooper, *Class: A View from Middle England* (London, 1993), p. 19.
7. G. Crossick, "From Gentleman to the Residuum: Languages of Social Description in Victorian Britain," in P. Corfield (ed.), *Language, History and Class* (Oxford, 1991), p. 176.
8. R. H. Tawney, *Equality* (London, 1931), pp. 65, 69; A. Marwick, *Class: Image and Reality in Britain, France and the USA since 1930* (London, 1980), p. 54.

1. INTRODUCTION:
   BEYOND CLASS—FORWARD TO CLASS?

1. P. Joyce, *Visions of the People: Industrial England and the Question of Class, 1848–1914* (Cambridge, 1991), pp. 1, 23; J. Alt, "Beyond Class: The Decline of Industrial Labor and Leisure," *Teleos*, 28 (1976), pp. 55–80.
2. A. Adonis and S. Pollard, *A Class Act: The Myth of Britain's Classless Society* (London, 1997), is much the most suggestive recent treatment. For other books explicitly or implicitly concerned with class, see P. Joyce (ed.), *Class* (Oxford, 1995); R. Marris, *How to Save the Underclass* (London, 1996); P. Saunders, *Unequal but Fair? A Study of Class Barriers in Britain* (London, 1996); P. Johnson and H. Reed, *Two Nations? The Inheritance of Poverty and Affluence* (London, 1996); D. J. Lee and B. S. Turner (eds.), *Conflicts About Class* (London, 1996); Lord Bauer, *Class on the Brain: The Cost of a British Obsession* (London, 1997); S. Brook, *Class: Knowing Your Place in Modern Britain* (London, 1997).
3. Quoted in *The Independent on Sunday*, 4 April 1993. See also P. Junor, *The Major Enigma* (London, 1993), pp. 202, 253–54; S. Hasler, "Britannia Rules—But She's Still Enslaved to Class," *Sunday Times*, 22 December 1991.
4. Consider, for example, this (surely incontrovertible) remark by Gabrielle Annan: "Not many English writers can manage a novel in which class is not an issue at all" ("Only the Drop," *London Review of Books*, 17 October 1996, p. 16).
5. K. Marx and F. Engels, *Manifesto of the Communist Party* (New York, 1964), p. 2, quoted in R. J. Morris, *Class and Class Consciousness in the Industrial Revolution, 1780–1850* (London, 1979), p. 10; M. Thatcher, "Don't Undo My Work," *Newsweek*, 27 April 1992, p. 37.
6. "Held sway" but was never totally dominant. For the survival of an alternative, more conservative tradition that stressed hierarchy and subordination, rather than class and conflict, as the key themes in the British past, see M. Taylor, "The Beginnings of Modern British Social History?" *HW*, no. 43 (1997), pp. 155–76.
7. Marx's thought on these subjects was neither systematic nor consistent and, as one scholar has observed, "any historian who wishes to come to grips with Marx's concepts of class and class consciousness in order to refute or substantiate either or both through empirical inquiry must familiarise himself with the whole corpus of Marx's writings" (R. S. Neale, *Class in English History, 1680–1850* [Oxford, 1981], p. 46). The literature on Marx and class is vast. See especially A. Giddens, *The Class*

Structure of the Advanced Societies, 2d ed. (London, 1981); P. Calvert, *The Concept of Class: An Historical Introduction* (London, 1982); F. Parkin, *Marxism and Class Theory: A Bourgeois Critique* (New York, 1979).

8. L. Stone, *The Causes of the English Revolution, 1529–1642* (London, 1972), p. 33.

9. K. Marx, *The Eighteenth Brumaire of Louis Bonaparte* (New York, 1963), p. 124; K. Marx and F. Engels, *The German Ideology* (New York, 1947), pp. 48–49.

10. J. R. Vincent, *Pollbooks: How Victorians Voted* (Cambridge, 1967), pp. 27–28.

11. S. R. Szreter, "The Genesis of the Registrar-General's Social Classification of Occupations," *British Journal of Sociology*, 35 (1984), pp. 522–46; J. H. Goldthorpe and P. Bevan, "The Study of Social Stratification in Great Britain, 1946–76," *Social Science Information*, 16 (1977), pp. 279–334; G. Marshall, H. Newby, D. Rose, and C. Vogler, *Social Class in Modern Britain* (London, 1988); W. G. Runciman, "How Many Classes Are There in Contemporary British Society?" *Sociology*, 29 (1990), pp. 377–96; G. Marshall and J. Goldthorpe, "The Promising Future of Class Analysis," *Sociology*, 26 (1992), pp. 381–400; R. E. Pahl, "Does Class Analysis Without Class Theory Have a Promising Future? A Reply to Goldthorpe and Marshall," *Sociology*, 27 (1993), pp. 253–58.

12. For two recent studies along these lines, see A. Walder, "The Re-Making of the Chinese Working Class, 1949–1981," *Modern China*, 10 (1984), pp. 3–48; I. Katznelson and A. R. Zolberg (eds.), *Working-Class Formation: Nineteenth-Century Patterns in Western Europe and the United States* (Princeton, 1986).

13. For two recent discussions (and revivals?) of this term, see P. Anderson, "The Notion of Bourgeois Revolution," in *English Questions* (London, 1992), pp. 105–18; R. Brenner, "Bourgeois Revolution and Transition to Capitalism," in A. L. Beier, D. Cannadine, and J. M. Rosenheim (eds.), *The First Modern Society: Essays in English History in Honour of Lawrence Stone* (Cambridge, 1989), pp. 271–304.

14. In *The Communist Manifesto*, Marx and Engels predicted that the imminent proletarian revolution would overthrow the "old conditions of production" and would thus "have swept away the condition for the existence of class antagonisms, and of classes generally, and will thereby have abolished its own supremacy as a class. In place of the old bourgeois society, with its classes and class antagonisms, we shall have an association in which the free development of each is the condition for the free development of all" (p. 41).

15. This interpretation is most famously associated with the work of two historians: R. H. Tawney, "The Rise of the Gentry, 1558–1640," *EcHR*, II (1941), pp. 1–38; and C. Hill, *The English Revolution of 1640* (London, 1940), *The Century of Revolution, 1603–1714* (London, 1961). See also P. Zagorin, "The Social Interpretation of the English Revolution," *Journal of Economic History*, 19 (1959), pp. 376–401; L. Stone, *Social Change and Revolution in England, 1540–1640* (London, 1965); idem, *Causes of the English Revolution*, pp. 26–48; R. C. Richardson, *The Debate on the English Revolution Revisited* (London, 1988), pp. 98–133.

16. J. H. Plumb, *The Growth of Political Stability in England, 1675–1725* (London, 1967); E. P. Thompson, "Eighteenth-Century English Society: Class Struggle Without Class?" *SH*, 3 (1978), p. 162.

17. The depiction of the industrial revolution as the "great transformation" between the premodern and modern worlds can be found in W. W. Rostow, *The Stages of Economic Growth: A Non-Communist Manifesto* (Cambridge, 1960); P. Mathias, *The First Industrial Nation: An Economic History of Britain, 1700–1914* (London, 1969); D. S. Landes, *The Unbound Prometheus: Technological Change and Industrial Development in Western Europe from 1750 to the Present* (Cambridge, 1969); E. J. Hobsbawm, *Industry and Empire: From 1750 to the Present Day* (Harmondsworth, 1969). This phase in the historiography of the industrial revolution is discussed in D. Cannadine, "The Present and the Past in the English Industrial Revolution, 1880–1980," *P&P*, no. 103 (1984), pp. 149–59.

18. E. P. Thompson, *The Making of the English Working Class* (Harmondsworth, 1968); A. Briggs, *The Age of Improvement, 1783–1867* (London, 1959); idem, "Middle-Class Consciousness in English Politics, 1780–1846," *P&P*, no. 9 (1956), pp. 65–74; H. J. Perkin, *The Origins of Modern English Society, 1780–1880* (London, 1969); E. J. Hobsbawm, *Labouring Men: Studies in the History of Labour* (London, 1964).

19. E. J. Hobsbawm, *The Age of Capital, 1848–1875* (London, 1975). This is, inevitably, a much oversimplified account. Throughout the 1960s, a fierce and acrimonious debate raged among English Marxists as to whether the bourgeoisie was or was not dominant in mid-nineteenth-century Britain, a debate, incidentally, that reflected Marx's own uncertainty in the matter. See especially P. Anderson, "Origins of the Present Crisis," *New Left Review*, no. 23 (1964), pp. 26–51; E. P. Thompson, "The Peculiarities of the English," in R. Miliband and J. Saville (eds.), *The Socialist Register, 1965* (London, 1965), pp. 311–62; P. Anderson, *Arguments Within English Marxism* (London, 1980), passim; idem, *Eng-*

lish Questions, pp. 122–28.

20. A. Briggs (ed.), *Chartist Studies* (London, 1958); D. Thompson (ed.), *The Early Chartists* (London, 1971); J. F. C. Harrison, *The Early Victorians, 1832–51* (London, 1971); J. Foster, *Class Struggle and the Industrial Revolution: Early Industrial Capitalism in Three English Towns* (London, 1974); D. Jones, *Chartism and the Chartists* (London, 1975).

21. The literature on the laboring aristocracy thesis is vast. See especially E. J. Hobsbawm, "The Labour Aristocracy," in *Labouring Men*, pp. 272–315; idem, "Artisan or Labour Aristocrat," *EcHR*, 2d ser., 37 (1984), pp. 355–72; idem, "The Aristocracy of Labour Reconsidered," in *Worlds of Labour: Further Studies in the History of Labour* (London, 1984), pp. 227–51; A. E. Musson, "Class Struggle and the Labour Aristocracy, 1830–1860," *SH*, 1 (1976), pp. 335–56; H. F. Moorhouse, "The Marxist Theory of the Labour Aristocracy," *SH*, 3 (1978), pp. 61–82; A. J. Reid, "Politics and Economics in the Formation of the British Working Class," *SH*, 3 (1978), pp. 347–56; R. Q. Gray, *The Labour Aristocracy in Victorian England* (Oxford, 1976); idem, *The Aristocracy of Labour in Nineteenth-Century Britain, c. 1850–1914* (London, 1981); G. J. Crossick, *An Artisan Elite in Victorian Society: Kentish London, 1840–1880* (London, 1978).

22. The pioneering works here, which stressed the deeply rooted social divisions in Britain from the 1880s to 1914, were R. C. K. Ensor, "Some Political and Economic Interactions in Later Victorian England," *TRHS*, 4th ser., 31 (1949), pp. 17–28; G. Dangerfield, *The Strange Death of Liberal England* (London, 1935). For more recent work, built around the concept of deepening class divisions, see P. F. Clarke, "Electoral Sociology of Modern Britain," *History*, 57 (1972), pp. 31–55; H. J. Perkin, "Land Reform and Class Conflict in Victorian Britain," in *The Structured Crowd: Essays in Social History* (Brighton, 1981), pp. 100–135; idem, *The Rise of Professional Society: England Since 1880* (London, 1989), pp. 62–115, 171–85; E. J. Hobsbawm, "The Formation of British Working Class Culture" and "The Making of the Working Class, 1870–1914," both in *Worlds of Labour*, pp. 176–213; G. Stedman Jones, *Outcast London: A Study in the Relations Between Classes in Victorian Society* (Harmondsworth, 1976); idem, "Working-Class Culture and Working-Class Politics in London, 1870–1900: Notes on the Re-Making of a Working Class," in *Languages of Class: Studies in English Working-Class History, 1832–1982* (Cambridge, 1983), pp. 179–238; S. Meacham, *A Life Apart: The English Working Class, 1890–1914* (London, 1977). For a useful recent summary of this class-based interpretation, see J. Belchem,

Class, Party and the Political System in Britain, 1867–1914 (London, 1990), esp. pp. 1–6.

23. H. Pelling and A. J. Reid, *A Short History of the Labour Party*, 11th ed. (London, 1996), pp. 39–40; J. Klugmann, *History of the Communist Party of Great Britain*, vol. 2, *The General Strike, 1925–1926* (London, 1969); M. Morris, *The General Strike* (Harmondsworth, 1976); J. Skelley (ed.), *The General Strike, 1926* (London, 1976); N. Branson, *Britain in the Nineteen Twenties* (London, 1976); M. Crick, *Scargill and the Miners* (London, 1985); A. Callinicos and M. Simons, *The Great Strike: The Miners' Strike of 1984–5 and Its Lessons* (London, 1985); D. Reed and O. Adamson, *Miners' Strike, 1984–5: People Versus State* (London, 1985); M. Adney and J. Lloyd, *The Miners' Strike: Loss without Limit* (London, 1986).

24. But see the alternative tradition explored in Taylor, "Modern British Social History?" pp. 155–76.

25. Consider Morris's statement in *Class and Class Consciousness*: "Marx still dominates" (p. 10).

26. G. Lefebvre, *The Coming of the French Revolution, 1789* (Princeton, 1947); idem, *The French Revolution* 2 vols. (New York, 1962–64); A. Soboul, *The French Revolution, 1787–1799* (London, 1974); idem, *A Short History of the French Revolution, 1789–1799* (London, 1977). For a helpful survey, see G. Ellis, "The 'Marxist Interpretation' of the French Revolution," *EHR*, 93 (1978), pp. 353–76.

27. S. R. Ross, *Francisco I. Madero: Apostle of American Democracy* (New York, 1955); C. C. Cumberland, *The Mexican Revolution: Genesis Under Madero* (Austin, 1952); J. Womack, *Zapata and the Mexican Revolution* (New York, 1968); J. M. Hart, *Revolutionary Mexico* (Berkeley, CA, 1987); A. Knight, "Revisionism and Revolution: Mexico Compared to England and France," *P&P*, no. 134 (1992), pp. 158–65.

28. D. Koenker, *Moscow Workers and the 1917 Revolution* (Princeton, 1981); S. A. Smith, *Red Petrograd: Revolution in the Factories, 1917–1918* (Cambridge, 1983); D. Raleigh, *Revolution on the Volga: 1917 in Saratov* (Ithaca, NY, 1986); R. G. Suny, *The Baku Commune, 1917–1918: Class and Nationality in the Russian Revolution* (Princeton, 1972); idem, "Toward a Social History of the October Revolution," *AHR*, 88 (1983), pp. 31–52.

29. Interestingly enough, and despite Marx's original insight that it was bourgeois, the American Revolution was explained much more in terms of ideology than of class. See R. B. Morris, "Class Struggle and the American Revolution," *WMQ*, 3d ser., 19 (1962), pp. 3–29; B. Bailyn, *The Ideological Origins of the American Revolution* (Cambridge, MA, 1967).

30. D. Thompson, "Nineteenth-Century Hidden Agendas," *History Today*, February 1992, pp. 45–48; B. Palmer, "Is There Now, or Has There Ever Been, a Working Class?" *History Today*, March 1992, pp. 51–54; R. Price, "Historiography, Narrative and the Nineteenth Century," *JBS*, 35 (1996), pp. 220–56; J. Thompson, "After the Fall: Class and Political Language in Britain, 1780–1900," *HJ*, 39 (1996), pp. 785–806; C. Kent, "Victorian Social History: Post-Thompson, Post-Foucault, Post-Modern," *Victorian Studies*, 11 (1996), pp. 97–134.

31. This more nuanced interpretation of recent British economic history may be found in such works as P. L. Payne, *British Entrepreneurship in the Nineteenth Century* (London, 1978); R. Samuel, "The Workshop of the World: Steam Power and Hand Technology in Mid-Victorian Britain," *HW*, no. 3 (1977), pp. 6–72; A. E. Musson, *The Growth of British Industry* (London, 1978); R. C. Floud and D. N. McCloskey (eds.), *The Economic History of Britain since 1700*, 2 vols. (Cambridge, 1981); M. J. Weiner, *English Culture and the Decline of the Industrial Spirit, 1850–1980* (London, 1981). For a discussion of this "limits to growth" interpretation of British economic history for the period 1750 to 1850, see Cannadine, "Present and the Past," pp. 159–67.

32. For some suggestive ideas, see W. H. Sewell, Jr., "How Classes Are Made: Critical Reflections on E. P. Thompson's Theory of Working-Class Formation," in H. J. Kaye and K. McClelland (eds.), *E. P. Thompson: Critical Perspectives* (Philadelphia, 1990), pp. 50–77.

33. There is an extensive literature on aristocratic involvement in nonagricultural enterprises. See especially J. T. Ward and R. G. Wilson (eds.), *Land and Industry: The Landed Estate and the Industrial Revolution* (Newton Abbot, 1971); D. Cannadine, *Lords and Landlords: The Aristocracy and the Towns, 1774–1967* (Leicester, 1980), part 1; J. V. Beckett, *The Aristocracy in England, 1660–1914* (Oxford, 1986), part 2. The debate on purchases of landed estates by middle-class businessmen and professionals is still running. For the most recent contributions, see W. D. Rubinstein, "New Men of Wealth and the Purchase of Land in Nineteenth-Century Britain," *P&P*, no. 92 (1981), pp. 125–47; L. Stone and J. C. F. Stone, *An Open Elite? England, 1540–1880* (Oxford, 1984); D. Spring, "Social Mobility and the English Landed Elite," *Canadian Journal of History*, 21 (1986), pp. 333–51; F. M. L. Thompson, "Life After Death: How Successful Nineteenth-Century Businessmen Disposed of Their Fortunes," *EcHR*, 2d ser., 43 (1990), pp. 40–61; W. D. Rubinstein, "Cutting Up Rich: A Reply to F. M. L. Thompson," *EcHR*, 2d ser., 45 (1992), pp. 350–61; F. M. L. Thompson, "Stitching It Together

Again," *EcHR*, 2d ser., 45 (1992), pp. 362–75.

34. W. D. Rubinstein, *Men of Property: The Very Wealthy in Britain Since the Industrial Revolution* (London, 1981); G. Ingham, *Capitalism Divided? The City and Industry in Britain's Social Development* (London, 1984); G. R. Searle, *Entrepreneurial Politics in Mid-Victorian Great Britain* (Oxford, 1993), esp. pp. 1–16; E. H. H. Green, "Rentiers Versus Producers? The Political Economy of the Bimetallic Controversy, c. 1880–1898," *EHR*, 103 (1988), pp. 588–612; R. Harrison and J. Zeitlin (eds.), *Divisions of Labour: Skilled Workers and Technological Change in Nineteenth-Century England* (London, 1985); A. J. Mayer, "The Lower Middle Class as an Historical Problem," *JMH*, 47 (1975), pp. 409–31; G. Crossick (ed.), *The Lower Middle Class in Britain, 1870–1914* (London, 1977); G. Holmes, *Augustan England: Professions, State and Society, 1680–1730* (London, 1982); W. J. Reader, *Professional Men: The Rise of the Professional Classes in Nineteenth-Century England* (London, 1966); H. J. Perkin, *The Rise of Professional Society: England Since 1880* (London, 1989); P. Horn, *The Rise and Fall of the Victorian Servant* (London, 1975); T. McBride, *The Domestic Revolution: The Modernisation of Household Service in England and France, 1820–1920* (London, 1976).

35. L. Stone, *The Crisis of the Aristocracy, 1558–1641* (Oxford, 1965); J. A. Cannon, *Aristocratic Century: The Peerage in Eighteenth-Century England* (Cambridge, 1984); F. M. L. Thompson, *English Landed Society in the Nineteenth Century* (London, 1963); A. J. Mayer, *The Persistence of the Old Regime: Europe to the Civil War* (London, 1981).

36. R. I. McKibbin, "Why Was There No Marxism in Great Britain?" in *The Ideologies of Class: Social Relations in Britain, 1880–1950* (Oxford, 1990), pp. 1–41; A. J. Reid, "Class and Organisation," *HJ*, 30 (1987), pp. 225–38; idem, *Social Classes and Social Relations in Britain, 1850–1914* (Cambridge, 1995).

37. P. Earle, *The Making of the English Middle Class: Business, Society and Family Life in London, 1660–1730* (London, 1989); R. J. Morris, *Class, Sect and Party: The Making of the British Middle Class: Leeds, 1820–50* (Manchester, 1990); M. J. Weiner, *English Culture and the Decline of the Industrial Spirit, 1850–1980* (Cambridge, 1981); C. Jones, *International Business in the Nineteenth Century: The Rise and Fall of a Cosmopolitan Bourgeoisie* (London, 1987); D. Gunn, "The 'Failure' of the Victorian Middle Class: A Critique," in J. Seed and J. Wolff (eds.), *The Culture of Capital: Art, Power and the Nineteenth-Century Middle Class* (Manchester, 1988), pp. 17–39. See also J. H. Hexter, "The Myth of the Middle Class in Tudor England," in *Reappraisals in History* (London, 1961), pp.

71–116. For a sympathetic reappraisal of this reappraisal, see J. Barry, introduction to J. Barry and C. Brooks (eds.), *The Middling Sort of People: Culture, Society and Politics in England, 1550–1800* (London, 1994), pp. 1–2, 6–11.

38. Thompson, *Making of the English Working Class*, p. 11; idem, "Eighteenth-Century English Society," pp. 146–50. The fullest recent treatment of this subject is in P. Joyce (ed.), *Historical Meanings of Work* (Cambridge, 1987).

39. R. W. Malcolmson, *Popular Recreations in English Society, 1700–1850* (Cambridge, 1973); P. Bailey, *Leisure and Class in Victorian England: Rational Recreation and the Conflict for Control, 1830–1885* (London, 1978); H. Cunningham, *Leisure in the Industrial Revolution, 1780–1880* (London, 1980); B. Fine and E. Leopold, "Consumption and the Industrial Revolution," *SH*, 15 (1990), pp. 151–79; L. Tiersten, "Redefining Consumer Culture: Recent Literature on Consumption and the Bourgeoisie in Western Europe," *Radical History Review*, no. 57 (1993), pp. 116–59; G. Stedman Jones, "Class Expression Versus Social Control: A Critique of Recent Trends in the Social History of 'Leisure,'" in *Languages of Class*, pp. 76–89; F. M. L. Thompson, "Social Control in Victorian Britain," *EcHR*, 2d ser., 31 (1981), pp. 189–208; M. A. Simpson and T. H. Lloyd (eds.), *Middle-Class Housing in Britain* (Newton Abbot, 1977); M. J. Daunton, *Housing and Home in the Victorian City: Working-Class Housing, 1850–1914* (London, 1983); D. Cannadine, "Residential Differentiation in Nineteenth-Century Towns: From Shapes on the Ground to Shapes in Society," in J. H. Johnson and C. G. Pooley (eds.), *The Structure of Nineteenth-Century Cities* (London, 1982), pp. 235–52; R. Dennis, *English Industrial Cities of the Nineteenth Century* (Cambridge, 1984), pp. 186–249.

40. Stone, *Causes of the English Revolution*, pp. 26–43; L. J. Colley, *In Defiance of Oligarchy: The Tory Party, 1714–1760* (Cambridge, 1982), pp. 3–10, 15–16; Perkin, *Origins of Modern English Society*, pp. 315–16.

41. R. T. Mackenzie and A. Silver, *Angels in Marble: Working-Class Conservatives in Urban England* (London, 1968); E. A. Nordlinger, *The Working-Class Tories: Authority, Deference and Stable Democracy* (London, 1967); R. Price, *An Imperial War and the British Working Class: Working-Class Attitudes and Reactions to the Boer War, 1899–1902* (London, 1972).

42. J. Harris, *Private Lives, Public Spirit: A Social History of Britain, 1870–1914* (Oxford, 1993), p. 8; D. Tanner, *Political Change and the Labour Party, 1900–18* (Cambridge, 1990), pp. 10–16.

43. J. L. Newton, M. P. Ryan, and J. R. Walkowitz (eds.), *Sex and Class in*

Women's History (London, 1983); J. Kelly, *Women, History, and Theory* (Chicago, 1984); L. Davidoff and C. Hall, *Family Fortunes: Men and Women of the English Middle Class, 1780–1850* (London, 1987); J. Lown, *Women and Industrialization: Gender at Work in Nineteenth-Century England* (London, 1990); J. Lawrence, "Class and Gender in the Making of Urban Toryism, 1880–1914," *EHR*, 108 (1993), pp. 629–52; A. Clark, *The Struggle for the Breeches: Gender and the Making of the British Working Class* (London, 1995). For critiques of Davidoff and Hall, see A. Vickery, "Golden Age to Separate Spheres? A Review of the Categories and Chronology of English Women's History," *HJ*, 36 (1993), pp. 383–414; D. Wahrman, " 'Middle Class' Domesticity Goes Public: Gender, Class and Politics from Queen Caroline to Queen Victoria," *JBS*, 32 (1993), pp. 396–432.

44. S. Alexander, "Women, Class and Sexual Differences in the 1830s and 1840s: Some Reflections on the Writing of a Feminist History," *HW*, no. 17 (1984), pp. 133–49; J. W. Scott, *Gender and the Politics of History* (New York, 1988), esp. chs. 2, 3, and 4; K. Canning, "Gender and the Politics of Class Formation: Rethinking German Labor History," *AHR*, 97 (1992), pp. 736–68.

45. R. Rorty (ed.), *The Linguistic Turn: Recent Essays in Philosophical Method* (London, 1967); Stedman Jones, *Languages of Class*; R. Porter and P. Burke (eds.), *The Social History of Language* (Cambridge, 1987); P. Schoffler, "Historians and Discourse Analysis," *HW*, no. 17 (1989), pp. 37–65; P. Corfield (ed.), *Language, History and Class* (Oxford, 1991); R. Samuel, "Reading the Signs," *HW*, no. 32 (1991), pp. 88–109; L. Berlanstein (ed.), *Re-Thinking Labor History: Essays on Discourse and Class Analysis* (Urbana-Champaign, IL, 1993); Joyce, *Visions of the People*; idem, *Democratic Subjects: The Self and the Social in Nineteenth-Century England* (Cambridge, 1994).

46. Z. Lockman, "Imagining the Working Class: Culture, Nationalism, and Class Formation in Egypt, 1899–1914," *Poetics Today*, 15 (1994), pp. 157–90.

47. This is an excessively simplified summary of an extremely complex and controversial literature. The debates and disagreements may be followed—though not always clarified—in R. Gray, "The Deconstruction of the English Working Class," *SH*, 11 (1986), pp. 363–73; N. Kirk, "In Defence of Class: A Critique of Recent Revisionist Writing Upon the Nineteenth-Century English Working Class," *International Review of Social History*, 32 (1987), pp. 2–47; B. D. Palmer, *Descent into Discourse: The Reification of Language and the Writing of Social History* (Philadel-

phia, 1990); D. Mayfield and S. Thorne, "Social History and Its Discontents: Gareth Stedman Jones and the Politics of Language," *SH*, 17 (1992), pp. 165–87; J. Lawrence and M. Taylor, "The Poverty of Protest: Gareth Stedman Jones and the Politics of Language—A Reply," *SH*, 18 (1993), pp. 1–18; P. Joyce, "The Imaginary Discontents of Social History: A Note of Response to Mayfield and Thorne," *SH*, 18 (1993), pp. 81–85; J. Vernon, "Who's Afraid of the Linguistic Turn? The Politics of Social History and Its Discontents," *SH*, 19 (1994), pp. 81–87; P. Joyce, "The End of Social History?" *SH*, 20 (1995), pp. 74–91. See also the debate, initiated by Lawrence Stone, on "History and Postmodernism," in *P&P*, no. 131 (1991), pp. 217–18; no. 133 (1991), pp. 204–13; no. 135 (1992), pp. 189–208.

48. G. Eley and K. Nield, "Why Does Social History Ignore Politics?" *SH*, 5 (1980), pp. 249–71; T. Judt, "A Clown in Regal Purple: Social History and the Historians," *HW*, no. 7 (1979), pp. 66–94; S. Hochstadt, "Social History and Politics: A Materialist View," *SH*, 7 (1982), pp. 75–83.

49. See, for instance, M. Sonenscher's review of Katznelson and Zolberg, *Working-Class Formation*, in *SH*, 13 (1988), pp. 385–88, where teleology is detected.

50. S. Schama, *Citizens: A Chronicle of the French Revolution* (London, 1989), p. xvi. For one brave attempt to revive a master narrative of class formation and class conflict, albeit as a local study, see T. Koditschek, *Class Formation and Urban Industrial Society: Bradford, 1750–1850* (Cambridge, 1990).

51. E. J. Hobsbawm, *The Forward March of Labour Halted?* (London, 1981); G. Stedman Jones, "Why Is the Labour Party in a Mess?" in *Languages of Class*, pp. 239–56; D. Milband, *Reinventing the Left* (London, 1995); E. Shaw (ed.), *The Labour Party Since 1979: Crisis and Transformation* (London, 1995). For a work on the seventeenth century, with obvious contemporary resonances, see C. Hill, *The Experience of Defeat: Milton and Some Contemporaries* (London, 1984).

52. P. Jenkins, "Goodbye to All That," *New York Review of Books*, 14 May 1992, pp. 16–17; H. Young, "Only Blair Dares to Admit the Good Old Days Are Gone," *The Guardian*, 16 June 1994. For Blair's explicit rejection of Marxism, see A. Blair, *New Britain: My Vision of a Young Country* (London, 1996), pp. 30, 38, 58–59; J. Sopel, *Tony Blair: The Moderniser* (London, 1995), p. 3; A. Blair, *Socialism* Fabian Pamphlet no. 565 (London, 1994), pp. 2–3; P. Mandelson and R. Liddle, *The Blair Revolution: Can New Labour Deliver?* (London, 1996), p. 29.

53. Blair, *New Britain*, pp. 51–56; T. Rogaly, "Blair's Community Spirit," *Fi-*

nancial Times, 18 March 1995; K. Brown, "Socialist Leader Woos Middle Classes," *Financial Times*, 24 March 1995; G. Kelly, "Off the Shelf Sociology," *Times Higher Education Supplement*, 24 March 1995, p. 21; A. Etzioni, *The Spirit of Community: Rights, Responsibilities, and the Communitarian Agenda* (New York, 1993); Pelling and Reid, *Short History of the Labour Party*, pp. 189–92. For a fuller discussion of Blair, see Major, Blair, and Beyond, in chapter 5, below.

54. This is discussed more fully in "The Impact of Thatcher," in chapter five, below.

55. S. Collini, "Badly Connected: The Passionate Intensity of Cultural Studies," *Victorian Studies*, 36 (1993), pp. 455–60. I have found the following particularly helpful on the demise of Communism: B. Fowkes, *The Rise and Fall of Communism in Eastern Europe* (New York, 1993); D. S. Mason, *Revolution in East-Central Europe: The Rise and Fall of Communism and the Cold War* (Boulder, CO, 1992); P. Cipkowski, *Revolution in Eastern Europe: Understanding the Collapse of Communism in Poland, Hungary, East Germany, Czechoslovakia, Romania, and the Soviet Union* (New York, 1991); D. Pryce-Jones, *The War that Never Was: The Fall of the Soviet Empire, 1985–1991* (London, 1995); R. Skidelsky, *The World After Communism: A Polemic For Our Times* (London, 1995).

56. For the fall of Marxism, see A. Yakovlev, *The Fate of Marxism in Russia* (New Haven, 1993); J. H. Moore (ed.), *Legacies of the Collapse of Marxism* (Fairfax, VA, 1994); R. Aronson, *After Marxism* (New York, 1995); A. Callari, S. Cullenberg, and C. Biewener, *Marxism in the Post-Modern Age* (New York, 1995). See also P. Curry, "Towards a Post-Marxist Social History: Thompson, Clark and Beyond," in A. Wilson (ed.), *Rethinking Social History: English Society 1570–1920 and Its Interpretation* (Manchester, 1993): "The whole tradition dominated and inspired by the October Revolution has now come to an end" (p. 171).

57. Revisionist work on the French Revolution is extensive. Among the most famous and influential books are A. Cobban, *The Myth of the French Revolution* (London, 1955); idem, *The Social Interpretation of the French Revolution* (London, 1964); W. Doyle, *Origins of the French Revolution* (Oxford, 1980); idem, *The Oxford History of the French Revolution* (Oxford, 1989); W. H. Sewell, *Work and Revolution in France: The Language of Labour from the Old Regime to 1848* (Cambridge, 1980); F. Furet, *Interpreting the French Revolution* (London, 1981); T. C. W. Blanning, *The French Revolution: Aristocrats Versus Bourgeois?* (London, 1987); L. Hunt, *Politics, Culture and Class in the French Revolution* (London, 1986). For modifications and restatements of the earlier social in-

terpretation, see G. C. Comninel, *Rethinking the French Revolution: Marxism and the Revisionist Challenge* (London, 1987); E. J. Hobsbawm, *Echoes of the Marseillaise: Two Centuries Look Back on the French Revolution* (London, 1990); C. Jones, "Bourgeois Revolution Revivified: 1789 and Social Change," in C. Lucas (ed.), *Rewriting the French Revolution* (Oxford, 1991), pp. 69–118. The fullest recent summary of these historiographical developments is in T. C. W. Blanning (ed.), *The Rise and Fall of the French Revolution* (London, 1996).

58. R. Ruiz, *The Great Rebellion: Mexico, 1905–1924* (New York, 1980); P. V. N. Hendersson, *Felix Diaz, the Porfirians, and the Mexican Revolution* (Lincoln, NE, 1981); P. Vanderwood, *Disorder and Progress: Bandits, Police, and Mexican Development* (Lincoln, NE, 1991); Knight, "Revisionism and Revolution," pp. 165–79; idem, "The Mexican Revolution: Bourgeois? Nationalist? Or Just a 'Great Rebellion'?" *Bulletin of Latin American Research*, 4 (1985), pp. 1–37.

59. L. H. Haimson, "The Problem of Social Identities in Early Twentieth-Century Russia," *Slavic Review*, 47 (1988), pp. 1–20; E. Acton, *Rethinking the Russian Revolution* (London, 1990); R. Pipes, *The Russian Revolution* (New York, 1990); R. G. Suny, "Revision and Retreat in the Historiography of 1917: Soviet History and Its Critics," *Russian Review*, 53 (1994), pp. 165–82; L. H. Siegelbaum and R. G. Suny, "Class Backwards? In Search of the Soviet Working Class," in L. H. Siegelbaum and R. G. Suny (eds.), *Making Workers Soviet: Power, Class, and Identity* (Ithaca, NY, 1994), pp. 1–26; O. Figes, *A People's Tragedy: The Russian Revolution, 1891–1924* (London, 1997).

60. P. M. Kennedy, *The Rise and Fall of the Great Powers: Economic Change and Military Conflict from 1500 to 2000* (London, 1988), esp. pp. xv–xxv.

61. W. G. Runciman, *A Treatise on Social Theory*, vol. 2, *Substantive Social Theory* (Cambridge, 1989), pp. 47–48, 181, 416. I am much indebted for this formulation to an unpublished paper by G. Stedman Jones, "The Rise and Fall of 'Class Struggle': Middle Class and Bourgeoisie, 1789–1850." A postmodern, postsocialist, postcommunist Marx has yet to emerge. No doubt he will appear before too long.

62. W. Reddy, *Money and Liberty in Europe: A Critique of Historical Understanding* (New York, 1987), pp. 30–31; idem, "The Concept of Class," in M. L. Bush (ed.), *Social Orders and Social Classes in Europe Since 1500: Studies in Social Stratification* (London, 1992), pp. 13–25. For the counterargument that "talk of its [i.e., class's] death is greatly exaggerated," see H. Benyon, "Class and Historical Explanation," in Bush, *Social Orders and Social Classes*, p. 249.

63. This is the general argument advanced in both McKibbin, *Ideologies of Class*, and Reid, *Social Classes*.

64. Jenkins, "Goodbye to All That," pp. 16–17; Curry, "Towards a Post-Marxist Social History," pp. 158–200. For dissenting views reasserting the continued importance, both historical and contemporary, of class (in a Marxist sense) and the class struggle, see E. M. Wood, *The Retreat from Class* (London, 1986); N. Geras, "Post Marxism?" *New Left Review*, no. 163 (1987), pp. 40–82; N. Kirk (ed.), *Social Class and Marxism: Defences and Challenges* (Aldershot, 1996); E. O. Wright (ed.), *Class Counts: Comparative Studies in Class Analysis* (Cambridge, 1997).

65. F. M. L. Thompson (ed.), *The Cambridge Social History of Britain, 1750–1950* 3 vols. (Cambridge, 1990). See also idem, *The Rise of Respectable Society: A Social History of Victorian Britain, 1830–1900* (London, 1988), as well as the following (mildly skeptical) reviews and discussions D. Cannadine, "The Way We Lived Then," *Times Literary Supplement*, 7 September 1990, pp. 934–35; P. Addison, "Dismantling the Class War," *London Review of Books*, 25 July 1991, pp. 12–13; G. Crossick, "Consensus, Order and the Social History of Modern Britain," *HJ*, 35 (1992), pp. 945–51; T. Koditschek, "A Tale of Two Thompsons," *Radical History Review*, no. 56 (1993), pp. 68–84. See also (and compare with his remarks quoted in note 25, above) R. J. Morris, "Class," in J. Cannon (ed.), *The Oxford Companion to British History* (Oxford, 1997): "Social class has lost its privileged position in the narrative of British social history" (p. 217).

66. C. Hill, "A Bourgeois Revolution?" in J. G. A. Pocock (ed.), *Three British Revolutions* (Princeton, 1980), pp. 109–39. See L. Stone, "The Bourgeois Revolution of Seventeenth-Century England Revisited," *P&P*, no. 109 (1985), pp. 44–54. See also A. McInnes, "When Was the English Revolution?" *History*, 67 (1982), pp. 377–92; B. Coward, "Was There an English Revolution in the Middle of the Seventeenth Century?" in C. Jones, M. Newitt, and S. Roberts (eds.), *Politics and People in Revolutionary England* (Oxford, 1986), pp. 9–40; C. S. R. Russell, *Unrevolutionary England* (London, 1990); J. S. Morrill, *The Nature of the English Revolution* (London, 1993). For attempts to modify and rehabilitate the concept, see B. Manning, *The English People and the English Revolution* (London, 1988); G. Eley and W. Hunt (eds.), *Reviving the English Revolution* (London, 1988); R. Brenner, *Merchants and Revolution: Commercial Change, Political Conflict, and London Overseas Traders, 1550–1653* (Princeton, NJ, 1993), esp. pp. 638–716.

67. E. J. Hobsbawm, *Nations and Nationalism Since 1780: Programme, Myth,*

Reality, 2d ed. (Cambridge, 1992); idem, *The Age of Extremes: The Short Twentieth Century* (London, 1994); E. P. Thompson, "The Making of a Ruling Class," *Dissent*, summer 1993, p. 380. For studies of Hill, Thompson, Hobsbawm, and others that implicitly recognize that they are no longer setting the scholarly agenda, see H. J. Kaye, *The British Marxist Historians* (Oxford, 1984); R. Samuel, "British Marxist Historians, 1880–1980," *New Left Review*, no. 120 (1980), pp. 42–55. For Hobsbawm's recent reflections on Marxism, see *On Historians* (London, 1997).

68. Some (perhaps most) sociologists are convinced that "class still matters," that it is "still the most common source of social identity," that "the class structure itself remains an obvious feature of life in late twentieth-century Britain," that "modern Britain is a society shaped predominantly by class," and that "classes have not withered away, and class identities exert a powerful influence on electoral choice" (Marshall et al., *Social Class in Modern Britain*, pp. 137, 143, 147, 183, 248). But the rarefied and arcane classes they think still matter bear scarcely any relation to the vernacular categories of social description and identity that are the subject of this book and with which, presumably, John Major was concerned. At the same time, they also recognize that "this does not mean that Britain is a nation of class warriors, resolutely pursuing a struggle to preserve or usurp power, in order to achieve specifically class objectives" (p. 155): i.e., Marx is dead. This does leave matters very uncertain. For some valuable comments (and criticisms) of British sociologists' continuing (and confused) obsession with class, see S. Ringen, "The Open Society and the Closed Mind," *Times Literary Supplement*, 24 January 1997, p. 6.

69. B. Anderson, *Imagined Communities: Reflections on the Origin and Spread of Nationalism* (London, 1983); G. Himmelfarb, *The Idea of Poverty: England in the Early Industrial Age* (London, 1984), p. 304. As with many fashionable methodologies, the "linguistic turn" is also a less original approach to the past than some of its proponents claim. Consider these words, written two generations ago, by a historian of nineteenth-century Britain: "Language is an inescapable part of the environment. In any situation, we see not the material facts of that situation, but what the particular vocabulary of our time and our group has taught us to look for" (H. M. Lynd, *England in the Eighteen Eighties* [London, 1945], p. 61).

70. Runciman, *Substantive Social Theory*, p. 108.

71. P. H. Lindert, "English Occupations, 1670–1811," *Journal of Economic*

History, 40 (1980), pp. 685–712; idem, "Unequal English Wealth since 1670," *Journal of Political Economy*, 94 (1986), pp. 1127–62; P. H. Lindert and J. G. Williamson, "Revising England's Social Tables, 1688–1812," *Explorations in Economic History*, 19 (1982), pp. 385–408; idem, "Reinterpreting Britain's Social Tables, 1688–1913," *Explorations in Economic History*, 20 (1983), pp. 94–109; N. F. R. Crafts, *British Economic Growth During the Industrial Revolution* (Oxford, 1985), pp. 1–8, 48–70; Runciman, "How Many Classes Are There in Contemporary British Society?" pp. 377–96; R. V. Jackson, "Inequality of Incomes and Lifespans in England Since 1688," *EcHR*, 2d ser., 47 (1994), pp. 508–24.

72. G. Kitson Clark, *An Expanding Society: Britain, 1830–1900* (Cambridge, 1967); J. G. A. Pocock, "British History: A Plea for a New Subject," *JMH*, 47 (1975), pp. 601–28; idem, "The Limits and Divisions of British History: In Search of the Unknown Subject," *AHR*, 87 (1982), pp. 311–36.

73. This remains a much understudied subject. For some suggestive hints, see W. H. McNeill, *The Great Frontier: Freedom and Hierarchy in Modern Times* (Princeton, 1983); L. Hartz, K. D. McRae, R. M. Morse, and R. N. Rosecrance, *The Founding of New Societies* (New York, 1969); G. Martin, *Bunyip Aristocracy: The New South Wales Constitution Debate of 1853 and Hereditary Institutions in the British Colonies* (London, 1986); H. Liebersohn, "Discovering Indigenous Nobility: Tocqueville, Chamisso, and Romantic Travel Writing," *AHR*, 99 (1994), pp. 746–66; I. Copland, *The Princes of India and the Endgame of Empire, 1917–1947* (Cambridge, 1997).

74. R. Darnton, "A Bourgeois Puts His World in Order," in *The Great Cat Massacre and Other Episodes in French Cultural History* (New York, 1985), pp. 107–43. For a discussion of this approach, see R. Chartier, "Texts, Symbols and Frenchness," *JMH*, 57 (1985), pp. 682–95; R. Darnton, "The Symbolic Element in History," *JMH*, 58 (1986), pp. 218–34.

75. Marshall et al., *Social Class in Modern Britain*, p. 187. For the distinction between formal and informal languages of social description, see K. Wrightson, "The Social Order of Early Modern England: Three Approaches," in L. Bonfield, R. Smith, and K. Wrightson (eds.), *The World We Have Gained: Histories of Population and Social Structure: Essays Presented to Peter Laslett on His Sevientieth Birthday* (Oxford, 1986), pp. 178–83.

76. G. Watson, *The English Ideology* (London, 1973), p. 174. In this regard, note these two comments by P. N. Furbank, which appear in "Sartre's Absent Whippet," *London Review of Books*, 24 February 1994, p. 26.

Here is the first: "In reality, everyone in England belonged to a criss-cross of hierarchies, occupying a different place in each." And here is the second: "Many people, at least in Britain, entertain simultaneously in their head a three-class system ('upper class,' 'middle class' and 'working class') and a two-class system ('bourgeoisie' and 'proletariat'), accommodating or masking the mismatch between the two as best they can." The author had previously explored some of the contradictions among these three mental models of British social structure in P. N. Furbank, *Unholy Pleasure: The Idea of Social Class* (Oxford, 1985). For an earlier attempt to explore the contradictions and discrepancies between the dichotomous and hierarchical models of society, see D. Lockwood, "Sources of Variation in Working Class Images of Society," *The Sociological Review*, new ser., 14 (1966), pp. 249–67. For a more recent attempt to deal with all three models, see B. Waites, *A Class Society at War: England, 1914–1918* (Leamington Spa, 1987).

77. E. Gellner, "Knowledge of Nature and Society," in M. Teich, R. Porter, and B. Gustaffsson (eds.), *Nature and Society in Historical Context* (Cambridge, 1997), pp. 9–17.

78. Consider, in this regard, the remarks of F. W. Maitland, *Township and Borough* (Cambridge, 1898): "Mere numbers are important. . . . There are some thoughts which will not come to men who are not tightly packed" (pp. 22–24).

79. K. Wilson, "Whiggery Assailed and Triumphant: Popular Radicalism in Hanoverian England," *JBS*, 34 (1995), p. 126.

80. M. Thatcher, *The Revival of Britain* (London, 1989), p. 98.

81. For example, G. D. Squibb, *Precedence in England* (Oxford, 1981).

82. M. Weber, "Class, Status and Party," in H. H. Gerth and C. Wright Mills (eds.), *From Max Weber* (London, 1946), pp. 180–95.

83. L. Dumont, *Homo Hierarchicus: The Caste System and Its Implications* (Chicago, 1991); R. Burghart, "Hierarchical Models of the Hindu Social System," *Man*, 13 (1978), pp. 519–36; A. Appadurai, "Is Homo Hierarchicus?" *American Anthropologist*, 13 (1986), pp. 754–61. For an attempt to write the history of Britain around the organizing principle of hierarchy, see R. Strong, *The Story of Britain* (London, 1996), esp. pp. 79–83, 205, 210, 259, 333, 335, 431–41, 489, 502–3, 527, 538, 568. Strong, of course, established his academic reputation as an art historian of pageantry and spectacle in early modern England, pageantry and spectacle explicitly designed to celebrate, proclaim, and reinforce a hierarchical view of the world.

84. M. Kawai, "On the System of Social Ranks in a Natural Group of

Japanese Monkeys," *Primates*, 1 (1958), pp. 11–48; M. R. A. Chance and C. J. Jolly, *Social Groups of Monkeys, Apes and Men* (London, 1970), pp. 202–5; F. De Waal, *Chimpanzee Politics: Power and Sex among Apes* (London, 1982), pp. 13–14, 86–87, 182–88, 210–13; P. C. Lee and J. A. Johnson, "Sex Differences in Alliances, and the Acquisition and Maintenance of Dominance Status Among Immature Primates," in A. H. Harcourt and F. De Waal (eds.), *Coalitions and Alliances in Humans and Other Animals* (Oxford, 1992), pp. 445–75; W. G. Runciman, introduction to W. G. Runciman, J. Maynard Smith, and R. I. M. Dunbar (eds.), *Evolution of Social Behaviour Patterns in Primates and Man, Proceedings of the British Academy*, 88 (1996), pp. 1–4.

85. In which regard, it is worth recalling Lord Runciman's observation that "in twentieth- as in fifteenth-century England, there are systematically observable inequalities of economic, ideological and political power, *to which the contemporary rhetoric relates in all sorts of still understudied ways*" (*London Review of Books*, 10 March 1994, p. 5). My italics.

2. THE EIGHTEENTH CENTURY:
CLASS WITHOUT CLASS STRUGGLE

1. E. P. Thompson, "Patrician Society, Plebeian Culture," *Journal of Social History*, 7 (1974), pp. 382–405; idem, "Eighteenth-Century English Society: Class Struggle Without Class?" *SH*, 3 (1978), pp. 133–65. For a recent reevaluation, sympathetic yet critical, see P. King, "Edward Thompson's Contribution to Eighteenth-Century Studies: The Patrician-Plebeian Model Re-Examined," *SH*, 21 (1996), pp. 215–28. For another interpretation, which also sees eighteenth-century society as deeply divided, but in an aspirational rather than adversarial way, see D. C. Coleman, "Gentlemen and Players," *EcHR*, 2d ser., 26 (1973), pp. 92–116; N. McKendrick, " 'Gentleman [sic] and Players' Revisited: The Gentlemanly Ideal, the Business Ideal, and the Professional Ideal in English Literary Culture," in N. McKendrick and R. B. Outhwaite (eds.), *Business Life and Public Policy: Essays in Honour of Donald Coleman* (Cambridge, 1986), pp. 98–136.

2. P. Earle, *The Making of the English Middle Class: Business, Society and Family Life in London* (London, 1989); P. G. M. Dickson, *The Financial Revolution in England: A Study in the Development of Public Credit* (London, 1967); G. Holmes, *Augustan England: Professions, State and Society, 1680–1730* (London, 1982); J. Brewer, *The Sinews of Power: War,*

Money and the English State, 1688–1783 (London, 1988); idem, *The Plea-sures of the Imagination: English Culture in the Eighteenth Century* (London, 1997); P. Borsay, *The English Urban Renaissance: Culture and Society in the Provincial Town, 1660–1770* (Oxford, 1989); P. Langford, *A Polite and Commercial People: England, 1727–1783* (Oxford, 1989); idem, *Public Life and the Propertied Englishman, 1689–1798* (Oxford, 1991); L. Weatherill, *Consumer Behaviour and Material Culture in Britain, 1660–1760* (London, 1968); J. Barry, "Consumers' Passions: The Middle Class in Eighteenth-Century England," *HJ*, 34 (1991), pp. 207–16; idem, "The State and the Middle Classes in Eighteenth-Century England," *Journal of Historical Sociology*, 4 (1991), p. 85; J. Barry and C. Brooks (eds.), *The Middling Sort of People: Culture, Society and Politics in England, 1550–1800* (Basingstoke, 1994).

3. P. Laslett, *The World We Have Lost*, 2d ed. (London, 1971); J. A. Cannon, *Aristocratic Century: The Peerage in Eighteenth-Century England* (Cambridge, 1984); J. V. Beckett, *The Aristocracy in England, 1660–1914* (Oxford, 1986); J. C. D. Clark, *English Society, 1688–1832: Ideology, Social Structure and Political Practice During the Ancien Régime* (Cambridge, 1985); L. Stone and J. C. Fawtier Stone, *An Open Elite? England, 1540–1880* (Oxford, 1984). Note also this comment on the Stones's book by R. A. Houston, in "British Society in the Eighteenth Century," *JBS*, 25 (1986): "Its wider implication is that English society is best understood as a finely graded hierarchy in which snobbery was the most important divisive factor" (p. 461).

4. The classic articles here are J. G. A. Pocock, "British History: A Plea for a New Subject," *JMH*, 47 (1975), pp. 601–28; idem, "The Limits and Divisions of British History: In Search of the Unknown Subject," *AHR*, 87 (1982), pp. 311–36. See also D. Cannadine, "British History as 'A New Subject': Politics, Perspectives and Prospects," *Welsh History Review*, 17 (1995), pp. 313–331.

5. For a recent and (inevitably) inconclusive attempt to discuss the relative merits of these three historical interpretations of the Hanoverian social order, see D. Hay and N. Rogers, *Eighteenth-Century English Society: Shuttles and Swords* (Oxford, 1997), pp. 17–36, 188–208. For an even more inconclusive debate on the popularity and appropriateness of the hierarchical and the three-stage models as more "accurate" guides, see the following exchange between J. M. Innes and J. C. D. Clark: Innes: "I would happily wager that a thousand contemporary references will be found characterising eighteenth-century England as a 'commercial society' to every one characterising it as landed, aristocratic, noble, hi-

erarchical or the like" ("Jonathan Clark, Social History, and England's 'Ancien régime,'" *P&P*, no. 115 [1987], p. 181). Clark: "I happily accept: but, alas, Innes has not yet named the stake" ("On Hitting the Buffers: The Historiography of England's Ancien Régime," *P&P*, no. 117 [1987], p. 206 n. 34). It cannot be said that such exchanges seriously advance the cause of historical understanding. For another display of equally irreconcilable views about the Hanoverian social order, see Langford, *Public Life and the Propertied Englishman*, p. 510, and J. A. Cannon, *Samuel Johnson and the Politics of Hanoverian England* (Cambridge, 1994), p. 262. I have discussed of these historiographical contradictions more fully in D. Cannadine, "Beyond Class? Social Structures and Social Perceptions in Modern England," *Proceedings of the British Academy*, forthcoming, 1998.

6.   D. A. L. Morgan, "The Individual Style of the English Gentleman," in M. Jones (ed.), *Gentry and Lesser Nobility in Late Medieval Europe* (Gloucester, 1986), pp. 15–35; M. H. Keen, *English Society in the Later Middle Ages, 1348–1500* (London, 1990), pp. 1–24; D. Crouch, *The Image of Aristocracy in Britain, 1000–1300* (London, 1992), pp. 15–38, 41–44, 344–47. See also P. Boyde, *Dante Philomythes and Philosopher: Man in the Cosmos* (Cambridge, 1981), pp. 222–24.

7.   E. M. W. Tillyard, *The Elizabethan World Picture* (London, 1943); D. Cressy, "Describing the Social Order of Elizabethan and Stuart England," *Literature and History*, 3 (1976), pp. 29–44; G. Aylmer, "Caste, Ordre (ou Statut) et Classe dans les Premiers Temps de l'Angleterre Moderne," in R. Mousnier (ed.), *Problèmes de Stratification Sociale* (Paris, 1968), pp. 137–57. A. H. Halsey, *Change in British Society*, 3d ed. (Oxford, 1986), p. 55. For the broader European context, see P. Burke, "The Language of Orders in Early Modern Europe," and W. Doyle, "Myths of Order and Ordering Myths," both in M. L. Bush (ed.), *Social Orders and Social Classes in Europe Since 1500: Studies in Social Stratification* (London, 1992), pp. 1–12, 218–229.

8.   A. O. Lovejoy, *The Great Chain of Being: A Study in the History of an Idea* (Cambridge, MA, 1936); W. F. Bynum, "The Great Chain of Being After Forty Years," *History of Science*, 13 (1975), pp. 1–28; K. Wrightson, *English Society, 1580–1680* (London, 1982), pp. 18–23; idem, "Estates, Degrees and Sorts: Changing Perceptions of Society in Tudor and Stuart England," in P. Corfield (ed.), *Language, History and Class* (Oxford, 1991), pp. 32–35; R. B. Schlatter, *The Social Ideas of Religious Leaders, 1660–1688* (Oxford, 1940), pp. 106–23.

9.   R. W. Malcolmson, *Life and Labour in England, 1700–1780* (London,

1981), pp. 14–17; F. A. Pottle (ed.), *Boswell's London Journal, 1762–3* (London, 1950), p. 320; P. Corfield, "Class by Name and Number in Eighteenth-Century Britain," in idem, *Language, History and Class*, pp. 103–4; Cannon, *Samuel Johnson*, pp. 154–70.

10. R. Gough, *The History of Myddle*, ed. D. Hay (Harmondsworth, 1981); K. Wrightson, " 'Sorts of People' in Tudor and Stuart England," in Barry and Brooks, *The Middling Sort of People*, p. 30; N. Rogers, *Whigs and Cities: Popular Politics in the Age of Walpole and Pitt* (Oxford, 1984), p. 279.

11. E. Gellner, "Knowledge of Nature and Society," in M. Teich, R. Porter, and B. Gustafsson (eds.), *Nature and Society in Historical Context* (Cambridge, 1997), p. 14; Corfield, "Class by Name and Number," pp. 102–3.

12. S. Wallech, "The Emergence of the Modern Concept of 'Class' in the English Language" (Ph.D. diss., Claremont Graduate School, 1981), pp. 16–66; H. J. Perkin, *The Origins of Modern English Society, 1780–1880* (London, 1969), p. 26.

13. G. Watson, *The English Ideology* (London, 1973), p. 180.

14. For an incisive critique of hierarchy as a way of seeing society, see P. N. Furbank, *Unholy Pleasure: The Idea of Social Class* (Oxford, 1985), pp. 75–83. See also his remarks in "Sartre's Absent Whippet," *London Review of Books*, 24 February 1994: "Social historians tend to mis-represent 'hierarchy,' I think, and it is a comedy to see them struggling with the aid of Gregory King's table of 1690 and of much fudging, to demonstrate that there was a single social hierarchy in 17th century England—whereas all that magistrates and divines meant to declare was that there *ought* to be one (so that everyone should 'know their place')" (p. 26). My italics.

15. B. Bailyn, *Voyagers to the West* (New York, 1986), pp. 83, 147–49.

16. L. Stone, "Social Mobility in England, 1500–1700," *P&P*, no. 33 (1966), p. 18.

17. J. Thirsk and J. P. Cooper (ed.), *Seventeenth-Century Economic Documents* (Oxford, 1972), pp. 780–81; Malcolmson, *Life and Labour in England*, pp. 11–12; idem, " 'Sorts of People,' " p. 30; Corfield, "Class in Eighteenth-Century Britain," pp. 115–18; P. Mathias, "The Social Structure in the Eighteenth Century: A Calculation by Joseph Massie," in *The Transformation of England: Essays in the Economic and Social History of England in the Eighteenth Century* (London, 1979), pp. 171–85.

18. Aristotle, *The Poetics*, book 4, ch. 2; G. Duby, *The Three Orders: Feudal Society Imagined* (Chicago, 1980); R. H. Mohl, *The Three Estates in Me-*

dieval and Renaissance Literature (New York, 1933); T. E. Powell. "The 'Three Orders' of Society in Anglo-Saxon England," *Anglo-Saxon England*, 33 (1994), pp. 103–32; Furbank, *Unholy Pleasure*, pp. 8–9; E. Power, "What Feudalism Meant in England," *The Listener*, 20 October 1938, pp. 817–18.

19. Wrightson, "Estates, Degrees and Sorts," pp. 30–52; idem, " 'Sorts of People,' " pp. 28–51; idem, "The Social Order of Early Modern England: Three Approaches," in L. Bonfield, R. M. Smith, and K. Wrightson (eds.), *The World We Have Gained: Histories of Population and Social Structure: Essays Presented to Peter Laslett on His Seventieth Birthday* (Oxford, 1986), pp. 178–84, 196 n. 49; Wallech, "Emergence of the Modern Concept of 'Class,' " pp. 24–25, 56.

20. E. Royle and J. Walvin, *English Radicals and Reformers, 1760–1848* (Brighton, 1982), p. 19; Rogers, *Whigs and Cities*, p. 129.

21. Corfield, "Class by Name and Number," pp. 107, 113; Furbank, *Unholy Pleasure*, p. 11; K. Wilson, *The Sense of the People: Politics, Culture and Imperialism, 1715–1785* (Cambridge, 1995), p. 352; N. McKendrick, "Josiah Wedgwood and the Commercialization of the Potteries," in N. McKendrick, J. Brewer, and J. H. Plumb, *The Birth of a Consumer Society: The Commercialization of Eighteenth-Century England* (London, 1982), p. 131.

22. For the medieval background, see R. H. Hilton, *Class Conflict and the Crisis of Feudalism: Essays in Medieval Social History* (London, 1985), pp. 114–19, 122–23, 152–55, 164, 217–25, 246–52. For the Civil War, see D. E. Underdown, *Revel, Riot and Rebellion: Popular Politics and Culture in England, 1603–1660* (Oxford, 1985), in which he describes the Civil War as the result of "two quite different constellations of social, political and cultural forces": "on the one side stood those who had put their trust in the traditional conception of the harmonious, vertically-integrated society. . . . On the other stood those . . . who wished to emphasise the moral and cultural distinctions which marked them off from their poorer, less disciplined neighbours" (p. 40). See also Corfield, "Class by Name and Number," pp. 117–18; Wrightson, " 'Sorts of People,' " pp. 34–40; Wilson, *Sense of the People*, pp. 231, 354.

23. Rogers, *Whigs and Cities*, p. 340; Wilson, *Sense of the People*, p. 287.

24. Corfield, "Class by Name and Number," p. 119; Borsay, *English Urban Renaissance*, pp. 96, 166, 293; Hay and Rogers, *Eighteenth-Century English Society*, p. 25.

25. Wilson, *Sense of the People*, pp. 128, 143.

26. Corfield, "Class by Name and Number," pp. 117–19; J. Brewer, *Party Ide-*

ology and Popular Politics at the Accession of George III (Cambridge, 1976), p. 168.

27. Corfield, "Class by Name and Number," pp. 102, 114.

28. Ibid., pp. 101–2.

29. Many Anglican justifications of hierarchy and subordination are quoted in Clark, *English Society*, pp. 93–118, 216–35; G. Holmes, "Gregory King and the Social Structure of Pre-Industrial England," *TRHS*, 5th ser., 27 (1977), pp. 41–68; Wallech, "The Emergence of the Modern Concept of 'Class,' " pp. 56–57; M. Shinagel, *Daniel Defoe and Middle-Class Gentility* (Cambridge, MA, 1968); J. McVeagh, *Tradeful Merchants: The Portrayal of the Capitalist in Literature* (London, 1981), pp. 53–82; D. Wahrman, *Imagining the Middle Class: The Political Representation of Class in Britain, c. 1780–1840* (Cambridge, 1995), p. 66.

30. The concept of "ideologically determined class stereotypes" is suggestively discussed in R. McKibbin, *Ideologies of Class: Social Relations in Britain, 1880–1950* (Oxford, 1990), pp. 270–74. See also Wahrman, *Imagining the Middle Class*, pp. 63–64; J. G. A. Pocock, "The History of Political Thought: A Methodological Enquiry," in P. Laslett and W. G. Runciman (eds.), *Philosophy, Politics and Society: Second Series* (Oxford, 1962), p. 199.

31. R. Porter, *English Society in the Eighteenth Century* (Harmondsworth, 1990), p. 74; L. Sutherland, "The City of London in Eighteenth-Century Politics," in R. Pares and A. J. P. Taylor (eds.), *Essays Presented to Sir Lewis Namier* (London, 1956), p. 66; Wilson, *Sense of the People*, p. 199. For another example of this usage, see Horace Walpole: "There was nowhere but in England the distinction of the middling people" (quoted in Stone and Stone, *Open Elite*, pp. 408–9).

32. L. Colley, *Britons: Forging the Nation, 1707–1837* (London, 1992), p. 92; R. Harris, " 'American Idols': Empire, War and the Middling Ranks in Mid Eighteenth-Century Britain," *P&P*, no. 150 (1996), p. 140.

33. G. Newman, *The Rise and Fall of English Nationalism: Cultural History, 1740–1830* (London, 1987), pp. 100–102.

34. Wilson, *Sense of the People*, pp. 18, 19, 231, 235, 265, 267; H. T. Dickinson, *The Politics of the People in Eighteenth-Century Britain* (London, 1995).

35. R. Kelso, *The Doctrine of the English Gentleman in the Sixteenth Century* (Urbana, IL, 1929); G. C. Brauer, *The Education of a Gentleman: Theories of Gentlemanly Education in England, 1660–1775* (New York, 1959).

36. Clark, *English Society*, p. 105; Shinagel, *Defoe and Middle-Class Gentility*, pp. 82–86.

37. P. J. Corfield, "The Rivals: Landed and Other Gentlemen," in N. Harte

and R. Quinault (eds.), *Land and Society in Britain, 1700–1914* (Manchester, 1996), pp. 1–33.

38. Hanoverian historians have also sometimes been inclined to do this: Clark, *English Society*, pp. 43, 90; King, "Edward Thompson's Contribution to Eighteenth-Century Studies," p. 221.

39. For some suggestive hints, see D. Wahrman's review of Langford's *Public Life and the Propertied Englishman* in *SH*, 17 (1992), pp. 500–501; E. H. Gould, "American Independence and Britain's Counter Revolution," *P&P*, no. 154 (1997), p. 134 n. 92.

40. J. P. Greene, "Search for Identity: An Interpretation of the Meaning of Selected Patterns of Social Response in Eighteenth-Century America," *Journal of Social History*, 3 (1970), pp. 205–19; idem, *Pursuits of Happiness: The Social Development of Early Modern British Colonies and the Formation of American Culture* (Chapel Hill, NC, 1988).

41. S. Foster, *The Solitary Way: The Puritan Social Ethic in the First Century of Settlement in New England* (New Haven, 1971), pp. 14–15; R. L. Bushman, *From Puritan to Yankee: Character and the Social Order in Connecticut* (Cambridge, MA, 1967), pp. 1–13, 184, 264, 267–68, 272–73, 279. For an outstanding study of one colony as a functioning hierarchical society, see R. Isaac, *The Transformation of Virginia, 1740–1790* (Chapel Hill, 1982), part 1.

42. R. L. Bushman, *King and People in Provincial Massachusetts* (Chapel Hill, NC, 1985), pp. 3–54; J. T. Main, *The Social Structure of Revolutionary America* (Princeton, 1965), pp. 219, 226–27; E. S. Morgan, *Inventing the People: The Rise of Popular Sovereignty in England and America* (New York, 1988), pp. 170–73; Isaac, *Transformation of Virginia*, pp. 104–10; N. H. Dawes, "Titles as Symbols of Prestige in Seventeenth-Century New England," *WMQ*, 6 (1949), pp. 69–83.

43. A. M. Schlesinger, "The Aristocracy in Colonial America," *Proceedings of the Massachusetts Historical Society*, 74 (1962), pp. 3–21; T. Woodcock and J. M. Robinson, *The Oxford Guide to Heraldry* (Oxford, 1989), pp. 156–70; Greene, "Search for Identity," p. 217; B. Bailyn, *The Ideological Origins of the American Revolution* (Cambridge, MA, 1967), pp. 278–79; Edmund S. Morgan and Helen M. Morgan, *The Stamp Act Crisis: Prologue to Revolution* (Chapel Hill, NC, 1953), pp. 16–18.

44. B. Bailyn, *The Origins of American Politics* (New York, 1970), pp. 131–32; idem, *Ideological Origins of the American Revolution*, p. 275; Main, *Social Structure*, p. 198.

45. Bushman, *King and People*, p. 84; C. N. Degler, *Out of Our Past* (New York, 1959), pp. 49–50. For other comments on colonial America being

"short in words of dignity and names of honour," see J. H. St. John de Crevecoeur, *Letters from an American Farmer* (London, 1971), pp. 39–41.

46. Main, *Social Structure*, pp. 222–23, 230–34; C. Bridenbaugh, *Cities in Revolt: Urban Life in America, 1743–1776* (New York, 1955), p. 79.

47. C. Rossiter, *Seedtime of the Republic* (New York, 1953), p. 106.

48. Bushman, *Puritan to Yankee*, p. 13; idem, *King and People*, p. 203; Main, *Social Structure*, p. 237.

49. Main, *Social Structure*, p. 228; Isaacs, *Transformation of Virginia*, pp. 43–44, 131–35; Bushman, *King and People*, passim; idem, " 'This New Man': Dependence and Independence, 1776," in R. Bushman, N. Harris, D. Rothman, B. M. Solomon, and S. Thernstrom (eds.), *Uprooted Americans: Essays in Honour of Oscar Handlin* (Boston, 1979), pp. 77–96; M. Zuckerman, "Identity in British America: Unease in Eden," in N. Canny and A. Pagden (eds.), *Colonial Identity in the Atlantic World, 1500–1800* (Princeton, 1987), p. 143.

50. See, for instance, the argument put forward by L. Hartz and W. H. McNeill that the colonial American frontier was a place whose social order could simultaneously be described as hierarchical, bourgeois, and egalitarian: W. H. McNeill, *The Great Frontier: Freedom and Hierarchy in Modern Times* (Princeton, 1983), pp. 3–31; L. Hartz, K. D. McRae, R. M. Morse, and R. N. Rosecrance, *The Founding of New Societies* (New York, 1969), pp. 4–10.

51. For colonial America as a hierarchical society, see J. R. Pole, "Historians and the Problem of Early American Democracy," *AHR*, 67 (1962), pp. 626–46; G. S. Wood, *The Radicalism of the American Revolution* (New York, 1992), part 1, esp. pp. 11–23; R. L. Beeman, "Deference, Republicanism, and the Emergence of Popular Politics in Eighteenth-Century America," *WMQ*, 49 (1990), pp. 401–30; R. Berthoff and J. M. Murrin, "Feudalism, Communalism, and the Yeoman Freeholder: The American Revolution Considered as a Social Movement," in S. G. Kurtz (ed.), *Essays on the American Revolution* (New York, 1973), pp. 256–88; G. J. Kornblith and J. M. Murrin, "The Making and Unmaking of an American Ruling Class," in A. F. Young (ed.), *Beyond the American Revolution: Explorations in the History of American Radicalism* (De Kalb, IL, 1993), pp. 27–79. For colonial America as a triadic, middle-class dominated society, see J. Clive and B. Bailyn, "England's Cultural Provinces: Scotland and America," *WMQ*, 11 (1954), pp. 202–5; B. Bailyn, "Politics and Social Structure in Virginia," in J. Morton Smith (ed.), *Seventeenth-Century America: Essays in Colonial History* (Chapel Hill, 1959), pp. 90–115; R. Hofstadter, *America at 1750: A Social Portrait*

(London, 1972), esp. pp. 131–79. For colonial America as a polarized society, see J. A. Henretta, "Economic Development and Social Structure
in Colonial Boston," *WMQ*, 22 (1965), pp. 75–92; K. Lockridge, "Land,
Population and the Evolution of New England Society, 1630–1790,"
P&P, no. 39 (1968), pp. 62–80; G. B. Nash, *The Urban Crucible: Social
Change, Political Consciousness, and the Origins of the American Revolution* (Cambridge, MA, 1979).

52. For discussion of changing standards of gentility, see Wood, *Radicalism
of the American Revolution*, pp. 193–212.

53. In practice, of course, colonial America, like eighteenth-century Eng-
land, was simultaneously a hierarchical, triadic, and polarized society.
See McNeill, *The Great Frontier*, pp. 3–31; Hartz, *The Founding of New
Societies*, pp. 4–10.

54. Hofstadter, *America at 1750*, pp. 143–44; A. H. Smyth (ed.), *The Writings of Benjamin Franklin*, vol. 5 (New York, 1906), p. 362; Clive and
Bailyn, "England's Cultural Provinces," p. 203; F. A. Pottle (ed.),
Boswell on the Grand Tour: Germany and Switzerland, 1764 (New York,
1953), p. 259; Cannon, *Samuel Johnson*, pp. 182–84.

55. N. McLeod, "Interpreting Early Irish Law: Status and Currency," in
Zeitschrift für celtische Philologie, 41 (1986), pp. 46–65; 47 (1987), pp.
41–115; G. W. S. Barrow, *The Anglo-Norman Era in Scottish History* (Oxford, 1980), pp. 120–21; R. R. Davies, *Conquest, Coexistence and Change:
Wales, 1063–1415* (Oxford, 1987), pp. 115–22.

56. G. H. Jenkins, *Literature, Religion and Society in Wales, 1660–1730*
(Cardiff, 1978), pp. 18–20, 58, 238–99; idem, *The Foundations of Modern
Wales: Wales, 1642–1780* (Oxford, 1987), pp. 390–92.

57. R. A. Houston and I. D. Whyte, "Introduction: Scottish Society in Perspective," in R. A. Houston and I. D. Whyte (eds.), *Scottish Society,
1500–1800* (Cambridge, 1989), p. 23.

58. D. Miller, "Hume and Progressive Individualism," *History of Political
Thought*, 1 (1980), pp. 269–74; idem, *Philosophy and Ideology in Hume's
Political Thought* (Oxford, 1981), pp. 132–37, 193, 196.

59. Corfield, "Class by Name and Number," pp. 126–27; Brewer, *Party Ideology and Popular Politics*, pp. 183–84; A. Ferguson, *An Essay on the History of Civil Society, 1767*, ed. D. Forbes (Edinburgh, 1966), pp. 72, 121–35,
174, 188, 249; A. Smith, *An Inquiry into the Nature and Causes of the
Wealth of Nations*, ed. R. H. Campbell and A. S. Skinner, with W. B.
Todd (Oxford, 1976), 2:714.

60. A. P. W. Malcomson, "Absenteeism in Eighteenth-Century Ireland,"
Irish Economic and Social History, 1 (1974), pp. 15–35.

61. Jenkins, *Foundations of Modern Wales*, pp. 226–27, 235, 261–67, 312–14; S. J. Connolly, *Religion, Law and Power: The Making of Protestant Ireland, 1660–1760* (Oxford, 1992), p. 60; J. Adam Smith, "Some Eighteenth-Century Ideas of Scotland," in N. T. Phillipson and R. Mitchison (eds.), *Scotland in the Age of Improvement* (Edinburgh, 1970), p. 110.

62. There was, of course, a considerable amount of absenteeism in England as well, because of government service, multiple estates, and so on. But its nationalistic-cum-political import was much less. See P. Roebuck, "Absentee Landownership in the Late Seventeenth and Early Eighteenth Centuries: A Neglected Factor in English Agrarian History," *Agricultural History Review*, 21 (1973), pp. 11–14; F. T. Melton, "Absentee Land Management in Seventeenth-Century England," *Agricultural History*, 52 (1978), pp. 147–59; J. V. Beckett, "Absentee Landownership in the Later Seventeenth and Early Eighteenth Centuries: The Case of Cumbria," *Northern History*, 19 (1983), pp. 87–107.

63. B. Lenman, *The Jacobite Clans of the Great Glen, 1650–1784* (London, 1984), p. 23.

64. D. Forbes, *Hume's Philosophical Politics* (Cambridge, 1975), pp. 175–79; Miller, "Hume and Progressive Individualism," pp. 270–72; idem, *Hume's Political Thought*, pp. 124–26; I. Hont and M. Ignatieff, "Needs and Justice in *The Wealth of Nations*: An Introductory Essay," in I. Hont and M. Ignatieff (eds.), *Wealth and Virtue: The Shaping of Political Economy in the Scottish Enlightenment* (Cambridge, 1983), pp. 1–15. For other examples of tripartite social description in eighteenth-century Edinburgh, see R. A. Houston, *Social Change in the Age of Enlightenment: Edinburgh, 1660–1760* (Oxford, 1994), pp. 83, 144, 206.

65. D. Dubisson, "L'Irlande et la théorie médiévale des 'trois ordres,'" *Revue de l'Histoire des Religions*, 188 (1975), pp. 35–63; T. E. Powell, "The Idea of the Three Orders of Society and Social Stratification in Early Medieval Ireland," *Irish Historical Studies*, 29 (1995), pp. 475–89; Connolly, *Religion, Law and Power*, pp. 63, 71; G. E. Mingay (ed.), *Arthur Young and His Times* (London, 1975), pp. 165–69.

66. This might also be because social description has been less well studied in Scotland, Ireland, and Wales than in England or colonial America for the modern period. But it seems unlikely that this is the only (or major) explanation for the relative absence of the three-layer model on the Celtic fringe. See Corfield, "Class by Name and Number," pp. 126–27 n. 71.

67. Connolly, *Religion, Law and Power*, pp. 47, 129, 140–42; P. Jenkins, *The Making of a Ruling Class: The Glamorgan Gentry, 1640–1740* (Cam-

bridge, 1983), p. 178; Jenkins, *Foundations of Modern Wales*, p. 107.

68. Houston and Whyte, "Scottish Society in Perspective," pp. 23–24; Ferguson, *History of Civil Society*, p. 249; Smith, *Wealth of Nations*, 2:795; R. H. Campbell, "The Enlightenment and the Economy," in R. H. Campbell and A. S. Skinner (eds.), *The Origins and Nature of the Scottish Enlightenment* (Edinburgh, 1982), p. 9.

69. Jenkins, *Foundations of Modern Wales*, pp. 221–22, 265–69; Jenkins, *Making of a Ruling Class*, p. xix; Connolly, *Religion, Law and Power*, pp. 104, 115, 119, 126; R. F. Foster, *Modern Ireland, 1600–1972* (London, 1988), pp. 170, 211.

70. For Scotland, Ireland, and Wales as hierarchical societies dominated by the traditional order, see Connolly, *Religion, Law and Power*; Jenkins, *The Making of a Ruling Class*; L. Timperley, "The Pattern of Landholding in Eighteenth-Century Scotland," in M. L. Parry and T. R. Slater (eds.), *The Making of the Scottish Countryside* (Edinburgh, 1980), pp. 137–54. For the tripartite social division, see T. M. Devine, "The Social Composition of the Business Class in the Larger Scottish Towns, 1680–1740," in T. M. Devine and D. Dickson (eds.), *Ireland and Scotland, 1600–1850* (Edinburgh, 1983), pp. 163–76; S. Nenadic, "The Rise of the Urban Middle Class," in T. M. Devine and R. Mitchison (eds.), *People and Society in Scotland*, vol. 1, *1760–1830* (Edinburgh, 1988), pp. 109–26; idem, "Middle-Rank Consumers and Domestic Culture in Edinburgh and Glasgow, 1720–1840," *P&P*, no. 145 (1994), pp. 122–56; M. Wall, "The Rise of a Catholic Middle Class in Eighteenth-Century Ireland," *Irish Historical Studies*, 11 (1958), pp. 91–115; D. Dickson, "Middlemen," in T. Bartlett and D. W. Hayton (eds.), *Penal Era and Golden Age: Essays in Irish History, 1690–1800* (Belfast, 1979), pp. 162–85; L. M. Cullen, "The Dublin Merchant Community in the Eighteenth Century," in P. Butel and L. M. Cullen (eds.), *Cities and Merchants: French and Irish Perspectives on Urban Development, 1500–1800* (Dublin, 1986), pp. 195–210; Jenkins, *Foundations of Modern Wales*, pp. 115–19, 269–74, 285–89, 302, 368, 386. For these societies as polarized societies, see Connolly, *Religion, Law and Power*, p. 128; Jenkins, *Making of a Ruling Class*, pp. 194–96; Houston and Whyte, "Scottish Society in Perspective," p. 17.

71. R. F. Foster, introduction to C. H. E. Philpin (ed.), *Nationalism and Popular Protest in Ireland* (Cambridge, 1987), p. 14.

72. Porter, *English Society in the Eighteenth Century*, p. 48.

73. N. F. R. Crafts, *British Economic Growth During the Industrial Revolution* (Oxford, 1985), pp. 9–17, 48–69, 115–40; J. Hoppit, "Counting the

Industrial Revolution," *EcHR*, 2d ser., 43 (1990), pp. 176–85. The once-fashionable idea that preindustrial England was like an underdeveloped nation of the 1950s or 1960s, with a small, rich elite but widespread poverty, owed much to the mistaken analysis of Gregory King. That analysis and the interpretation based on it are now largely discredited: see Holmes, "Gregory King," pp. 54–68.

74. Cannon, *Samuel Johnson*, p. 252.

75. E. A. Wrigley, "A Simple Model of London's Importance in Changing English Society and Economy, 1675–1750," *P&P*, no. 37 (1967), pp. 45–70; idem, "Urban Growth and Agricultural Change: England and the Continent in the Early Modern Period," *Journal of Interdisciplinary History*, 15 (1985), pp. 683–728; P. J. Corfield, *The Impact of English Towns, 1700–1800* (Oxford, 1982); Houston and Whyte, "Scottish Society in Perspective," p. 6; L. M. Cullen, "Scotland and Ireland, 1600–1800: Their Role in the Evolution of British Society," in Houston and Whyte, *Scottish Society*, p. 232.

76. J. Boulton, *Neighbourhood and Society: A London Suburb in the Seventeenth Century* (Cambridge, 1987), pp. 99–119, 166–205; M. J. Power, "The Social Topography of Restoration London," in A. L. Beier and R. A. P. Finlay (eds.), *The Making of the Metropolis: London, 1500–1700* (London, 1986), p. 221; Houston, *Social Change in the Age of Enlightenment*, pp. 104–46.

77. Cannon, *Aristocratic Century*, pp. 93–125; idem, *Samuel Johnson*, pp. 248–98.

78. J. A. Phillips, *Electoral Behaviour in Unreformed England: Plumpers, Splitters, and Straights* (Princeton, 1982), pp. 168–211; F. O'Gorman, *Voters, Patrons and Parties: The Unreformed Electorate in Hanoverian England, 1734–1832* (Oxford, 1989), pp. 172–223; I. R. Christie, *British "Non-Elite" MPs, 1715–1820* (Oxford, 1995).

79. J. H. Langbein, "Albion's Fatal Flaws," *P&P*, no. 98 (1983), pp. 96–120; P. King, "Decision-Makers and Decision-Making in the English Criminal Law, 1750–1800," *HJ*, 27 (1984), pp. 25–58; J. Innes and J. Styles, "The Crime Wave: Recent Writing on Crime and Criminal Justice in Eighteenth-Century England," *JBS*, 25 (1986), pp. 402–9, 420–30.

80. D. Hay, "Property, Authority and the Criminal Law," in D. Hay, P. Linebaugh, J. G. Rule, E. P. Thompson, and C. Winslow, *Albion's Fatal Tree: Crime and Society in Eighteenth-Century England* (London, 1975), pp. 17–63; idem, "Poaching and the Game Laws on Cannock Chase," in ibid., pp. 189–254; idem, *The London Hanged: Crime and Civil Society*

in the Eighteenth Century (London, 1992), parts 1–3; P. B. Munsche, *Gentlemen and Poachers: the English Game Laws, 1671–1831* (Cambridge, 1981), esp. pp. 76–105, 159–68; D. W. Howell, *Patriarchs and Parasites: The Gentry of South-West Wales in the Eighteenth Century* (Cardiff, 1986), p. 168; Connolly, *Religion, Law and Power*, pp. 264–313.

81. R. A. Houston, "The Literacy Myth? Illiteracy in Scotland, 1630–1760," *P&P*, no. 96 (1982), pp. 81–102; idem, *Scottish Literacy and Scottish Identity* (Cambridge, 1985), pp. 20–83. See also idem, "British Society in the Eighteenth Century," where Houston observes: "There was a clear hierarchy of reading and writing abilities that closely followed the divisions of British society" (p. 446).

82. Cannon, *Aristocratic Century*, pp. 34–59; Jenkins, *Making of a Ruling Class*, pp. 218–26; L. Stone, "The Size and Composition of the Oxford Student Body, 1580–1910," in L. Stone (ed.), *The University in Society*, 2 vols. (Princeton, 1974), 1:37–57; V. Neuberg, *Popular Education in Eighteenth-Century England* (London, 1971), p. 2.

83. Houston, *Social Change in the Age of the Enlightenment*, pp. 54–67; Q. R. D. Skinner, "Language and Social Change," in J. Tully (ed.), *Meaning and Context: Quentin Skinner and His Critics* (Cambridge, 1988), p. 132.

84. R. O. Bucholz, " 'Nothing but Ceremony': Queen Anne and the Limitations of Royal Ritual," *JBS*, 30 (1991), pp. 288–323; G. S. Rousseau, " 'This Grand and Sacred Solemnity': Of Coronations, Republics and Poetry," *British Journal for Eighteenth-Century Studies*, 5 (1982), pp. 1–19; Clark, *English Society*, pp. 166–78; Houston, *Social Change in the Age of Enlightenment*, pp. 50–53; Wilson, *Sense of the People*, pp. 87–88, 295–96; Bushman, *King and People*, pp. 14–25.

85. F. O'Gorman, "Campaign Rituals and Ceremonies: The Social Meaning of Elections in England, 1780–1860," *P&P*, no. 135 (1992), pp. 79–115; J. L. McCracken, "The Social Structure and Social Life, 1714–60," in T. W. Moody and W. E. Vaughan (eds.), *A New History of Ireland*, vol. 4, *Eighteenth-Century Ireland, 1691–1800* (Oxford, 1986), 49; Connolly, *Religion, Law and Power*, pp. 133–36; S. Lukes, "Political Ritual and Social Integration," in *Essays in Social Theory* (London, 1977), pp. 52–73.

86. C. Phythian-Adams, "Ceremony and the Citizen: The Communal Year at Coventry," in P. Clark and P. Slack (eds.), *Crisis and Order in English Towns* (London, 1972), pp. 57–85; P. Borsay, " 'All The Town's a Stage': Urban Ritual and Ceremony, 1660–1800," in P. Clark (ed.), *The Transformation of English Provincial Towns, 1600–1800* (London, 1984), pp. 228–58.

87. Houston, *Social Change in the Age of Enlightenment*, pp. 214–23; Cannon, *Samuel Johnson*, p. 263.

88. E. P. Thompson, "The Moral Economy of the English Crowd in the Eighteenth Century," *P&P*, no. 50 (1971), pp. 76–136; Houston, *Social Change in the Age of Enlightenment*, pp. 290–331.

89. Jenkins, *Making of a Ruling Class*, pp. 18–19, 96–100; Wilson, *Sense of the People*, pp. 84–236; Brewer, *Party Ideology and Popular Politics*, esp. pp. 139–272; Hay and Rogers, *Eighteenth-Century English Society*, pp. 63–70, 135–42, 216–17.

90. J. Brewer, "Clubs, Commercialisation and Politics," in McKendrick, Brewer, and Plumb, *Birth of a Consumer Society*, pp. 197–262; idem, "English Radicalism in the Age of George III," in J. G. A. Pocock (ed.), *Three British Revolutions: 1641, 1688, 1776* (Princeton, 1980), p. 332; N. Rogers, "The Middling Sort in Eighteenth-Century Politics," in Barry and Brooks, *The Middling Sort of People*, pp. 159–80. Brewer's effort to tie the Wilkite agitation specifically to the "middling sorts" has been criticized in O'Gorman, *Voters, Patrons and Parties*, pp. 284, 293–95, 301–3; Wahrman, *Imagining the Middle Class*, pp. 66–67.

91. Brewer, *Sinews of Power*, p. 203; J. G. A. Pocock, "Cambridge Paradigms and Scotch Philosophers: A Study of the Relations Between the Civic Humanist and the Civil Jurisprudential Interpretation of Eighteenth-century Social Thought," in Hont and Ignatieff, *Wealth and Virtue*, p. 237; Colley, *Britons*, pp. 71, 100.

92. Connolly, *Religion, Law and Power*, p. 198.

93. J. Ellis, "A Dynamic Society: Social Relations in Newcastle-upon-Tyne, 1660–1760," in Clark, *Transformation of English Provincial Towns*, p. 217; Cannon, *Aristocratic Century*, pp. 148–79; D. Howell, "Society, 1660–1793," in B. Howells (ed.), *Early Modern Pembrokeshire, 1536–1815* (Haverfordwest, 1987), pp. 256, 298; Connolly, *Religion, Law and Power*, pp. 198–233; idem, "Albion's Fatal Twigs: Justice and the Law in the Eighteenth Century," in R. Mitchison and P. Roebuck (eds.), *Economy and Society in Scotland and Ireland, 1500–1939* (Edinburgh, 1988), pp. 117–25; Houston and Whyte, "Scottish Society in Perspective," pp. 25–28.

94. Porter, *English Society in the Eighteenth Century*, pp. 53–54; Wrightson, "The Social Order of Early Modern England," pp. 196–201; R. Pares, *King George III and the Politicians* (Oxford, 1953), p. 3; J. A. Sharpe, *Early Modern England: A Social History, 1550–1760* (London, 1987), pp. 120–23. For a recent attempt to rehabilitate the idea that there was a British working class and, before 1776, a transatlantic proletariat, see P.

Linebaugh and M. Rediker, "The Many-Headed Hydra: Sailors, Slaves and the Atlantic Working Class in the Eighteenth Century," in D. Segal (ed.), *Crossing Cultures: Essays in the Displacement of Western Civilization* (London, 1992), pp. 105–41.

95. Bailyn, "1776: A Year of Challenge—A World Transformed," *Journal of Law and Economics*, 19 (1976), pp. 437–66; J. P. Greene, *All Men Are Created Equal: Some Reflections on the Character of the American Revolution* (Oxford, 1976).

96. This argument has been most recently, eloquently, and comprehensively made in Wood, *Radicalism of the American Revolution*, pp. 229–369. For discussion of these ideas, see J. Appleby, B. C. Smith, M. Zuckerman, and G. Wood, "Forum: How Revolutionary Was the Revolution? A Discussion of Gordon S. Wood's *The Radicalism of the American Revolution*," *WMQ*, 51 (1994), pp. 677–716.

97. Berthoff and Murrin, "Feudalism, Communalism, and the Yeoman Freeholder," pp. 276–88; Kornblith and Murrin, "Making and Unmaking of an American Ruling Class," pp. 45–65; Morgan, *Inventing the People*, pp. 247–52, 263–87, 288–306.

98. B. Bailyn, "Political Experience and Enlightenment Ideas in Eighteenth-Century America," *AHR*, 67 (1961–62), pp. 348–51.

99. There is a massive literature on the making of the American working class and middle class. I have found the following especially suggestive: S. V. Salinger, "Artists, Journeymen, and the Transformation of Labor in Late Eighteenth-Century Philadelphia," *WMQ*, 40 (1983), pp. 62–84; D. Montgomery, "The Working Classes of the Pre-Industrial American City, 1780–1830," *Labor History*, 9 (1968), pp. 3–22; S. Wilentz, "Artisan Origins of the American Working Class," *International Labor and Working Class History*, 18 (1981), pp. 1–22; idem, *Chants Democratic: New York City and the Rise of the American Working Class, 1788–1850* (New York, 1984), pp. 4–19; S. Blumin, *The Emergence of the Middle Class: Social Experience in the American City, 1760–1900* (Cambridge, MA, 1989).

100. G. S. Wood, *The Creation of the American Republic, 1776–1787* (Chapel Hill, 1969), pp. 483–99, 569–74; J. L. Huston, "The American Revolutionaries, the Political Economy of Aristocracy, and the American Concept of the Distribution of Wealth, 1765–1900," *AHR*, 98 (1993), pp. 1079–105; J. H. Hutson, "Country, Court, and Constitution: Antifederalism and the Historians," *WMQ*, 38 (1981), pp. 337–68; S. Cornell, "Aristocracy Assailed: The Ideology of Backcountry Anti-Federalism," *Journal of American History*, 76 (1990), pp. 1148–172; J. Appleby, *Capital-*

ism and a New Social Order: The Republican Vision of the 1790s (New York, 1984), pp. 51–78. For the demise of hierarchy in one colony/state, see Isaac, *Transformation of Virginia*, pp. 299–322.

101. Bushman, "Dependence and Independence," pp. 91–92; idem, *King and People*, pp. 235–52; M. Ryan, "The American Parade: Representations of the Nineteenth-Century Social Order," in L. Hunt (ed.), *The New Cultural History* (Los Angeles, 1989), pp. 131–53.

102. Nineteenth-century America, though evolving very differently from nineteenth-century England, remained dependent on the English language of class. For a recent symposium that stimulatingly addresses some of these matters, see B. E. Shafer (ed.), *Is America Different? A New Look at American Exceptionalism* (Oxford, 1991), especially the essays by S. M. Lipset and D. Bell.

103. Pole, "Historians and the Problem of Early American Democracy," p. 64; Bushman, *From Puritan to Yankee*, p. 11; Wood, *Radicalism of the American Revolution*, pp. 347–48.

104. For an introduction to American self-mythologizing about social structure, see R. Sennett and J. Cobb, *The Hidden Injuries of Class* (New York, 1973); P. Fussell, *Class: A Guide to the American Status System* (New York, 1983). Interestingly enough, Fussell's book was published in Britain as *Caste Marks: Style and Status in the U.S.A.* (London, 1984).

105. I take up this point again in chapter five.

106. For the subsequent history of ideas (and denials) of class in the United States, see M. J. Burke, *The Conundrum of Class: Public Discourse on the Social Order in America* (Chicago, 1995).

107. Smith, *Wealth of Nations*, 2:181–82; N. T. Phillipson, "Adam Smith as Civic Moralist," in Hont and Ignatieff, *Wealth and Virtue*, p. 191.

108. Smith, *Wealth of Nations*, 1:265; 2:423, 714.

109. Houston, *Social Change in the Age of Enlightenment*, pp. 19–20; Porter, *English Society in the Eighteenth Century*, pp. 53–54.

110. Perkin, *Origins of Modern English Society*, p. 26; Wallech, "Emergence of the Modern Concept of 'Class,'" pp. 425–29; D. Winch, *Adam Smith's Politics: An Essay in Historiographic Revision* (Cambridge, 1978), pp. 99–102; D. Ricardo, *On the Principles of Political Economy* (London, 1817), pp. 5, 49; M. Ignatieff, "John Millar and Individualism," in Hont and Ignatieff, *Wealth and Virtue*, pp. 322, 342; D. McClellan (ed.), *Karl Marx: Selected Writings* (Oxford, 1977), p. 341.

111. Winch, *Adam Smith's Politics*, pp. 99–102. Cf. D. A. Reisman, *Adam Smith's Sociological Economics* (London, 1976), pp. 93, 100, 194–99.

3. THE NINETEENTH CENTURY:
A VIABLE HIERARCHICAL SOCIETY

1. J. Vernon, *Politics and the People: A Study in English Political Culture, c. 1815–1867* (Cambridge, 1993); P. Joyce, *Democratic Subjects: The Self and the Social in Nineteenth-Century England* (Cambridge, 1984); J. Epstein, *Radical Expression: Political Language, Ritual, and Symbol in England, 1790–1850* (New York, 1994); M. W. Steinberg, "Culturally Speaking: Finding a Commons Between Post-Structuralism and the Thompsonian Perspective," *SH*, 11 (1996), pp. 193–214; D. Wahrman, "The New Political History: A Review Essay," *SH*, 21 (1996), pp. 342–54.

2. This is a (very simplified) summary of the views put forward in many books and articles. For the most influential accounts, see E. J. Hobsbawm, *The Age of Revolutions, 1789–1848* (London, 1962); H. J. Perkin, *The Origins of Modern English Society, 1780–1880* (London, 1969); A. Briggs, *The Age of Improvement, 1783–1867* (London, 1959); idem, "Middle-Class Consciousness in English Politics, 1780–1846," *P&P*, no. 9 (1956), pp. 65–74; E. P. Thompson, *The Making of the English Working Class* (Harmondsworth, 1968); J. Foster, *Class Struggle and the Industrial Revolution: Early Industrial Capitalism in Three English Towns* (London, 1974); D. Thompson, *The Early Chartists* (London, 1971). For a different argument, which nevertheless shares the same class-based paradigm, see R. S. Neale, "Class and Class Consciousness in Early Nineteenth-Century England: Three Classes or Five?" in *Class and Ideology in the Nineteenth Century* (London, 1972), pp. 15–40.

3. A. Briggs, "The Language of 'Class' in Nineteenth-Century England," in M. W. Flinn and T. C. Smout (eds.), *Essays in Social History* (Oxford, 1974), pp. 154–77.

4. A. Briggs, *Victorian People: A Reassessment of Persons and Themes, 1851–1867* (Harmondsworth, 1965); W. L. Burn, *The Age of Equipoise: Study of the Mid-Victorian Generation* (London, 1964); E. J. Hobsbawm, *The Age of Capital, 1848–1875* (London, 1975); Perkin, *Modern English Society*, pp. 340–47.

5. For two particularly powerful pieces of skeptical scholarship, see C. Calhoun, *The Question of Class Struggle: Social Foundations of Popular Radicalism During the Industrial Revolution* (Chicago, 1982); D. Wahrman, *Imagining the Middle Class: The Political Representation of Class in Britain, c. 1780–1840* (Cambridge, 1995).

6. See Wahrman, *Imagining the Middle Class*: "The French Revolution explicitly politicised social class" (p. 35). What he really means is that it

explicitly politicized social *description*. Lord Liverpool, in 1819, certainly thought that "the events of the French Revolution had directed the attention of the lower orders of the community, and those immediately above them, to political considerations" (P. Mandler, *Aristocratic Government in the Age of Reform: Whigs and Liberals, 1830–1852* (Oxford, 1990), p. 98.

7. E. A. Wrigley, *Continuity, Change and Chance: The Character of the Industrial Revolution in England* (Cambridge, 1988); M. Berg and P. Hudson, "Rehabilitating the Industrial Revolution," *EcHR*, 2d ser., 45 (1992), pp. 24–50; J. Hoppitt, "Counting the Industrial Revolution," *EcHR*, 2d ser., 43 (1990), pp. 173–93; P. K. O'Brien, "Modern Conceptions of the Industrial Revolution," in P. K. O'Brien and R. Quinault (eds.), *The Industrial Revolution and British Society* (Cambridge, 1993), pp. 1–30; C. Tilly, *Popular Contention in Great Britain, 1758–1834* (London, 1995). For a survey of the historiography, see D. Cannadine, "The Present and the Past in the English Industrial Revolution, 1880–1980," *P&P*, no. 103 (1984), pp. 159–67.

8. Briggs, "Language of 'Class,'" pp. 154–77. Here are three famous examples of contemporary observers writing in the language of class: Thomas Gisborne, *Enquiry into the Duties of Men in the Higher Rank and Middle Classes of Society in Great Britain* (London, 1795); J. Wade, *History of the Middle and Working Classes* (London, 1833); F. Engels, *The Condition of the Working Class in England* (London, 1845).

9. J. Seed, "From 'Middling Sort' to 'Middle Class' in Late Eighteenth- and Early Nineteenth-Century Britain" in M. L. Bush (ed.), *Social Orders and Social Classes in Europe since 1500: Studies in Social Stratification* (London, 1992), pp. 114–35, rather overestimates the extent and inevitability of this development. John Wade used "middle classes," "middle orders," and "middle ranks" interchangeably in his writings. See Wahrman, *Imagining the Middle Class*, p. 356 n. 59.

10. G. Himmelfarb, *The Idea of Poverty: England in the Early Industrial Age* (London, 1984), pp. 288–304; G. Crossick, "From Gentlemen to the Residuum: Languages of Social Description in Victorian Britain," in P. Corfield (ed.), *Language, History and Class* (Oxford, 1991), pp. 150–61. When the Home Office described the Luddites as belonging to "the very lowest orders of the people," they were not only not using the "language of class"; they were also implying, correctly, that workmen better off and higher up the social scale were not involved. See M. I. Thomis, *The Luddites: Machine Breaking in Regency England* (Newton Abbot, 1970), p. 111.

11. Burke's belief that a divinely sanctioned and aristocracy-dominated so-

cial and political hierarchy was the best of all possible worlds did not prevent him from taking a low view of certain individual peers, most famously the duke of Bedford, the recipient in 1796 of his *Letter to a Noble Lord*. See J. A. Cannon, *Aristocratic Century: The Peerage in Eighteenth-Century England* (Cambridge, 1984), pp. 167–68.

12. H. T. Dickinson, *Liberty and Property: Political Ideology in Eighteenth-Century Britain* (London, 1977), p. 306; I. R. Christie, *Stress and Stability in Late Eighteenth-Century Britain: Reflections on the British Avoidance of Revolution* (Oxford, 1984), p. 169. J. C. D. Clark, *English Society, 1688–1832: Ideology, Social Structure and Political Practice During the Ancien Régime* (Cambridge, 1985), pp. 80, 93–99, 247–58; D. Roberts, *Paternalism in Early Victorian England* (New Brunswick, 1979), pp. 30, 187; L. Colley, *Britons: Forging the Nation, 1707–1837* (London, 1992), pp. 252–53; M. Girouard, *The Return to Camelot: Chivalry and the English Gentleman* (London, 1981), p. 19.

13. Thompson, *English Working Class*, pp. 100–101. My italics.

14. Himmelfarb, *Idea of Poverty*, p. 98; Clark, *English Society*, pp. 324–30; J. A. Cannon, *Parliamentary Reform, 1640–1832* (Cambridge, 1972), p. 119.

15. Thompson, *English Working Class*, pp. 26–27, 120; Himmelfarb, *Idea of Poverty*, p. 97.

16. Christie, *Stress and Stability*, p. 57; Clark, *English Society*, p. 87.

17. Perkin, *Modern English Society*, p. 23; Clark, *English Society*, p. 91.

18. R. Porter, *English Society in the Eighteenth Century* (Harmondsworth, 1990), pp. 298–99, 340–43, 354–55; D. Eastwood, *Governing Rural England: Tradition and Transformation in Local Government, 1780–1840* (Oxford, 1994), pp. 15–21. For another example, see these comments by the earl of Radnor in 1793: "With respect to difference of rank, all the inhabitants of this kingdom are interested in the maintenance of it, for it is essential and fundamental to our form of government, and it remains to be proved that any government in the world is, or ever was, comparable to ours" (A Cobban [ed.], *The Debate on the French Revolution, 1789–1800*, 2d ed. [London, 1960], pp. 399–400).

19. Dickinson, *Liberty and Property*, pp. 292, 303; Clark, *English Society*, p. 234; Thompson, *English Working Class*, p. 442. For a general discussion of the bishops' views on revolution and subordination, see R. A. Solway, *Prelates and People: Ecclesiastical Social Thought in England, 1783–1852* (London, 1969), pp. 19–84.

20. Roberts, *Paternalism*, p. 30; Perkin, *Modern English Society*, p. 282; Clark, *English Society*, pp. 268–70, 350–52; Girouard, *Return to Camelot*, pp. 36, 57–65; C. A. Bayly, *Imperial Meridian: The British Empire and the*

World, 1780–1830 (London, 1989), p. 194. Southey's attachment to hierarchy is discussed in D. Eastwood, "Robert Southey and the Intellectual Origins of Romantic Conservatism," *EHR*, 104 (1989), pp. 308–31.

21. Wahrman, *Imagining the Middle Class*, p. 159; A. Mitchell, "The Association Movement of 1792–93," *HJ*, 4 (1961), pp. 56–68; D. E. Ginter, "The Loyalist Association Movement," *HJ*, 9 (1966), pp. 179–90; Perkin, *Modern English Society*, pp. 30–31, 195.

22. Eastwood, *Governing Rural England*, p. 20; Girouard, *Return to Camelot*, pp. 20–25, 49–50; Wahrman, *Imagining the Middle Class*, p. 165; Colley, *Britons*, pp. 146–93; D. Cannadine, *Aspects of Aristocracy: Grandeur and Decline in Modern Britain* (London, 1994), pp. 25–33.

23. Bayly, *Imperial Meridian*, p. 196; J. R. Hill, "National Festivals, the State and Protestant Ascendancy in Ireland, 1790–1829," *Irish Historical Studies*, 24 (1984), pp. 30–51; Girouard, *Return to Camelot*, pp. 26–28.

24. M. Harrison, *Crowds and History: Mass Phenomena in English Towns, 1790–1835* (Cambridge, 1988), pp. 234–67, investigates the celebrations of peace with France (1801), the coronation of George IV (1821), and the coronation of William IV (1831) as staged in Bristol, Liverpool, Norwich, and Manchester. See also L. Colley, "The Apotheosis of George III: Loyalty, Royalty and the British Nation, 1760–1820," *P&P*, no. 102 (1984), pp. 94–129; idem, *Britons*, pp. 194–236.

25. *English Society*, p. 216; J. Ehrman, *The Younger Pitt: The Years of Acclaim* (London, 1969), pp. 360–71; B. Bailyn, *The Ideological Origins of the American Revolution* (Cambridge, MA, 1967), p. 280 n. 47; G. Martin, *Bunyip Aristocracy: The New South Wales Constitution Debate of 1853 and Hereditary Institutions in the British Colonies* (London, 1986), pp. 21–30. Even that self-styled "friend of the people" Charles James Fox supported the introduction of aristocracy into Canada; see Cannon, *Aristocratic Century*, p. 164. For broader discussion of empire and hierarchy in Canada, see H. Temperley, "Frontierism, Capital, and the American Loyalists in Canada," *Journal of American Studies*, 13 (1979), pp. 11–12.

26. Bayly, *Imperial Meridian*, pp. 110–112, 194–216; M. Francis, *Governors and Settlers: Images of Authority in the British Colonies, 1820–60* (London, 1992), esp. pp. 1–71; T. R. Metcalf, "Imperial Towns and Cities," in P. J. Marshall (ed.), *The Cambridge Illustrated History of the British Empire* (Cambridge, 1996), pp. 239–40.

27. Bayly, *Imperial Meridian*, pp. 142–63, 220–24; R. B. Sheridan, "The Rise of a Colonial Gentry: A Case Study of Antigua, 1730–1775," *EcHR*, 2d ser., 13 (1960–61), pp. 342–56; G. C. Bolton, "The Idea of a Colonial Gentry," *Historical Studies*, 12 (1968), pp. 307–28; D. Washbrook, "Eco-

nomic Depression and the Making of 'Traditional' Society in Colonial India, 1820–1855," *TRHS*, 6th ser., 3 (1993), pp. 237–63.

28. P. J. Marshall, "Imperial Britain," *Journal of Imperial and Commonwealth History*, 23 (1995), p. 385. The antislavery movement was also much preoccupied with the preservation of hierarchy: see D. Brion Davis, *The Problem of Slavery in the Age of Revolution, 1770–1823* (Ithaca, NY, 1975), p. 377; A. D. Kriegal, "A Convergence of Ethics: Saints and Whigs in British Antislavery," *JBS*, 26 (1987), pp. 441, 449. For a discussion of European perceptions of hierarchy in the non-European world, see H. Liebersohn, "Discovering Indigenous Nobility: Tocqueville, Chamisso, and Romantic Travel Writing," *AHR*, 99 (1994), pp. 746–66.

29. Dickinson, *Liberty and Property*, pp. 247–48, 240–58.

30. Thompson, *English Working Class*, p. 103; Cannon, *Aristocratic Century*, pp. 163–65.

31. Himmelfarb, *Idea of Poverty*, pp. 209, 220; Thompson, *English Working Class*, pp. 679–80, 819, 823, 825; I. Dyck, *William Cobbett and Rural Popular Culture* (Cambridge, 1992), pp. 71–73.

32. Cannon, *Aristocratic Century*, pp. 167, 169; Briggs, "Language of 'Class,'" p. 156.

33. J. Wade, *The Extraordinary Red Book* (London, 1816); idem, *The Extraordinary Black Book* (London, 1819); W. D. Rubinstein, "The End of 'Old Corruption' in Britain, 1780–1860," *P&P*, no. 101 (1983), pp. 55–86; Thompson, *English Working Class*, pp. 108, 848; G. Claeys, "The Reaction to Political Radicalism and the Popularisation of Political Economy in Early Nineteenth-Century Britain: The Case of 'Productive' and 'Unproductive' Labour," in T. Shinn and R. Whitley (eds.), *Expository Science: Forms and Functions of Popularisation* (Dordrecht, 1985), pp. 119–36; I. J. Prothero, "William Benbow and the Concept of the 'General Strike,'" *P&P*, no. 63 (1974), pp. 142–43, 158–59.

34. Harrison, *Crowds and History*, pp. 268–88; J. Stevenson, "Food Riots in England, 1792–1818," in J. Stevenson and R. Quinault (eds.), *Popular Protest and Public Order* (London, 1974), pp. 33–74; A. Booth, "Food Riots in the North-West of England, 1790–1801," *P&P*, no. 77 (1977), pp. 84–107.

35. Prothero, "William Benbow," p. 157; J. R. Dinwiddy, "The 'Black Lamp' in Yorkshire, 1801–1802," *P&P*, no. 64 (1974), pp. 113–23; idem, "Luddism and Politics in the Northern Counties," *SH*, 4 (1979), pp. 33–63; D. Hay and N. Rogers, *Eighteenth-Century English Society: Shuttles and Swords* (Oxford, 1997), pp. 179–208.

36. J. Belchem, "Republicanism, Popular Constitutionalism and the Radical Platform in Early Nineteenth-Century England," *SH*, 6 (1981), pp. 1–32; J. Epstein, "Understanding the Cap of Liberty: Symbolic Practice and Social Conflict in Early Nineteenth-Century England," *P&P*, no. 122 (1989), pp. 75–118.

37. J. P. Parry, *The Rise and Fall of Liberal Government in Victorian Britain* (London, 1993), pp. 33–34; Calhoun, *Question of Class Struggle*, pp. 105–15; I. J. Prothero, *Artisans and Politics in Early Nineteenth-Century London: John Gast and His Times* (London, 1981), pp. 132–55; T. W. Laqueur, "The Queen Caroline Affair: Politics as Art in the Reign of George IV," *JMH*, 54 (1982), pp. 417–66; A. Clark, "Queen Caroline and the Sexual Politics of Popular Culture in London, 1820," *Representations*, no. 31 (1990), pp. 47–68.

38. M. Elliott, "The Origin and Transformation of Early Irish Republicanism," *International Review of Social History*, 23 (1978), p. 411, quoted in Christie, *Stress and Stability*, p. 16.

39. J. Smith, *The Men of No Property: Irish Radicals and Popular Politics in the Late Eighteenth Century* (London, 1992), p. 6; G. Stedman Jones, "The Rise and Fall of 'Class Struggle': Middle Class and Bourgeoisie, 1789–1850" (unpublished paper), p. 5; R. F. Foster, *Modern Ireland, 1600–1972* (London, 1988), pp. 299–301.

40. E. Richards, *A History of the Highland Clearances:* vol. 1, *Agrarian Transformation and the Evictions, 1746–1886* (London, 1982), pp. 170, 194, 198, 200, 203, 210, 215, 219, 249, 251, 264, 268–69, 273–74, 299, 303, 319, 321–22, 355; W. H. Fraser, *Conflict and Class: Scottish Workers, 1700–1838* (Edinburgh, 1988), pp. 83, 103.

41. D. J. V. Jones, *Before Rebecca: Popular Protest in Wales, 1793–1835* (London, 1973), pp. 53, 63, 91; D. W. Howell, *Patriarchs and Parasites: The Gentry of South West Wales in the Eighteenth Century* (Cardiff, 1986), pp. 229–30.

42. T. M. Devine, "Unrest and Stability in Rural Ireland and Scotland, 1760–1840," in R. Mitchison and P. Roebuck (eds.), *Economy and Society in Scotland and Ireland, 1500–1939* (Edinburgh, 1988), pp. 126–39; T. Bartlett, "An End to Moral Economy: The Irish Militia Disturbances of 1793," *P&P*, no. 99 (1983), pp. 41–64.

43. T. M. Devine, "Social Responses to Agrarian 'Improvement': The Highland and Lowland Clearances in Scotland," in R. A. Houston and I. D. Whyte (eds.), *Scottish Society, 1500–1800* (Cambridge, 1989), pp. 148–68; E. Richards, "Patterns of Highland Discontent, 1790–1860," in Stevenson and Quinault, *Popular Protest and Public Order*, pp. 75–114;

Richards, *History of the Highland Clearances*, pp. 249–362; K. J. Logue, *Popular Disturbances in Scotland, 1780–1815* (Edinburgh, 1979); Jones, *Before Rebecca*, pp. 13–94.

44. Briggs, "Language of 'Class,'" p. 155; Thompson, *English Working Class*, p. 60; F. O'Gorman, *Voters, Patrons and Parties: The Unreformed Electorate of Hanoverian England, 1734–1832* (Oxford, 1989), pp. 236–37; E. A. Wasson, "The Great Whigs and Parliamentary Reform, 1809–1830," *JBS*, 24 (1985), p. 457; idem, *Whig Renaissance: Lord Althorp and the Whig Party, 1782–1845* (London, 1987), p. 80; E. A. Smith, *Lord Grey, 1764–1845* (Oxford, 1990), p. 217. For Lord Holland's later (1826) fear that "the divisions of classes and great interests are arrayed against each other," see Wahrman, *Imagining the Middle Class*, p. 233.

45. Clark, *English Society*, p. 372; Perkin, *Modern English Society*, p. 180; Cannon, *Parliamentary Reform*, p. 167, quoting Sydney Smith writing in 1819.

46. Richards, *History of the Highland Clearances*, pp. 66, 77, 357.

47. S. J. Connolly, *Priests and People in Pre-Famine Ireland, 1780–1845* (New York, 1982), p. 19; K. T. Hoppen, *Ireland Since 1800: Conflict and Community* (London, 1989), pp. 10, 44, 47; Smith, *Men of No Property*, pp. 7–8, 25–25.

48. Thompson, *English Working Class*, pp. 64, 304; Himmelfarb, *Idea of Poverty*, p. 304; Calhoun, *Question of Class Struggle*, pp. 3–23, 32–59.

49. Thompson, *English Working Class*, pp. 753, 836, 838; Himmelfarb, *Idea of Poverty*, pp. 228–29; Calhoun, *Question of Class Struggle*, pp. 95–126.

50. Wahrman, *Imagining the Middle Class*, pp. 40–46; Briggs, "Language of 'Class,'" p. 160.

51. Wahrman, *Imagining the Middle Class*, pp. 47–48; Parry, *Rise and Fall of Liberal Government*, p. 28.

52. Wahrman, *Imagining the Middle Class*, pp. 158–59, 162, 197–98, 217–18.

53. Perkin, *Modern English Society*, p. 294; Wahrman, *Imagining the Middle Class*, pp. 257–59.

54. Cannon, *Parliamentary Reform*, pp. 166, 183; Wahrman, *Imagining the Middle Class*, pp. 253–54.

55. Briggs, "Language of 'Class,'" p. 162; Wahrman, *Imagining the Middle Class*, pp. 254, 269.

56. L. Mugglestone, *"Talking Proper": The Rise of the Accent as Social Symbol* (Oxford, 1995), pp. 7–57, details the rise of "standard English" during the last quarter of the eighteenth century.

57. P. Lawson and J. Philips, "'Our Execrable Banditti': Perceptions of Nabobs in Mid-Eighteenth-Century Britain," *Albion*, 16 (1984), pp.

225–41; J. Raven, *Judging New Wealth: Popular Publishing and Responses to Commerce in England, 1750–1800* (Oxford, 1992), pp. 138–82, 201–12,

58. Raven, *Judging New Wealth*, pp. 221–48; P. J. Marshall, *The Impeachment of Warren Hastings* (Oxford, 1965).

59. Wahrman, *Imagining the Middle Class*, pp. 22, 27–29, 148–52, 227, 239–40; J. G. A. Pocock, "The Political Economy of Burke's Analysis of the French Revolution," *HJ*, 25 (1982), pp. 331–49. Burke, it should now be clear, used all three modes of social analysis: the hierarchical, the triadic, and the polarized, but as (by this time) a true conservative, his main concern was to defend hierarchy.

60. Girouard, *Return to Camelot*, p. 65; Wahrman, *Imagining the Middle Class*, pp. 164–68, 200–214, 250.

61. J. Barry, "Bourgeois Collectivism? Urban Association and the Middling Sort," in J. Barry and C. Brooks (eds.), *The Middling Sort of People: Culture, Society and Politics in England, 1550–1800* (Basingstoke, 1994), pp. 84–112; R. Price, "Historiography, Narrative and the Nineteenth Century," *JBS*, 35 (1996), pp. 245–46. See also the articles in the special issue of the *JBS*, 32 (1993), pp. 305–96, by Brown, Hunt, and Money, devoted to eighteenth century middle-class assertiveness and identity. There also seems less evidence than was once thought of the growth in late-eighteenth- and early-nineteenth-century middle-class wealth; see L. D. Schwartz, "Social Class and Social Geography: The Middle Classes in London at the End of the Eighteenth Century," *SH*, 7 (1982), pp. 167–85.

62. Wahrman, *Imagining the Middle Class*, pp. 60–63; Parry, *Rise and Fall of Liberal Government*, pp. 28–30. See also the remarks of T. C. Smout on the Scottish middle class in *A History of the Scottish People, 1560–1830* (London, 1969), pp. 338–40.

63. Cf. S. Nenadic, "The Rise of the Urban Middle Class," in T. M. Devine and R. Mitchison (eds.), *People and Society in Scotland*, vol. 1, *1760–1830* (Edinburgh, 1988): "By the 1830s, the language of class was well developed in Scotland, though the terminology of 'ranks and orders' had not vanished from smaller and non-industrial towns" (p. 120). Such a formulation is not only mistaken in supposing that the language of class drove away the language of ranks and orders; it also fails to recognize that the language of class was often used as an expression of hierarchy.

64. E. H. Hunt, *British Labour History, 1815–1914* (London, 1981), pp. 245–49; E. Royle and J. Walvin, *English Radicals and Reformers, 1760–1848* (Brighton, 1982), pp. 181, 189. Cf. S. Wallech, " 'Class Versus Rank': The Transformation of Eighteenth-Century English Social

Terms and Theories of Production," *Journal of the History of Ideas*, 47 (1986): "The concept of 'class' had by 1821 captured the imagination of Great Britain's thinking population" (p. 431). Indeed it had long since done so, but not just in the sense, as he uses it, of collective categories.

65. M. Brock, *The Great Reform Act* (London, 1973), p. 210.

66. Cannon, *Parliamentary Reform*, p. 215; Wahrman, *Imagining the Middle Class*, pp. 323–27.

67. R. W. Davis, "The Whigs and the Idea of Electoral Deference: Some Further Thoughts on the Great Reform Act," *Durham University Journal*, 67 (1974), pp. 83, 89; Parry, *Rise and Fall of Liberal Government*, p. 78; Smith, *Lord Grey*, pp. 255, 259–60.

68. Cannon, *Parliamentary Reform*, pp. 216, 224.

69. Parry, *Rise and Fall of Liberal Government*, p. 78; Thompson, *English Working Class*, p. 899.

70. Perkin, *Modern English Society*, pp. 230, 294; Cannon, *Parliamentary Reform*, pp. 250–52; Wahrman, *Imagining the Middle Class*, pp. 306–9.

71. N. McCord, "Some Difficulties of Parliamentary Reform," *HJ*, 10 (1967), pp. 376–85; idem, "Some Limitations of the Age of Reform," in H. Hearder and H. R. Loyn (eds.), *British Government and Administration: Studies Presented to S. B. Chrimes* (Cardiff, 1974), pp. 186–95. For the shortcomings and limitations of the censuses from 1801 to 1831 as guides to numbers, income, occupation, and rank, see M. Drake, "The Census, 1801–1891," in E. A. Wrigley (ed.), *Nineteenth-Century Society: Essays in the Use of Quantitative Methods for the Study of Social Data* (Cambridge), 1972, pp. 8–11, 32–33, 44–45; W. A. Armstrong, "The Use of Information About Occupation," in ibid., pp. 192–94.

72. Parry, *Rise and Fall of Liberal Government*, pp. 5, 343–44 n. 3; Mandler, *Aristocratic Government in the Age of Reform*, p. 29; R. W. Davis, "Deference and Aristocracy in the Time of the Great Reform Act," *AHR*, 81 (1976), p. 534; Thompson, *English Working Class*, p. 901.

73. Briggs, "Language of 'Class,'" p. 173 n. 32; D. J. Rowe, "Class and Political Radicalism in London, 1831–2," *HJ*, 13 (1970), p. 39.

74. J. Hamburger, *James Mill and the Art of Revolution* (New Haven, 1963); A. Briggs, "The Background of the English Parliamentary Reform Movement in Three English Cities," *Cambridge Historical Journal*, 10 (1950–52), pp. 293–317; G. A. Williams, *The Merthyr Rising* (London, 1978); F. Montgomery, "Glasgow and the Struggle for Parliamentary Reform, 1830–1832," *Scottish Historical Review*, 61 (1982), pp. 130–45; Thompson, *English Working Class*, pp. 888–900; G. Rude, "English Rural and Urban Disturbances on the Eve of the First Reform Bill,

1830–1831," *P&P*, no. 37 (1967), pp. 87–102; E. J. Hobsbawm and G. Rude, *Captain Swing* (London, 1969); Harrison, *Crowds and History*, pp. 289–314.

75. Thompson, *English Working Class*, p. 253; Parry, *Rise and Fall of Liberal Government*, p. 61; E. A. Smith, *Reform or Revolution? A Diary of Reform in England, 1830–2* (Stroud, 1992), pp. 70, 83–84.

76. Cannon, *Parliamentary Reform*, p. 261. This is also the claim made by J. C. D. Clark, namely, that 1832 spelled the "dissolution of the social order" of the eighteenth-century ancien régime. But now, as then, this was an excessively alarmist response. See Clark, *English Society*, p. 410; O'Gorman, *Voters, Patrons and Parties*, p. 393 n. 22.

77. Smith, *Reform or Revolution?* pp. 10–11, 27, 61, 72, 80.

78. Cannon, *Parliamentary Reform*, p. 257; Wahrman, *Imagining the Middle Class*, pp. 18, 328–33.

79. Cannon, *Parliamentary Reform,* pp. 216, 257; Wahrman, *Imagining the Middle Class*, pp. 344–52; Thompson, *English Working Class*, pp. 903, 983; Himmelfarb, *Idea of Poverty*, p. 241; A. Briggs, "National Bearings," in *Chartist Studies* (London, 1959), p. 295.

80. Smith, *Reform or Revolution?* pp. 143–44; G. Stedman Jones, *Languages of Class: Studies in English Working-Class History, 1832–1982* (Cambridge, 1983) pp. 104–6, 173; P. Joyce, *Visions of the People: Industrial England and the Question of Class, 1840–1914* (Cambridge, 1991) pp. 13, 37.

81. Wahrman, *Imagining the Middle Class*, pp. 333–43; R. J. Morris, *Class, Sect and Party: The Making of the British Middle Class: Leeds, 1820–1850* (Manchester, 1990), p. 10.

82. Wahrman, *Imagining the Middle Class*, pp. 352–66; G. K. Lewis, "From Aristocracy to Middle Class: Bulwer-Lytton's *England and the English*," in *Slavery, Imperialism, and Freedom: Studies in English Radical Thought* (New York, 1978), pp. 81–107.

83. D. Fraser, "Introduction: Municipal Reform in Historical Perspective," in idem (ed.), *Municipal Reform and the Industrial City* (Leicester, 1982), pp. 2–3, 10–11; V. A. C. Gatrell, "Incorporation and the Pursuit of Liberal Hegemony in Manchester, 1790–1839," in ibid., pp. 50–51.

84. N. McCord, *The Anti–Corn Law League, 1838–1846* (London, 1958), pp. 23, 115, 117, 127, 136; Wahrman, *Imagining the Middle Class*, pp. 409–10.

85. Briggs, "Language of 'Class,'" p. 163; Royle and Walvin, *English Radicals and Reformers*, pp. 175–76; McCord, *Anti–Corn Law League*, p. 127; G. M. Trevelyan, *The Life of John Bright* (London, 1913), p. 141.

86. Briggs, "National Bearings," p. 298; McCord, *Anti–Corn Law League*, p. 215; J. Saville, *1848: The British State and the Chartist Movement*

(Cambridge, 1987), p. 7.

87. Fraser, "Municipal Reform in Historical Perspective," pp. 2–8; idem, *Urban Politics in Victorian Britain: The Structure of Politics in Victorian Cities* (Leicester, 1976); E. P. Hennock, *Fit and Proper Persons: Ideal and Reality in Nineteenth-Century Urban Government* (London, 1973), pp. 183–85.

88. D. Nicholls, "The English Middle Class and the Ideological Significance of Radicalism, 1760–1886," *JBS*, 24 (1985), p. 417.

89. Briggs, "Language of 'Class,'" p. 154; Perkin, *Modern English Society*, p. 257.

90. Stedman Jones, *Languages of Class*, p. 104; D. Goodway, *London Chartism, 1838–1848* (Cambridge, 1982), p. 28; J. F. C. Harrison, "Chartism in Leicester," in Briggs, *Chartist Studies*, p. 104.

91. J. Epstein, "Some Organisational and Cultural Aspects of the Chartist Movement in Nottingham," in J. Epstein and D. Thompson (eds.), *The Chartist Experience: Studies in Working-Class Radicalism and Culture, 1830–60* (London, 1982), p. 244; Saville, *1848*, p. 146; Himmelfarb, *Idea of Poverty*, pp. 259–61.

92. A. Briggs, "Local Background of Chartism," in idem, *Chartist Studies*, p. 19; D. Thompson, *The Chartists* (London, 1984), pp. 31, 251; J. T. Ward, *The Chartists* (London, 1973), p. 74; Stedman Jones, *Languages of Class*, p. 104.

93. D. Read, "Chartism in Manchester," in Briggs, *Chartist Studies*, p. 35; Goodway, *London Chartism*, p. 120; J. Belchem, "1848: Fergus O'Connor and the Collapse of the Mass Platform," in Epstein and Thompson, *Chartist Experience*, p. 273.

94. R. N. Soffer, "Attitudes and Allegiances in the Unskilled North, 1830–1850," *International Review of Social History*, 10 (1965), pp. 429–54; Briggs, "Local Background of Chartism," pp. 4–5; idem, "National Bearings," pp. 289–92.

95. Calhoun, *Question of Class Struggle*, pp. 116–36; Stedman Jones, *Languages of Class*, pp. 25–75; Joyce, *Visions of the People*, pp. 95–109, 112–13; J. R. Dinwiddy, *Chartism* (London, 1987). Recently, A. Clark, in *The Struggle for the Breeches: Gender and the Making of the British Working Class* (London, 1995), reasserted that "in the 1830s and 1840s, Chartists expressed a distinct class antagonism" (p. 267). But the evidence does not really bear this out.

96. Stedman Jones, *Languages of Class*, pp. 90–178; Ward, *The Chartists*, pp. 74–75.

97. Himmelfarb, *Idea of Poverty*, pp. 192–201, 279–84, 492; Briggs, "Lan-

guage of 'Class,' " p. 157.

98. Wahrman, *Imagining the Middle Class*, pp. 411–13; Armstrong, "Use of Information About Occupation," p. 199. The key passages are in *The Manifesto of the Communist Party* (1848) and *The Eighteenth Brumaire of Louis Bonaparte* (1852); many of them are collected in A. Giddens and D. Held (eds.), *Classes, Power and Conflict: Classical and Contemporary Debates* (London, 1982), pp. 12–38.

99. R. Blake, *Disraeli* (London, 1966), pp. 190–220.

100. Himmelfarb, *Idea of Poverty*, pp. 492–93, 504–6.

101. Himmelfarb, *Idea of Poverty*, p. 356; Perkin, *Modern English Society*, p.

173. Thompson, *English Working Class*, p. 356; P. A. Pickering, *Chartism and the Chartists in Manchester and Salford* (London, 1955), pp. 9–12; Morris, *Class, Sect and Party*, p. 38.

102. T. Koditschek, *Class Formation and Urban Industrial Society: Bradford, 1750–1850* (Cambridge, 1990), p. 389; Himmelfarb, *Idea of Poverty*, pp. 435–37; Briggs, "Local Background of Chartism," p. 1.

103. Roberts, *Paternalism*, pp. 3, 58.

104. Blake, *Disraeli*, p. 179; Saville, *1848*, pp. 32, 164–65.

105. Wahrman, *Imagining the Middle Class*, pp. 412–13; Stedman Jones, "Rise and Fall of 'Class Struggle,' " pp. 1–3, 13–24.

106. Armstrong, "Use of Information About Occupation," p. 200.

107. Morris, *Class, Sect and Party*, pp. 39–56; Koditschek, *Bradford*, pp. 312, 377, 419; D. Ward, "Environs and Neighbours in the 'Two Nations': Residential Differentiation in Mid-Nineteenth-Century Leeds," *Journal of Historical Geography*, 6 (1980), pp. 133–34; R. Lawton, "An Age of Great Cities," *Town Planning Review*, 43 (1972), pp. 199–221; D. Cannadine, "Victorian Cities: How Different?" *SH*, 2 (1977), pp. 199–221; C. G. Pooley, "Residential Differentiation in Victorian Cities: A Reassessment," *Transactions of the Institute of British Geographers*, new ser., 9 (1984), pp. 131–44.

108. K. T. Hoppen, *Ireland since 1800: Conflict and Conformity* (London, 1989), pp. 35–38.

109. G. Kitson Clark, *Churchmen and the Condition of England, 1832–1885: A Study in the Development of Social Ideas and Practice from the Old Regime to the Modern State* (London, 1973), pp. 3–23.

110. Crossick, "From Gentleman to the Residuum," p. 160; G. Martin and B. E. Kline, "British Emigration and New Identities," in Marshall, *British Empire*, p. 268. Lord Durham's viceregal regime in Canada was also very authoritarian, hierarchical, and ceremonial; see G. Martin, *The Durham Report and British Policy: A Critical Essay* (Cambridge, 1972), pp. 22–23.

111. Himmelfarb, *Idea of Poverty*, pp. 459–60, 486–88; A. Welsh, *The City of Dickens* (London, 1986), pp. 7–8, 31, 80–81, 145.

112. K. C. Phillips, *Language and Class in Victorian England* (Oxford, 1984), p. 3.

113. Kitson Clark, *Churchmen and the Condition of England*, p. 9; Roberts, *Paternalism*, pp. 111, 151–52.

114. Roberts, *Paternalism*, pp. 68–72; Girouard, *Return to Camelot*, p. 83.

115. J. T. Ward, *The Factory Movement, 1830–1855* (London, 1962).

116. E. Bulwer Lytton, *King Arthur* (London, 1848), 2:169, 173; Girouard, *Return to Camelot*, pp. 74, 86, 87–110, 111–28; Blake, *Disraeli*, pp. 167–72.

117. Parry, *Rise and Fall of Liberal Government*, p. 3; Saville, *1848*, pp. 107–8; Smith, *Lord Grey*, pp. 36–37, 141, 255, 259, 307, 321; D. Cecil, *Melbourne* (New York, 1954), p. 192; R. Brent, *Liberal Anglican Politics: Whiggery, Religion and Reform, 1830–1841* (Oxford, 1987), pp. 27, 121–22, 219, 234–37; R. Johnson, "Educational Policy and Social Control in Early Victorian England," *P&P*, no. 49 (1970), pp. 96–119.

118. J. P. Parry, "Past and Future in the Later Career of Lord John Russell," in T. C. W. Blanning and D. Cannadine (eds.), *History and Biography: Essays in Honour of Derek Beales* (Cambridge, 1996), p. 171. See P. Ziegler, *Melbourne* (London, 1976), pp. 138, 349; Parry, *Rise and Fall of Liberal Government*, p. 134.

119. Wahrman, *Imagining the Middle Class*, pp. 223, 341–43; D. Read, *Peel and the Victorians* (Oxford, 1987), pp. 3–4; N. Gash, *Reaction and Reconstruction in English Politics, 1832–1852* (Oxford, 1965), p. 139.

120. N. Gash, *Sir Robert Peel: The Life of Sir Robert Peel after 1830* (London, 1972), pp. xx, 96–97, 130, 235–37, 589, 608, 714; G. R. Searle, *Entrepreneurial Politics in Mid-Victorian Britain* (Oxford, 1993), pp. 39–42.

121. Ward, *The Chartists*, p. 203; Saville, *1848*, p. 102.

122. R. Brown, *Change and Continuity in British Society, 1800–1850* (Cambridge, 1987), p. 168.

123. C. Fairfield, *Some Account of George William Wilshire Baron Bramwell of Hever and His Opinions* (London, 1898), p. 124; D. Abraham, "Liberty and Property: Lord Bramwell and the Political Economy of Liberal Jurisprudence, Individualism, Freedom, and Liberty," *The American Journal of Legal History*, 38 (1994), p. 306.

124. M. Arnold, *Culture and Anarchy and Other Writings*, ed. S. Collini (Cambridge, 1993), pp. 102–25; R. Harrison, *Before the Socialists: Studies in Labour and Politics, 1861–1881* (London, 1965), pp. 21, 27.

125. H. C. G. Matthew, *Gladstone, 1809–1874* (Oxford, 1986), pp. 3–5, 53, 122–23, 130, 210.

126. H. J. Perkin, *The Age of the Railway* (London, 1971), pp. 151–75; F. M. L. Thompson, "English Landed Society in the Nineteenth Century," in P. Thane, G. Crossick, and R. Floud (eds.), *The Power of the Past: Essays for Eric Hobsbawm* (Cambridge, 1984), pp. 195–96.

127. Perkin, *Modern English Society*, pp. 299–301; Kitson Clark, *Churchmen and the Condition of England*, pp. 102–3; N. J. Smelser, *Social Paralysis and Social Change: British Working-Class Education in the Nineteenth Century* (Los Angeles, 1991), pp. 45–46. This was less so in Scotland, where the poor had a better chance of a good education than they did in England; see W. H. Mathew, "The Origins and Occupations of Glasgow University Students, 1740–1839," *P&P*, no. 33 (1966), pp. 74–94.

128. Perkin, *Modern English Society*, p. 374; J. Vincent, *The Formation of the Liberal Party, 1859–1868* (London, 1966), p. 2. See also *The Economist*, 28 April 1855: "There is a prevailing and well-founded belief that our Government, since the Reform Act, has been virtually in the hands of the middle classes."

129. Blake, *Disraeli*, p. 273; N. McCord, "Cobden and Bright in Politics, 1846–1857," in R. Robson (ed.), *Ideas and Institutions of Victorian Britain: Essays in Honour of Dr. G. Kitson Clark* (London, 1967), p. 113; Briggs, "Language of 'Class,'" p. 177 n. 109.

130. For a helpful discussion of these contradictions and full references to the quotations in this paragraph, see P. Anderson, "The Figures of Descent," reprinted in his *English Questions* (London, 1992), pp. 121–26.

131. W. L. Arnstein, "The Survival of the Victorian Aristocracy," in F. C. Jaher (ed.), *The Rich, the Well-Born, and the Powerful* (New York, 1973), pp. 203–57; idem, "The Myth of the Triumphant Middle Class," *The Historian*, 37 (1975), pp. 205–21; W. D. Rubinstein, *Men of Property: The Very Wealthy in Britain since the Industrial Revolution* (London, 1981); M. J. Weiner, *English Culture and the Decline of the Industrial Spirit, 1850–1980* (Cambridge, 1981); S. Nenadic, "Businessmen, the Urban Middle Classes and the 'Dominance' of Manufacturers in Nineteenth-Century Britain," *EcHR*, 2d ser., 44 (1991), pp. 66–85; G. Searle, *Entrepreneurial Politics in Mid-Victorian Britain* (Oxford, 1993).

132. E. P. Thompson, "The Peculiarities of the English," in *The Poverty of Theory* (London, 1978), esp. pp. 35–56; R. Q. Gray, "Bourgeois Hegemony in Victorian Britain," in J. Bloomfield (ed.), *Class, Hegemony and Party* (London, 1977), pp. 73–93; R. H. Trainor, "Urban Elites in Victorian Britain," *Urban History Yearbook*, 11 (1985), p. 1–17; S. Gunn, "The 'Failure' of the Victorian Middle Class: A Critique," in J. Wolff and J. Seed (eds.), *The Culture of Capital: Art, Power and the Nineteenth-Cen-*

tury Middle Class (Manchester, 1988), pp. 17–43; E. J. Hobsbawm, "The Example of the English Middle Class," in J. Kocka and A. Mitchell (eds.), *Bourgeois Society in Nineteenth-Century Europe* (Oxford, 1993), pp. 127–50; D. S. Macleod, *Art and the Victorian Middle Class: Money and the Making of Cultural Identity* (Cambridge, 1996).

133. P. Warwick, "Did Britain Change? An Inquiry into the Causes of National Decline," *Journal of Contemporary History*, 20 (1985), pp. 115–22; P. Thane, "Aristocracy and Middle Classes in Victorian England: The Problem of Gentrification," in A. M. Birke and L. Kettenacher (eds.), *Middle Classes, Aristocracy and Monarchy* (Munich, 1989), pp. 93–107.

134. P. Joyce, *Work, Society and Politics: The Culture of the Factory in Later Victorian England* (London, 1980); Searle, *Entrepreneurial Politics*, p. 211.

135. F. M. L. Thompson, *The Rise of Respectable Society: A Social History of Victorian Britain, 1830–1900* (London, 1988), p. 138; Himmelfarb, *Idea of Poverty*, pp. 316, 322, 353, 378–81.

136. G. Best, *Mid-Victorian Britain, 1851–75* (London, 1971), pp. 95–97; B. Harrison, *Peaceable Kingdom: Stability and Change in Modern Britain* (Oxford, 1982), pp. 159–60.

137. See, for instance, the two inconsistent divisions of society advanced, apparently unawares, by Frederic Harrison, which are quoted in Harrison, *Before the Socialists*, p. 28 n. 2.

138. Burn, *Age of Equipoise*, p. 255, 260; Best, *Mid-Victorian Britain*, pp. 245–47; Briggs, *Victorian People*, pp. 142–44; Crossick, "From Gentleman to the Residuum," pp. 163–65.

139. Best, *Mid-Victorian Britain*, pp. xvi, 260–63.

140. Mugglestone, *"Talking Proper,"* pp. 106–59.

141. For examples of British condescension to Canadian colonials, see G. W. Martin, *Britain and the Origins of Canadian Confederation, 1837–67* (Cambridge, 1995), pp. 139–42, 240, 259–61.

142. Perkin, *Modern English Society*, pp. 174–75, 446; G. Stedman Jones, *Outcast London: A Study in the Relationship Between the Classes in Victorian Society* (Harmondsworth, 1976) pp. 12–14, 241–70.

143. Parry, *Rise and Fall of Liberal Government*, p. 227; Harrison, *Peaceable Kingdom*, p. 281; Joyce, *Visions of the People*, pp. 245–52; P. Keating (ed.), *Into Unknown England, 1866–1913: Selections from the Social Explorers* (Glasgow, 1976), pp. 11–32; D. Nord, "The Social Explorer as Anthropologist: Victorian Travellers among the Urban Poor," in W. Sharp and L. Wallock (eds.), *Visions of the Modern City* (Baltimore, 1987), pp. 122–34.

144. Searle, *Entrepreneurial Politics*, pp. 51–88, 167–200; Parry, *Rise and Fall of Liberal Government*, p. 179.

145. O. Anderson, *A Liberal State at War: English Politics and Economics During the Crimean War* (London, 1967), pp. 101–18; idem, "The Administrative Reform Association," in P. Hollis (ed.), *Pressure from Without in Early Victorian England* (London, 1974), pp. 262–88; Searle, *Entrepreneurial Politics*, pp. 89–125.

146. Searle, *Entrepreneurial Politics*, pp. 103–5, 131–32; Anderson, *Liberal State at War*, pp. 118–28.

147. Perkin, *Modern English Society*, p. 391.

148. E. D. Steele, *Palmerson and Liberalism, 1855–65* (Cambridge, 1991), p. 122; Vincent, *Liberal Party*, pp. 169–74.

149. Joyce, *Visions of the People*, pp. 56–65, 70–74. For broader discussion of the popular hero on the platform, articulating the politics of populism, see J. Belchem and J. Epstein, "The Nineteenth-Century Gentleman Leader Revisited," *SH*, 22 (1977), pp. 174–93.

150. K. O. Morgan, *Wales in British Politics, 1868–1923*, 3d ed. (Cardiff, 1980), pp. 22–27; M. Cragoe, "Conscience or Coercion? Clerical Influence at the General Election of 1868 in Wales," *P&P*, no. 149 (1995), pp. 140–69; K. T. Hoppen, *Elections, Politics and Society in Ireland, 1832–1885* (Oxford, 1984), pp. 464–65; Foster, *Modern Ireland*, pp. 390–99.

151. McCord, "Cobden and Bright in Politics," pp. 107–9; D. Read, *Cobden and Bright: A Victorian Political Partnership* (London, 1967), pp. 158–61.

152. Foster, *Modern Ireland*, p. 392; R. V. Comerford, *The Fenians in Context, 1848–82* (Dublin, 1985), p. 40.

153. Searle, *Entrepreneurial Politics*, pp. 290–321; Briggs, "Language of 'Class,'" p. 171, quoting *Essays on Reform* (London, 1867), p. 74; Burn, *Age of Equipoise*, pp. 265–66, 286; Best, *Mid-Victorian Britain*, pp. 150, 158; F. Bedarida, *A Social History of England, 1851–1990*, 2d ed. (London, 1991), pp. 36–72.

154. Best, *Mid-Victorian Britain*, pp. xv–xvi; G. Watson, *The English Ideology* (London, 1973), pp. 174–75. For a general analysis of nineteenth-century British society that builds on this insight, see Thompson, *Rise of Respectable Society*, esp. pp. 152–53, 173–74, 177, 181–82, 193–96, 360–361.

155. Briggs, *Victorian People*, pp. 99–100; M. Cowling, *1867: Disraeli, Gladstone and Revolution: The Passing of the Second Reform Bill* (Cambridge, 1967), p. 8.

156. Joyce, *Work, Society and Politics*, p. 296; Best, *Mid-Victorian Britain*, pp. xv–xvi, 232–38; R. Strong, *The Story of Britain* (London, 1996), pp. 439–40; Kitson Clark, *Churchmen and the Condition of England*, pp. 166–68; Lord Willoughby de Broke, *The Passing Years* (London, 1924), pp. 56–58. Here is one quotation from the eponymous character in Trollope's *The Prime*

Minister (1876; rpt., Oxford, 1983): "The Conservative . . . thinks that God has divided the world as he finds it divided, and that he may best do his duty by making the inferior man happy and contented in his position, teaching him that the place which he holds is by God's ordinance" (p. 24). The same view of the social order might, not unreasonably, have been attributed to many Whigs.

157. Parry, *Rise and Fall of Liberal Government*, pp. 5, 175.

158. Watson, *English Ideology*, p. 180; Perkin, *Modern English Society*, pp. 408–9; Briggs, *Victorian People*, p. 106; Steel, *Palmerston*, p. 36; Best, *Mid-Victorian Britain*, p. 233. See also A. H. Halsey, *Change in British Society*, 4th ed. (Oxford, 1995), pp. 200–201, where he reproduces a passport signed by Palmerston in 1851, with its "confident description of social hierarchy," extending through the social fabric from the queen to a man and maidservant.

159. R. Blake, *Disraeli and Gladstone* (Cambridge, 1969), pp. 17, 22; idem, *Disraeli*, pp. 278–84, 762–63.

160. Vincent, *Liberal Party*, pp. 211–12, 224; Matthew, *Gladstone, 1809–1874*, pp. 26, 29, 34–35; R. Jenkins, *Gladstone* (London, 1995), pp. ix, 406, 426; Joyce, *Visions of the People*, p. 56.

161. Crossick, "From Gentleman to the Residuum," p. 161; Joyce, *Visions of the People*, p. 57; Himmelfarb, *Idea of Poverty*, p. 533; Steele, *Palmerston*, p. 177.

162. Searle, *Entrepreneurial Politics*, pp. 296–97; Parry, *Rise and Fall of Liberal Government*, pp. 168–69; Steele, *Palmerston*, pp. 41–42; Vincent, *Liberal Party*, p. 79.

163. Vincent, *Liberal Party*, p. 218; Parry, *Rise and Fall of Liberal Government*, p. 3.

164. Briggs, "Language of 'Class,' " p. 169, quoting *The Times*, 10 August 1861.

165. Searle, *Entrepreneurial Politics*, pp. 129, 224; Steele, *Palmerston*, pp. 128–29, 206, 229.

166. Cowling, *1867*, pp. 95–96.

167. Harrison, *Before the Socialists*, p. 109; Briggs, *Victorian People*, pp. 280, 296.

168. Matthew, *Gladstone*, p. 139; Parry, *Rise and Fall of Liberal Government*, p. 209; Harrison, *Before the Socialists*, p. 66.

169. Matthew, *Gladstone*, p. 140; McCord, "Difficulties of Parliamentary Reform," pp. 383–84.

170. Briggs, *Victorian People*, pp. 255–62, 292–303.

171. Harrison, *Peaceable Kingdom*, p. 266; Harrison, *Before the Socialists*, pp. 115–16.

172. Cowling, *1867*, pp. 40, 57–58, 188; Harrison, *Before the Socialists*, p. 120.

173. Searle, *Entrepreneurial Politics*, pp. 226–27; Briggs, *Victorian People*, pp. 286, 302–3; F. B. Smith, *The Making of the Second Reform Bill* (Cambridge, 1966), p. 225.

174. Harrison, *Before the Socialists*, p. 124; Briggs, *Victorian People*, pp. 299–301.

175. D. Spring, introduction to J. Bateman, *The Great Landowners of Great Britain and Ireland*, 4th ed. (London, 1883; rpt., Leicester, 1971), pp. 8–13; D. Cannadine, *The Decline and Fall of the British Aristocracy* (London, 1990), pp. 54–56.

176. Briggs, *Victorian People*, p. 262.

177. Watson, *English Ideology*, p. 188.

178. J. Austen, *Pride and Prejudice* (New York, 1961), p. 138; J. Harris, *Private Lives, Public Spirit: A Social History of Britain, 1870–1914* (Oxford, 1993), p. 224.

179. B. Cohn, *Colonialism and Its Forms of Knowledge: The British in India* (Princeton, 1996), pp. 8, 119–27; I. Copland, *The Princes of India and the Endgame of Empire, 1917–1947* (Cambridge, 1997), p. 17.

180. L. A. Knight, "The Royal Titles Act and India," *HJ*, 11 (1968), p. 488; B. Cohn, "Representing Authority in Victorian India," in E. J. Hobsbawm and T. Ranger (eds.), *The Invention of Tradition* (Cambridge, 1983), pp. 165–210.

4. THE TWENTIETH CENTURY:
SOCIAL IDENTITIES AND POLITICAL IDENTITIES

1. P. G. J. Pulzer, *Political Representation and Elections: Parties and Voting in Great Britain* (New York, 1967), p. 102; B. Waites, *A Class Society at War: England, 1914–1918* (Leamington Spa, 1987), p. 2. For the general application of this view to modern Britain, see D. Butler and D. Stokes, *Political Change in Britain* (London, 1969), pp. 65–94.

2. For the (much-debated) effects of these franchise extensions, see N. Blewett, "The Franchise in the United Kingdom, 1885–1918," *P&P*, no. 32 (1965), pp. 27–56; B. M. Walker, "The Irish Electorate, 1865–1915," *Irish Historical Studies*, 18 (1973), pp. 359–406; H. C. G. Matthew, R. I. McKibbin, and J. A. Kay, "The Franchise Factor and the Rise of the Labour Party," *EHR*, 91 (1976), pp. 723–52; M. Hart, "The Liberals, the War and the Franchise," *EHR*, 97 (1982), pp. 820–31; D. M. Tanner, "The Parliamentary Electoral System, the 'Fourth' Reform Act and the

Rise of Labour in England and Wales," *Bulletin of the Institute of Historical Research*, 56 (1983), pp. 205–19.

3. D. Tanner, *Political Change and the Labour Party, 1900–18* (Cambridge, 1990), pp. 10–16, well summarizes the recent literature on this. As he notes, "The logic of much recent analysis is to recognise the difficulties of making connections between 'social' experience and 'political' responses" (p. 11).

4. J. Harris, *Private Lives, Public Spirit: A Social History of Britain, 1870–1914* (Oxford, 1993), p. 8; D. Jarvis, "British Conservatism and Class Politics in the 1920s," *EHR*, 111 (1996), p. 69. The argument that the 1880s were a major turning point was originally made by H. M. Lynd, *England in the Eighteen Eighties* (London, 1945). For a recent restatement of this view, see E. J. Feuchtwanger, *Democracy and Empire: Britain 1865–1914* (London, 1985), pp. 112–191; D. Cannadine, *The Decline and Fall of the British Aristocracy* (London, 1990), pp. 25–31. For a very different interpretation of this decade, which nevertheless sees it as pivotal, see J. Walkowitz, *City of Dreadful Delight: Narratives of Sexual Danger in Late-Victorian London* (Chicago, 1992).

5. J. A. Winter and D. M. Joslin (eds.), *R. H. Tawney's Commonplace Book* (Cambridge, 1972), p. 18. For Tawney's own view of contemporary society, see J. M. Winter, "R. H. Tawney's Early Political Thought," *P&P*, no. 47 (1970), pp. 71–96.

6. J. Stevenson, *British Society, 1914–45* (Harmondsworth, 1984), p. 22; R. I. McKibbin, *The Ideologies of Class: Social Relations in Britain, 1880–1950* (Oxford, 1990), p. vii.

7. Cannadine, *Decline and Fall*, pp. 57–60; R. Douglas, *Land, People and Politics: A History of the Land Question in the United Kingdom, 1878–1952* (London, 1976), p. 27; L. P. Curtis, Jr., *Coercion and Conciliation in Ireland, 1880–1892: A Study in Constructive Unionism* (Princeton, 1963), pp. 239–58. This antilandlord agitation in Ireland was accompanied by, and no doubt helped to provoke, similar outbursts in Wales and Scotland; see D. W. Crowley, "The 'Crofters Party,' 1885–1892," *Scottish Historical Review*, 35 (1956), pp. 110–26; H. J. Hanham, "The Problem of Highland Discontent, 1880–1885," *TRHS*, 5th ser., 19 (1970), pp. 21–65; K. O. Morgan, *Wales in British Politics, 1868–1922* (Cardiff, 1970), pp. 94–96; D. W. Howell, *Land and People in Nineteenth-Century Wales* (London, 1977), pp. 85–89.

8. For the most recent analysis of the land war in these collective class terms, see S. Clark, *Social Origins of the Irish Land War* (Princeton, 1979), esp. pp. 225–349. For one way in which it both articulated and

widened the gap between "the landlords" and "the people," see L. P. Curtis, Jr., "Stopping the Hunt, 1881–1882: An Aspect of the Irish Land War," in C. H. E. Philpin (ed.), *Nationalism and Popular Protest in Ireland* (Cambridge, 1987), pp. 349–402. For a shrewd critique, see L. P. Curtis, Jr., "On Class and Class Conflict in the Land War," *Irish Economic and Social History*, 8 (1981), pp. 86–94.

9. In which regard, consider these remarks of Gladstone's friend and colleague John Morley: "In my heart, I feel the [Land] League has done downright good work in raising up the tenants against their truly detestable tyrants" (Cannadine, *Decline and Fall*, p. 65). Here was ideological stereotyping with a vengeance.

10. P. F. Clarke, *A Question of Leadership: Gladstone to Thatcher* (London, 1991), pp. 34–35; H. C. G. Matthew (ed.), *The Gladstone Diaries*, vol. 11, *July 1883–December 1886* (Oxford, 1990), pp. 538, 560, 571, 629.

11. E. F. Biagini, *Liberty, Retrenchment and Reform: Popular Liberalism in the Age of Gladstone, 1860–1880* (Cambridge, 1990), pp. 50–60; P. Joyce, *Visions of the People: Industrial England and the Question of Class, 1848–1914* (Cambridge, 1991), pp. 56, 68–84, 245–55, 294–309; G. Stedman Jones, *Languages of Class: Studies in English Working-Class History, 1832–1982* (Cambridge, 1983), p. 229; J. P. Parry, *The Rise and Fall of Liberal Government in Victorian England* (London, 1993), pp. 296, 302.

12. P. Guedalla (ed.), *The Queen and Mr. Gladstone*, 2 vols. (London, 1933), 2:446–52; P. Magnus, *Gladstone: A Biography* (London, 1954), pp. 414–22.

13. Lord Salisbury, "Disintegration," reprinted in P. Smith (ed.), *Lord Salisbury on Politics: A Selection From His Articles in the Quarterly Review, 1860–1883* (London, 1972), pp. 338–76; P. Marsh, *The Discipline of Popular Government: Lord Salisbury's Domestic Statecraft, 1881–1902* (Hassocks, 1978), pp. 10–17; A. Offer, *Property and Politics, 1870–1914: Landownership, Law, Ideology and Urban Development in England* (Cambridge, 1981), p. 153. In this regard, see also this comment by G. Kitson Clark, *Churchmen and the Condition of England, 1832–1885* (London, 1973): "An era was beginning in which the old hierarchy would no longer be tolerated" (p. 267). He is, of course, describing the old order in the countryside.

14. Marsh, *Discipline of Popular Government*, pp. 69, 99; A. Jones and M. Bentley, "Salisbury and Baldwin," in M. Cowling (ed.), *Conservative Essays* (London, 1978), pp. 26, 28; Clarke, *Question of Leadership*, pp. 45, 50, 56–57; E. H. H. Green, *The Crisis of Conservatism: The Politics, Economics and Ideology of the Conservative Party, 1880–1914* (London, 1995), pp. 78–119; N. Soldon, "Laissez-Faire as Dogma: The Liberty and

Property Defence League," in K. D. Brown (ed.), *Essays in Anti-Labour History* (London, 1974), pp. 234–61; W. H. Mallock, *Classes and Masses* (London, 1896); idem, *Aristocracy and Evolution* (London, 1898), pp. 42, 46, 323, 347–48, 352, 376–77; idem, *Memoirs of Life and Literature* (London, 1920), pp. 1–16, 21, 25–26, 106–24, 133–43, 161, 251.

15. W. C. Lubenow, "Irish Home Rule and the Social Basis of the Great Separation in the Liberal Party in 1886," *HJ*, 28 (1985), pp. 125–27; Green, *Crisis of Conservatism*, p. 86; P. Thompson, *The Edwardians: The Re-Making of British Society*, 2d ed. (London, 1992), p. 212; Jarvis, "British Conservatism," pp. 65–68

16. Thompson, *The Edwardians*, p. 236; J. Grigg, *Lloyd George: The People's Champion, 1902–1911* (London, 1978), pp. 224–25; B. K. Murray, *The People's Budget of 1909–10: Lloyd George and Liberal Politics* (Oxford, 1980), p. 199.

17. Green, *Crisis of Conservatism*, p. 272; G. D. Phillips, *The Diehards: Aristocratic Society and Politics in Edwardian England* (London, 1979), p. 125; N. Blewett, *The Peers, the Parties and the People: The General Elections of 1910* (London, 1972), p. 155; A. Adonis, *Making Aristocracy Work: The Peerage and the Political System in Britain, 1884–1914* (Oxford, 1993), p. 149.

18. Grigg, *Lloyd George*, pp. 211, 304; Murray, *The People's Budget*, p. 256.

19. H. M. Pelling, *A Short History of the Labour Party*, 3d ed. (London, 1968), pp. 5–6; D. Powell, *The Edwardian Crisis: Britain, 1901–14* (London, 1996), p. 102.

20. H. J. Perkin, *The Rise of Professional Society: England since 1880* (London, 1989), pp. 111, 174–75, 178; E. H. Phelps Brown, *The Growth of British Industrial Relations* (London, 1965), p. 330; S. Meacham, " 'The Sense of an Impending Clash': English Working-Class Unrest Before the First World War," *AHR*, 77 (1972), pp. 1343–64; Thompson, *The Edwardians*, p. 241.

21. E. J. Hobsbawm, *Worlds of Labour: Further Studies in the History of Labour* (London, 1984), p. 190; R. I. McKibbin, *The Evolution of the Labour Party, 1910–1924* (Oxford, 1974); Tanner, *Political Change and the Labour Party*, pp. 3–4; Powell, *Edwardian Crisis*, p. 108.

22. A. Wright, *British Socialism* (London, 1983), p. 77; D. Howell, *British Workers and the ILP* (Manchester, 1983), pp. 352–62; G. Foote, *The Labour Party's Political Thought: A History* (London, 1985), pp. 43–45; C. Tsuzuki, *H. M. Hyndman and British Socialism* (Oxford, 1961), pp. 153–54; D. Marquand, *Ramsay MacDonald* (London, 1977), pp. 34, 37.

23. G. Himmelfarb, *Poverty and Compassion: The Moral Imagination of the*

Late Victorians (New York, 1991), pp. 357–78; B. Webb, *My Apprentice-ship* (Harmondsworth, 1971), pp. 64–65, 346–48; A. M. McBriar, *Fabi-an Socialism and English Politics, 1884–1918* (Cambridge, 1962), pp. 63–71; P. F. Clarke, "The Social Democratic Theory of the Class Strug-gle," in J. Winter (ed.), *The Working Class in Modern British History: Es-says in Honour of Henry Pelling* (Cambridge, 1983), pp. 3–8.

24. Tsuzuki, *Hyndman and British Socialism*, pp. 46, 83–86, 97, 179; K. Willis, "The Introduction and Critical Reception of Marxist Thought in Britain, 1850–1900," *HJ*, 20 (1977), pp. 417–59; M. Bevir, "The British Social Democratic Federation, 1880–1885: From O'Brienism to Marx-ism," *International Review of Social History*, 37 (1992), pp. 207–29; J. Schneer, *Ben Tillett: Portrait of a Labour Leader* (London, 1982), p. 133.

25. A. Mearns, *The Bitter Cry of Outcast London* (London, 1883); W. Booth, *In Darkest England and the Way Out* (London, 1890); C. F. G. Master-man, "The Social Abyss," *Contemporary Review*, 81 (1902).

26. H. George, *Progress and Poverty* (London, 1883), pp. 6–7; M. Bulmer, K. Bales, and K. Kish Sklar, "The Social Survey in Historical Perspective," in M. Bulmer, K. Bales, and K. Kish Sklar (eds.), *The Social Survey in Historical Perspective, 1880–1940* (Cambridge, 1991), p. 24; D. Epstein Nord, *The Apprenticeship of Beatrice Webb* (London, 1985), p. 186.

27. P. Keating (ed.), *Into Unknown England, 1866–1913: Selections from the Social Explorers* (Glasgow, 1976), pp. 24–31; Himmelfarb, *Poverty and Compassion*, p. 32; E. P. Hennock, "Poverty and Social Theory in Eng-land: The Experience of the 1880s," *SH*, 1 (1976), p. 75.

28. Powell, *Edwardian Crisis*, p. 35; Mallock, *Aristocracy and Evolution*, p. 42.

29. Himmelfarb, *Poverty and Compassion*, p. 158; Webb, *My Apprenticeship*, pp. 186, 191–96, 231–32. In 1895 J. A. Hobson was attacked in the *Na-tional Review* for preaching "the gospel of hatred . . . hatred between class and class, between master and men, between rich and poor," an-other set of polarities that were not at all the same. See Green, *Crisis of Conservatism*, p. 144.

30. R. F. Roster, introduction to Philpin, *Nationalism and Popular Protest*, pp. 9–10; K. T. Hoppen, "Landlords, Society and Electoral Politics in Mid-Nineteenth-Century Ireland," in ibid., 284–319; W. E. Vaughan, *Landlords and Tenants in Ireland, 1848–1904* (Dundalk, 1984), pp. 13–26; E. Richards, *A History of the Highland Clearances*, vol. 1, *Agrarian Trans-formations and the Evictions 1746–1886* (London, 1982), 7–11, 29–32; Howell, *Land and People of Nineteenth-Century Wales*, pp. 43–45, 64–65, 68–71, 85–91.

31. Foster, introduction, pp. 10–12; D. Jordan, "Merchants, 'Strong Farmers' and Fenians: The Post-Famine Political Elite and the Irish Land War," in Philpin, *Nationalism and Popular Protest*, 320–48; R. F. Foster, *Modern Ireland, 1600–1972* (Harmondsworth, 1989), pp. 405–15; P. Bew, *Land and the National Question in Ireland, 1858–82* (Dublin, 1978), pp. 4–5, 121–26, 188–90, 220–24; A. W. Orridge, "Who Supported the Land War? An Aggregate-Data Analysis of Irish Agrarian Discontent, 1879–1882," *Economic and Social Review*, 12 (1980–81), pp. 203–33; K. T. Hoppen, *Elections, Politics and Society in Ireland, 1832–1885* (Oxford, 1984), pp. viii, 473–79; D. S. Jones, "The Cleavage Between Graziers and Peasants in the Land Struggle, 1890–1910," in S. Clark and J. S. Donnelly, Jr. (eds.), *Irish Peasants: Violence and Political Unrest, 1780–1914* (Manchester, 1983), pp. 374–417.

32. Thompson, *The Edwardians*, p. 213; Green, *Crisis of Conservatism*, pp. 120–56; M. Pugh, *The Tories and the People, 1880–1935* (Oxford, 1935), pp. 139–74; H. Cunningham, "The Conservative Party and Patriotism," in R. Colls and P. Dodd (eds.), *Englishness: Politics and Culture, 1880–1920* (Beckenham, 1986), pp. 283–307; J. Lawrence, "Class and Gender in the Making of Urban Toryism, 1880–1914," *EHR*, 108 (1993), pp. 629–52; Jarvis, "British Conservatism," p. 66.

33. Harris, *Private Lives, Public Spirit*, p. 9; Powell, *Edwardian Crisis*, p. 169; Tanner, *Political Change and the Labour Party*, pp. 5, 421; Murray, *The People's Budget*, pp. 5–15; G. R. Searle, *Corruption in British Politics, 1895–1930* (Oxford, 1987), p. 139.

34. C. Shaw, "The Large Manufacturing Employers of 1907," *Business History*, 25 (1983), pp. 24–60; P. L. Payne, "The Emergence of the Large Scale Company in Great Britain," *EcHR*, 2d ser., 20 (1967), pp. 519–42.

35. R. I. McKibbin, *The Ideologies of Class: Social Relations in Britain, 1880–1950* (Oxford, 1990), pp. 6–8; S. Baldwin, *On England* (London, 1926), pp. 34–35.

36. Harris, *Private Lives, Public Spirit*, pp. 128–29; Joyce, *Visions of the People*, pp. 124–41; McKibbin, *Ideologies of Class*, pp. 4, 37; A. J. Reid, "The Division of Labour and Politics in Britain, 1880–1920," in W. J. Mommsen and H.-G. Husung (eds.), *The Development of Trade Unionism in Great Britain and Germany, 1880–1914* (London, 1985), pp. 150–65; idem, "Class and Organisation," *HJ*, 30 (1987), pp. 235–38; idem, *Social Classes and Social Relations in Britain, 1850–1914* (Cambridge, 1995), pp. 18–29; R. Harrison and J. Zeitlin (eds.), *Divisions of Labour: Skilled Workers and Technological Change in Nineteenth-Century England* (London, 1985).

37. Harris, *Private Lives, Public Spirit*, pp. 140–41; McKibbin, *Ideologies of Class*, pp. 2–3; Joyce, *Visions of the People*, pp. 114–41. See also Tanner, *Political Change and the Labour Party*: "The rise of Labour between 1885 and 1931 cannot be explained by an expanding class consciousness" (p. 441).

38. Willis, "Marxist Thought in Britain," pp. 419, 441–48, 455–59. McKibbin, *Ideologies of Class*, pp. 1–41; E. J. Hobsbawm, "Dr. Marx and the Victorian Critics," in *Labouring Men* (London, 1964), pp. 239–49.

39. McKibbin, *Ideologies of Class*, p. 14; P. F. Clarke, *Liberals and Social Democrats* (London, 1978), pp. 145–46; H. Pelling, "The Labour Unrest, 1911–14," in *Popular Politics and Society in Late Victorian Britain* (London, 1968), pp. 147–64; G. A. Phillips, "The Triple Industrial Alliance in 1914," *EcHR*, 2d ser., 24 (1971), pp. 55–67; E. H. Hunt, *British Labour History, 1815–1914* (London, 1981), pp. 329–34; Thompson, *The Edwardians*, p. 206.

40. Hennock, "Poverty and Social Theory in England," pp. 72–77; Himmelfarb, *Poverty and Compassion*, pp. 103–4.

41. McKibbin, *Ideologies of Class*, pp. 167–96; Bulmer, Bales, and Sklar, "The Social Survey," p. 22; K. Bales, "Charles Booth's *Survey of Life and Labour of the People in London*, 1889–1903," in Bulmer, Bales, and Sklar, *Social Survey in Historical Perspective*, p. 91; J. Lewis, "The Place of Social Investigation, Social Theory and Social Work in the Approach to Late Victorian and Edwardian Social Problems: The Case of Beatrice Webb and Helen Bosanquet," in ibid., pp. 148–69.

42. Phillips, *The Diehards*, p. 102; Thompson, *The Edwardians*, p. 78.

43. Perkin, *Rise of Professional Society*, p. 101; Powell, *Edwardian Crisis*, p. 11; C. F. G. Masterman, *The Condition of England* (London, 1909).

44. J. F. C. Harrison, *Late Victorian Britain, 1870–1901* (London, 1990), pp. 80–81; A. Clarke, *The Effects of the Factory System* 3d ed. (London, 1913), pp. 27–28.

45. Thompson, *The Edwardians*, p. 284–85.

46. A. J. Mayer, "The Lower Middle Class as a Historical Problem," *JMH*, 47 (1975), pp. 409–31; G. Anderson, *Victorian Clerks* (Manchester, 1975); G. Crossick (ed.), *The Lower Middle Class in Britain, 1870–1914* (London, 1977); idem, "Metaphors of the Middle: The Discovery of the Petit Bourgeoisie, 1880–1914," *TRHS*, 6th ser., 4 (1994), pp. 251–79.

47. W. J. Reader, *Professional Men: The Rise of the Professional Classes in Nineteenth-Century England* (London, 1966); T. R. Gourvish, "The Rise of the Professions," in T. R. Gourvish and A. O'Day (eds.), *Later Victorian Britain* (London, 1988), pp. 18–23; Perkin, *Rise of Professional*

Society, esp. pp. 78–101, 116–22.

48. J. Camplin, *The Rise of the Rich* (New York, 1979); W. D. Rubinstein, *Men of Property: The Very Wealthy in Britain since the Industrial Revolution* (London, 1981), pp. 38–43, 60, 74; Cannadine, *Decline and Fall*, pp. 90–91.

49. G. K. Chesterton, *Autobiography* (London, n.d.), p. 13.

50. G. Huxley, *Victorian Duke: The Life of Hugh Lupus Grosvenor, First Duke of Westminster* (London, 1967), p. 164.

51. P. Addison, "Winston Churchill and the Working Class, 1900–1914," in Winter, *Working Class in Modern British History*, p. 48.

52. J. R. Green, *A Short History of the English People*, new ed., revised and enlarged, with epilogue by Alice Stopford Green (London, 1916), p. 838; S. Webb, "The Basis of Socialism: Historic," in G. B. Shaw (ed.), *Fabian Essays on Socialism* (New York, 1891), pp. 12, 14; A. V. Dicey, *Lectures on the Relation Between Law and Public Opinion in England During the Nineteenth Century* (New Brunswick, 1981), pp. 185–86; G. M. Trevelyan, *Lord Grey of the Reform Bill* (London, 1920), p. 245.

53. W. L. Blease, *A Short History of English Liberalism* (London, 1913), pp. 73, 168; D. Wahrman, *Imagining the Middle Class: The Political Representation of Class in Britain, c. 1780–1840* (Cambridge, 1995), pp. 413–17.

54. H. V. Emy, *Liberals, Radicals and Social Politics, 1892–1914* (Cambridge, 1973), pp. 171–73; J. Cooper: *Class: A View from Middle England* (London, 1993), p. 29.

55. Epstein Nord, *Apprenticeship of Beatrice Webb*, p. 49; D. Cannadine, "The Present and the Past in the English Industrial Revolution, 1880–1980," *P&P*, no. 103 (1984), pp. 133–39.

56. Kitson Clark, *Churchmen and the Condition of England*, p. 287; Wahrman, *Imagining the Middle Class*, pp. 414–15 n. 11; M. J. Weiner, *English Culture and the Decline of the Industrial Spirit, 1850–1980* (Cambridge, 1981), pp. 82–86.

57. Searle, *Corruption in British Politics*, pp. 103–237; Cannadine, *Decline and Fall*, pp. 329–35.

58. R. A. Rempel, *Unionists Divided: Arthur Balfour, Joseph Chamberlain and the Unionist Free Traders* (Newton Abbot, 1972), p. 109; Weiner, *English Culture*, pp. 99–100.

59. E. E. Williams, *"Made in Germany,"* ed. A. Albu (London, 1896; rpt., Brighton, 1973), pp. xxi, 1; Sir J. H. Clapham, *An Economic History of Modern Britain* (Cambridge, 1938), 3:42–43, 130.

60. C. Wilson, "Economy and Society in Late Victorian Britain," *EcHR*, 2d ser., 18 (1965), p. 194; D. H. Aldcroft and H. W. Richardson, *The*

British Economy, 1870–1939 (London, 1969), p. 113 n. 2.

61. Masterman, *Condition of England*, pp. 14, 71, 80–82.

62. Masterman, *Condition of England*, pp. 12, 18, 96, 112; B. Crick, *George Orwell: A Life*, new ed. (Harmondsworth, 1992), pp. 52–53, 58–60.

63. Keating, *Into Unknown England*, p. 124; Himmelfarb, *Poverty and Compassion*, p. 111.

64. Phillips, *The Diehards*, pp. 57, 111, 113; Masterman, *Condition of England*, p. 12.

65. R. Harrison, *Before the Socialists: Studies in Labour and Politics, 1861–1881* (London, 1965), p. 196; Joyce, *Visions of the People*, pp. 160, 173.

66. M. Pugh, *The Tories and the People, 1880–1935* (Oxford, 1985), pp. 2, 6, 13, 20–22, 27, 141–42. It can scarcely be coincidence that during this period the Conservatives also espoused the "ramparts of property" policy, whereby they sought to promote owner occupation among a much larger proportion of the population than hitherto. It was hoped that this finely graded and securely established propertied order would underpin and support the finely graded but no-longer securely established social order, a policy that it has been argued came to its fullest fruition under Margaret Thatcher in the 1980s, with the sale of council houses. See Cannadine, *Decline and Fall*, pp. 453–54; Offer, *Property and Politics*, pp. 148–49, 353, 362, 380, 406; Green, *Crisis of Conservatism*, pp. 290–91.

67. Sir I. De la Bere, *The Queen's Orders of Chivalry* (London, 1964), pp. 15–16, 129, 143, 144, 149, 168, 171, 177–78; W. D. Rubinstein, "The Evolution of the British Honours System since the Mid-Nineteenth Century," in *Elites and the Wealthy in Modern British History: Essays in Social and Economic History* (New York, 1987), pp. 222–61; Cannadine, *Decline and Fall*, pp. 198–202, 299–302, 307.

68. A. Marwick, *Class: Image and Reality in Britain, France and the USA since 1930* (London, 1980), p. 30; Harris, *Private Lives, Public Spirit*, pp. 6, 234–35.

69. B. Cohn, "Representing Authority in Victorian India," in E. J. Hobsbawm and T. Ranger (eds.), *The Invention of Tradition* (Cambridge, 1983), pp. 165–210; D. Cannadine, *Aspects of Aristocracy: Grandeur and Decline in Modern Britain* (London, 1994), pp. 78–90; S. Khilnani, *The Idea of India* (London, 1997), pp. 122, 134.

70. D. A. Washbrook, "Caste, Class and Dominance in Modern Tamil Nadu: Non-Brahmanism, Dravidianism and Tamil Nationalism," in F. R. Frankel and M. S. A. Rao (eds.), *Dominance and State Power in Modern India: Decline of a Social Order* (Delhi, 1989), p. 248; I. Copland, *The*

Princes of India in the Endgame of Empire, 1917–1947 (Cambridge, 1997), p. 21.

71. G. C. Bolton, "The Idea of a Colonial Gentry," *Historical Studies*, 13 (1968), pp. 307, 323; R. Hubbard, *Rideau Hall: An Illustrated History of Government House, Ottawa* (Montreal, 1977); C. Cunneen, *King's Men: Australia's Governors General* (London, 1983); Cannadine, *Decline and Fall*, pp. 588–601; idem, *Aspects of Aristocracy*, pp. 109–10; idem, "Imperial Canada: Old History—New Problems," in C. M. Coates (ed.), *Imperial Canada, 1867–1917* (Edinburgh, 1997), pp. 8–9;

72. McKibbin, *Ideologies of Class*, pp. 17–20; Pugh, *Tories and The People*, p. 163.

73. A. C. Benson, *The Life of Edward White Benson, Sometime Archbishop of Canterbury* (London, 1899), p. 133; D. Cannadine, "The Context, Performance and Meaning of Ritual: The British Monarchy and the 'Invention of Tradition,' c. 1820–1977," in Hobsbawm and Ranger, *Invention of Tradition*, pp. 129–38. At the time of the coronation of Edward VII, in 1902, the Social Democratic Federation sent a loyal address specifically denying any intention of replacing the monarchy by a republic; see Stedman Jones, *Languages of Class*, p. 211.

74. Joyce, *Visions of the People*, pp. 182–83; D. Cannadine and E. Hammeron, "Conflict and Consensus on a Ceremonial Occasion: The Diamond Jubilee in Cambridge," *HJ*, 24 (1981), pp. 111–46.

75. D. Cannadine, "The Transformation of Civic Ritual in Modern Britain: The Colchester Oyster Feast," *P&P*, no. 94 (1982), pp. 107–30; idem, *Aspects of Aristocracy*, pp. 90–99; T. B. Smith, "In Defense of Privilege: The City of London and the Challenge of Municipal Reform, 1875–1900," *Journal of Social History*, 27 (1993–94), pp. 59–83; M. Sanderson, *The Universities and British Industry, 1850–1970* (London, 1972), p. 81.

76. Cannadine, *Decline and Fall*, pp. 559–72. Labour councillors were as attracted to mayoral chains of office and aldermanic robes as Liberals or Conservatives; see McKibbin, *Ideologies of Class*, p. 25 n. 79.

77. J. W. Burrow, *Evolution and Society* (Cambridge, 1966); G. Weber, "Science and Society in Nineteenth-Century Anthropology," *History of Science*, 12 (1974), pp. 260–83.

78. S. R. Szreter, *Fertility, Class and Gender in Britain, 1860–1940* (Cambridge, 1996), pp. 165–73.

79. Lynd, *England in the Eighteen Eighties*, pp. 77–78, 179; Mallock, *Aristocracy and Evolution*, p. 49; idem, *Memoirs of Life and Literature*, p. 197; H. Cecil, *Liberty and Authority* (London, 1910), p. 56.

80. Cf. G. Crossick, "From Gentleman to the Residuum: Languages of Social Description in Victorian Britain," in P. Corfield (ed.), *Language, History and Class* (Oxford, 1991), p. 171.

81. A. Briggs, "The Language of 'Class' in Nineteenth-Century England," in M. W. Flinn and T. C. Smout (eds.), *Essays in Social History* (Oxford, 1974), p. 171.

82. R. Roberts, *The Classic Slum: Salford Life in the First Quarter of the Century* (Harmondsworth, 1990), pp. 13, 17, 19, 21, 41, 153, 167, 184–85.

83. Ibid., pp. 13, 17, 23, 28, 91.

84. A. Marwick, *The Deluge: British Society and the First World War* (London, 1978); Waites, *Class Society at War.*

85. Perkin, *Rise of Professional Society*, pp. 192, 207; P. Renshaw, *The General Strike* (London, 1975), pp. 67–68. This was also, of course, the view articulated in the novels of John Buchan.

86. Cannadine, *Aspects of Aristocracy*, pp. 156–57; M. Cowling, *Religion and Public Doctrine in Modern England* (Cambridge, 1980), pp. 320–28; W. S. Churchill, *The World Crisis*, vol. 1, *1911–14* (London, 1923), p. 188; ibid., vol. 4, *The Eastern Front* (London, 1931), pp. 17–32; idem, *My Early Life* (New York, 1939), pp. 89–92, 122; idem, *Marlborough: His Life and Times*, vol. 1, *1650–1688* (London, 1933), pp. 37–40.

87. P. Addison, "The Political Beliefs of Winston Churchill," *TRHS*, 5th ser., 30 (1980), p. 46; M. Gilbert, *Winston S. Churchill*, vol. 5, *1922–39* (London, 1977), pp. 914–15.

88. McKibbin, *Ideologies of Class*, p. 298; Cannadine, *Decline and Fall*, pp. 103–25, 230–31, 266–69.

89. E. D. Goldstein, "*Quis Separabit?* The Order of St. Patrick and Anglo-Irish Relations, 1922–34," *Historical Research*, 62 (1989), pp. 70–80; Cannadine, *Decline and Fall*, pp. 177–79, 485–87.

90. A. L. Gleason, *What The Workers Want* (London, 1920), p. 250; Roberts, *Classic Slum*, pp. 220, 225, 227.

91. Perkin, *Rise of Professional Society*, pp. 219, 268; Pugh, *Tories and the People*, pp. 175–91; J. B. Priestley, *English Journey* (London, 1934), pp. 401–3.

92. C. F. G. Masterman, *England After War* (London, 1923), pp. 33–34, 42, 96; Perkin, *Rise of Professional Society*, p. 393.

93. G. D. H. Cole and M. I. Cole, *The Condition of Britain* (London, 1937), pp. 65, 79.

94. A. A. Jackson, *The Middle Classes, 1900–1950* (Nairn, 1991), p. 11; Cole and Cole, *Condition of Britain*, p. 79.

95. G. Orwell, *The Lion and the Unicorn: Socialism and the English Genius* (1941; rpt., Harmondsworth, 1982), p. 66.

96. McKibbin, *Ideologies of Class*, p. 268; J. Ramsden, *The Age of Balfour and Baldwin, 1902–1940* (London, 1978), p. 98–99; Cannadine, *Decline and Fall*, pp. 189–95; G. R. Searle, *Country Before Party: Coalition and the Idea of 'National Government' in Modern Britain, 1885–1987* (London, 1995), pp. 103–4.

97. Quoted in J. Cooper, *Class: A View from Middle England* (London, 1993), p. 29; Cannadine, *Decline and Fall*, pp. 228–29.

98. Masterman, *England After War*, pp. 71–122; McKibbin, *Ideologies of Class*, pp. 272–73; M. Petter, " 'Temporary Gentlemen' in the Aftermath of the Great War: Rank, Status and the Ex-Officer Problem," *HJ*, 37 (1994), pp. 127–52.

99. T. Jeffrey and K. McClelland, "A World Fit to Live in: The *Daily Mail* and the Middle Classes, 1918–39," in J. Curran, A. Smith, and P. Wingate (eds.), *Impacts and Influences: Essays on Media Power in the Twentieth Century* (London, 1987), pp. 27–52; McKibbin, *Ideologies of Class*, p. 268.

100. Cannadine, *Decline and Fall*, pp. 221, 229, 295; P. Williamson (ed.), *The Modernisation of Conservative Politics: The Diaries and Letters of William Bridgeman, 1904–1935* (London, 1988), pp. 126–27.

101. B. Crick, *George Orwell: A Life*, new ed. (Harmondsworth, 1992), p. 52; Jackson, *Middle Classes*, p. 316.

102. A. M. Carr-Saunders and D. Caradog Jones, *A Survey of the Social Structure of England and Wales* (London, 1927), pp. 70–73; ibid., 2d ed. (Oxford, 1937), p. 67.

103. Waites, *Class Society at War*, pp. 47, 74; G. Askwith, *Industrial Problems and Disputes* (London, 1920), pp. 67, 470. Even Masterman admitted "the struggle between Capital and Labour has become more fierce and uncompromising" (*England After War*, p. 13).

104. N. Branson, *Britain in the Nineteen Twenties* (London, 1976), pp. 143–45; L. Hannah, *The Rise of the Corporate Economy* (London, 1976), pp. 78–141.

105. Stevenson, *British Society*, p. 195; Marquand, *MacDonald*, p. 243; S. Macintyre, *A Proletarian Science: Marxism in Britain, 1917–1933* (Cambridge, 1980), p. 11.

106. Branson, *Nineteen Twenties*, pp. 196–97; A. J. P. Taylor, *English History, 1914–1945* (Oxford, 1965), p. 245; Renshaw, *The General Strike*, pp. 180, 187; M. Morris, *The General Strike* (Harmondsworth, 1976), p. 91; K. Laybourn, *The General Strike of 1926* (Manchester, 1993), pp. 55–56, 65, 100–101.

107. Marquand, *MacDonald*, p. 488.

108. Macintyre, *Proletarian Science*, pp. 161, 165; H. M. Pelling and A. J. Reid, *A Short History of the Labour Party*, 11th ed. (London, 1996), pp. 39–40.

109. Marquand, *MacDonald*, pp. 288–89, 395, 450.

110. S. Brooke, *Labour's War: The Labour Party During the Second World War* (Oxford, 1992), pp. 17–18, 271; J. Campbell, *Aneurin Bevan and the Mirage of British Socialism* (New York, 1987), pp. 8–16, 43, 48–49, 52, 60, 70.

111. Mcintyre, *Proletarian Science*, pp. 24, 31, 58, 76, 81, 87.

112. Taylor, *English History*, pp. 170–71; Branson, *Nineteen Twenties*, pp. 122–23.

113. Stevenson, *British Society*, p. 345; Cole and Cole, *Condition of Britain*, p. 72.

114. R. Hoggart, *The Uses of Literacy* (London, 1957), pp. 62–66. It was precisely this anxiety about the split in society between "them" and "us," or capital and labour, that prompted the duke of York to undertake his annual summer camps, which brought together equal numbers of public-school and working-class boys "to promote a sense of equality and comradeship between the upper and lower classes." See J. W. Wheeler-Bennett, *King George VI: His Life and Reign* (London, 1957), pp. 157–86; S. Bradford, *King George VI* (London, 1989), pp. 78–83.

115. M. Cowling, *The Impact of Labour, 1920–1924: The Beginning of Modern British Politics* (London, 1971), pp. 15–44; K. O. Morgan, *Consensus and Disunity: The Lloyd George Coalition Government, 1918–1922* (Oxford, 1979), pp. 298–300.

116. J. M. Keynes, *Essays in Persuasion* (London, 1931), p. 324; P. Addison, *Churchill on the Home Front, 1900–1955* (London, 1992), pp. 201, 208, 212–15.

117. McKibbin, *Ideologies of Class*, pp. 270–75, 282–85, 288–92, 299–300; Jarvis, "British Conservatism," pp. 63, 72–75.

118. McKibbin, *Ideologies of Class*, pp. 271–72; Masterman, *England After War*, pp. 79–81, 106–7.

119. Crick, *Orwell*, p. 52; McKibbin, *Ideologies of Class*, pp. 126–30, 233–36.

120. Perkin, *Rise of Professional Society*, pp. 269, 274; Stevenson, *British Society*, pp. 342, 344; Macintyre, *Proletarian Science*, pp. 173–74.

121. Branson, *Nineteen Twenties*, p. 53; Renshaw, *General Strike*, p. 187.

122. Jarvis, "British Conservatism," pp. 79–84; Macintyre, *Proletarian Science*, p. 11; Cole and Cole, *Condition of Britain*, p. 390; I. McLean, *The Legend of Red Clydeside* (Edinburgh, 1983).

123. Masterman, *England After War*, pp. 203–9; Renshaw, *General Strike*, pp. 250–51.

124. Marquand, *MacDonald*, p. 520; Macintyre, *Proletarian Science*, p. 198; P.

Addison, *The Road to 1945: British Politics and the Second World War* (London, 1975), p. 24.

125. Marquand, *MacDonald*, p. 258; Jarvis, "British Conservatism," pp. 83–84.

126. A. Duff Cooper, *Why Workers Should Be Tories* (London, 1926), quoted in Marwick, *Class*, p. 91; Jarvis, "British Conservatism," p. 59; J. P. Parry, "From the Thirty-Nine Articles to the Thirty-Nine Steps: Reflections on the Thought of John Buchan," in M. Bentley (ed.), *Public and Private Doctrines: Essays in British History Presented to Maurice Cowling* (Cambridge, 1993), p. 217.

127. P. Williamson, "The Doctrinal Politics of Stanley Baldwin," in Bentley, *Public and Private Doctrines*, p. 184.

128. S. Baldwin, *Our Inheritance* (London, 1928), p. 17; idem, *Service of Our Lives* (London, 1937), p. 117; idem, *On England*, pp. 4, 17, 27, 29, 58.

129. S. Baldwin, *An Interpreter of England* (London, 1939), p. 89; idem, *On England*, pp. 4, 12–13, 40, 181; idem, *Our Inheritance*, p. 111.

130. S. Baldwin, *Service of Our Lives* (London, 1937), p. 136; idem, *Our Inheritance*, pp. 30, 34, 88.

131. S. Baldwin, *This Torch of Freedom* (London, 1935), p. 169; idem, *On England*, pp. 34–35, 80; idem, *Our Inheritance*, p. 210; D. Cannadine, "Politics, Propaganda and Art: The Case of Two 'Worcestershire Lads,'" *Midland History*, 4 (1977), pp. 97–123.

132. Baldwin, *Our Inheritance*, p. 88; Williamson, "Doctrinal Politics of Stanley Baldwin," pp. 192–95, 198.

133. McKibbin, *Ideologies of Class*, pp. 51–55; Macintyre, *Proletarian Science*, p. 175.

134. Clarke, "Social Democratic Theory," pp. 7–8; S. Brooke, "Evan Durbin: Reassessing a Labour 'Revisionist,'" *Twentieth-Century British History*, 7 (1996), pp. 29–31, 42–44; idem, *Labour's War*, pp. 296–99.

135. Macintyre, *Proletarian Science*, pp. 53, 175; Marquand, *MacDonald*, pp. 226, 278–79, 283, 312, 450–62.

136. McKibbin, *Ideologies of Class*, pp. 25–26; Marquand, *MacDonald*, pp. 246–47, 312–14, 401–6, 410–11, 493, 495–99, 624, 674, 686–92, 774–78, 783–84, 788.

137. Cannadine, *Decline and Fall*, p. 301.

138. McKibbin, *Ideologies of Class*, p. 19.

139. Cannadine, "Context," pp. 139–52.

140. McKibbin, *Ideologies of Class*, pp. 24–25; M. Thatcher, *The Path to Power* (London, 1995), pp. 20–21; H. Young, *Iron Lady: A Biography of Margaret Thatcher* (New York, 1990), p. 8.

141. E. J. Hobsbawm, "Mass-Producing Traditions: Europe, 1870–1914," in Hobsbawm and Ranger, *Invention of Tradition*, pp. 303–4; Cannadine, *Aspects of Aristocracy*, pp. 100–107; idem, "War and Death, Grief and Mourning in Modern Britain," in J. Whaley (ed.), *Mirrors of Mortality: Studies in the Social History of Death* (London, 1981), pp. 219–25.

142. Cannadine, *Decline and Fall*, pp. 175–76, 600–602; N. Mansergh, *The Government of Northern Ireland* (London, 1936), pp. 169–76;

143. P. Scott, *Staying On* (London, 1994), pp. 96–98, 169. Copland, *Princes of India*, pp. 41–43; Khilnani, *Idea of India*, pp. 122, 134; G. Studdert-Kennedy, "The Christian Imperialism of the Die-Hard Defenders of the Raj, 1926–35," *Journal of Imperial and Commonwealth History*, 18 (1990), pp. 342–62.

144. H. Cecil, *Natural Instinct as the Basis for Social Institutions* (London, 1926), pp. 14–15.

145. H. Belloc, *The Contrast* (London, 1923), pp. 88, 275–78; idem, *An Essay on the Nature of Contemporary England* (London, 1937), pp. 5–6, 18, 22, 28, 35, 38, 42, 78.

146. R. H. Tawney, *Equality* (London, 1931), pp. 25–26, 28, 50, 88, 97, 123.

147. Ibid., pp. 27–28, 31, 38–39, 87.

148. E. Power, "What Feudalism Meant in England," *The Listener*, 20 October 1938, pp. 817–18; J. H. Hutton, "What Caste Means in India," *The Listener*, 20 October 1938, pp. 819–20; D. Forde, "Primitive Societies and Class Distinctions," *The Listener*, 1 December 1938, pp. 1176–78; J. B. Condliffe and B. Braatoy, "Class in New Zealand and Scandinavia," *The Listener*, 8 December 1938, pp. 1233–35; R. Gram Swing, "Class in the USA," *The Listener*, 15 December 1938, pp. 1308–10.

149. E. Salter Davies and D. G. Perry, "Does Education Create Barriers?" *The Listener*, 27 October 1938, pp. 874–77; B. Thomas, "Jobs as Class Labels," *The Listener*, 3 November 1938, pp. 939–41; J. Jewkes, "How Wealth Affects Class," *The Listener*, 10 November 1938, pp. 997–99; "How Class Affects Manners," *The Listener*, 17 November 1938, p. 1075.

150. A. Ludovici, G. A. Isaacs, and T. Harrison, "What Do We Mean by 'Class'?" *The Listener*, 13 October 1938, pp. 765–67; T. H. Marshall, "Class: An Enquiry into Social Distinctions," *The Listener*, 22 December 1938, pp. 1353–55; Condliffe and Braatoy, "Class in New Zealand and Scandinavia," p. 1233.

151. A. Horner and M. M. Postan, "The Class Struggle," *The Listener*, 24 November 1938, pp. 1109–11.

152. Orwell, *Lion and the Unicorn*, p. 52.

153. Ibid., pp. 40–45, 48–49, 51–53, 55–56, 66–67, 70, 77–78, 81–83, 102, 106,

109.

154. Ibid., p. 58; Crick, *George Orwell*, pp. 52–53, 57–60, 73, 107, 128, 148–49, 180, 184–85, 206–7, 281–82, 287–94, 305–6, 342–44, 380, 403–8, 432, 518–19, 559; R. Pearce, "Revisiting Orwell's *Wigan Pier*," *History*, 82 (1997), pp. 410–28.

155. B. Crick, introduction to Orwell, *Lion and the Unicorn*, pp. 25, 30; Orwell, *Lion and the Unicorn*, pp. 66–69, 95, 100.

156. A. Marwick, *British Society since 1945* (Harmondsworth, 1982); K. O. Morgan, *The People's Peace: British History, 1945–1989* (Oxford, 1990); P. F. Clarke, *Hope and Glory: Britain, 1900–1990* (Harmondsworth, 1996), pp. 216 ff.

157. P. Hennessy, *Never Again: Britain, 1945–51* (London, 1992), p. 38; P. Addison, *Churchill on the Home Front, 1900–1955* (London, 1992), pp. 327, 380; Marwick, *Class*, p. 214.

158. Morgan, *People's Peace*, p. 17; P. Summerfield, "The 'Levelling of Class,'" in H. L. Smith (ed.), *War and Social Change: British Society in the Second World War* (Manchester, 1986), pp. 179–207; H. L. Smith, *Britain in the Second World War: A Social History* (Manchester, 1996), pp. 1–3, 9–10, 41–50.

159. Brooke, *Labour's War*, p. 88; Addison, *Road to 1945*, pp. 131–32, 140–41, 152–53, 161–63.

160. P. Fussell, *Caste Marks: Style and Status in the USA* (London, 1984), p. 25; Addison, *Road to 1945*, p. 126; I. Gilmour, *Whatever Happened to the Tories? The Conservatives Since 1945* (London, 1997), p. 16.

161. Morgan, *People's Peace*, pp. 63, 81; Marwick, *Class*, p. 279; H. Thomas (ed.), *The Establishment* (London, 1994); A. Sisman, *A. J. P. Taylor: A Biography* (London, 1994), p. 214.

162. Morgan, *People's Peace*, pp. 198–200; N. Mitford, "The English Aristocracy," *Encounter*, September 1955, pp. 5–6.

163. Marwick, *Class*, p. 309; M. Kahan, D. Butler, and D. Stokes, "On the Analytical Division of Social Classes," *British Journal of Sociology*, 17 (1966), pp. 124, 128, 130.

164. Butler and Stokes, *Political Change in Britain*, p. 67.

165. Brooke, *Labour's War*, pp. 124, 131, 189, 272, 323; Morgan, *People's Peace*, p. 19; Addison, *Road to 1945*, p. 154; N. Nicolson (ed.), *Harold Nicolson: Diaries and Letters, 1939–1945* (London, 1967), p. 465.

166. K. O. Morgan, *Labour in Power, 1945 to 1951* (Oxford, 1984), pp. 79, 88–91, 152, 484; idem, *People's Peace*, pp. 35, 63, 81; Clarke, *Question of Leadership*, p. 237; R. Rhodes James (ed.), *"Chips": The Diaries of Sir Henry Channon* (London, 1967), p. 516; T. Burridge, *Clement Attlee: A*

Political Biography (London, 1985), p. 197.

167. K. Harris, *Attlee* (London, 1982), p. 257; Burridge, *Attlee*, p. 293.

168. A. Gamble, *The Conservative Nation* (London, 1974), p. 66; A. Sampson, *The Anatomy of Britain* (London, 1962), pp. 108–9; idem, *Macmillan: A Study in Ambiguity* (London, 1967), p. 165.

169. B. Pimlott, *Harold Wilson* (London, 1992), pp. 273–75, 300–307, 313, 317; P. Ziegler, *Wilson: The Authorized Life of Lord Wilson of Riveaulx* (London, 1993), pp. 143–44, 150; Morgan, *People's Peace*, pp. 142–43, 177; Clarke, *Hope and Glory*, pp. 293–94.

170. J. Campbell, *Edward Heath: A Biography* (London, 1993), p. 414; Gilmour, *The Tories*, pp. 267–68; Morgan, *People's Peace*, pp. 345, 354, 389–90; Pelling and Reid, *History of the Labour Party*, pp. 147, 159; Gamble, *Conservative Nation*, pp. 231–32.

171. Butler and Stokes, *Political Change in Britain*, p. 77; Brooke, *Labour's War*, pp. 338–39.

172. The strongest academic case for embourgeoisement was made in F. Zweig, *The Worker in an Affluent Society* (London, 1961). But there have been many powerful criticisms, among them J. H. Goldthorpe and D. Lockwood, "Affluence and the British Class Structure," *Sociological Review*, new ser., 11 (1963), pp. 133–66; W. G. Runciman, "Embourgeoisement, Self-Rated Class and Party Preference," *Sociological Review*, new ser., 12 (1964), pp. 137–54; J. H. Goldthorpe, D. Lockwood, F. Bechhofer, and J. Platt, *The Affluent Worker: Political Attitudes and Behaviour* (Cambridge, 1968); idem, *The Affluent Worker in the Class Structure* (Cambridge, 1969); Butler and Stokes, *Political Change in Britain*, pp. 101–4.

173. Butler and Stokes, *Political Change in Britain*, pp. 80–94; Brooke, *Labour's War*, pp. 275, 296–302; C. A. R. Crosland, *The Future of Socialism* (London, 1956), p. 20; Brooke, "Evan Durbin," pp. 27–31; Clarke, "Social Democratic Theory," pp. 3, 5, 7, 15–16; R. Plant, "Social Democracy," in D. Marquand and A. Seldon (eds.), *The Ideas that Shaped Post-War Britain* (London, 1996), pp. 165–70.

174. R. Millward, "The 1940s Nationalisation in Britain: Means to an End or the Means of Production?" *EcHR*, 2d ser., 50 (1997), pp. 209–34; Morgan, *Labour in Power*, p. 95–96, 136; C. R. Attlee, *The Granada Historical Records Interview* (London, 1967), p. 55.

175. R. Mackenzie and A. Silver, *Angels in Marble: Working-Class Conservatives in Urban England* (Chicago, 1968), p. 240; G. Hutchinson, *The Last Edwardian at Number 10: An Impression of Harold Macmillan* (London, 1980), p. 179.

176. Campbell, *Heath*, p. 420; Gilmour, *The Tories*, p. 268; M. Moran, *The Politics of Industrial Relations* (London, 1977), p. 152; A. J. Davies, *We, The Nation: The Conservative Party and the Pursuit of Power* (London, 1989), p. 196.

177. H. Fairlie, "The BBC," in Thomas, *The Establishment*, p. 202.

178. Sampson, *Macmillan*, p. 176; W. G. Runciman, *Relative Deprivation and Social Justice* (Berkeley, CA, 1966), pp. 45–52; M. Young, *The Rise of the Meritocracy, 1870–2033* (London, 1958); M. Shanks, *The Stagnant Society* (Harmondsworth, 1961); Perkin, *Rise of Professional Society*, p. 449.

179. M. Stacey, *Tradition and Change: A Study of Banbury* (Oxford, 1960), pp. 144–65; F. M. Martin, "Some Subjective Aspects of Social Stratification," in D. V. Glass (ed.), *Social Mobility in Britain* (Glencoe, IL, 1954), p. 58.

180. A. M. Carr-Saunders, D. Caradog Jones, and C. A. Moser, *A Survey of Social Conditions in England and Wales* (Oxford, 1958), p. 116; A. S. C. Ross, " 'U and Non-U': An Essay in Sociological Linguistics," *Encounter*, November 1955, p. 11.

181. Marwick, *Class*, p. 229; Gamble, *Conservative Nation*, p. 59.

182. R. Lewis and A. Maude, *The English Middle Classes* (New York, 1950), pp. vii, 337, 341, 346.

183. Ibid., pp. vii, 111, 113, 247, 250, 302, 313, 324, 334.

184. Gilmour, *The Tories*, pp. 107, 170; Gamble, *Conservative Nation*, p. 78; J. Bonham, "The Middle Class Revolt," *Political Quarterly*, 33 (1962), pp. 238–46.

185. Hutchinson, *The Last Edwardian*, p. 365; A. Horne, *Harold Macmillan*, vol. 2, *1957–1986* (London, 1989), p. 62.

186. A. Horne, *Harold Macmillan*, vol. 1, *1894–1956* (London, 1988), pp. 105, 115; ibid., vol. 2, *1957–1986*, pp. 156–57; Clarke, *Question of Leadership*, pp. 215, 219; Davies, *We, The Nation*, p. 110.

187. J. Harris, " 'Contract' and 'Citizenship,' " in Marquand and Seldon, *Post-War Britain*, p. 132.

188. I. Crewe, B. Sarvlik, and J. Alt, "Partisan Dealignment in Britain, 1964–1974," *British Journal of Political Science*, 7 (1977), pp. 135–68.

189. S. H. Beer, *Britain Against Itself: The Political Contradictions of Collectivism* (London, 1982), pp. 175–80; Sir K. Joseph, *Reversing the Trend: A Critical Reappraisal of Conservative Economic and Social Policies* (London, 1975). See also Quintin Hogg's speech of 1974, "I am myself passionately a defender of the middle class. . . . I will maintain to my last gasp the right of the middle class . . . to its own way of life" (quoted in K. Baker [ed.], *The Faber Book of Conservatism* [London, 1993], p. 124).

190. Lewis and Maude, *English Middle Classes*, pp. 3–21.

191. Martin, "Subjective Aspects of Social Stratification," pp. 58–63.

192. See above, ch. 1, pp. 5–6, and ch. 3, pp. 59–60.

193. Marwick, *Class*, p. 309; H. Thomas, "The Establishment and Society," in Thomas, *The Establishment*, p. 9; M. Stacey, E. Batstone, C. Bell, and A. Murcott, *Power, Persistence and Change: A Second Study of Banbury* (London, 1975), pp. 121, 131–35.

194. R. Scase, "English and Swedish Concepts of Class," in F. Parkin (ed.), *The Social Analysis of Class Structure* (London, 1974), pp. 149–77. Compare the slightly different figures given in Goldthorpe et al., *Affluent Worker in the Class Structure*, pp. 145–46.

195. Butler and Stokes, *Political Change in Britain*, p. 66.

196. H. Macmillan, *Pointing the Way, 1959–61* (London, 1972), p. 18; Lewis and Maude, *English Middle Classes*, pp. 18–19.

197. Davies, *We, The Nation*, p. 333; A. Howard, " 'We Are The Masters Now,' " in M. Sissons and P. French (eds.), *Age of Austerity* (London, 1963), p. 31; Morgan, *Labour in Power*, p. 327.

198. Rhodes James, *"Chips,"* p. 580; Fairlie, "The BBC," p. 191.

199. Quoted in Marwick, *Class*, p. 244.

200. K. O. Morgan, *Labour People: Leaders and Lieutenants, Hardie to Kinnock* (Oxford, 1987), pp. 146–47; Burridge, *Attlee*, pp. 2, 4, 7, 10, 16, 313–14; Harris, *Attlee*, pp. 544–56; Ziegler, *Wilson*, 96–97, 215, 367, 499, 513–14.

201. Crosland, *Future of Socialism*, pp. 41, 116, 169, 171, 177–78, 186–88, 217. Perhaps this explains why, as minister of education, he was eager to get rid of "every fucking grammar school in England and Wales and Northern Ireland" but left the public schools alone (S. Crosland, *Tony Crosland* [London, 1982], p. 148). See Clarke, *Hope and Glory*, p. 286.

202. Addison, *Churchill on the Home Front*, pp. 47, 52–53, 211, 311–15, 439; V. Bonham Carter, *Winston Churchill As I Knew Him* (London, 1965), p. 161; I. Berlin, "Mr Churchill in 1940," in H. Hardy and R. Hausheer (eds.), *Isaiah Berlin, The Proper Study of Mankind: An Anthology of Essays* (London, 1997), pp. 609, 612, 619, 621, 625.

203. A. Eden, *Another World, 1870–1914* (London, 1970); Sampson, *Macmillan*, pp. 173–76; Lord Home, *The Way the Wind Blows* (London, 1976).

204. Stevenson, *British Society*, pp. 259–62; Addison, *Road to 1945*, pp. 237–38; J. Ramsden, " 'A Party for Owners or a Party for Earners?' How Far Did the British Conservative Party Really Change after 1945?" *TRHS*, 5th ser., 37 (1987), pp. 49–63.

205. D. Clarke, *The Conservative Faith in a Modern Age* (first published 1947), in R. A. Butler (ed.), *Conservatism, 1945–50* (London, 1950), esp.

pp. 7, 9, 10, 15–18, 24–25, 41–42; A. D. Cooper, *Old Men Forget* (London, 1953), pp. 65–66; G. Butler, *The Tory Tradition* (London, 1914; rpt., London, 1957), pp. 67–71; Gamble, *Conservative Nation*, pp. 111–13; A. Sampson, *The New Anatomy of Britain* (London, 1971), p. 37.

206. In which regard it is worth recalling Orwell's regretful (but correct) recognition of "the British preference for doing things slowly and not stirring up class hatred" (G. Orwell, "London Letter," *Partisan Review*, summer 1946, p. 321). See also Young, *Rise of the Meritocracy*: "Britain . . . remained rural minded long after eighty per cent of its population were collected together in towns" (p. 22).

207. Runciman, *Relative Deprivation*, pp. 170–87; E. A. Nordlinger, *The Working-Class Tories* (London, 1967); F. Parkin, "Working-Class Conservatives: A Theory of Political Deviance," *British Journal of Sociology*, 18 (1967), pp. 278–290; Mackenzie and Silver, *Angels in Marble*; R. Waller, "Conservative Electoral Support and Social Class," in A. Seldon and S. Ball (eds.), *Conservative Century: The Conservative Party since 1900* (Oxford, 1994), p. 583.

208. Campbell, *Heath*, pp. 144, 171, 177; Cannadine, *Decline and Fall*, pp. 675–76; Sampson, *New Anatomy of Britain*, pp. 103–7; Clarke, *Hope and Glory*, p. 359.

209. Campbell, *Heath*, p. 189; Beer, *Britain Against Itself*, pp. 169–75; I. Gilmour, *Inside Right: A Study of Conservatism* (London, 1977); W. Waldegrave, *The Binding of Leviathan: Conservatism and the Future* (London, 1978).

210. J. G. Darwin, "The Fear of Falling: British Politics and Imperial Decline since 1900," *TRHS*, 5th ser., 36 (1986), pp. 27–43.

211. Cannadine, *Decline and Fall*, pp. 686, 723–25; Copland, *Princes of India*, pp. 261–68.

212. P. Worsthorne, "Class and Conflict in British Foreign Policy," *Foreign Affairs*, 37 (1959), pp. 419–31.

213. Beer, *Britain Against Itself*, pp. 5, 105; D. Kavanagh, "Political Culture in Great Britain: The Decline of the Civic Culture," in G. A. Almond and S. Verba (eds.), *The Civic Culture Revisited* (Boston, 1980), p. 170; Marwick, *British Society*, pp. 205–15.

214. J. Deverson and K. Lindsay, *Voices from the Middle Class* (London, 1975); P. Bauer, *Class on the Brain: The Cost of a British Obsession* (London, 1978); Beer, *Britain Against Itself*, pp. 158–65; Clarke, *Hope and Glory*, pp. 355–57.

215. D. Lockwood, "Sources of Variation in Working-Class Images of Society," *Sociological Review*, new ser., 14 (1966), pp. 249–67; Goldthorpe

et al., *Affluent Worker in the Class Structure*, pp. 118–20; E. Bott, "The Concept of Class as a Reference Group," *Human Relations*, 7 (1954), p. 259; Martin, "Subjective Aspects of Social Stratification," pp. 51–75; Runciman, *Relative Deprivation*, p. 160; Butler and Stokes, *Political Change in Britain*, pp. 66, 94; R. Dahrendorf, *Class and Class Conflict in Industrial Society* (Stanford, CA, 1959), p. 284.

216. Cooper, *Class*, passim, esp. pp. 11–14, 17, 149, 242, 318. My italics.

5. CONCLUSION:
TOWARD A "CLASSLESS SOCIETY"?

1. For an alternative vocabulary describing the same polarized model, in which historians are divided into "lumpers" and "splitters," see J. H. Hexter, *On Historians* (London, 1979), p. 242; J. A. Cannon, "The Historian at Work," in idem (ed.), *The Historian at Work* (London, 1980), p. 3.

2. F. Stern (ed.), *The Varieties of History* (New York, 1956), pp. 55–62.

3. W. H. McNeill, *The Great Frontier: Freedom and Hierarchy in Modern Times* (Princeton, 1983), pp. 8–9.

4. A. H. Halsey, *Change in British Society*, 4th ed. (Oxford, 1995), p. 144.

5. G. Marshall, H. Newby, D. Rose, and C. Vogler, *Social Class in Modern Britain* (London, 1988), p. 187.

6. G. Watson, *The English Ideology* (London, 1973), p. 181; M. C. Finn, *After Chartism: Class and Nation in English Radical Politics, 1848–1874* (Cambridge, 1993), p. 11; F. M. L. Thompson, *The Rise of Respectable Society: A Social History of Victorian Britain, 1830–1900* (London, 1988), p. 361; E. Gellner, "Knowledge of Nature and Society," in M. Teich, R. Porter, and B. Gustafsson (eds.), *Nature and Society in Historical Context* (Cambridge, 1997), p. 17.

7. P. Fussell, *Caste Marks: Style and Status in the U.S.A.* (London, 1984), p. 24.

8. One more example, already mentioned in chapter 2: James Nelson's observation of 1753 that "every nation has its custom of dividing people into classes" (P. Corfield, "Class by Name and Number in Eighteenth-Century Britain," in idem [ed.], *Language, History and Class* [Oxford, 1991], pp. 101–2). It is not at all clear from this remark what model(s) of society he had in mind.

9. For the dangers of a "very literal reading of language," see D. Wahrman, "The New Political History: A Review Essay," *SH*, 21 (1996), p. 345; S.

O. Rose, "Respectable Men, Disorderly Others: The Language of Gender and the Lancashire Weavers' Strike of 1878 in Britain," *Gender and History*, 5 (1993), p. 393; M. W. Steinberg, "Culturally Speaking: Finding a Commons Between Post-Structuralism and the Thompsonian Perspective," *SH*, 21 (1996), pp. 194–201.

10. E. P. Thompson, *The Making of the English Working Class* (Harmondsworth, 1968), pp. 195, 201, 915; Halsey, *Change in British Society*, pp. 57–59; S. Edgell, *Class* (London, 1993), p. 1; A. Marwick, *Class: Image and Reality in Britain, France and the USA since 1930* (London, 1980), p. 16; idem, *British Society since 1945* (Harmondsworth, 1982), p. 39.

11. The only book I know that has tried to treat hierarchy as a serious subject in the history of Britain is R. Strong, *The Story of Britain* (London, 1996), pp. 79–83, 205, 210, 259, 333, 335, 431–41, 489, 502–3, 527, 538, 568. In strictly analytical terms, of course, hierarchy is a complex phenomenon that can be varyingly discussed in terms of wealth, power, or prestige—or careers. But throughout this book, I have been dealing with it in its vernacular sense. See J. H. Goldthorpe and K. Hope, "Occupational Grading and Occupational Prestige," *Social Science Information*, 11 (1972), pp. 21–22; H. J. Perkin, *The Rise of Professional Society: England since 1880* (London, 1989), pp. 2–3, 9.

12. M. Taylor, "The Beginnings of Modern British Social History?" *HW*, no. 43 (1997), p. 162; E. M. W. Tillyard, *The Elizabethan World Picture* (London, 1943), pp. 101–2. For two suggestive and stimulating uses of hierarchy as a way of understanding the past, with reference to jewelry and food, see G. Clark, *Symbols of Excellence: Precious Metals as Expressions of Status* (Cambridge, 1986), esp. pp. 9–11, 27–30, 65–67, 104–5; J. Goody, *Cooking, Cuisine and Class: A Study in Comparative Sociology* (Cambridge, 1982), esp. pp. vii, 99–111, 133–53. On occasion, Goody also uses the triadic and polarized models of society.

13. M. Thatcher, "Don't Undo My Work," *Newsweek*, 27 April 1992, p. 37.

14. Edgell, *Class*, p. 2; K. Marx and F. Engels, *Selected Works*, 2 vols. (Moscow, 1962), 2:34–35.

15. For an earlier discussion of Marx as a special case of a more general formulation of social analysis, see R. Dahrendorf, *Class and Class Conflict in Industrial Society* (Stanford, 1959), pp. 136–37, 245.

16. R. I. McKibbin, *Ideologies of Class: Social Relations in Britain, 1880–1950* (Oxford, 1990), pp. 270–74.

17. It bears repeating that we do not know—and may well never be able to know—whether this is actually the case. But the fact that many people *believe* it to be true means that there is something that needs to be explained.

18. P. Gottschalk and T. M. Smeeding, "Cross-Cultural Comparisons of Earning and Income Inequality," *Journal of Economic Literature*, 35 (1997), pp. 633–87; J. H. Goldthorpe, C. Llewellyn, and C. Payne, *Social Mobility and Class Structure in Modern Britain*, 2d ed. (Oxford, 1987), pp. 303–23. Hence this remark of Stein Ringen: "There is nothing exceptional about Britain. . . . Britain is a pretty open society without strong barriers to social or economic mobility. . . . The British, however, punish themselves by *believing* that their society is one of unusually strong and rigid class distinctions" ("The Great British Myth," *Times Literary Supplement*, 23 January 1998, p. 3).

19. M. Thatcher, *The Revival of Britain* (London, 1989), p. 98.

20. M. Thatcher, *The Path to Power* (London, 1995), pp. 24, 47.

21. M. Thatcher, *The Downing Street Years* (London, 1993), p. 10; idem, *Path to Power*, pp. 5, 19, 23, 546.

22. Thatcher, *Path to Power*, pp. 4, 13, 566, 568.

23. P. Jenkins, *Mrs. Thatcher's Revolution: The Ending of the Socialist Era* (Cambridge, MA, 1988), pp. 82–83; H. Young, *Iron Lady: A Biography of Margaret Thatcher* (New York, 1990), pp. 28–36.

24. Thatcher, *Downing Street Years*, p. 285; Young, *Iron Lady*, pp. 489–90; S. Bradford, *Elizabeth: A Biography of Her Majesty the Queen* (London, 1996), pp. 380–81; B. Pimlott, *The Queen* (London, 1996), p. 495.

25. J. Ranelagh, *Thatcher's People: An Insider's Account of the Politics, the Power and the Personalities* (London, 1991), p. 64; Thatcher, *Path to Power*, pp. 20–21; idem, *Downing Street Years*, p. 23; Young, *Iron Lady*, p. 8; P. Riddell, *The Thatcher Decade* (Oxford, 1989), pp. 3, 150.

26. Young, *Iron Lady*, p. 322; Thatcher, *Path to Power*, p. 546; idem, *Downing Street Years*, p. 627; Ranelagh, *Thatcher's People*, pp. 179–80.

27. Thatcher, *Path to Power*, p. 243.

28. Jenkins, *Thatcher's Revolution*, pp. 178, 334; Thatcher, *Revival of Britain*, p. 56.

29. M. Holmes, *Thatcherism: Scope and Limits, 1983–87* (Basingstoke, 1989), D. Kavanagh, *Thatcherism and British Politics: The End of Consensus?* (Oxford, 1987), p. 291; R. Skidelsky, introduction to idem (ed.), *Thatcherism* (London, 1988), p. 22; R. Dahrendorf, "Changing Social Values Under Mrs. Thatcher," in ibid., pp. 198–99; Thatcher, *Revival of Britain*, pp. 56–57.

30. Jenkins, *Thatcher's Revolution*, p. 323; Thatcher, *Revival of Britain*, pp. 116–17, 230. This phrase had been in Labour's election manifesto in October 1974.

31. P. F. Clarke, *Hope and Glory: Britain, 1900–1990* (London, 1996), p. 379;

idem, *A Question of Leadership: Gladstone to Thatcher* (London, 1991), pp. 299, 318, 319.

32. J. Campbell, *Edward Heath: A Biography* (London, 1993), p. 654; D. Marquand, "The Paradoxes of Thatcherism," in Skidelsky, *Thatcherism*, pp. 163–72; R. Levitas (ed.), *The Ideology of the New Right* (Cambridge, 1986); I. Buruma, "Action Anglaise," *New York Review of Books*, 20 October 1994, pp. 66–71.

33. Corfield, "Class by Name and Number": "A tradition of not referring explicitly to social class is continued today in some political circles, especially among economic liberals; but it is still difficult to avoid some aggregative groupings" (p. 111 n. 37). See also Thatcher, "Don't Undo My Work": "The more you talk about class—or even about 'classlessness'—the more you fix the idea in people's minds" (p. 37).

34. Thatcher, *Path to Power*, pp. 58–59, 73; idem, *Downing Street Years*, p. 371; idem, *Revival of Britain*, pp. 69, 74, 182, 199.

35. See Class as History, in chapter 1, above.

36. Jenkins, *Thatcher's Revolution*, p. 53; Thatcher, *Revival of Britain*, pp. 54, 56, 141, 186, 196, 218; idem, *Path to Power*, p. 47.

37. Young, *Iron Lady*, pp. 143, 412, 490; Clarke, *Hope and Glory*, p. 380; Ranelagh, *Thatcher's People*, p. 296; Thatcher, *Revival of Britain*, p. 155; Bradford, *Elizabeth*, pp. 379–81, 387–90; Pimlott, *The Queen*, pp. 461–69, 494–515.

38. Thatcher, *Path to Power*, p. 51; Ranelagh, *Thatcher's People*, p. 39; I. Gilmour, *Dancing with Dogma: Britain Under Thatcherism* (London, 1992), p. 140; W. Whitelaw, *The Whitelaw Memoirs* (London, 1989), pp. 2, 12, 19, 32–34, 204, 245; J. Prior, *A Balance of Power* (London, 1986), pp. 252–54, 269–70; Lord Carrington, *Reflect on Things Past* (London, 1988), pp. 12, 20–21, 31, 45–48, 374–75.

39. Young, *Iron Lady*, pp. 118, 331; Ranelagh, *Thatcher's People*, p. 24; Thatcher, *Downing Street Years*, pp. 28–29, 129; Jenkins, *Thatcher's Revolution*, pp. 53–54.

40. Young, *Iron Lady*, pp. 220–21; Thatcher, *Downing Street Years*, pp. 104–5, 150–51, 832.

41. Young, *Iron Lady*, pp. 108, 115–16, 127.

42. Thatcher, *Downing Street Years*, pp. 625–26.

43. Thatcher, *Downing Street Years*, pp. 339–78; Jenkins, *Thatcher's Revolution*, p. 232; A. Horne, *Harold Macmillan*, vol. 2, *1957–1986* (New York, 1989), p. 626.

44. Jenkins, *Thatcher's Revolution*, p. 13, 225–27; Young, *Iron Lady*, pp. 366–67; Clarke, *Hope and Glory*, pp. 378–79; Holmes, *Thatcherism*, p. 46;

M. Crick, *Scargill and the Miners* (Harmondsworth, 1985), pp. 28–31, 147–48. This Scargillite view has made its way into surviving Marxist analysis of Thatcher, which sees her prime ministership, far too simplistically, as a "hegemonic project" of waging ruling-class war against the working class; see Riddell, *Thatcher Decade*, pp. 4–5; A. Gamble, *The Free Economy and the Strong State: The Politics of Thatcherism* (London, 1988); S. Hall and M. Jacques (eds.), *The Politics of Thatcherism* (Edinburgh, 1983); R. Jessop, K. Bonnett, S. Bromley, and T. Ling, *Thatcherism: A Tale of Two Nations* (Oxford, 1988).

45. Jenkins, *Thatcher's Revolution*, p. 228; Thatcher, *Downing Street Years*, pp. 352–53, 377.

46. Riddell, *Thatcher Decade*, p. 171; Young, *Iron Lady*, p. 490; Thatcher, *Downing Street Years*, p. 626.

47. Young, *Iron Lady*, p. 536.

48. Riddell, *Thatcher Decade*, pp. 8, 212–13; Young, *Iron Lady*, pp. 410–12, 525–26.

49. Holmes, *Thatcherism*, pp. 138–51; Kavanagh, *Thatcherism*, pp. 145–46; Jenkins, *Thatcher's Revolution*, pp. 133–34, 317–19; D. Bell, *The Coming of the Post-Industrial Society* (London, 1974).

50. P. Junor, *The Major Enigma* (London, 1993), pp. 202, 253.

51. D. Kavanagh, "A Major Agenda?" in D. Kavanagh and A. Seldon (eds.), *The Major Effect* (London, 1994), pp. 14, 17.

52. Junor, *Major*, pp. 146–47, 176–77, 254; Kavanagh, "Major Agenda?" p. 15; H. Young, "The Prime Minister," in Kavanagh and Seldon, *Major Effect*, p. 22; R. Harris, "And Is There Honey Still for Tory Tea?" *The Sunday Times*, 23 February 1997.

53. Junor, *Major Enigma*, pp. 53–54, 60, 85, 112, 114, 153; Young, "The Prime Minister," p. 22; R. Holt and A. Tomlinson, "Sport and Leisure," in Kavanagh and Seldon, *Major Effect*, pp. 444–45; W. Rees-Mogg, "Class Politics Is Below the Salt," *The Times*, 14 October 1996.

54. For Cowling's stress on the importance of inequality in Conservative thinking, see M. Cowling, "The Present Position," in idem (ed.), *Conservative Essays* (London, 1978), pp. 10–11; idem, *A Conservative Future* (London, 1997).

55. *Troilus and Cressida*, 3.3.101–110. I am most grateful to the Rt. Hon. Michael Portillo for kindly allowing me to see a copy of this speech, which was delivered on 14 January 1994. This passage from Shakespeare is also reprinted in K. Baker (ed.), *The Faber Book of Conservatism* (London, 1993), pp. 19–20, and is approvingly quoted by Lord Lawson in his foreword to Lord Bauer, *Class on the Brain: The Cost of a British*

Obsession (London, 1977). It is not coincidence that E. M. W. Tillyard begins the first chapter in *Elizabethan World Picture*, entitled "Order," with a discussion of it (pp. 7–9).

56. Kavanagh, *Thatcherism*, p. 107. This goes back to F. A. Hayek, *The Constitution of Liberty* (Chicago, 1960) pp. 402–3, which discussed the contradictions between neoconservatives and neoliberals. For an attempt to claim there is no such contradiction, see D. Willetts, *Modern Conservatism* (London, 1992), p. 47. For the more plausible insistence that there is, see J. Gray, "The Strange Death of Tory England," *Dissent*, fall 1995, pp. 447–52. See also A. J. Davies, *We, The Nation: The Conservative Party and the Pursuit of Power* (London, 1995), where he argues that "the indifference of the free market to hierarchy could be dangerous" for the Tories (p. 279). It has been—and still is).

57. A. Adonis, "The Transformation of the Conservative Party in the 1980s," in A. Adonis and T. Hames (eds.), *A Conservative Revolution? The Thatcher-Reagan Decade in Perspective* (Manchester, 1994), pp. 145–67.

58. Kavanagh, "A Major Agenda?" p. 11; J. Gray, "Labour's Struggle to Avoid Class War," *The Guardian*, 10 August 1995; A. Blair, *New Britain: My Vision of a Young Country* (London, 1996), pp. 6, 216.

59. A. Blair, "Introduction: My Vision for Britain," in G. Radice (ed.), *What Needs to Change: New Visions of Britain* (London (1996), pp. 7, 10; idem, *New Britain*, pp. 45, 65, 69, 237, 298.

60. J. Rentoul, *Tony Blair* (London, 1995), p. 424; Blair, "My Vision for Britain," p. 6; idem, *New Britain*, pp. 6, 22, 139, 209, 301.

61. Thatcher, *Downing Street Years*, pp. 129–30; Bradford, *Elizabeth*, p. 379. See the definitions of Middle America and Middle England offered in J. Pearsall and W. Trumble (eds.), *The Oxford English Reference Dictionary*, 2d ed. (Oxford, 1996): "The middle class in the US, especially as a conservative political force"; "the middle classes in England outside London, especially as representative of conservative political views" (p. 914).

62. Junor, *Major*, p. 112; M. Balen, *Kenneth Clarke* (London, 1994), p. 5; Holt and Tomlinson, "Sport and Leisure," pp. 444–45; R. Hewison, "The Arts," in Kavanagh and Seldon, *Major Effect*, p. 419. For an earlier use of the phrase "Middle England" in connection with Thatcher (at the time of the miners' strike), see Young, *Iron Lady*, pp. 377, 489.

63. M. Jacques, "The Rebel Alliance of British Talents," *The Guardian*, 20 February 1997. *The Observer*, 3 November 1996, claimed that Chester was "the statistical heart of middle England," whatever that meant.

64. J. Sopel, *Tony Blair: The Moderniser* (London, 1995), p. 32; Rentoul,

Blair, pp. 40–44; Blair, *New Britain*: "We are not just isolated figures struggling to compete against each other, but human beings, members of a community and a society" (p. 56).

65. Rentoul, *Blair*, pp. 304, 454; Blair, *New Britain*, pp. 29, 37; D. Marquand, "Community and the Left," in Radice, *What Needs to Change*, pp. 67–68; B. Anderson, *Imagined Communities: Reflections on the Origin and Spread of Nationalism* (London, 1983).

66. Sopel, *Tony Blair*, pp. 159, 244–46. See also the many references to Middle England as the constituency Labour needed to attract in M. Perryman (ed.), *The Blair Agenda* (London, 1996), pp. 13, 39, 77, 93–94.

67. I. Jack, "The Model of a Modern Middle Englander," *The Independent on Sunday*, 27 April, 1997.

68. M. Jacques, "Caste Down," *The Sunday Times*, 12 June 1994.

69. Blair, *New Britain*, pp. 65, 121.

70. A. Sampson, *The Essential Anatomy of Britain* (London, 1992), pp. 63–64; R. Hoggart, *The Way We Live Now* (London, 1995), pp. 3–11, 193–212; A. Marwick, *British Society since 1945*, new ed. (Harmondsworth, 1996), pp. 449–57; F. McDonough, "Class and Politics," in M. Storry and P. Childs (eds.), *British Cultural Identities* (London, 1997), pp. 208–20. For some of the contradictions and complexities inherent in the idea of the "classless society," see W. G. Runciman, *Relative Deprivation and Social Justice* (Berkeley, CA, 1966), p. 40.

71. Since 1978 inequality has been rising much faster in the USA than in the UK (K. Bradsher, "Gap in Wealth in U.S. Called Widest in West," *New York Times*, 17 April 1995).

72. A. J. P. Taylor, *English History, 1914–1945* (Oxford, 1965), p. 310.

73. In this regard, consider these remarks of Martin Kettle, "What's in a Name," *The Guardian*, 10 May 1997: "Names are an extraordinarily potent starting point for any cultural revolution. How we address one another is always a resonant matter, and the right has always favoured formal hierarchies which emphasise class and other forms of power, while the left has always tended towards democratic informality. Whole volumes of etiquette still exist—and are regularly consulted—to ensure that language and title are 'correctly' used in order to maintain networks of deference and support the mystique of authority." See also W. Rees-Mogg, "History, Privilege, Class and a Matter of Honour," *Daily Mail*, 1 January 1994: "A government which wanted to create a genuinely classless society would no doubt abolish the Honours List altogether, along with the House of Lords and the monarchy, all of which tend to support a class structure." "It is," he concludes, "a plau-

sible but probably dangerous objective." He may well be right.

74. G. Walden, "Kick Class Out of the Schoolroom," *The Observer*, 18 August 1996: "While other European countries have a single national culture of education, in Britain there are two: a superior one for a social and moneyed caste, and an inferior one for the rest. The ethos of the first is aspirational; of the second, egalitarian." These arguments are developed more fully in G. Walden, *We Should Know Better* (London, 1996).

75. R. Harris, "Deference Is Alive and Well and Killing Us," *The Sunday Times*, 21 July 1996. See also R. Hoggart, *Townscape with Figures* (London, 1994): "In all things English, there is a pecking order" (p. 150).

76. S. Boseley, "Labour's Class Question," *The Guardian*, 7 December 1994; B. Appleyard, "Divided We Stand," *The Independent*, 18 April 1996.

77. Holt and Tomlinson, "Sport and Leisure," p. 455.

78. L. O'Kelly, "So Much for the Death of Class," *The Sunday Times*, 21 August 1994.

79. H. M. Hyndman, *The Record of an Adventurous Life* (London, 1911), pp. 244–45; C. Tsuzuki, *H. M. Hyndman and British Socialism* (Oxford, 1961), p. 35; D. Aitkenhead, "Empty Promises of a Classless Warrior," *The Guardian*, 21 March 1997.

80. S. Schama, *Landscape and Memory* (New York, 1995), pp. 10–18.

81. J. Dimbleby, *The Prince of Wales: A Biography* (London, 1994), p. 523; A. Bennett, *Writing Home* (London, 1994), p. 33; J. K. Galbraith, *The Good Society: The Humane Agenda* (London, 1996), pp. 6–9.

INDEX

Absentee landlords, 42, 223n62
Accents, 96
Act of Union (1707), 42
Adams, John, 37
Administrative Reform
  Association, 97
Adversarial politics, 98
Age of mass democratic politics, 109
American culture, 55; *see also*
  Colonial America; United States
American Invasion scare, 123
American Revolution, 55–56
Anatomy of Britain, The
  (Sampson), 151
Anderson, Benedict, 188
Animals, social organization, 23
Anti-Corn Law League, 81, 82
Antihierarchical models of social
  structure, 34; *see also* Social
  models
Applegarth, Robert, 95
Aristocracy, 5, 111, 180–81; *see also*
  Titles; Tory Party; Upper classes
Aristotle, 30
Arnold, Matthew, 91
Art of Colonization (Wakefield), 88
Atkin, John, 72
Attlee, Clement Richard, 1st Earl

Attlee, 152, 154, 160
Attlee government, 152
Attwood, Thomas, 77
Australia, 19

Bagehot, Walter, 93
Baines, Edward Jr., 80, 102
Baldwin, Stanley: relationship with
  workers, 118; rhetoric, 142, 165;
  social vision, 143; views on busi-
  ness consolidations, 135; views
  on House of Commons, 133;
  views on social structure, 141–42
Ballantyne, Bill, 135
Banbury, 155, 159
Bankes, Henry, 70
Barber, Walter, 135
Baring, Alexander, 78
Barnett, Samuel, 115–16
Barton, John (fict.), 85
Baxter, R. D., 95
BBC, programs on class, 147–48
Beales, Edmund, 104
Beaverbrook, William Maxwell
  Aitken, 1st Baron, 190
Beckford, William, 33
Bedford, Francis Russell, 7th duke
  of, 98

275

Milton, Viscount, later 5th Earl
Fitzwilliam, 73
Miners, 153, 182
Mitford, Nancy, 151, 156
Models, *see* Hierarchical model;
Polarized model; Triadic model
Monarchy, 127, 144–45, 177
Monthly Magazine, 72
Montpellier, 19–20, 76
Morgan, Kenneth, 150, 159
Morley, Stephen (fict.), 85
Morris, Desmond, 23
Morris, Lewis, 41
Morrison, Herbert, 156
Municipal Corporations Act (1835),
81, 82
Mutiny of 1857, 108
Mysteries of London, The
(Reynolds), 86

Nabobs, 73
Names, 273*n*73; *see also* Titles
National Union of Mineworkers,
153; *see also* Miners
Nelson, James, 29, 33
Neoconservatives in Conservative
Party, 187
Neopopulists in Conservative
Party, 187
Newcastle Commission, 92
New England (U.S.), 40
New Labour Party, 187, 188; *see also*
Labour Party
New Zealand, 19
Nicolson, Harold, 152
Nineteenth century, 59–108; to
1820, 59–75; 1820s and 1830s,
75–91; mid-Victorian era,
91–106; summary, 106–8
Nobility, 63; *see also* Aristocracy

Nonroyal public life, 145
Northern Ireland, 146
Northern Star (newspaper), 83
O'Brien, Bronterre, 79
*Observations Concerning the
Distinction of Ranks* (Millar), 42
*Observations on the Causes of the
Dissolution Which Reigns among
the Lower Classes of the People*
(Hanway), 31–32
Obsession with class, 175
Occupational groups, 9
Occupations, 56
Old Corruption, 84, 178
"On the Analytical Division of
Social Classes," 151–52
Order of St. Patrick, 131
Order of the British Empire, 144
Order of the Star of India, 108
Orders of knighthoods, 126; *see also*
Honors system
Organized labor, *see* Trade unions
Orwell, George: characterization of
Britain, 175; description of social
structures, 148–49; views on
middle class, 124–25, 132–33, 134;
views on working classes, 139
Oswald, James, 67
Otter, William, 64, 70
Oxbridge, 49

Paine, Thomas, 62, 63
Palmerston, Henry John Temple, 3d
Viscount, 95–96, 100–101, 102
Pan-British community, 36, 37, 164;
see also Celtic fringe; Colonial
America
Parachutists, scholars as, 167
Parades, 55
Pares, Richard, 52

Index compiled by Fred Leise